Julius Caesar on stage
in England and America, 1599–1973

Julius Caesar on stage in England and America, 1599–1973

JOHN RIPLEY
Associate Professor, Department of English
McGill University

CAMBRIDGE UNIVERSITY PRESS
CAMBRIDGE
LONDON   NEW YORK   NEW ROCHELLE
MELBOURNE   SYDNEY

Published by the Press Syndicate of the University of Cambridge
The Pitt Building, Trumpington Street, Cambridge CB2 1RP
32 East 57th Street, New York, NY 10022, USA
296 Beaconsfield Parade, Middle Park, Melbourne 3206, Australia

First published 1980

Set, printed and bound in Great Britain by
Fakenham Press Limited
Fakenham, Norfolk

Library of Congress Cataloguing in Publication Data
Ripley, John, 1936–
Julius Caesar on stage in England and America,
1599–1973.
Bibliography: p.
1. Shakespeare, William, 1564–1616. Julius
Caesar. 2. Shakespeare, William, 1564–1616 – Stage
history. 3. Theatre – England – History. 4. Theatre
– United States – History. I. Title.
PR2808.R56   822.3'3   79–10822
ISBN 0 521 22781 X

For Judi

CONTENTS

ILLUSTRATIONS

ACKNOWLEDGEMENTS

It is a pleasure to thank the many theatre-lovers on both sides of the footlights for their contributions to my research.

I am indebted more deeply than I can say to the late Professor Allardyce Nicoll who encouraged me in the early stages of this study, and to Professor John Russell Brown and the late Professor T. J. B. Spencer who supervised part of it as a doctoral dissertation. Professor Charles Shattuck has been a source of inspiration and practical aid throughout. I am particularly grateful to him for reading the manuscript, and for invaluable hints for its improvement.

From the outset Miss Eileen Robinson of the Shakespeare Centre Library has been unfailingly generous of time and expertise. In specific and varied ways I have been graciously assisted by Mr Lindsay Anderson, the late Mr W. Bridges-Adams, Mr John Houseman, Professor Leo Hughes, Mr Norman Lloyd; Mr George Nash of the Enthoven Collection, Victoria and Albert Museum; Mrs Allardyce Nicoll, Miss Lyn Oxenford; Mr Louis Rachow, Librarian of the Walter Hampden Memorial Library, The Players; Mr Dennis Roberts and the late Mrs Roberts, Miss Sybil Rosenfeld, Mr Gerald Simms, Mr George Skillan, Professor A. C. Sprague, the late Mr Robert Speaight CBE, Mrs Carol Stairs, and Mrs Michael Warren.

Theatre collections and libraries on both sides of the Atlantic have made me welcome, and their staffs have gone well beyond the call of duty in locating elusive research materials. Especially helpful have been The British Library; the Enthoven Collection (Victoria and Albert Museum); the Folger Shakespeare Library; the Garrick Club Library; the Guthrie Theatre; the Harvard Theatre Collection; the libraries of the Historical Society of New York and the Historical Society of Pennsylvania; the Library of Congress; the McLennan Library (McGill University); the Metropolitan Toronto Public Library (Theatre Section); the Museum of the City of New York; the Shakespeare Centre Library; the Shakespeare Institute Library; the Shakespeare Memorial Library (Birmingham Public Library); the University of Bristol Theatre Collection; the University of London Library; the Walter Hampden Memorial Library, The Players; and the Wilmington, Delaware, Public Library.

My wife's confidence and enthusiasm prompted me to undertake this book; and her research assistance, critical judgement, and endless patience now make possible its completion.

Last, but far from least, I gratefully acknowledge the financial support of the Canada Council, the Faculty of Graduate Studies, McGill University, and the Imperial Order Daughters of the Empire.

NOTE

All books and periodicals referred to are published in London unless otherwise stated.

Whenever possible promptbooks bear the numbers allotted them by Charles H. Shattuck in *The Shakespeare Promptbooks*, Urbana and London, 1965. Professor Shattuck's catalogue contains full descriptions of each.

All *Julius Caesar* line numbers refer to *The Riverside Shakespeare*, ed. G. Blakemore Evans, Boston, 1974.

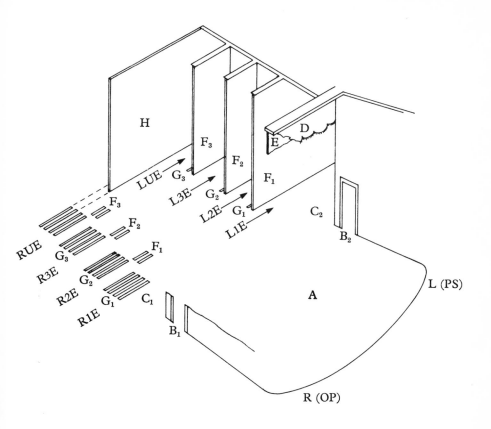

GUIDE TO EIGHTEENTH-CENTURY AND
EARLY NINETEENTH-CENTURY STAGE TERMS

A – forestage or apron; B_1 B_2 – proscenium doors; C_1, C_2 – proscenium arch; D –
curtain; E – act drop; F_1, F_2, F_3 – paired side wings or sideshutters in grooves; G_1,
G_2, G_3 – bisected backshutters in grooves 1, 2 and 3. Entrances (L1E, L2E, etc.) are
designated by the number of the backshutter groove immediately upstage. H –
backscene, drop, or sky cloth. PS – prompt side; OP – opposite prompt.

Introduction

Julius Caesar's sensational action, straightforward characters, and absence of sex have long made it a popular school text; so much so that hardly a literate member of English-speaking society can claim ignorance of it, even if 'Friends, Romans, countrymen' constitutes his only sure recollection. Critics, however, have been less taken with it than educators. As early as the seventeenth century Thomas Rymer brought Shakespeare to book for sinning 'not against nature and Philosophy only, but against the most known History';[1] while as late as the end of the nineteenth, Shaw indicted him for 'this travestying of a great man [Caesar] as a silly braggart, whilst the pitiful gang of mischief-makers who destroyed him are lauded as statesmen and patriots'.[2] Yet from the moment the Globe actors first spouted and jigged for Thomas Platter, *Caesar* has been, save for a couple of brief interludes, a perennial hit at the box-office and a challenge to most major performers – with the notable exceptions of Garrick, Kean, Irving, and Olivier. And this in spite of grave theatrical drawbacks: a titular hero who dies before the play is half over; three other roles of greater interest competing one with another for a share of the audience's sympathy; a mob which if small or inactive saps the play's vitality, but if large or boisterous swamps the action; two final acts which threaten momentarily to dwindle into anti-climax; and little feminine interest to balance its defects.

Neither critics nor men of the theatre would deny that the play bristles with difficulties. From the late seventeenth century until the work of Ulrici, Hudson, Gervinus, and Moulton two hundred years later, study and stage regarded the piece as successful merely in parts. Only in this century has there been a widespread academic recognition of *Caesar*'s wholeness, and a willingness on the part of the theatre to offer more than piecemeal solutions to its problems.

The play and its critics

Predictably, the prime concern of neo-classical commentators was the title role – the unhistoric figure Caesar cuts, and the relatively brief period in which he cuts it. Rymer thought it downright 'Sacriledge' on the part of the dramatist to put Caesar and Brutus in 'Fool's Coats', to reduce titans of antiquity to mere 'Jack-puddens in the Shakespear dress'.[3] John Dennis, scandalized at Shakespeare's 'gross Mistakes in the Characters which he has drawn from History', asks caustically, 'How could it be that seeing *Caesar*, we should ask for Caesar?'[4] Even Mrs Montague, Shakespeare's defender against the censure of Voltaire, conceded Caesar's 'historical character . . . ought certainly have been more attended to'.[5] In the first decades of the nineteenth century, sporadic outcries were still heard. Hazlitt, for example, regretted to find the 'mighty Julius' unworthy of his admiration and unfaithful to the portraits of him in his *Commentaries*.[6]

Dissatisfaction with Caesar's dramatic inconsequence, as distinct from his historic inaccuracy, took its rise with Charles Gildon's complaint that '*Caesar* is the shortest and most inconsiderable Part . . . and he is killed in the beginning of the Third Act.'[7] 'How could [Shakespeare] have made so very little of the first and greatest of Men', demanded an outraged Dennis, 'as that *Caesar* should be put a Fourth-rate Actor in his own Tragedy?'[8] A century later Leigh Hunt remarked only that 'Caesar appears but in two short scenes and is dismissed at the beginning of the third act.'[9] So minor a character seemed to him unworthy of further comment.

Once Caesar had been judged inadequate, critics cast about for another hero. Rymer was dissatisfied with all the candidates, but Gildon plumped solidly for Brutus. In fact, maintained Gildon, the play is not Caesar's tragedy at all, but that of Brutus; and consequently should bear his name. 'Brutus', he contended, 'is plainly the shining and darling Character of the Poet; and is to the end of the Play the most considerable Person.'[10] Mrs Montague agreed that 'the principal object of our poet was to interest the spectator for Brutus';[11] and Coleridge came to the same conclusion, although he confessed he could not see 'into Shakespeare's motive, the *rationale* – or in what point he meant Brutus's character to appear'.[12] For Hunt Brutus' primacy was unequivocal. 'Brutus', he insisted, 'after his interview with *Cassius* in the commencement of the play is the arbiter of all that succeeds, and the predominant spirit to the last.'[13] And his view remained the popular one throughout much of the nineteenth century. Swinburne's notion of him as the 'very noblest figure of a typical and ideal republican in all the literature of the world'[14] would have met with little opposition, except for Rymer and Shaw, until comparatively recent times.

Although most critics awarded Brutus the palm, the decision for neo-classical critics was tantamount to indicting the play's structure. A drama in which the titular hero gets only a few lines could hardly be judged well-wrought. 'If it had been properly call'd *Julius Caesar* it ought to have ended at his Death', declared Gildon, 'and then it had been much more regular, natural and beautiful.'[15] David Erskine Baker's lament in 1782 that the piece failed to close 'with the most natural and affecting catastrophe, viz. the death of Caesar'[16] is one of the latest survivals of this objection. It need hardly be added that Shakespeare's neglect of the unities in *Caesar*, as elsewhere, was relentlessly scolded.

The mob offered another target for Augustan displeasure. Gildon concluded that the dramatist had limned 'the Commons of Rome' as if they were 'the Rabble of an *Irish* Village, as senseless, ignorant, silly and cowardly, not remembring, that the Citizens of *Rome* were the Soldiers of the Common-wealth, by whom they Conquer'd the World; and who in Julius Caesar's time were at least, as Polite, as our Citizens of London'.[17] Dennis objected not so much to the historical misrepresentation of the mob as to their presence in the play at all, including it among the things '*Shakespear* has introduced ... into his Tragedies, which are against the Dignity of that noble Poem.'[18] Mrs Montague found the 'mechanics' altogether 'too loquacious' and wished that 'the part of the mob had been shorter';[19] while Francis Gentleman, although he guardedly approved the 'pathetically persuasive' speeches of the tribunes, dismissed the crowd sequences as 'ludicrous matter'[20] which the tragedy might well have been spared.

An age as conscious of language as of history and rules was hardly likely to find *Caesar*'s idiom entirely as it ought to be. Rymer contended that the 'Language which Shakespeare puts into the Mouth of Brutus would not suit, or be convenient, unless from some son of the Shambles or some unnatural offspring of the Butchery.'[21] Gentleman concurred with Ben Jonson's dictum that the 'quaint remark upon the leanness of Cassius deserves to be sneered at' and termed Caesar's allusion to his deafness 'unessential and ridiculous'. He similarly disparaged the reference to 'sweaty nightcaps' and the 'bashaw stile' of Caesar's reply to Metellus in the Assassination scene, and asked why the dictator should speak English elsewhere and yet say '*Et tu Brute?*' at his death.[22] Examples could be multiplied.

Throughout the eighteenth century, then, and well into the nineteenth, *Caesar* was regarded less as a unified work of art than a series of loosely-connected episodes featuring inaccurate portraits of Roman historical figures, the chief of which is Brutus. Certain scenes, however, were wholeheartedly admired. Charles Gildon's enthusiasm for the Quarrel scene initiated a century and a half of critical eulogy.[23] Dryden shared Gildon's excitement, comparing the quarrel with the confrontation of Agamemnon and Menelaus in Euripides' *Iphigenia* to the advantage of Shakespeare.[24] Dr Johnson, no great admirer of the play, grudgingly conceded that 'the contention and reconcilement of *Brutus* and *Cassius* is universally celebrated',[25] while Baker demanded rhetorically whether there could be 'a finer scene of resentment and reconciliation between friends' than this.[26]

Hazlitt warmly applauded the scene's construction, and Coleridge lauded it on all counts. 'I know of no part in Shakespeare', he maintained, 'that more impresses on me the belief of his genius being superhuman than this scene.'[27]

Next in order of popularity was the Forum sequence without, of course, for all but Romantic critics, the unapt mob. Gildon included this scene with the quarrel as 'the two best things in the play'. Although, in Gildon's view, the orations of Brutus and Antony 'have nothing (in a Dramatic Sense) to do with the Death of *Caesar* which is the first Action', he accorded strong praise to the speeches themselves, especially Antony's: 'What *Mark Antony* says to the imaginary people of *Shakespear*'s Rome, are so artful, so finely taken from the very Nature of the thing, that I question whether what the real *Mark Antony* spoke cou'd be more moving or better calculated to that Effect.'[28] Mrs Montague, if reluctant to commend the episode in its entirety, was nonetheless captivated by Antony's astuteness. 'Is there any oration extant', she asked, 'in which the topics are more skillfully selected for the minds and temper of the persons to whom it is spoken?'[29]

Hazlitt gave his blessing to two further scenes relatively unpraised heretofore – 'the well-known dialogue between Brutus and Cassius, in which the latter breaks the design of the conspiracy to the former', and the 'short scene . . . when Caesar enters with his train'. The latter Hazlitt judged 'more expressive of the genius of Shakespear' than almost any other passage in his work.[30]

In general the neo-classical critic tended to censure *Caesar* more severely than did his Romantic successor. Gildon concluded that if the play were revised to give Caesar his proper place and regularize the design 'there cannot be so much of this [Shakespeare's play] remaining as to rob the Alterer of the Honour of the whole'.[31] And his verdict epitomizes the Augustan viewpoint. The more liberal Romantic assessment is typified by Hazlitt's estimate that although *Caesar* is 'not equal as a whole to either of his other plays taken from Roman history', 'it . . . abounds in admirable and affecting passages'.[32] Hunt found himself charmed by the richness of individual personalities which 'seem to bring at once before us the result of a thousand different educations, or of a thousand different habits, induced by situation, passion, or reflection'.[33] And Coleridge and Hazlitt echoed his sentiments. In essence, however, neo-classical and Romantic reaction to *Caesar* differed more in degree than in kind. Both schools of criticism admired the play in part rather than as a whole; and neither was prepared to allow it any measure of dramatic unity.

Dr Johnson, it should be noted, challenged two of the charges against *Caesar*: (1) its historic inaccuracy and (2) its want of classical structure. In answer to the first objection Johnson insisted that Shakespeare 'always makes nature predominate over accident, and, if he preserves the essential character, is not very careful of distinctions superimposed and adventitious. His story requires *Romans* as kings, but he thinks only on men.'[34] *Caesar*, he suggested, is not a dramatized historical document, as the Augustan commentators argued, but a study of human kind and its relationships. The fact that the locale is Julian Rome is of relatively minor significance. Johnson's defence of *Caesar*'s irregularities was hardly less radical. In his opinion, 'a play written with a nice observation of critical rules is to be contemplated as an elaborate curiosity . . . by which is shown, rather what is possible than what is necessary'. While, he argued, the observation of the unities 'may sometimes conduce to pleasure, they are always to be sacrificed to the nobler beauties of variety and instruction'.[35] Unfortunately Johnson stopped short of spelling out *Caesar*'s design; but at least he asserted with all the authority at his command that lack of classical form did not necessarily imply formlessness.

How much Hermann Ulrici owed to Dr Johnson is unclear; but knowingly or not, he took up the cudgels on *Caesar*'s behalf in 1839 exactly where the Great Cham had dropped them seventy-five years earlier. Ulrici found himself not only convinced of the play's wholeness, but prepared to define its nature. 'The want of unity of interest is the common objection that has been most frequently brought against *Julius Caesar*', he began.

Now if the unity of interest ought to centre entirely in one *personage* of the drama, then no doubt the objection is just, for it is divided between Caesar, Brutus and Cassius, and Antony and Octavius. But we cannot for a moment concede that poetical interest is invariably personal; we believe rather that it attaches as frequently to an idea . . . Now in 'Julius Caesar' this interest is one throughout, and possesses a true and organic unity.[36]

For Ulrici *Caesar*'s unifying theme was the idea of history in 'its despotic power and energy of development' and the attempts of individuals to tamper with it, a viewpoint one need not profess to appreciate its landmark importance.

Once the play was allowed to have a form, a fresh examination of the characters and their relationship to it naturally followed. In the third quarter of the century, Gervinus, Lindner, and Dowden took a close look at Caesar himself, and argued his claim to the title role with varying degrees of enthusiasm.[37] H. N. Hudson's support, however, was wholehearted and unequivocal. 'Caesar', he contended, 'is not only the subject [of the play] but also the governing power of it throughout'.

He is the centre and spring-head of the entire action, giving law and shape to every thing that is said and done. This is manifestly true in what occurs before his death; and it is true in a still deeper sense afterwards, since his genius then becomes the Nemesis of retributive Providence, presiding over the whole course of the drama.[38]

With the role of Caesar to some degree clarified and a unifying principle of one kind or another admitted, Victorian scholarship embraced *Caesar* with relative ease as a political and personal study as distinct from a mere dramatization of history, as an ensemble drama rather than a hero-play, and as a carefully-contrived work of art instead of a flawed collection of bravura scenes. Richard G. Moulton's 1885 analogy between *Caesar*'s form and grouping techniques in painting and sculpture represents a culmination toward which criticism had been groping for over a century. 'The four leading figures', he argued, 'all on the grandest scale, have the elements of their characters thrown into relief by comparison with one another, and the contrast stands out boldly when the four are reviewed in relation to one single idea.'[39]

Moulton's confident assertion of *Caesar*'s structural soundness was but the first swallow in a century-long summer of critical admiration; and there is as yet no sign of wane. Reckoned for generations among the most straightforward of Shakespeare's works, *Caesar* in our times has acquired a reputation for complexity. Roman history, Renaissance politics, and Elizabethan stage practice have all been pressed into service to reveal its subtle splendours and resolve its enigmas. There are, however, a fair number of critics who dissociate themselves from attempts to unravel the play's mysteries by any means whatever; ambiguity, they contend, is used by Shakespeare as a deliberate artistic device.[40] A detailed survey of contemporary *Caesar* criticism is beyond the scope of this study; but a few landmark works may serve to illustrate the major approaches canvassed.[41]

M. W. MacCallum's *Shakespeare's Roman Plays* (1910), this century's first important *Caesar* critique, examined at length Shakespeare's debt to Plutarch and his transmutation of his source material into the makings of dramatic conflict. Granville-Barker, in his 1927 Preface, was little interested in the play's historical basis or lack of it.[42] As a playwright and director he set himself to peer over Shakespeare's shoulder as he worked, to recapture *Caesar*'s form and flow as revealed in the Elizabethan playhouse. His findings take the form of a running commentary on the play's structure and characters, almost as if given to actors at rehearsal. Wilson Knight's *Wheel of Fire* (1930) and *The Imperial Theme* (1931), R. A. Foakes's 'An Approach to *Julius Caesar*' (1954),[43] and Maurice Charney's *Shakespeare's Roman Plays* (1963) all probe *Caesar*'s central issues through its language and images. D. A. Traversi's *Shakespeare's Roman Plays* (1963) espouses no single methodology but reflects discursively on the play in a manner at once wonderfully catholic and individualistic. Traversi addresses us as unashamedly from the study as Granville-Barker does from the stage. All the above critics, however divergent their methods and conclusions, share the conviction that *Caesar*'s apparent confusions are susceptible of clarification and resolution. Adrien Bonjour (*The Structure of Julius Caesar*, 1958) does not; and asks us, on the contrary, to accept *Caesar*'s ambiguity and ambivalence as calculated dramatic devices (p. 24).

No serious twentieth-century critic would deny Caesar's pivotal position in the dramatic action or dispute his claim to the title role; but his character remains a vexed topic. Sir Mark Hunter argued in 1931 that 'the personality of Julius moves before us as something right royal; a character, not indeed immune from calumnious stroke, but sufficiently great to render the impassioned eulogy of Antony and the calm tribute of Brutus not inconsistent with what we have actually heard and seen of the object of their praise.'[44] John Dover Wilson took a diametrically opposite view. In his introduction to the New Shakespeare edition of *Julius Caesar* (Cambridge, 1949) he imagined Shakespeare putting the final touches to 'a Roman Tamburlaine of illimitable ambition and ruthless irresistible genius; a monstrous tyrant who destroyed his country and ruined "the mightiest and most flourishing commonwealth that the world will ever see" – one feature remained to add before the sixteenth century stage-figure of the great dictator was complete, that of a braggart'. More recently Ernest Schanzer suggested, diplomatically enough, that Shakespeare's Caesar may be both or neither of these figures. What, he asked, if the dramatist was consciously ambiguous? It is just possible that 'there *is* no real Caesar, that he merely exists as a set of images in other men's minds and his own'.[45] Most modern commentators take their bearings from one of these three compass points.

The critic's notion of Caesar inevitably conditions his reading of Brutus. Hunter firmly pooh-poohed the Romantic image of Brutus as a gentle idealist; here was no 'nobly-natured mistaken man', but an 'intellectually dishonest' one. John Dover Wilson, predictably enough, found Brutus the altogether heroic and ill-fated defender of Rome against Caesarism. Most modern critics have sided with Hunter rather than Wilson, with the result that Brutus has been thrust from his pedestal to rub elbows with flawed humanity. 'The fine man is a coarse thinker, the saint of self-denial has very little self left to deny', jibed Mark Van Doren.[46] 'Brutus' faults are seated at the very heart of his character', asserted Gordon Ross Smith. 'Although his behaviour, even to himself, is clothed in the habit ... of virtue, his basic motivation is egotistical satisfaction of his will.'[47] William R. Bowden considered him 'the self-righteous, opinionated, humorless, intellectually limited do-gooder in public life'.[48] Ernest Schanzer's conclusion that he is 'a bad judge of character but by no means devoid of political shrewdness and practical wisdom'[49] represents an unusually charitable assessment for these times.[50]

Antony and Cassius have enjoyed nothing like the attention lavished upon Caesar and Brutus. Both remain substantially as the Romantic commentators left them, save perhaps for some elaboration of their imperfections. The majority of critics cited above have something worthwhile to say about them, but Granville-Barker's remarks have become classic.

Undoubtedly the most productive approach to *Caesar* since the Second

World War has been its analysis in the context of Elizabethan conceptions of
Roman politics. As T. J. B. Spencer reminds us, 'Caesar and Brutus in the
play are not merely dramatic creations; they were also historical figures
which were firmly established in the popular imagination. Shakespeare's
audience inevitably brought pre-conceptions which guided their impressions from the play.'[51] Major insights in this area have been provided
by J. E. Phillips, Brents Stirling, T. J. B. Spencer, Geoffrey Bullough,
Northrop Frye, and L. C. Knights.[52]

Most of *Julius Caesar*'s stage history has been shaped and coloured by the
Augustan and Romantic notion of the play as seriously defective overall,
although thoroughly fine in parts. The fondness for particular scenes which
dominated criticism from Gildon to Montague is paralleled by a similar
emphasis in the theatre from Betterton to Quin. Nineteenth-century productions reflect the impact of Romantic character-analysis. One figure or
another is forever highlighted at the expense of the rest, although the
predilection for individual scenes continues. The new-found respect for
Shakespeare's craftsmanship characteristic of Ulrici, Hudson, and Gervinus touches other plays in the late nineteenth century via William Poel,
but fails to influence *Caesar* productions to any degree until Bridges-
Adams's first full-text revival at Stratford-upon-Avon in 1919.

No sooner had *Caesar*'s theatrical unity been recognized and demonstrated during the 1920s and 1930s at Stratford and the Old Vic when the
rise of director's theatre contorted it anew; and critics have offered little
opposition to the trend. Indeed, apart from a common tendency to down-
grade Brutus and upgrade Caesar, the contemporary stage and study show
little awareness of each other, Scholarship pays scant heed to the play in
performance; and directors seem content to be their own critics.

The play in the theatre

From the late seventeenth century onwards, managers prepared to stage
Caesar faced a choice: on the one hand, the script might be rewritten; on the
other, the text might be retained and its faults camouflaged by cuts,
role-manipulation, and ingenious stagecraft.

The only attempts to rewrite *Caesar* date from the first half of the
eighteenth century; and none had any success. Early in the century Thomas
Killigrew, a minor playwright, attempted a rough adaptation which was
never published or acted.[53] John Sheffield, Duke of Buckingham, rewrote
the tragedy as two plays, with Caesar as the hero of the first and Brutus as
protagonist of the second. Both were published in 1723 to hoots of critical
derision, and neither was staged.[54] Voltaire's *La Mort de César* (1736) was
published and performed in Paris,[55] and would find no mention in this study
save that it outraged Aaron Hill sufficiently to prompt his own version titled

Caesar's Revenge (*c.* 1738). Despite Hill's importunity, Garrick fought shy of the piece; and after an uneventful première at Bath it disappeared.[56]

These alterations were one and all mere exercises in possibility, not products of necessary dramatic truth. Form was arbitrarily imposed upon theme; theme did not dictate form. And in every case the theme suffered. It is to the credit of theatre managers from Shakespeare's time to our own that they were shrewd enough to recognize that the power of the text lay in its purity; and, although they cut it severely, they did not, save for the Dryden–Davenant version and its aftermath, permit interpolations.

For almost four hundred years, in defiance of critical sniffs, *Caesar* has kept the English and American boards; and its chequered history illuminates both the play and the theatres which staged it. At one moment it has served as a star-vehicle; at another, a clothes-horse for pageantry; at still another, a political medium. The script has been endlessly chopped and changed; individual roles have been adjusted up or down to suit the whims of stars; and spectacle has been added or subtracted as fashion dictated. Yet audiences remained consistently loyal, whatever its form. Early seventeenth-century theatre-goers were ravished by the play and left the theatre in wonder, Leonard Digges tells us. Three centuries on, their successors made it the most frequently-requested item in the Old Vic repertoire.

My reasons for organizing the tale chronologically should be self-evident. The relative importance, or lack of it, accorded particular productions requires perhaps a word of clarification.

The seventeenth century receives only one chapter because that is all our scanty knowledge can provide. The eighteenth century, an era of frequent performances and mediocre interpretation, merits no more than a chapter. The nineteenth century saw most leading actor-managers bring their talents to *Caesar*'s service; and the contributions of Kemble, Young, Macready, Phelps, Tree, and Benson deserve extensive discussion.

Some of the most colourful interludes in *Caesar*'s stage history are American. Throughout the first hundred years of the new republic audiences packed playhouses in Philadelphia, New York, Boston, and elsewhere to revel in its libertarian sentiments. In the second half of the nineteenth century, when the play was a virtual stranger to London, Edwin Booth and Lawrence Barrett took it to every corner of America by rail. Their respective interpretations of Brutus and Cassius challenge comparison with the finest of all time. In 1937 Orson Welles's anti-Fascist revival achieved a New York run of 157 performances, the longest on record; and its influence on later productions is well-nigh incalculable. *Caesar*'s transatlantic career, then, receives substantial attention.

During the first half of this century, *Caesar* enjoyed a.more than moderate popularity in England. Bridges-Adams, the first director of the play in the

modern sense of the term, pioneered at Stratford between 1919 and 1934 the
application of Elizabethan theatre techniques to commercial productions of
it.[57] London performances prior to the Second World War, although
perhaps better acted, represented little advance on Bridges-Adams's innovations. I have accordingly given Bridges-Adams's revivals an entire chapter, and surveyed the work of his metropolitan contemporaries in another.

The past few decades have had their splendid moments, beginning with
Gielgud's Cassius in 1950; however, since most modern interpretations
have been widely seen and well documented, I have treated them in outline
rather than in detail. I have, nevertheless, tried to highlight the salient
features of each. Today the theatre is not so much a national as an international phenomenon; consequently, I felt no useful purpose would be
served by separating contemporary English and North American revivals.

My approach is the same for all productions. I have attempted to determine what text was spoken, to record distribution of speeches, reduction of
cast, major cuts and their impact on theatrical form, and additions on the
rare occasions when they occur. Stagecraft receives equal attention – settings, costumes, stage business, crowd scenes, and lighting when it is
noteworthy. The interpretation of the four major roles – Caesar, Brutus,
Cassius, and Antony –[58] constitutes a third area of interest. The prominence
given to each feature naturally varies from revival to revival: Macready's
productions, for example, were *tours de force* of acting, while Beerbohm
Tree's were marvels of stagecraft.

No performance, of course, takes place in a vacuum, but is profoundly
conditioned by its physical environment, the aesthetic notions of its actor-
manager or director, and the tastes of its audience. These factors all constitute collateral interests in the reconstruction of any given production.

Wherever possible I have relied upon promptbooks and other theatre
documents as prime sources of information. All too often, however,
promptbooks are silent upon what we most need to know – exactly how an
actor looked or sounded at any particular moment. Inevitably I have been
obliged to draw upon secondary sources – letters, diaries, reviews, and
interviews – with the ever-present risk of seeing not the performance itself
but what some eyewitness thought he saw. Whenever I could I have
attempted to correlate the testimony of several witnesses and to weigh their
findings against the overall tone of theatre documents. Although one can
never catch the stage moment exactly as it happened, I hope that my
reconstructions, if sometimes inadequate, are not seriously inaccurate.

The general reader may find the detail excessive, while the specialist may
wish for more. I have tried to reconcile the need for a readable narrative with
the awareness that much of the raw material of this study is not easy to come
by. To include as much detail as seemed relevant without being over-
tedious has been my aim, if not always my achievement. The non-specialist

may wish to read fairly selectively, while the enthusiast will find additional notes at the end of the book and full documentation of my sources should he desire to consult them further.

I have not attempted to suggest a definitive interpretation of the play; rather I have tried to record what has been done with it in the theatre and the effects which followed. From that record may emerge perhaps a greater appreciation of *Caesar*'s literary and theatrical potential, some assessment of how much of that potential has been realized, and just possibly some directions for future exploration.

I

Seventeenth-century productions

The first recorded performance of *Julius Caesar* took place on 21 September, 1599, quite possibly at the Globe Theatre. Thomas Platter, a Swiss traveller, spent the period from 18 September to 20 October in England where he saw two plays, one of which, it would appear, was *Julius Caesar*. He writes:

After dinner on the 21st of September, at about two o'clock, I went with my companions over the water, and in the strewn roof-house saw the tragedy of the first Emperor Julius with at least fifteen characters very well acted. At the end of the comedy they danced according to their custom with extreme elegance. Two in men's clothes and two in women's gave this performance, in wonderful combination with each other.[1]

Since *Julius Caesar* is not included in Francis Meres's list of Shakespeare's plays in *Palladis Tamia: Wits Treasury* (entered Stationers' Register, September 1598), it is probable that it was not then written. Contemporary scholarship suggests that it was completed a few months after Meres's work was registered.[2] Thus, the performance of 21 September 1599 was, in all likelihood, one of the first, if not the first, representations.

Shakespeare's play was by no means the first to deal with Caesar's life and times. The Revels Accounts for 1581 record that the 'children of Pawles' played 'a storie of Pompey' at Court on Twelfth Night, 6 January.[3] There also survives an epilogue, in Latin prose, belonging to a play called *Caesar Interfectus* which may have been acted at Christ Church, Oxford, in 1582.[4] Stephen Gosson's *Playes Confuted in Five Actions* (entered Stationers' Register, 6 April 1582) makes mention of a 'history of Caesar and Pompey' which was played at 'the Theater'.[5] The existence of a number of plays on the Caesar theme points to a considerable interest in the subject on the part of dramatic writers and, by inference, on the part of audiences.

Some evidence of *Julius Caesar*'s popularity may be adduced from frequent satirical allusions to it in contemporary dramas. The fairly sophisticated games played with certain of Caesar's lines suggest that authors assumed a thorough-going knowledge of the piece on the part of their audiences. And where was familiarity to be acquired save in the theatre since no published version appeared before the First Folio in 1623? An excellent example is found in Ben Jonson's *Every Man Out of His Humour* when Antony's lines:

> O judgment! thou art fled to brutish beasts,
> And men have lost their reason. (III.ii.104–5)

are mockingly introduced into Clove's conversation with Orange: 'Then comming to the pretty *Animall, as Reason long since is fled to animalls* you know.'[6] Surely Jonson would not have satirized this phrase unless he was reasonably certain that the audience would perceive the connection; and if *Every Man Out of His Humour* was first performed in 1599, as the Jonson First Folio suggests, then *Julius Caesar* must have become known to the public fairly quickly. In 1907 E. Koeppel[7] drew attention to another echo in *The Wisdome of Doctor Dodypoll* (Stationers' Register 1600) when the potion-crazed Alberdure exits shouting, 'Then reason's fled to animals I see, / And Ile vanish like Tobaccco smoake.'[8] Two other speeches in the same work, not previously noticed, I think, may also gibe at passages in *Julius Caesar*. The first, the words of the Doctor:

Be garr, dis Earle be de chollericke complection; almost skipshack, be garr; he no point staie for one place: Madame me be so laxatiue: mee be bound for no point mooue.[9]

seems humorously reminiscent of the speech in which Caesar asserts his inflexibility (III.i.58–70). Again, the Doctor's speech: 'Know? what you know? you see your selfe, by garr me see you; me speake vatt me see; you no point speake so',[10] recalls Cassius' offer to act as Brutus' mirror at I.ii.67–70.

Firm confirmation of *Julius Caesar*'s grip on the Jacobean audience is contained in two poems (or possibly two versions of the same poem) by Leonard Digges. In his prefatory verses entitled 'To the Memorie of the deceased Authour Maister W. Shakespeare', and prefixed to the First Folio, he writes:

> Nor shall I e're beleeue, or thinke thee dead
> (Though mist) vntill our bankrout Stage be sped
> (Impossible) with some new straine t'out-do
> Passions of *Iuliet*, and her *Romeo*;
> Or till I heare a Scene more nobly take,
> Then when thy half-Sword parlying *Romans* spake.

In this passage Digges has obviously in mind the Quarrel scene as performed in the theatre; and some tradition of Brutus and Cassius threatening each other with half-drawn swords is suggested.

This popularity apparently continued throughout the succeeding years, and in a second poem (or another version of the first) which prefaced the 1640 edition of Shakespeare's poems, Digges records in more detail the reaction of the audience to *Julius Caesar*:

> So have I seen, when Caesar would appeare,
> And on the Stage at half-sword parley were
> *Brutus* and *Cassius*: oh how the Audience,
> Were ravish'd, with what wonder they went thence. . . .[11]

Although the latter poem must have been written before 1635 (the year of Digges's death), yet the fact that it could be published in 1640, supposedly for reader-appeal, and continue to express the same kind of enthusiasm revealed in the Folio poem seventeen years earlier, must surely indicate a fairly constant popularity throughout almost two intervening decades.

In addition to Platter's diary entry, only three records survive of performances prior to the Restoration. The first occurs in the Chamber Accounts for 1613 in which record is made of a payment to John Heminges for presenting 'Caesars Tragedye'[12] during the marriage festivities of Princess Elizabeth and the Elector Palatine sometime in the winter of 1612–13.[13] It was performed on at least two other occasions before 'the Kinge and Queene', once on 31 January 1636/7 at St James, and again at the Cockpit on 13 November 1638,[14] both times by the King's company.

These scattered references, however inadequate, suggest that *Julius Caesar* during the reigns of James and Charles was well-established in both royal and public favour. Noteworthy, too, is the emergence of the Quarrel scene as one of the play's most admired features.

It is possible that the King's Men performed *Julius Caesar* at Gibbon's Tennis Court between 1660 and 1663,[15] but no positive record of its performance occurs until Downes includes it as one of the plays performed in 1663 following the opening of Killigrew's new theatre in Brydges Street, Drury Lane.[16] In January 1668/9 *Julius Caesar* was one of the plays allotted to the King's company by royal warrant,[17] and it must be supposed that it was performed exclusively by them thereafter.

Downes provides us with our first cast-list for *Julius Caesar*, probably for a performance at about the time of the issuing of the warrant.[18] The roster of principal performers reads as follows:

Julius Caesar	Mr. Bell
Cassius	Major Mohun
Brutus	Mr. Hart
Antony	Mr. Kynaston
Calphurnia	Mrs. Marshal
Portia	Mrs. Corbet[19]

The actors Hart and Mohun, however, had probably been acting their roles throughout the decade since both had been members of the King's company since its organization.

Charles Hart, who played Brutus, was one of the company's leading actors. Wright tells us that Hart acted first as a boy at the Blackfriars in women's parts, and was an apprentice to Robinson.[20] During the Civil War he entered the King's Army and became a Lieutenant of Horse in Prince Rupert's Regiment.[21] It comes, then, as no surprise to find that on his return to the stage he made his reputation in military and statesmanlike roles, including Alexander in Lee's *The Rival Queens*, Arbaces in *A King and No King*, Amintor in *The Maid's Tragedy*, Duke Rollo in *The Bloody Brother*, and *Othello*.[22] Contemporary accounts of Hart's temperamental range, technique, and naturalness, buttress Downes's claim that if he acted Brutus 'but once in a Fortnight, the House was fill'd as at a New Play'.[23]

While Brutus was clearly the hero-role in revivals by the King's company, Cassius was not less ably played. Michael Mohun, who took the part, had also acted in pre-Commonwealth performances,[24] and, like Hart, had seen military service during the Civil War.[25] No doubt scenes in tent and battle were still fresh in his memory when he enacted Cassius in the first post-Restoration performances. Downes tells us that Cassius was one of his greatest roles, although he was in all 'most Accurate and Correct'.[26]

Among Mohun's most successful parts, Downes cites Mardonius in *A King and No King*, Melantius in *The Maid's Tragedy*, and Volpone. The briefest examination of these characters shows that his talents lay in quite a different direction from those of Hart. Where the latter excelled in portraying physical grandeur and depth and intensity of emotion, Mohun seems to have been at his best in depicting uncouth force and temperamental volatility.

No record survives of Mohun's movement and general stage deportment, but his elocution and interpretation were inimitable. Special mention is made of his rendering of Cassius' death (v.iii) in the epilogue to Fane's *Love in the Dark* (1675) wherein certain players who attempted to caricature his gait while he was suffering from some foot complaint (Genest suggests gout) are censured for their pains:

> Those Blades indeed are cripples in their art,
> Mimick his foot, but not his speaking part.
> Let them the Traytor or Volpone try?
> Could they –
> Rage like Cethegus, or like Cassius die?[27]

Edward Kynaston, who played Antony to the Brutus and Cassius of Hart and Mohun, was a much younger actor, who, according to Bellchambers,[28] began his stage career at the Cockpit in 1659. At the time of joining the

King's company he played mainly female roles, but by 1670 he had established an enviable reputation in male parts. It is doubtful that he partnered Hart and Mohun in performances immediately following the Restoration, but within the next decade, while still under 25, he had become a worthy third to the above actors, and one of the youngest Antonys in *Julius Caesar*'s stage history. He continued to play the part until near the turn of the century.[29]

It is unfortunate that no detailed account of any of these three performances survives; yet sufficient evidence remains to establish their substantial contribution to *Julius Caesar*'s stage history. Without doubt, Mohun and Hart brought to their interpretations elements of pre-Commonwealth stage practice, providing a bridge between Jacobean and Restoration productions. The fact that their names were associated with the play must have gone a considerable way toward securing its financial success and reputation;[30] and their interpretations (certainly that of Hart, at least)[31] provided a standard to be striven after throughout the rest of the seventeenth century and well on into the next. Also, the fact that at least three of the chief roles[32] were played by leading actors can hardly be overstressed; it is a happy circumstance all too seldom to be recorded.

From the time of the organization of the King's Men in 1660 until the union of the companies in 1682, *Julius Caesar* apparently went the way of stock plays, being revived at regular intervals and received with popular favour.[33] It is probable that Hart, Mohun, and Kynaston continued to perform until the union in 1682, after which Hart and Mohun retired, and were succeeded by the Brutus of Betterton and the Cassius of Smith.

Of the acting version used in the period 1660–82 we know nothing at all, but it seems likely that Hart and Mohun spoke something close to the Folio text, in keeping with the Blackfriars traditions. This assumption is to some extent borne out by the inclusion of Cinna the Poet in the manuscript cast-list for *c*.1669–72, a part which was consistently cut later, and by the 1684 acting edition which suggests little intervening alteration between the Folio text and itself.[34]

Only one performance for the period 1660–82 can be firmly dated. This was a performance before royalty, but whether at court or not is uncertain.[35] It is mentioned in a warrant dated 1 June 1677 which records a payment of twenty pounds for a performance of *Julius Caesar* on 4 December 1676.[36]

With the union of the companies in 1682 our picture of *Julius Caesar* in performance becomes somewhat clearer; for two years after the merger appeared the first acting version. Between the years 1684 and 1691 Miss Bartlett traces six separate printings of the play, and thinks there may well have been more. This, in itself, suggests an immense popularity for *Julius Caesar*;[37] and the fact that all editions contain the same cast-list indicates that for at least seven years the cast remained fairly static. The 1684 edition

claims to present the play 'As it is Now ACTED AT THE Theatre Royal', and
contains the following cast-list on the verso of the title-page:

Julius Caesar	By Mr. Goodman
Octavius Caesar	Mr. Perin
Antony	Mr. Kynaston
Brutus	Mr. Betterton
Cassius	Mr. Smith
Caska	Mr. Griffin
Trebonius	Mr. Saunders
Ligarius	Mr. Bowman
Decius Brutus	Mr. Williams
Metellus Cimber	Mr. Montfort
Cinna	Mr. Carlile
Artimedorus [sic]	Mr. Percival
Mesala	Mr. Wiltshire
And	*And*
Titinius	Mr. Gillo
Cinna the Poet	Mr. Jevon
Flavius	Mr. Norris
Plebeians	(Mr. Underhill
	(Mr. Lee
	(Mr. Bright
Women	
Calphurnia	Md. Slingsby
Portia	Mrs. Cook

Guards and Attendants

It is generally agreed that this edition represents something very close to
the actual acting text used at this time. Miss Bartlett concludes that these
acting editions were 'issued in quick succession to supply the demand
created by Betterton's fine presentation of the great tragedy', and suggests
that it was taken 'from a copy of the First Folio corrected for acting'.[38]
Hazelton Spencer, like Miss Bartlett, maintains that 'it appeared in
response to renewed public interest in the play because of Betterton's
revival'.[39] Odell carries its history a step farther back and believes that it
represents the acting text of Mohun and Hart, as transmitted to Betterton.[40]
In defence of its claim to be a theatrical version of the play, it seems highly
unlikely that the play would have run through six editions in roughly the
same form if the assertion were not basically true. Then, too, the cast-list is
surprisingly full, even to the inclusion of Cinna the Poet, which sorts well
with the fullness of the text. But, while it probably represents the play
substantially as it was acted, it is unlikely to have been printed from a
prompt-copy, unless that prompt-copy was very sparsely marked indeed.
The text is basically that of the First Folio, complete with the Folio
misprints and confusions.

Furthermore, while certain alterations are made in speech prefixes, inconsistencies are by no means eliminated. At I.iii.4–5, although Trebonius takes Cicero's speeches, Casca says, as in the Folio, 'O Cicero, / I have seen Tempests'; and again at I.iii.40, at the departure of Trebonius, the Folio direction 'Exit Cicero' is left standing. Again, although both Marullus and Cicero are eliminated, they appear in the stage direction at I.ii as in the Folio.

There is no evidence of prompter's directions nor of theatrical cutting. While the absence of cuts may indicate merely that a full text was played, the lack of notes is significant. The Folio directions are reprinted throughout, save for the alteration of 'Marullus' to 'Caska' in the direction for entry at I.i. and the substitution of 'Trebonius' for 'Cicero' in the entry for I.iii; if the text were printed from a theatre version it seems highly probable that the book-holder's instructions would have been apparent at some point. On the whole it seems likely that the text was printed from a First Folio copy in which the publisher had marked certain theatre practices he had noted in performances, and to which he appended the current cast-list.

Although the 1684 acting edition offers little specific information about stage practice, several significant observations can be made. First, the fullness of the cast-list indicates that the play must have been acted in something like its entirety. It is particularly noteworthy that Cinna the Poet appears, played by Mr Jevon, a part which was almost invariably cut a hundred years later.[41] If one assumes that Lucilius, Young Cato, Volumnius, Varro, Clitus, Claudius, Strato, Lucius, and Dardanius would be included with 'Guards and Attendants', then Publius, Popilius Lena, the Soothsayer, Pindarus, and the Camp Poet are the only parts unaccounted for. Whether or not their omission is significant, it is difficult to say. On the one hand, they may have been considered too minor for printing or they may have been played at various times by various people as the occasion required; but on the other hand, they may have been eliminated from the play altogether or their speeches may have been redistributed among other characters, without the publisher of the acting version taking note of it.

In any case, the 1684 acting version establishes the elimination of Marullus from I.i., his speeches being given to Casca. This practice marks but the beginning of a long series of speech redistributions, many of which fall to Casca's share regardless of their appropriateness to his character. It would appear that the intention was partly to decrease the size of the cast and thus expenses, and partly to amplify the character of Casca, so as to attract a major actor to the part. The fact that Marullus' 'Wherefore rejoice?' speech with its impassioned appeal is completely foreign to the sour and laconic Casca apparently mattered not a whit. In I.iii, the character of Cicero is also eliminated, his speeches being taken by Trebonius, another convention which became standard practice in the eighteenth and early nineteenth centuries.

Caesar's chief interpreters throughout the period of union, the cast-list tells us, were Thomas Betterton as Brutus and William Smith as Cassius. Edward Kynaston continued to perform Antony as he had done for at least a decade past.

From 1684 onwards *Julius Caesar* performance is inseparable from the name of Thomas Betterton, who performed Brutus from at least as early as 1684[42] until 1707, when he appeared in the role for the last time at the Queen's Theatre in the Haymarket.

Betterton brought to Brutus, it would seem, a massive dignity in spite of a somewhat ungainly body, a face 'serious, venerable, and majestic', a voice capable of almost infinite variation of tone and colour, all of which were dominated by an intelligence which understood the value of restraint. But Betterton's dignity by no means implied turgidity; when occasion required, fire was not lacking. Cibber, looking back on Betterton's Brutus, recalled that

> he could vary his Spirit to the different Characters he acted. Those wild impatient Starts, that fierce and flashing Fire, which he threw into *Hotspur*, never came from the unruffled Temper of his *Brutus* ... when the Betterton Brutus was provok'd in his Dispute with *Cassius*, his Spirit flew only to his Eye; his steady Look alone supply'd that Terror which he disdain'd an Intemperance in his Voice should rise to. Thus with a settled Dignity of Contempt, like an unheeding Rock he repelled upon himself the Foam of Cassius ... Not but some part of this Scene, where he reproaches *Cassius*, his Temper is not under this Suppression, but opens into that Warmth which becomes a Man of Virtue; yet this is that *Hasty Spark* of Anger which Brutus himself endeavours to excuse.[43]

In this brief account of Betterton's Brutus several points are worthy of note. First, we see established the tradition of Brutus as the 'Philosopher and the Heroe';[44] and the contrast between the 'unruffled Temper' of Brutus and the fiery disposition of Cassius is highlighted. Also important is the fact that Betterton did allow Brutus' anger some rein in the Quarrel scene, thus heightening the impression of restraint created throughout the rest of the play. Significant, too, is the indication of ensemble acting between Brutus and Cassius, a suggestion that neither attempted to dominate the scene – a phenomenon all too common in the next century.

Throughout the years of the Union and for some time thereafter at Lincoln's Inn Fields, Betterton's Brutus was ably seconded by Kynaston's Antony.[45] Of Smith, the Cassius of performances during the era of the United Company, we know very little indeed. He was an associate with Betterton in theatre management during the union, and was apparently highly regarded as an actor.[46] No record of his interpretation survives save for the hint conveyed by Cibber's phrase 'Foam of Cassius'. Of Cardell

Goodman's Caesar we know next to nothing, save that Goodman's style was characterized by force and restraint.[47]

Before turning from *Julius Caesar* performances during the union it is worth noting the practice, made clear by the acting edition, of allotting the parts of the citizens to the comedians of the company. Of the three mentioned – Underhill, Lee (Leigh), and Bright – some record of the first two survives. Leigh is commended by Cibber for his ability to 'attack' rather than 'court' the applause of the audience,[48] and is described as possessing a 'farcical Vivacity' which prevented his performance from becoming languid. In contrast to Leigh's effervescence was Underhill's excellence in 'Characters that may be called Still-life'. He specialized in 'the Stiff, the Heavy, and the Stupid'[49] types with remarkable success. The citizens, then, were not lacking in individuality; and it speaks well for the overall quality of Betterton's productions that even these comparatively small parts were played by principal comedians.

Only one performance for the period 1682–95 can be firmly dated. This was given at Whitehall on Monday, 18 April 1687, and is listed in a warrant dated 30 June of the same year.[50]

In 1695, after a salary dispute, the leading actors (headed by Betterton) seceded from the Theatre Royal and obtained a patent from William III to act in a new theatre on the site of a tennis court in Lincoln's Inn Fields. They began playing there on 29 April 1695.[51] and Betterton appeared almost exclusively at this theatre throughout the remainder of his career. There, too, Kynaston remained until his retirement. No doubt *Julius Caesar* was revived at intervals by the two veterans, but who played Cassius after the death of Smith is not known.[52] The next recorded performance took place on Monday, 14 February 1703/4 when the following theatrical advertisement appears:

At the New Theatre in *Little-Lincolns-Inn-Fields*, this present *Monday* being the 14th of *February*, will be presented *Julius Caesar, with the Death of Brutus and Cassius.*[53]

No cast-list is provided for this performance, nor for the next which took place two years later (14 March 1705/6) 'at the Desire of several Ladies of Quality'.

No further announcement of performances is made until Tuesday, 14 January 1707/8 when *The Daily Courant* carries the following notice:

For the Encouragement of the Comedians Acting in the Hay-Market, and to enable them to keep the Diversion of Plays under a seperate [*sic*] Interest from Operas.

At the Queen's Theatre in the Hay-Market, this present Tuesday, being the 14th of January, will be reviv'd the Tragedy of Julius Caesar. By Subscription. With a new Prologue. The parts of Julius Caesar by Mr. Booth, Octavius Caesar by Mr. Mills, Mark Antony by Mr. Wilks, Brutus by Mr. Betterton, Cassius by Mr.

Verbruggen, Caska by Mr. Keene, Ligarius by Mr. Boman, Decius Brutus by Mr. Husbands, Cinna the Poet by Mr. Bowen, four Plebians by Mr. Johnson, Mr. Bullock, Mr. Norris, Mr. Cross, Calphurnia by Mrs. Barry, Portia by Mrs. Bracegirdle.

It was repeated the following day.

This production marks very sharply the end of one era and the beginning of another. Kynaston, Goodman, and Smith had all left the stage; only Betterton remained of the actors who had performed the play at the beginning of the union; and this seems to have been his last performance. In the same cast, however, were the figures destined to become *Caesar*'s stars in the new century. Already Robert Wilks had taken the role of Antony, and Booth was temporarily playing Caesar while he marked time before assuming the role of Brutus, as Betterton's successor.

In the little more than a century traversed so far we have observed *Julius Caesar* firmly establish itself in the public taste, first in the pre-Commonwealth period, and then in the post-Restoration era. In a sense it is surprising that the play achieved such popularity during the reign of Charles II when it could not have been politically apt: the age had factions enough already, and the revolt against authority was still fresh in the minds of both king and populace. The secret of its success, one must assume, was its Roman subject matter[54] and exceptionally powerful acting by the best actors of the day. To the eighteenth century was transmitted a full text and a high standard of interpretation – a gift that the eighteenth century was hardly able to pass on to the nineteenth.

2

Eighteenth-century productions

In the first half of the eighteenth century, from Betterton's last performance in 1707 to the final appearance of James Quin as Brutus in 1751, only five years were without at least one *Julius Caesar* revival. Among Shakespeare's plays *Caesar* stands ninth in order of theatrical popularity, surpassed by *Hamlet*, *Macbeth*, *Othello*, *1 Henry IV*, *The Merry Wives*, *Richard III*, *The Tempest*, and *King Lear*.[1] Performances were neither exclusively at one theatre nor by any one major actor: all four leading playhouses – Drury Lane, Covent Garden, Lincoln's Inn Fields, and Goodman's Fields – staged revivals which featured most actors of any reputation, with the notable exception of David Garrick.[2]

The reasons for *Julius Caesar*'s popularity are several. The classical subject matter was eminently to the taste of an age which identified with, and sought its political and literary models in, the Rome of the Caesars. Even more important, perhaps, was the resurgence of nationalism in the first decades of the century which drew its inspiration from examples of Roman *amor patriae* and found theatrical expression in patriotic plays[3] like *Cato*. Closely allied with this upsurge of patriotic fervour, and perhaps the cause of it, was the ever-present fear of domestic or foreign tyranny. The prologue to the subscription performance of 1706/7 (Drury Lane, 14 January), written by Dennis and spoken by 'the Ghost of Shakespear', makes clear the consonance of Shakespeare's play with the temper of the times:

> Hail, my lov'd Britons! how I'm pleas'd to see
> The great assertors of fair Liberty,
> Assembled here upon this solemn day,
> To see this *Roman* and this *English* play!
> This tragedy in great Eliza's reign,
> Was writ, when Philip plagu'd both land and main,
> To subjugate the western world to Spain.
> Then I brought mighty Julius on the stage,
> Then Britain heard my godlike Roman's rage,
> And came in crouds, with rapture came, to see,

The world from its proud tyrant freed by me.
Rome he enslav'd, for which he died once there;
But for his introducing slav'ry here,
Ten times I sacrifice him ev'ry year.
                    . . .

Those glorious happy years [of Elizabeth] roll round again,
France struggles for a fifth monarchic reign,
Like our own mad fanatics here, in vain,
For a more fam'd, more great Eliza's here,
A wiser Cecil, and a nobler Vere.[4]

Of course, contemporary aptness is not sufficient in itself to account for
Julius Caesar's stage success; popular subject matter must be vivified by
adequate performance. To the interpretations of Barton Booth and Robert
Wilks, as Brutus and Antony, belongs much of the credit for the frequent
revivals of the play in the years 1712–28.[5] After the death of Booth (1733),
James Quin, although far from a first-rate actor, contrived to preserve the
play from desuetude until the mid-century.

The reafter the stage history of *Julius Caesar* is not so happy. From Quin's
last performance (1751) to the end of the century, the play was presented
only twenty-three times, with no revivals at all from 1781 onwards. This fall
from favour was no doubt due to Garrick's failure to perform it and the lack
of a sufficient number of actors of suitable calibre to undertake it without
him. Perhaps some weight may also be attached to Mrs Inchbald's suggestion that the political climate was such as to make the play an unhappy
choice.[6]

Text

To determine the text of *Julius Caesar* spoken at any given eighteenth-
century performance is impossible; nevertheless, on the evidence of two
almost certainly authentic acting editions and a promptbook, one can
roughly ascertain the state of the script at three time-points.[7] The
Dryden–Davenant edition (1719) probably represents the version played in
the early years of the century. A Covent Garden promptbook used for a
production in January 1766 (*JC* 4) records the character of the playhouse
copy some fifty years on. Bell's edition (1773), prepared and annotated by
Francis Gentleman, incorporates revisions associated with the next-to-last
revivals of the period.[8]

The legitimacy of the title-page claim of the Dryden–Davenant version to
represent the play 'As it is now Acted' is patent. The theatricality
of line-rearrangement, the vivid stage directions (e.g. 'Scene draws,
and discovers the Capitol; they seat themselves' at III.i.12 or 'Ring
down' for Caesar's ghost at IV.iii.286), and the applause-directed rants

inserted for Brutus carry their own conviction. The origins of this version and its connection with Davenant and Dryden are much less certain.

Until the researches of R. C. Bald and William Van Lennep,[9] it was generally thought that the adaptation was made shortly prior to its publication. Montague Summers, for example, plumped for the hand of Cibber.[10] Bald, however, noted that in the remains of the Smock Alley Third Folio (used in the seventeenth century as a prompt-copy at the Smock Alley Theatre in Dublin, and now in the Folger Library) is a manuscript cast-list and a fragment of text containing the last two lines spoken by the dying Brutus, as in the Dryden–Davenant version:

> poor slavish rome, farwell: Ceasear now be still
> I Kild not thee wth half so good a will
>
>   *Dyes.*

This discovery places the earliest occurrence of these lines some time before 1676.[11] Somewhat superficially from the scant evidence, Van Lennep concludes that the play was performed in Dublin 'in a version which was printed in 1719 as the work of Davenant and Dryden'.[12] While it is true that the lines cited above are identical with the Dryden–Davenant version, there is no other evidence to indicate that the play was performed in full in the 1719 text. In fact, the cast-list would militate against this view, since 'Murillus' is included (played by Mr Williams),[13] a role which was allotted to 'Caska' in the Dryden–Davenant copy. Van Lennep goes on to conjecture that the play was given in London before it was presented in Dublin, but there is no evidence to support this supposition. Moreover, if the play was being performed at this time in London in the Dryden–Davenant version, how can the acting editions of 1684–91 be accounted for? These editions clearly indicate that throughout these years Marullus was eliminated, his lines being taken by Casca. Also, the Cinna the Poet scene was played, while Cinna appears neither in the Smock Alley cast-list nor in the Dryden–Davenant text.

It is more probable that the 1719 edition represents the state of the London prompt-copy in 1719 – a composite of the 1684–91 quartos and the Smock Alley version – although when it first assumed this form cannot be determined with any certainty. One is tempted to conjecture that John Richards[14] may have brought with him from Dublin Brutus' added death lines (and perhaps other inserted speeches) and that these were added to the Betterton copy sometime in the 1690s or the early 1700s. This theory would account for the elimination of Marullus (derived from the Betterton text) and the insertion of Brutus' death lines (derived from the Smock Alley copy), both of which are found in the 1719 version. Other alterations may have been derived from one or the other of the above copies or may merely represent an accumulation of stage practices over a period of almost three decades. All of the existing evidence points toward the conclusion of David Erskine Baker who made the earliest comment on this text: 'This seems to be a publication of the play-house copy, with alterations for the stage, which perhaps were traditionally ascribed to Davenant and Dryden, how truly, let any person determine, after reading the . . . ridiculous rant which is added at the close of the fourth act.'[15]

Compared with the ravages suffered by other Shakespearian plays during this period, the Dryden–Davenant version touches *Julius Caesar* comparatively lightly. The practice of redistributing speeches, initiated with the 1684 version, continues. About one hundred and sixty lines are cut, and twenty-eight new ones are added.

Perhaps it is the character of Casca which is most strikingly altered. He takes not only the speeches of Marullus (as in the 1684 edition) but those of Titinius as well. Casca now not only volubly berates the plebeians, but also goes off on Cassius' reconnaissance mission and later kills himself with dog-like devotion by Cassius' body. How ill these actions sort with the sour and laconic Roman of I.ii is too obvious for comment.

Trebonius continues to take Cicero's speeches as in the 1684 edition, while young Cato, Volumnius, Strato, and Clitus are all eliminated. Their speeches are either omitted or redistributed among Messala, Dardanius, Popilius, and Lucilius. The roles of Artemidorus and the Soothsayer are merged (with the Soothsayer taking the speeches), and Cinna the Poet and the Camp Poet are both eliminated. The three latter innovations persisted until the present century. In all, the Dryden–Davenant version reduces the speaking parts by ten.

The cuts are modest when compared, for example, with the drastic excisions of Tree or Welles; they are for the most part purposeful,[16] and are characteristic of the tastes of the age. Not unexpectedly, Shakespeare's language comes in for some revision aimed at modernizing the vocabulary, clarifying the syntax, and preserving decorum of expression.[17] No mention is made of hats, nightgowns, or walking unbraced; and Portia decorously wounds herself in the arm rather than the thigh. An attempt is also made to reduce the number of references to the supernatural, which apparently struck the age as excessive. When Francis Gentlemen, in his notes to Bell's *Julius Caesar*, commented that 'omens and prodigies are too much insisted upon in this play',[18] he was no doubt voicing a long-held theatrical view. Cassius' speech to Casca, in which he reiterates the omens and suggests that they are 'instruments of fear and warning' (I.iii.59–71) is omitted, as is his similar observation at I.iii.126–30.

A large number of cuts may be attributed to an attempt to 'excise language and ideas unsuited to the elevation of tragedy',[19] particularly those which would tend to lower the heroic tone of the leading characters. Brutus receives most of the attention. His somewhat dubious injunction to the conspirators:

> And let our hearts, as subtle masters do,
> Stir up their servants to an act of rage,
> And after seen to chide 'em. (II.i.175–7)

is eliminated, partly to clarify syntax, but particularly because it tends to destroy Brutus' claim to perfect rationality. The short scene in which Brutus soliloquizes to the sleeping Lucius after the departure of the conspirators (II.i.229–33) is also removed. This cut was apparently standard throughout the century,[20] and, taken in conjunction with others (see below), initiates a trend toward a straight-line interpretation of Brutus as a cold-blooded idealist which reached its culmination with John Philip Kemble's performance in 1812. Portia makes no reference to his 'impatience'; nor does he promise to tell her his 'engagements'. After the assassination his reference to 'the bleeding business' done by the hands of the conspirators (III.i.168) and the line 'As fire drives out fire, so pity pity –' (III.i.171) are cut to clear Brutus of any suggestion of callousness. In the Quarrel scene, the somewhat swaggering exchange:

Bru. I say you are not.
Cas. Urge me no more, I shall forget myself;
      Have mind upon your health; tempt me no farther. (IV.iii.34–6)

is excised, prompting one to wonder whether the criticism of Rymer[21] was entirely without effect. No mention is made of the lost book or Brutus' forgetfulness, and prior to his death Clitus' comment, 'Now is that noble vessel full of grief, / That it runs over even at his eyes' (V.v.13–14), disappears. Brutus may well emerge as a more convincing Stoic, but without touches of frailty his humanity lacks credibility.

Brutus is not the only character to be purged of improprieties. Caesar's braggadocio beginning 'Danger knows full well' (II.ii.44–8) is eliminated, together with Antony's rather unsportsmanlike reference to Lepidus (IV.i.34–9). Cassius is not permitted his diatribe against the decadence of contemporary Romans (I.iii.80–4), nor does Metellus refer to the youth and wildness of the conspirators (II.i.147–9).

A number of excisions are designed to accelerate pace and heighten theatrical effect. In I.iii Cassius and Casca exit on the strong curtain lines

> . . . Three parts of him
> Is ours already, and the man entire
> Upon the next encounter yields him ours. (I.iii.154–6)

and the rest of the scene is cut. The Cinna the Poet scene is removed to allow the action to move directly from Antony's 'Bring me to Octavius' to the scene in which the triumvirate meet at Antony's house; and at IV.iii.124ff the interlude of the Camp Poet is eliminated. From the military sequences the brief exchange between Antony and Octavius (V.i.23–6) about whether they should 'give sign of battle' is removed, and the first fifteen lines of V.iv, in which young Cato proclaims his name about the field and Lucilius impersonates Brutus, vanish. The scene begins with the entry of Antony and the soldiers with Lucilius prisoner. Gentleman's explanation, although half a century later, clearly elucidates both cuts. 'The hurry of battle is necessarily confused', he explains, 'wherefore as little dialogue should be introduced as possible; wherefore the original is in representation considerably reduced, and the catastrophe brought on with more spirit.'[22]

The eighteenth-century theatre-goer regarded *Caesar*, it will be recalled, as a patriotic play. Caesar was presented as the villain who suppressed liberty, and Brutus as the hero who asserted it. More often than not Caesar appeared as the stock stage tyrant, a conventional figure of rant and strut. Brutus, on the other hand, was considered the ideal patriot with whom English lovers of liberty identified themselves and their causes. 'My Lord,' says one of Mrs Centlivre's characters in *The Wonder* (Drury Lane 1714), 'the *English* are by nature, what the ancient *Romans* were by discipline – courageous, bold, hardy, and in love with Liberty.' (I.i.)[23]

If cuts provide some indication of the impression Brutus was intended to make in the eighteenth-century theatre, additions to the text put the point beyond all doubt. The first insertion occurs after Brutus questions Claudius and Varro following the exit of the ghost. Once they have departed in search of Cassius, Brutus remains alone on stage (save for the sleeping Lucius), and brings the act to a stirring end with

> Sure they have raised some Devil to their aid,
> And think to frighten *Brutus* with a shade.
> But ere night closes this fatal Day,
> I'll send more Ghosts this visit to repay.

Not only does this speech allow the actor a strong curtain, but Brutus' defiance of Caesar's spirit is well-calculated to appeal to an audience who expected his response to tyranny, whether physical or spiritual, to be prompt and devastating.

But there was more to come. The ghost at IV.iii.283 promises Brutus another visit at Philippi, and the eighteenth-century audience was not to be disappointed. After Brutus' lines:

> O Julius Caesar, thou art mighty yet!
> Thy spirit walks abroad, and turns our swords
> In our own proper entrails.

which are transposed from V.iii.94–6 to come after Brutus' instructions for the burial of Cassius, appears the direction: '*Enter* Caesars *Ghost* –,' and the following exchange ensues:

Ghost Cassius, my three and thirty wounds are now reveng'd.
Brut. What art thou, why com'st thou.
Ghost To keep my word and meet thee in *Philippi* fields.
Brut. Well, I will see thee then.
Ghost Next, ungrateful *Brutus*, do I call.
Brut. Ungrateful, *Caesar*, that wou'd Rome enthral.
Ghost The Ides of March Remember – I must go.
          To meet thee on the burning Lake below.

                                                    [sinks]
Brut. My Spirits come to me – Stay thou bloody Apparition, come back, I wou'd
          converse Longer with thee – 'tis gone, this fatal shadow
          Haunts me still.

Beyond the spectacular appeal offered by the appearance of a ghost, the scene assures the audience of the ultimate fate of tyrants and permits Brutus one more opportunity to assert the purity of his motives.

The alterations to Brutus' death scene (V.v), however, were even more drastic and longer-lived.[24] Immediately after Brutus invites Volumnius (in Dryden–Davenant, Popilius) to kill him and Volumnius refuses, Lucilius breaks in:

Luc. Fly my Lord.
Brut. Why do you stay to save his Life
          That must not live.
Luc. After you, what *Roman* wou'd Live?
Brut. What *Roman* wou'd not live that may
          To serve his Country in a nobler day.
          You are not above pardon, tho' Brutus is.
Luc. I'm not afraid to die.
Brut. Retire and let me think a while.
          Now one last look, and then farewel to all.
          That wou'd with the unhappy Brutus fall.
          Scorning to view his Country's Misery,
          Thus *Brutus* always strikes for Liberty.

                                              [Stabs himself]
          Poor slavish *Rome* farewel, Caesar now be still.
          I kill'd not thee with half so Good a will.

                                                    [Dies]
Enter Anthony, Octavius, Messala, *and Soldiers.*
Anth. Whom mourn you over?
Luc. 'Tis Brutus.
Mess. So Brutus shou'd be found – I thank
          Thee *Brutus*, that thou hast prov'd
          Messala's saying true.
Anth. This was the noblest Roman [etc.]

The handling of this final scene leaves little doubt that Brutus is intended to emerge as the play's hero; with Strato eliminated, Brutus alone com-

mands the audience's attention in the final moments. The last lines of
Lucilius clearly establish Brutus' stature as a leader of men; his own present
him as magnanimous patriot and martyr to the cause of freedom. The taking
of his own life not only heightens the dramatic intensity but constitutes
behaviour somewhat more consonant with heroic tragedy. The cutting of
most of the lines following Brutus' death hurries the play to its close while
the tragic impression is still fresh.

Although the Dryden–Davenant alterations are comparatively minor,
their influence upon later productions is profound. This version confirms
the tradition of reducing the cast by elimination of characters and redistribution of speeches, continues the expansion of the character of Casca, and
initiates the practice of cutting the Cinna the Poet and Camp Poet episodes.
Its concern for propriety of language and consistency of tragic tone affects
the state of the theatre text until the close of the nineteenth century. Finally,
it clearly demonstrates the emergence of Brutus as the leading character in
the tragedy. Where Betterton apparently established Brutus' predominance
by sheer acting skill, this version secures him the plum role by textual
alteration.

The 1766 Covent Garden promptbook, in the Folger Shakespeare
Library,[25] attests to the continued use of the Dryden–Davenant arrangement, albeit with slight alterations, throughout the first half of the century.
Such changes as there are serve merely to underline the trend toward cast
reduction, simplification of syntax, tragic propriety, and swiftness of action
evident in the 1719 text.

All the characters eliminated from the Dryden–Davenant version, save
for Volumnius and Artemidorus, are omitted from the Covent Garden text.
In addition, Flavius is replaced by Cinna in I.i; Messala's lines are taken by
Trebonius throughout; and Dardanius is replaced by Volumnius in the last
scene. Although Lucilius is retained elsewhere, it is Trebonius who is taken
prisoner by Mark Antony at v.iv. Otherwise the speech redistribution and
cast-list are identical with the Dryden–Davenant copy. Cuts in the interests
of tragic decorum multiply; and the distaste for supernatural references
intensifies.

To the list of Dryden–Davenant pace cuts, the Covent Garden text adds
several fresh ones. The Caius Ligarius scene is more heavily blue-pencilled
than previously, and now ends with Brutus' promise to Ligarius to unfold
'What it is . . . as we are going' (II.i.329–30). The citizens' ejaculations in
the Forum scene are drastically curtailed to speed up the action and permit
comparatively uninterrupted declamation. Swiftness of movement is, of
course, achieved, but with a lamentable loss of naturalness.

A further regrettable cut occurs at the end of the Ghost scene (IV.iii).
After the disappearance of the ghost, Brutus calls Lucius, adding 'Lucius, I
say' to Shakespeare's text; Lucius, however, does not awaken. When

Brutus calls Claudius and Varro, he does not ask if either saw anything, but simply instructs them to proceed to Cassius. Here a pathetic and intensely human picture of the Stoic struggling with mounting panic is sacrificed in a rush to end the scene with all possible speed.

For many of Shakespeare's plays, Bell's edition provides the first genuine theatre text; in the case of *Caesar*, however, it serves mainly to confirm the authenticity of the Dryden–Davenant and Covent Garden scripts and to record an ever more rigorous application of the aesthetic principles which shaped the play in earlier decades. Still in evidence is an attempt to reduce the size of the cast, and most of the cuts and alterations in the interest of propriety and consistency of tragic tone are retained. Cuts to ensure dramatic pace are considerably heavier.

Where the Covent Garden text reduces the speaking parts by twelve, Bell's decreases the cast by seventeen, or roughly half the number of Shakespeare's named characters. Perhaps the most striking alteration is the increasing importance given to Casca and Trebonius. Casca continues to take the lines of Marullus (now companioned by Decius Brutus who replaces Flavius) and Titinius, but in addition he assumes Pindarus' role in the preliminaries to the Quarrel scene[26] (although Pindarus himself kills Cassius). Trebonius takes the speeches of Cicero and Messala as in the Covent Garden version, and to these adds the lines of Publius at II.ii and those of Lucilius throughout. Artemidorus and the Soothsayer are once more merged, with the former speaking the lines. Eliminated in addition to those already mentioned are Young Cato, Strato, Volumnius, Clitus, and Dardanius. When necessary, their short speeches are redistributed among Decius, Cinna, and Metellus. Popilius Lena and Caius Ligarius[27] disappear entirely.

References to the supernatural are further reduced. The concern to elevate the tragic stature of Brutus also continues. In addition to preserving the earlier omissions, Bell's edition does not permit him to go to Caesar's house to bring the Dictator to the Capitol, thus clearing him of one more possible charge of base conduct.

Most of the Covent Garden pace cuts remain, and a good many new ones are added. In I.i the citizens now exit at I.i.56, immediately after Marullus' (Bell–Casca's) impassioned speech. Their cue is Flavius' (Bell–Decius Brutus') 'Go, go, good countrymen.' The rest of the speech is deleted. Flavius' order to 'disrobe the images' is retained, but Marullus' (Casca's) query, 'May we do so?' and all but Flavius' (Decius Brutus') four final lines (I.i.72–5) are cut. These excisions are, of course, meant to hurry the action forward to the entrance of Caesar, but the texture of the dramatic experience suffers. Marullus' organ-like swell of impassioned declamation needs the more sympathetic, lower-keyed appeal of Flavius to complete its effect. The cutting of the conversation between the tribunes, or in this case, the

conspirators, is also unwise. Their colloquy offers a brief respite between
the excitement of the mob scene and the imminent arrival of the procession.
Without it, the impact of Caesar's first entry is bound to be lessened.

In order to provide a more dramatic exit for Brutus in I.ii, his lines at
I.ii.171–5:

> Till then, my noble friend, chew upon this:
>
> . . .
>
> Is like to lay upon us.

are transposed to I.ii.306 to come after his rather prosaic invitation to
Cassius: 'or, if you will, / Come home to me, and I will wait for you', upon
which he would ordinarily quit the stage. Again, Shakespeare's stagecraft is
sounder than the eighteenth-century manager's. Cassius, after all, has the
final speech in the scene which he must build to the highly dramatic finale
'And after this let Caesar seat him sure, / For we will shake him, or worse
days endure' (I.ii.321–2). If Brutus is given too striking an exit, Cassius'
outburst inevitably comes as something of an anti-climax.

Several lines (I.iii.146–51) are cut from the exchange between Cassius
and Cinna at I.iii to hasten the end of this scene. The audience was thus left
uninformed of the names of the conspirators and the meeting to take place at
Pompey's theatre – essential information if they are fully to appreciate what
follows. The meeting between Brutus and Caius Ligarius (II.i.309–34) is
cut, as much, no doubt, to connect the conspiracy and the assassination with
minimum delay as to reduce the size of the cast.

Further attempts to unify the action are evident in the handling of the
Assassination scene. Caesar's procession to the Capitol, the Soothsayer's
warning, Artemidorus' futile attempt to make his suit to Caesar, and the
conspirators' fear of betrayal by Popilius are all deleted. The scene opens
with Cassius' 'Trebonius knows his time. . .' (III.i.25). In order not to
distract attention from the major figures in the crucial moments following
the assassination, all reference to Publius is cut. The drastic reduction of the
first part of the scene destroys the gradual build-up of dramatic tension,
while the omission of Publius robs the audience of a moment of much-
needed relaxation before a fresh movement begins.

Brutus' lines beginning 'How many times shall Caesar bleed in sport'
(III.i.114–16) and Cassius' 'So oft as that shall be' (III.i.116–18) speech are
excised. Gentleman allows that these speeches, 'though seldom delivered
on the stage, certainly deserve preservation, as they tend to naturalize
representation, in the same manner the mock tragedy in *Hamlet*
does'.[28]

The Forum scene, too, is more heavily hacked than in the Covent Garden
version. Besides the cuts discussed earlier, there is no division of the
audience between Brutus and Cassius at the start of the scene. The last lines

of the exchange between Antony and the servant (III.ii.268–71) are removed to spare an allusion to Brutus and Cassius in unseemly flight and to allow Antony a more effective exit on

> Fortune is merry,
> And in this mood will give us anything. (III.ii.266–7)

The Cinna the Poet episode is once more omitted.

In act IV a number of excisions are made to secure greater speed and coherence. The Camp Poet is again eliminated from the Quarrel scene. Gentleman finds the character 'without any meaning, unless that of turning a noble reflection into ill-timed laughter'; and notes with some satisfaction that 'the rhiming excrescence is justly consigned to oblivion'.[29] The character probably disappeared not long after the publication of the Dryden–Davenant version. He does not appear in the Covent Garden copy.

Later in the same scene, after the exit of the ghost, the lines in which Brutus awakens Lucius (IV.iii.289–98) are cut altogether. He now speaks only to Claudius and Varro. The scene once more ends with the long-standing interpolated rant beginning 'Sure they have raised some devil'.

Act V generally follows the Dryden–Davenant text with several further excisions, not the least of which is Cassius' birthday speech (V.i.70–91). By the omission of this redeeming glimpse of Cassius shortly before his death, his dramatic stature cannot but suffer. The cut was designed to permit the action to move directly from the challenge of Octavius to the farewells of Brutus and Cassius. Gentleman was not much in favour of the omission. 'This short conversation between *Cassius* and *Casca* [who took Messala's lines]', he remarks, 'is sometimes, but very improperly rejected by the stage; it is a fine picture of the impression which ominous appearances made on the bravest Romans.'[30] Indeed it is all of this, and infinitely more.

Cassius' death scene closely parallels the Dryden–Davenant version, but several changes are made in the sequence in which the bodies are discovered. Messala's apostrophe to Error (V.iii.67–71) is deleted as are Cato's lines at V.iii.93, 96–7, 'He is slain' and 'Brave Titinius! / Look whe'er he have not crown'd dead Cassius!' The latter lines were probably omitted to focus dramatic concentration solely upon the corpse of Cassius. The speech in which Brutus arranges for Cassius' funeral is omitted (V.iii.104–6). The most significant change, however, is the deletion of the second appearance of Caesar's ghost; by 1773 it seems to have served its purpose. Gentleman notes that he had seen it on stage, probably in the early years of his theatre career (c. 1750), but two decades later the addition was considered 'insufferable ignorance'.[31]

Brutus' death scene is essentially that of the Dryden–Davenant and Covent Garden versions, with a somewhat altered, although clearly derivative, death-speech:

I shall have glory by this losing day.
Retire and let me think a while –
Now, one last look, and then, farewell to all;
Scorning to view his country's wrongs,
Thus Brutus always strikes for liberty.
Poor slavish Rome, farewel.
Caesar now be still;
I killed not thee with half so good a will. Oh!

Gone is the exchange between Brutus and Lucilius; but that final outburst of patriotism and the histrionic suicide were not so easily to be surrendered by Brutuses who felt, no doubt, that the dramatic honours were too widely distributed already.

On the whole, the eighteenth-century theatre text of *Caesar* remains remarkably faithful to the original when one considers the amount of critical detraction to which the play was subjected throughout the period. Admittedly, it is given a patriotic slant, but cuts and additions effect a heightening of certain aspects rather than a basic alteration of direction. Perhaps the most striking feature is the consistent predominance of Brutus with his excellent curtains, stirring rant, and lurid death-scene. Cassius' speeches, it will be noted, are more heavily cut than Antony's, possibly because, in the age of Cibber at least, the roles of Brutus and Antony were usually taken by the leading players. Significant also is the downgrading of the crowd by reducing their time on stage in I.i, cutting their lines in the Forum scene, and eliminating the Cinna the Poet sequence altogether.

Stagecraft

A detailed analysis of staging and interpretation for each eighteenth-century revival would be both tedious and unnecessary, even if materials were available for such a study. The stock status of the play implies a fairly standardized method of presentation; thus some reconstruction of Covent Garden settings and business will demonstrate basic production methods valid for all London theatres of the period. Here the 1766 promptbook[32] is the chief source of information.

At the beginning of the performance the curtain rises to reveal a back-shutter described as 'Iron Gate Town'. This was doubtless a stock flat[33] placed in the first grooves and depicting an iron gate with a town in the background. Cinna and Casca enter PS (prompt side, i.e. stage left) and the mob enters OP (opposite prompt, i.e. stage right). The entry was no doubt made through the doors flanking the proscenium, and they meet on the apron. The prompter's direction states that 'The mob hallow when Curtain rises.' The nondescript backshutter offers a kind of pictorial relief to the action without distracting from it.[34]

In all likelihood the mob was small, comprising merely a few comedy actors who took the parts of citizens. Cast-lists in 1721 provide three citizens for Drury Lane and four for Lincoln's Inn Fields; but in 1722, Lincoln's Inn Fields increases the number to five and, in 1723, to six. The largest number recorded is for the Goodman's Fields revival in 1732 when nine citizens are listed. For most performances thereafter an estimate of six would not be far wrong. The mob was thus suggestive of the Roman populace, rather than representative as in nineteenth-century performances. After Casca's harangue, the mob exits PS and the tribunes depart in opposite directions shortly after, leaving a clear stage for the entry of Caesar and his entourage.

Before and during Caesar's arrival, 'Musick plays a March.' Caesar enters OP with his party, and a small show they must have made. In addition to the characters specified in the text, the promptbook calls for only 'Guards Mob etc.' On Caesar's 'He is a dreamer, let us leave him. Pass.' (I.ii.24), the march is resumed, and the procession exits PS. Brutus and Cassius now have the apron to themselves for the intimate dialogue in which Cassius sounds Brutus.

Until 1766 Caesar apparently re-entered on Brutus' 'But look you, Cassius' (I.ii.182); the Covent Garden book has him reappear on 'Casca will tell us what the matter is' (I.ii.189). Brutus comments on 'the angry spot' while looking off PS, thus keeping the attention of the audience focussed upon himself at the expense of Caesar. Uneventfully the Dictator crosses the apron and exits OP. Casca, after passing on his information, exits OP and Brutus exits PS. The side from which Cassius departs is not indicated. The lowering of the lights and a clear stage marked the end of the first act.

The second act begins with the modern I.iii. No change of scene is indicated. The stage remains darkened ('Lamps down continues') while Casca enters OP and Trebonius PS to the accompaniment of thunder and lightning. Cassius arrives from PS and Trebonius goes off OP. Later Cinna enters OP and exits from the same side.

After the exit of Cassius and Casca (OP), the 'Iron Gate Town' flat is drawn off revealing behind (probably in groove 2)[35] a backshutter representing 'Court by Gar [?den]'. Brutus enters PS, followed a moment later by Lucius. During Brutus' soliloquy 'Lightning frequently' illuminates the semi-darkness. Brutus no doubt played the scene as far forward as possible. After Lucius enters PS with 'Sir, March is wasted fifteen days' (II.i.59), the conspirators' knock follows at OP. They enter OP and leave from the same side. One interesting direction at II.i.191 reminds the person in charge of sound effects to 'Ring C [urtain] Bell to strike Clock.' After the exit of the conspirators Portia enters and exits PS, and later Ligarius enters OP.

Following the exit of Brutus and Ligarius (OP), a shutter described as 'Marble Hall' ('chamber' crossed out), was run on in groove 1.[36] As the flat appears the lamps come up. Caesar enters OP; and when he bids the servant (who enters and exits PS) to order the priests to do 'present sacrifice' thunder is heard. There are few other directions for this scene, save that Calphurnia enters PS and exits from the opposite side. The conspirators enter OP and exit with Caesar PS. With their exit act II ends.

Act III commences with the modern II.iii. The withdrawal of Marble Hall reveals a flat identified only as 'Town', probably in groove 2 where Brutus' garden had previously been.[37] Artemidorus enters OP and no doubt reads his paper fairly well forward. After his 'If not, the Fates with traitors do contrive' (II.iii.16), he exits OP, leaving a clear stage for the entry of Portia and Lucius (PS). Artemidorus again enters after Lucius' 'Sooth, Madam, I hear nothing' (II.iv.20) to speak the Soothsayer's lines. Once Portia has directed Lucius to run to the Capitol, she exits PS and Lucius follows Artemidorus off OP.

Now that the stage is cleared, a 'March of Musick & Trumpets' heralds the approach of the procession. There is no scene change: the Dictator enters OP with his following ('Attend[ts]' are now included) and stops on the forestage in front of the Town flat for his exchanges with the Soothsayer and Artemidorus. Popilius enters OP alone immediately before his 'I wish your enterprise to-day may thrive' (III.i.13), and exits with Caesar and his train at PS. The separate entry for Popilius markedly heightens the dramatic impact of this relatively minor incident.

Caesar and his company then apparently go between the wing flats and arrange themselves in state behind the Town backshutter. Meanwhile, Brutus and Cassius conduct their brief conversation on the apron. The audience now has opportunity to observe the conspirators at close range in the crucial moments before the assassination without the visual distraction of the Dictator and his attendants. After Cinna's 'Casca, you are the first that rears your hand' (III.i.30), the conspirators exit PS and return to a new scene. While they are off the Town flat is withdrawn to reveal Caesar (probably seated) with his attendants before a backshutter described as 'Dalls Palace' ('Hall' crossed out).[38] Because some properties were necessary (e.g. Pompey's statue) and a fairly large number of characters had to be accommodated, the scene must have been run on in groove 3, or perhaps Dall's Palace was a backscene placed at extreme upstage.

No directions are provided for the business of the assassination; and the absence of such details may suggest that it was handled in a fairly impromptu manner. Davies warns that 'from the great number of persons on the stage, during the representation of Caesar's murder, much difficulty in the action may arise, unless great accuracy is observed in the direction of those who are employed. The several conspirators, pressing with eagerness to have a share in stabbing the victim, must be so regulated as to avoid confusion.'[39] One wonders if he is here speaking from unfortunate experience.

In the moments following the assassination the conspirators do not wash their hands in Caesar's blood. While the sight of a bloodthirsty Brutus may have offended against eighteenth-century notions of decorum,[40] its absence cost the audience an invaluable insight into the sacrificial fanaticism underlying Brutus' act – the practical expression, in fact, of his earlier injunction to the conspirators to be 'sacrificers, but not butchers' (II.i.166).[41]

At the end of the scene Antony does not ask the servant to assist him with Caesar's body; '4 Gents with the Bier' are provided PS to relieve him of the labour. After Antony's exit the curtain is lowered to allow the Forum setting to be positioned.

In all probability the Forum scene occupied roughly the same stage area as that used for the Assassination sequence.[42] It was not the Roman Forum which confronted the audience, however, but the 'Town' backshutter of previous scenes with a 'pulpit' in front. The mob apparently rioted near the proscenium opening and on the apron. According to Voltaire, Brutus entered with his dagger still dripping with blood. 'Avec quel ravissement je voyais Brutus', he recalls, 'tenant encore un poignard teint du sang de César, assembler le peuple romain, et lui parler . . . de haut de la tribune aux harangues.'[43] On the line 'Save I alone, till Antony have spoke' (III.ii.61), Brutus exits PS and Antony enters OP with the '4 Gents' bearing Caesar's bier. It is worth noting that Antony enters much later than in the Folio text, presumably to allow Brutus to dominate the stage without the diversion caused by the presence of Antony and the dead Caesar. This arrangement, however, was not without its defects, for, lacking the corpse of Caesar to point to from time to time, the impact of Brutus' speech must have been considerably lessened.

There was apparently little attempt made to achieve co-ordination between Antony and the mob. The scene seems to have been regarded as merely a declamatory set-piece. As we noted earlier, the mob was small and was usually made up of a few comedians. While Antony concentrated on his applause points, the comedians found themselves with little to do, and, as one might expect, diverted themselves and the audience with comic business. Gentleman draws attention to one such piece of behaviour on Antony's 'lend me your ears': 'We have seen some very comical comedians put up their hands to their ears, as if *Antony* meant to be taken in a literal sense – wretched buffoonery.'[44] On Antony's exit (OP) the curtain once more falls to allow the pulpit to be taken off and the scene set for Antony's house.

Act IV opens with the triumvirate 'Disc[d][45] (presumably seated) before a flat designated only by the name of its painter, 'Laguerre'[46] ('Marble Hall' crossed out). Properties are merely a table and three chairs, with a 'Standish' on the table. At the end of the scene Antony and Octavius exit PS.

Following the conference, a backshutter described as 'Short Wood'[47] slides across in front of Antony's house, perhaps in the first grooves. To a march Brutus and soldiers enter OP, and Lucilius and Pindarus enter PS. Later Cassius enters to a march at PS. After their first brief exchange Brutus and Cassius exit OP and re-enter on a fresh setting.

While the front scene was taking place on the apron, Brutus' tent was mounted behind and its furnishings put in place. The front-shutters then slid back to reveal the set scene. Whether the tent was a functional one or merely a backshutter cannot be ascertained. Besides providing for a tent, the direction calls for 'Table Book Lres [?Letters] Candles 2 State Chairs 2 Cane Chairs'. State chairs were obviously provided for the generals and cane seats for their subordinates. Altogether the setting was simple, light, and cheap – eminently suited to the speed of the performance and adequate enough.

The remainder of the act is very sparsely marked indeed, save for one or two intriguing notes. It is clear that Lucius did not play the lute himself, and it is doubtful if he sang. The warning cue is 'One to play Lute', and a few lines later the direction reads 'One plays behind.' Noteworthy also is the method of entry for Caesar's ghost. He was originally intended to appear by way of the trap since the direction reads 'Caesar a taper below PS'. Later, however, the prompter crosses out 'below', indicating that the ghost should walk on PS bearing his candle. The trap was, it seems, used for his exit: a note reads 'Trap Bell to sink Ghost.'

After Brutus' exit at the end of act IV, the Short Wood backshutter was drawn on again for act V, thus allowing the action to move swiftly from Brutus' tent to the meeting of the rival armies. Presumably the confrontation was staged on the apron – the only possible place if the Short Wood scene was to mask the full tent setting behind. Also, the maximum area behind the proscenium would be needed to ready the 'Long Wood'[48] scene for use in a few moments.

Antony and Octavius enter OP through the proscenium door, and Brutus and Cassius enter similarly from PS. After the exchange between the rival generals, Octavius and Antony exit OP, leaving Brutus and Cassius the apron to themselves for their farewells. For this intimate type of scene the location could hardly have been better.

After the exit of Brutus and Cassius the Short Wood is drawn off to reveal the Long Wood occupying the area behind the proscenium. This setting remains on for the next three scenes (V.ii, V.iii, V.iv). At extreme upstage was probably placed a backscene or drop with a variety of freestanding tree pieces, or even tent pieces, in front to suggest a camp and wood as seen in perspective. As Brutus stands by Cassius' body, towards the end of the act, Caesar's ghost enters PS (with no taper this time), and once more exits by way of the trap. Interestingly enough, Brutus and his men do not carry off the bodies of their comrades; they exit, somewhat inexplicably, leaving them on stage. The direction reads 'Curtain down & up while Bodies are taken off.'[49]

The 'Short Wood' backshutter ('Long Wood' crossed out) is brought on for Brutus' death scene which is played on the apron. Since every effort was made to avoid placing scenic effects in this area, Brutus' 'rest on this rock' is altered to read 'let us rest here'. In Brutus' final moments his friends retire to somewhere near the proscenium, and Brutus stabs himself well downstage. As he dies a retreat is sounded. Antony and his men enter PS, and the eulogy is spoken downstage near the body.

Before turning to performances of the major roles, a word must be said about costume. Without attempting the degree of historic authenticity later advocated by Planché and furnished by Charles Kean, it is clear that managers attempted to dress their actors in a distinctive fashion for dramas with a classical setting. This à la romaine costume, which probably took its origins from Renaissance art,[50] was less historically correct than conventional. The first example of its elaboration in England occurs in the Peacham illustration for Titus Andronicus (1595), and it persists with some slight variations until John Kemble's time.[51]

Basically the outfit consisted of a lorica or cuirass ('the Roman breastplate, shaped to the figure and modelling the torso muscles')[52] and a 'base' or skirt below the cuirass which was overlaid with 'labels' or strips of material. Over the shoulders was flung a draped scarf or, sometimes, a cloak.[53] Antony wears this mode of dress in the frontispiece to Rowe's edition of 1709 (Illustration 1).[54] An engraving of William Smith as Mark Antony (Covent Garden 1773, Drury Lane 1780) shows him identically attired some seven decades later (Illustration 2). The use of the cloak instead of the scarf may be seen in Bell's 'Dramatick Character' plate of Sheridan as Brutus, dated 9 January, 1776, but probably drawn much earlier (Illustration 3). Noteworthy also are the close-fitting breeches which Sheridan wears beneath his mid-thigh-length base.

The Covent Garden inventory of 1744[55] lists an abundance of cuirasses (known as 'shapes'), clearly distinguished as 'Roman' and apparently made in all colours of the rainbow. In Lot No. A, for example, are Roman shapes 'out of wear' in 'scarlet silk', 'blue sattin', 'crimson', 'yellow Tabby', and 'bla[ck] velvet . . . trimmed with beads'. Their elaborateness is indicated by a contemporary account of a Brutus or Cato costume described as 'a crimson shape . . . adorned with thick-embossed plates of silver, and on the breast a gorgon's head, the face of which was flourished round with spangles, and, by way of eyes, two large red stones'.[56] These cuirasses were apparently

1. The Forum scene (III.ii). Rowe's edition, 1709

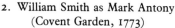

2. William Smith as Mark Antony
(Covent Garden, 1773)

3. Thomas Sheridan as Brutus.
Bell's 'Dramatick Character' Plate, 1776.

equipped with detachable sleeves, for recorded also are 'twenty six sleeves to the above shapes'. This entry helps explain an otherwise puzzling alteration of Casca's line in the Covent Garden promptbook from 'You pulled me by the cloak' to 'You pulled me by the sleeve'. A drawer full of 'roman boots' is also noted. Even the arms seem to have been conventional. '8 Roman foils' are carefully distinguished from '17 modern do. [ditto]'.

It must be remembered, of course, that while a considerable amount of costume was provided, its suitability to the wearer was often problematical. It was axiomatic that the leading character (in this play, Brutus) had always the grandest costume regardless of its appropriateness to his personality. Conversely, a royal character requiring considerable state, but with few lines, was frequently dressed in such penurious fashion that all verisimilitude was lost. Such seems to have been the lot of Caesar. Aaron Hill, in a letter to Benjamin Victor, expresses the surprise of both himself and Barton Booth that in dressing Caesar contemporary managers 'contriv'd to make his very laurel look ridiculous'.[57]

There is nothing to suggest that female characters wore anything but contemporary dress.

The actors

The most competent eighteenth-century *Caesar* performances took place in the two decades immediately following the death of Betterton in 1710, when his standard of interpretation was still fresh in the minds of actor and audience, and players of some ability were available to perpetuate the Betterton tradition. During these years Barton Booth succeeded Betterton as the leading Brutus, and Robert Wilks fell heir to Kynaston's Antony. Although neither was quite of the calibre of his predecessor, their renderings were not totally unworthy of comparison with their distinguished models.

When Booth first played Brutus at Drury Lane in 1709,[58] he was only 28; but he had already almost a decade of acting behind him, much of it spent in close association with Betterton.[59] He was acquainted with the older actor's interpretation of the role, and 'a professed admirer of Betterton almost to idolatry'.[60] While, according to Davies, he 'had too much judgement to copy or servilely imitate his action', he did not scruple to learn 'what he could from his great exemplar and fitted it to his own powers and manner'.[61]

In the years 1709–13 Booth played Brutus at intervals without establishing any great reputation in it or other classical characters. In 1713, however, at the age of 33, he took the title role in Addison's *Cato*; according to Whincop, his performance 'carried his Reputation to the full extent' and 'recommended him to the Favour of the whole Town'.[62] Henceforth his popularity was assured, and Brutus and Cato remained two of his favourite parts until his retirement in 1728.

Physically Booth was only 'of a middle Stature', but, according to Theophilus Cibber, 'there was such an exalted Dignity in his Appearance, no body on the Stage looked taller'.[63] Combined with this innate dignity was a countenance characterized by 'a manly sweetness', and trained in mobility 'to mark every Passion with a Strength to reach the Eye of the most distant Spectator'.[64] Cibber found 'the Tones of his Voice were all musical', and his ear so excellent that 'no one ever heard a dissonant Note come from him'.[65] Overriding and directing these gifts was a keen mind, disciplined by a Westminster schooling. According to Cooke, Booth's Brutus owed much of its effectiveness to 'a fine study of the part, which he acquired by his taste, and intimate knowledge of the classics'.[66]

Like Betterton he portrayed Brutus primarily as patriot and philosopher, with the latter predominating. No detailed record survives, but an account of his triumph in the Quarrel scene illustrates his general style of interpretation. Like his predecessor, he delineated the choler of the patriot through underplaying rather than overplaying. On the lines, 'For your *life* you durst not: / No! – for your *soul* you durst not,' 'Booth ... looking stedfastly at Cassius pronounced these words not much raised above a whisper, yet with such a firmness of tone as always produced the loudest effect.'[67] The announcement of Portia's death later in the same scene was carefully designed to secure the maximum effect with minimal force. Beginning with the line 'When I spoke that, I was ill-temper'd too' (IV.iii.116), 'he prepared the audience so for the cause of his *ill-temper*, by showing he had some private grief at heart, as to call up the utmost attention.' Then, subtly, he managed to change the mood of his audience from mere curiosity to profound sympathy with the line 'No man bears sorrow better. Portia is dead' (IV.iii.147). Cooke tells us that 'the expressive pause before he spoke the last words, and his heart-piercing manner in speaking them, forced every auditor to be a participator of his sorrows'.[68]

The first recorded performance of Robert Wilks as Antony took place at the 1707 subscription revival in which Booth and Betterton also appeared. His name does not again occur in cast-lists[69] until 1713 when, at the age of 43, he played Antony to Booth's 32-year-old Brutus. From this time onward he partnered Booth until the latter's retirement.

Where Booth was weak as a romantic and comic actor, Wilks made his reputation as a player of lovers and fine gentlemen; where Booth was a brilliant actor, Wilks may be described as useful and conscientious. Although possessed of a graceful figure and pleasing manners, he lacked both Booth's tragic dignity and vocal virtuosity.

If Wilks fell short of being a heavy tragedian, he was nevertheless unequalled in roles which called for the impersonation of nobility smitten by tragic grief. According to Steele, Wilks's chief strength lay in his power 'to beseech gracefully, to approach respectfully, to pity, to mourn, to love'.[70] Surely no better qualifications could be asked for the performer of Antony in the episode following the assassination. Davies preserves a tantalizing glimpse of the first moments:

Wilks ... as soon as he entered the stage, without taking any notice of the conspirators, walked swiftly up to the dead body of Caesar and knelt down; he paused some time before he spoke; and, after surveying the corpse with manifest tokens of the deepest sorrow, he addressed it in a most affecting and pathetic manner.[71]

While this sequence was without doubt superb, his Forum speech was less successful. Here he needed Booth's commanding presence and vocal technique. Although, according to Davies, 'his address through the whole was easy and eloquent', and his action 'was critically adapted to produce the intended consequences of the speaker', 'his voice wanted that fulness and variety, requisite to impress the sentiments and pathos with which the speech abounds'. 'Besides', Davies continues, 'Wilks was apt to strike the syllables too forcibly as well as uniformly.'[72]

Since, as in the Betterton era, the roles of Brutus and Antony were played by the two leading actors, the part of Cassius frequently fell to a player of considerably less competence. Little concrete information survives relating to the performances of George Powell, Thomas Elrington, or John Mills, but contemporary opinion indicates that none was of the calibre of either Booth or Wilks.

Caesar was little better served by his representatives than was Cassius. Theophilus Keene, the most talented actor to attempt the part during the period, seems to have been at least competent; he, however, apparently played it only once – in 1710. According to Bellchambers, 'his figure and voice, though neither elegant nor soft, were good, and his action was so complete, that it obtained for him the epithet of majestic'.[73] Whatever else Keene's Caesar may have lacked, he must have possessed authority, a quality all too often missing in subsequent performances. John Mills (1713, 1715, 1718–19) was probably a passable Dictator, if somewhat monotonous and lacking in spirit. Next to nothing is known of John Thurmond, who played the role from 1721 to 1726, nor of Charles Williams, who succeeded him in 1727.

Revivals at Drury Lane during the Booth era were patchy affairs at best. While Booth and Wilks captured certain facets of Brutus and Antony, their inherent weaknesses prevented them from giving completely satisfactory in-the-round interpretations. Booth's Brutus had dignity without requisite sensibility, and Wilks's Antony had sensibility without convincing dignity. As Cibber observed, 'If either of them could have borrowed a little of the other's Fault, they would Both have been improv'd by it.'[74] Moreover, since the role of Cassius was played by inferior actors, the characters of Brutus and Antony obtruded unduly to the detriment of the ensemble. The lack of a competent Caesar served only to compound the problem.

James Quin appeared as Brutus for the first time at the age of 23 on 1 November 1718 at Christopher Rich's rebuilt theatre in Portugal Street, Lincoln's Inn Fields; and here he challenged Booth's interpretation throughout the last decade of Booth's career. On the latter's retirement Quin became the principal Brutus of his day, and played the role regularly at both patent theatres until 1750.

Davies tells us that Quin was 'tall and bulky' in person with a manly countenance and a 'piercing and expressive' eye.[75] In natural dignity Sir John Hill found him superior even to Garrick,[76] while Davies commends him unreservedly for his 'well-regulated tone of voice' and judicious elocution, even going so far as to suggest that he 'understood propriety in speaking, better than any other actor of the time'.[77] Possessed of such gifts, natural and acquired, it appeared that with maturity Quin would become a superlative player; however, he failed to achieve first-rate stature, and enjoyed the position of leading actor more through lack of competition than desert.

Davies remarks that Quin 'had the good sense to admire and imitate Booth, and the honesty to own it',[78] but in this wholesale admiration lay the seeds of Quin's failure. As we noted earlier, the predominant trait in Booth's acting style was restraint. When Quin, lacking both Booth's educational advantages and discriminating judgement, attempted to copy Booth's reserved force, the effect was closer to turgidity. Davies considered him 'utterly unqualified for the striking and vigorous characters of tragedy', but in stoic characters making few demands for flexibility of emotion, his weaknesses were less obvious; consequently, his 'Cato and Brutus were remembered with pleasure by those who wished to forget his Lear and Richard'.[79]

In the scene with Cassius in the first act, in his meeting with the conspirators, and finally, in his death, Quin's Roman must have been majestic, if somewhat tumid. In the Quarrel scene, however, when called upon to represent noble and restrained anger, Booth's example was forgotten and all reserve vanished amid waves of histrionic rage and bluster. In *Peregrine Pickle* Smollett has the Knight of Malta describe Quin's performance thus:

In the character of the mild patriot Brutus, [he] loses all temper and decorum; nay, so ridiculous the behaviour of him and Cassius at their interview, that setting foot to foot and grinning at each other, with the aspect of two cobblers enraged, they thrust their left sides together with repeated shocks, that the hilts of their swords may clash for the entertainment of the audience; as if they were a couple of merry-andrews endeavouring to raise the laugh of the vulgar, on some scaffold at Bartholomew Fair. The despair of a great man, who falls a sacrifice to the infernal practices of a subtle traitor that enjoyed his confidence, this English Aesopus represents by beating his own forehead, and bellowing like a bull . . . In short, he seems to be a stranger to the more refined sensations of the soul, consequently his expression is of the vulgar kind, and he must often sink under the idea of the poet; so that he has recourse to such violence of affected agitation as imposes upon the undiscerning spectator.[80]

Even the line 'No, for your *soul*, you durst not', which Booth pronounced in a voice 'not raised much above a whisper', Quin spoke with 'a look of anger approaching to rage'.[81]

At moments, however, Quin's performance approached the greatness of his predecessors. Davies recalls that his 'look and tone of voice in uttering *Portia is dead*! were extremely affecting: his expressive pause before he spoke fixed the audience in deep attention'.[82] In Sir John Hill's opinion, his 'tone of majesty' as he made the announcement was such as to 'chill an audience'[83] rather than allow them to share his grief as Booth's reading had done.

On the whole the Betterton tradition, admittedly weakened by Booth, reached its final decadence with Quin. The 'Philosopher and the Heroe' degenerated into a majestic, ponderous mouther of lines. Unruffled temper was replaced by monotonous turgidity, and the spirit which flew only to

Betterton's eye now expressed itself in clashing swords and indecorous rant. Gone, too, were the ensemble effects of Betterton and Smith, leaving the role little more than a solo piece of declamation.[84]

Even had Quin been willing to play in close co-operation with his supporting actor, the calibre of his Cassiuses would have made such an attempt vain. All were of the useful, but uninspired, variety, and well below even Quin's standard. Antony Boheme, who played the role to Quin's Brutus from 1722 to 1729, and William Milward, who replaced him from 1737 to 1741,[85] were physically-convincing and full-voiced Romans; but brought little else to the role. Lacey Ryan, who partnered Quin both at Lincoln's Inn Fields (1718–21) and Covent Garden (1742–51), was probably the least offensive. Despite physical and vocal deficiencies, he captured admirably, if not excessively, Cassius' fire and turbulence.[86] Gentleman recalls Ryan as the one good Cassius he had seen, and commends him for his ability to hit off 'the techy degree of passion' and 'the general mode of mind which actuates it'.[87]

During his lengthy career, Quin's Brutus was partnered by a wide variety of Antonys (see chronological handlist). Since Antony seems to have been regarded as the second role, the quality of actor was rather higher than for Cassius. But to say this is not to say a very great deal. All were physically convincing as the noble young Roman, but few managed to compass anything like the complexity of Shakespeare's conception. Each man seemed to grasp one facet of the character or another – the pathos, or the oratorical power, or the military bearing – without effectively seizing the whole.

Milward's Antony (1734–6) was apparently the most polished interpretation between Wilks and Barry. In Davies' opinion, he had for the role 'every thing . . . which nature could bestow, person, look, voice'. Moreover, 'his action and address were easy without art, and his deportment . . . was far from ungraceful'.[88] Since his *forte* lay in 'characters where distress is dignified by superiority of rank',[89] his conduct of the Assassination sequence no doubt carried considerable conviction. In the Forum speech he managed to exercise more vocal control than was usually characteristic of him. Davies tells us that 'he opened the preparatory part of the oration in a low but distinct and audible voice . . . and, by gradual progress, rose to such a height, as not only to inflame the populace on the stage but to touch the audience with a kind of enthusiastic rapture' when he uttered the lines beginning 'But were I Brutus . . .' (III.ii.226–30).[90]

Certainly the best Antony since Wilks, and perhaps even the best since Kynaston, was Spranger Barry (1750, 1751). In person Barry was 'above five feet eleven inches high, finely formed, and possessing a countenance in which manliness and sweetness of feature were . . . happily blended'. His action was so pleasing that 'even his *exits* and *entrances* had peculiar graces from their characteristic ease and simplicity'.[91] From the very beginning of the play his height allowed him to command the attention of the audience, and his graceful movement lent credibility to the athleticism which characterizes Antony in the early scenes. At the age of 31, when Barry first partnered Quin, he must have seemed altogether the sort of noble young man Caesar would select as a friend.

Barry's talents were particularly apt for the scene following Caesar's assassination. His capacity to convey an almost unbearable distress upon seeing Caesar's corpse resembled that of Wilks. When he played Antony in the first act of *All For Love*, Thomas Wilkes found it 'impossible to see him stretched on the ground . . . overwhelmed with misfortune, without entering into all his grief'.[92]

The Forum scene, strangely enough, was probably the weakest part of Barry's performance. In the calmer moments of declamation at the commencement of the oration, Davies found Barry's voice not sufficiently sonorous nor 'flexible enough to express the full meaning of the author'. However, when roused by passion later in the address, 'Barry rose superior to all speakers', and 'his close of the harangue was as warm and glowing as the beginning was cold and deficient'.[93] Gentleman noted that although Barry provided 'all the plausibility of insinuation that SHAKESPEARE meant', he found 'judgement . . . not . . . so much his friend as might have been wished'.[94]

In the military scenes of the fourth and fifth acts, Barry's performance must have been superior to that of Wilks, for he possessed the weight that Wilks lacked.

Of the Caesars who partnered Quin, little need be said. The role was usually played by a relatively untalented performer, or was used by inexperienced actors as a stepping-stone to a larger part. Leigh (1718) and Boheme (1718, 1721) both played Caesar before undertaking Antony, and Ryan essayed the Dictator from 1725 to 1729 between two periods of playing Cassius. Of Ogden, who represented Caesar three times in the years 1718–20, nothing is known. Berry (1737, 1741) and Bridgwater (1742–51) both gave undistinguished performances.

William Mills, son of John Mills, probably played Caesar more often than any other eighteenth-century actor. In his father's opinion it was 'the part in tragedy which his son William acted with most propriety', and, in Davies' view, 'he gave such an idea of the part as Shakespeare intended'.[95] The operative phrase here is 'as Shakespeare intended'. In representing Caesar as a stock stage tyrant gloriously overthrown in the cause of liberty, no doubt Mills was eminently successful; but what Shakespeare intended is another matter. In Bajazet, according to Aaron Hill, Mills 'found out, that a great noise was one mark of anger; but he forgot, that all this noise in the anger of a sovereign, should take its measure from his dignity, and the decorum proper to his condition'.[96] It may have been Mills's performance

Hill had in mind when he bemoaned the 'scandalous figure he [Caesar] makes, on the stages of *Europe*'.[97]

With the retirement of Quin in 1751 *Julius Caesar* ended almost a century of unbroken popularity. Throughout the next three decades, revivals were widely spaced and lasted for only a night or two. Actors were generally of inferior quality, mere imitators of Quin or Garrick, and their insipid interpretations probably contributed as much to the play's final fall from favour after 1780 as the changing tastes of audiences.

Thomas Sheridan, who undertook Brutus during a visit to England in 1755 when his Dublin public was in revolt, provided the only performance of any note in the second half of the century. According to Thomas Wilkes, Nature was 'not very liberal to him in those practical gifts which are generally first regarded'; his voice was 'harsh and discordant', and his action was 'solemn', 'stiff', 'confined', and 'entirely . . . devoid of elegance'.[98] As Brutus, however, although inferior to Quin in appearance, 'his person, though unimportant, by the aid of dress was not totally void of respect',[99] and his reading, in Gentleman's opinion, maintained 'stricter equality through the whole than Mr. Quin; if he could not rise so high in the view of criticism, neither did he fall so low'.[100] Like Booth, and unlike Quin, Sheridan had the advantage of considerable education. According to one contemporary, he was 'an excellent Scholar' and 'an exceeding good Commentator on his Author'.[101] It is not surprising, then, to learn that Brutus' lines were delivered with admirable intelligibility, although their effect was somewhat marred by 'frequent, ungracious snip-snap breaks of voice, and a painful attempt to keep up the last syllable of every sentence'.[102]

Sheridan's Cato was much praised for its power to make the audience 'admire the Stoic', but 'pity the Parent'[103] and the same mixture of dignity and tenderness would have sat well on his Brutus. In the scenes with Portia and Lucius, Sheridan was obviously capable of providing an insight into Brutus' humanity which was quite beyond the powers of Quin. His greatest moments, however, came in the Forum scene. 'In his Brutus' Orations', wrote one critic, 'we *who are mute Spectators of the Scene*, are by his graceful and enforcing Manner enthusiastically warmed, and become almost accessory to the Deed.'[104]

Sparks (1753, 1754) strutted through a poor imitation of Quin's Brutus, while Walker's stilted patriot (1766–7) moved Hugh Kelly to warn that more than a 'frigid nicety of care / In heav'n-formed BRUTUS, constitutes a play'r'.[105] Robert Bensley (1773) tended to aim at 'vehemence of expression, without considering propriety of character, or the untrained extent of his natural powers', but mercifully played the role only once. Of Palmer's Brutus (1780), the last of the century, nothing is known.

After the retirement of Ryan as Cassius in 1755, Smith (1766, 1767), Hull

(1773), and Henry (1780)[106] successively attempted the part. Smith and Hull, both excellent players of fine gentlemen, appear to have been utter failures in this rough and fiery military character. Henry guest-starred in the role while on a visit from the United States. His performance will be examined later in its American context (see p. 102).

The Antonys of Ross (1766), Hull (1767), and Smith (1773, 1780), while engaging and pleasant enough, bore no comparison with Barry's. Of Clarke and Packer, who succeeded Bridgwater as Caesar, little is known. Gentleman lumps both together as actors who reached 'that insipid medium which just avoids censure, yet never can reach praise'.[107]

Although on the whole the eighteenth century was not an era of great *Caesar* productions, a fair number of accomplishments accrue to its credit. The flexibility of its stagecraft allowed the play to be performed at a speed which the nineteenth century, for all its scenic wonders and historic authenticity, could not approach. The sparsity of scenery and the utilization of the apron threw the weight, and rightly, upon the actor. As a result of the close contact between actor and audience, a high standard of movement, facial expression, and speech was demanded, and the way was thrown open for intensely detailed individual effects.

It is regrettable that the age failed to provide *Julius Caesar* with actors fully capable of meeting this challenge. Several actors were great in particular facets of their characters, but few, if any, could compass in-the-round interpretations. Brutus and Antony probably fared best. Booth captured much of Brutus' complexity, but fell just short of realizing the whole. The same could be said of Wilks's Antony. If these performances were not great *in toto*, they were great *in parte*, and these peak moments established a standard to be striven after by later actors with greater capabilities.

Undoubtedly Caesar, Cassius, and the crowd received less than justice. Caesars were not of sufficiently high calibre to lend the play requisite unity and tragic impetus, nor did any performer demonstrate the immense possibilities latent in Cassius. The crowd, ridiculously small and badly played, was given little prominence. It needs scarcely to be remarked that we look in vain for any suggestion of ensemble. Yet no better demonstration of the magnetism of Shakespeare's individual characters could be wished than the fact that Brutus without a satisfactory Cassius and Antony without a crowd could draw enthusiastic audiences without intermission over a period of more than fifty years.

3
John Philip Kemble (1812)

John Philip Kemble's revival at Covent Garden on 29 February 1812, hailed with enthusiasm by critics and public alike, marked a triumphant restoration of *Julius Caesar* to popular favour. The performance was repeated no less than sixteen times in the same season[1] and at regular intervals thereafter until Kemble's retirement in 1817. 'I have never spoken', maintained Julian Charles Young, 'with any one fortunate enough to have seen that play rendered, as it then was, who has not admitted it to have been the greatest intellectual recreation he has ever enjoyed.'[2]

While acting-manager at Drury Lane (1788–1802) Kemble attempted to convince the financially inept Sheridan that it was 'a waste of time and money' to lavish the theatre's resources on ephemeral pieces when 'a grand and permanent attraction might be given to Drury Lane by encreasing the power of Shakespeare'.[3] But it was only with his assumption of the Covent Garden management and a one-sixth share of the patent that he found himself completely free to stage Shakespeare as he saw fit. From 1804 to his retirement in 1817 one glittering revival followed another. Of these *Julius Caesar* was one of the most successful.

Kemble's notions of Shakespeare production owed much to the beau idéal school of painting of which Sir Joshua Reynolds was the most vocal member. Sir Joshua, a keen theatre-goer and admirer of Mrs Siddons, became an intimate friend of Kemble's in the 1780s, about the time he was completing his *Discourses to the Royal Academy* in which he urged (along with Barry, Opie, and Fuseli) the painting of ideal form rather than the slavish copying of nature. It is not the task of the artist, argued Reynolds, 'to amuse mankind with the minute neatness of his imitations' of nature as she is, but 'to improve them by the grandeur of his ideas'. The true artist must carefully 'distinguish the accidental deficiencies, and deformities of things, from their general figures' and so depict an 'abstract idea of their forms more perfect than any one original'.[4]

Kemble's search for the central form in Shakespeare's works started with the text. It was not Kemble's 'notion of the business' to order the prompter 'to write out the parts from some old mutilated copy lingering on his shelves', but 'to consider it attentively in the author's genuine book'.[5] To supplement his own research, he frequently sought the advice of the textual critics, Steevens, Malone, and Reed, although as often as not he ignored it. Once he felt confident of the correctness of his basic script, he proceeded to vitiate his pains by savagely carving it up to reveal a predetermined quintessential shape.

With the text of the play settled, Kemble turned his attention to matters of presentation; and he was as ill-satisfied with stock methods of Shakespearian stagecraft as he was with the traditional theatre text. In his opinion, 'too many and too considerable demands were made upon the imagination of the spectator, "to piece out with their thoughts" the imperfections of the stage. He saw no reason why the representation in the seeming magnificence of the action should yield to the reality; and that it should be *true* as well as splendid.'[6] Toward the achievement of correctness and artistic excellence in décor, Kemble felt that 'the prevailing studies of the times' had much to contribute. He was quick to utilize the innovations of the pantomime designers and avidly followed the work of contemporary artists and antiquaries for their further improvement. For the implementation of his scenic concepts, Kemble assembled the best artists available and supervised them meticulously.

Kemble's painted backgrounds owed much of their effect to his living scenery – processions and statuesque groupings of supernumeraries roughly comparable in function to drapery in beau idéal paintings. Costumes, based on antiquarian research, were relatively accurate, colours were simple and subdued, movement was kept to a minimum, and groupings were arranged according to the sculptural principles admired by Reynolds.

If the performer was not to be overwhelmed by the *mise en scène*, he must heighten his acting style comparably. Scenic grandeur demanded histrionic grandeur, in which 'everything should be raised and enlarged beyond its natural state; that the full effect may come home to the spectator, which otherwise would be lost in the comparatively extensive space of the theatre'.[7] With the models of classic art before them, Kemble and Mrs Siddons cultivated what became known as 'the grand style', characterized by a deliberate and majestic step, a statuesque grace of action, and formal, stately declamation.

Text

Just prior to a revival, Kemble usually published an acting text. His first edition of *Julius Caesar* appeared in 1811. This version, while substantially representing the play as it was acted, was not quite the final stage text. Kemble's own working-copy, an 1811 edition now in the Folger Shakespeare Library (*JC* 6), contains further alterations, presumably made while the play was in rehearsal. Some of these changes were incorporated in a second edition in 1812, and virtually all of them in a third edition in 1814. For purposes of this study I use the 1814 edition.[8] The appearance of this version established the text of *Julius Caesar* spoken in the theatre until the end of the century.

In general it may be said that Kemble's script bears a close resemblance to those of the eighteenth century; not, however, because Kemble accepted uncritically the eighteenth-century alterations (minute corrections throughout the copy bear strong evidence to the contrary), but because they fitted his conception of the central form of the play.

Where the Dryden–Davenant version reduced the speaking parts by ten, Kemble managed to eliminate no less than fourteen. The reasons for the curtailment, however, were very different. Where the eighteenth-century manager was forced by economic pressures to restrict the size of the cast, Kemble's reductions were designed to impose upon the play a unity which he felt it lacked. He sought mainly to eliminate the minor characters, who might be termed 'excrescences' (to use Reynolds's term), and to focus attention upon the conspirators who now play a much more prominent part. Casca, Trebonius, and Metellus are the particular gainers.

As in Bell's edition, the roles of Casca and Trebonius are much expanded; but Trebonius now assumes the greater stature. He takes the place of Messala at the conference table (IV.ii) and replaces Casca (Shakespeare–Titinius) as Cassius' observer in V.iii. Metellus is given Lucilius' lines in IV.ii, accompanies Varro in the vigil in Brutus' tent (replacing Claudius), and finally appears in Brutus' death-scene where he takes Volumnius' speeches.

Titinius also is accorded a little more importance. He, not Lucilius, is taken prisoner in V.iv, and, for good measure, he is granted several mute appearances not accorded him by Shakespeare.

Cicero is again eliminated, as in the eighteenth century; but his lines are now cut completely, not given to Trebonius as in Bell's edition. Caius Ligarius vanishes together with his scene, although casual references to him are preserved. Publius no longer appears at the Capitol; Popilius Lenas receives Brutus' reassurances. The roles of Artemidorus and the Soothsayer are again merged, and the Soothsayer takes the speeches. Cinna the Poet and the Camp Poet continue to be banned from the play altogether.

The reallocation of roles is most marked in Brutus' death scene (V.v) where the personnel comprises not Dardanius, Clitus, Strato, and Volumnius, but Metellus, Varro, and Lucius.

Kemble seems to have been greatly concerned at the apparent numerical imbalance of forces in the play: Shakespeare endows Brutus with almost a surfeit of friends and attendants while Antony has next to none. Having reduced Brutus' following, Kemble attempted to add a few to Antony's train. The two nameless servants are now given names and appear no longer to be so much servants as Antony's friend–attendants. The servant who goes to 'bid the priests do present sacrifice' at Caesar's request (II.ii.5) is designated as Flavius. He appears with Clitus and four guards in III.i. to announce the arrival of Octavius in Rome and frequently accompanies Antony thereafter as a mute. Antony's emissary to the conspirators in III.i is called Servius; he appears again in the Forum scene, at the capture of Titinius (v.iv), and on several other occasions, but remains mute. Clitus and Strato, too, retain their names, if not their personalities, and constantly companion Antony throughout the play.

Thus, visually at least, Kemble contrives to divide the dramatis personae into two fairly symmetrical groups. On the one side he places the conspirators – Brutus, Cassius, Casca, Trebonius, Decius, Metellus, and Cinna – and their followers – Lucius, Varro, and Pindarus; on the other stand Antony, Octavius, Lepidus, Flavius, Servius, Strato, and Clitus.

Kemble's cutting of *Julius Caesar* is more drastic than anything yet noted; in addition to a score or so of maddening alterations and deletions of words and phrases in the service of propriety, tragic and historic, he excises 450 lines, compared with 175 in the Dryden–Davenant version and 350 in Bell's edition.

Like his predecessors he found the supernatural references excessive and cut more drastically than previous versions. He omits the whole of Cicero's meeting with Casca (I.iii,1–40) and the interchange between Casca and Cassius regarding the impatience of the heavens (I.iii.46–71). He does, however, restore Cassius' reference to the night (I.iii.125–30).

The greater part of Kemble's cutting, however, is designed to regularize the form of the play. Having created two roughly symmetrical groups, he proceeds by cutting to symmetrize the major characters within each group, pruning away those facets of their personalities, which, though natural enough, might detract from the central core of each. His attention was mainly devoted to Brutus, Cassius, and Antony, with the major emphasis upon Brutus, played by himself.

Generally it may be said that he considered the play Brutus' tragedy, with Brutus seen as a self-possessed Stoic, a magnanimous philosopher and patriot. This Brutus was essentially the idealized creation of David or Reynolds, not the intensely human, and often inconsistent, character created by Shakespeare. Brutus, the self-deceived fanatic, the impatient husband, the frightened general, the almost maternal master, well nigh vanishes.

All significant eighteenth-century cuts are retained, and several new ones appear. For the first time, some attempt is made to clear Brutus of a charge of falsehood in IV.iii. When Trebonius (Shakespeare–Messala) asks him if he had letters from his wife, Brutus truthfully replies, 'No, Trebonius'; and the latter does not press the point. Brutus' fatherly promise to Lucius not to keep him long from sleep (IV.iii.264–5) is removed, and he does not awaken the boy after the appearance of the ghost. In V.iii the hero-patriot, renouncing the luxury of sentiment, makes no promise to the dead Cassius to weep for him when occasion allows. His fanatical invitation to the blood rite (III.i.105–7) is made to read more decorously:

> On Romans, on;
> With hands and swords besmear'd in Caesar's blood.

The interpolated lines of defiant rant at the end of the Tent scene are mercifully consigned to oblivion.

The traditional rendering of Brutus' death, however, proved a temptation too strong to resist. Once again, then, Brutus requests his companions to kill him – first Lucius (!), then Metellus – and when they refuse, he falls upon his own sword. Kemble preserves part of the Dryden–Davenant–Bell death-speech, but subjects it to some revision. It now runs:

> This was the justest cause that ever men
> Did draw their swords for; and the gods renounce it, –
> Disdaining life, to live a slave in Rome,
> Thus Brutus strikes his last – for liberty! –
> Farewell,
> Beloved country! – Caesar, now be still;
> I kill'd not thee with half so good a will.

These are the last words of a defiant hero-patriot. Those of Shakespeare's earth-weary philosopher:

> So fare you well at once; for Brutus' tongue
> Hath almost ended his life's history.
> Night hangs upon mine eyes; my bones would rest,
> That have but labour'd to attain this hour. (V.v.39–42)

are regrettably excised. With Kemble's words and in the Kemble manner, Brutus continued to die until the present century.

The character of Cassius, too, does not entirely escape Kemble's attack on extravagant or unheroic behaviour. In addition to the traditional cuts Kemble strikes out his somewhat hypocritical lines at I.ii.176–7:

> I am glad that my weak words
> Have struck but thus much show of fire from Brutus.

together with the rather vainglorious speech (I.iii.91–7) in which he asserts his determination to triumph over tyranny, by death if necessary. On the whole, however, Cassius suffers far less of a sea change than does Brutus.

Antony, on the other hand, undergoes a striking transformation. Not content with enhancing his position by an augmented following, Kemble sets out to render his character and motives more worthy of approbation as well. Shakespeare's highly-complex mixture of good and evil, of devoted friendship and shameless opportunism, held little charm for Kemble. His aim was to render Antony the chivalrous young athlete, the noble companion of Caesar, who, from the purest motives, sets out to revenge his friend's death and effects a successful revolution. At I.ii.1, Casca's 'Peace, ho! Caesar speaks.' is given to Antony to call attention to his presence at the very beginning of the tragedy. Brutus' description of him as 'but a limb of Caesar' (II.i.165) is deleted, together with the reference to his fondness for sports, wildness, and much company (II.i.185–9). Young Romans could not expect simultaneously to indulge themselves and claim the wholehearted admiration of the audience. The most important alteration, however, is effected by the excision of the whole of IV.i – the scene in which Antony reveals his corrupt and ruthless nature.

Most other cuts and revisions are designed to speed up the action and secure more flamboyant entrances and exits. As in Bell's edition, Brutus' 'Till then, my noble friend' lines (I.ii.171–5) are transposed to his exit. The Caius Ligarius scene is cut entirely to permit the domestic interviews between Brutus and Portia and Caesar and Calphurnia to follow each other without interruption. The Soothsayer's (Shakespeare–Artemidorus') speeches in II.iii and II.iv are somewhat abbreviated in the interests of pace. In III.i the first twenty-four lines, in which the Soothsayer accosts Caesar and Popilius dismays the conspirators, are restored.

To avoid interruption of Antony's Forum speech, the plebeians' interjections are drastically cut. The impressionistic, almost cinematic, sequence in which Brutus asks Messala to ride (V.ii) is sacrificed to speed and unity of action, and V.iii is drastically altered. The speeches by Titinius and Trebonius (Shakespeare–Titinius and Messala) are more severely cut than previously. Titinius' lament over Cassius (V.iii.59–65) vanishes and much of Messala's speech, just before he goes to inform Brutus of Cassius' death (V.iii.73–8), is deleted. Since Trebonius does not kill himself (Kemble no doubt wished to avoid three deaths in such close conjunction), his farewell speech (V.iii.85–90) is, of course, omitted. The arrangements for Cassius' funeral are also somewhat curtailed. The remainder of the play closely conforms to Bell's edition.

Stagecraft

No pictorial record survives of Kemble's décor for *Julius Caesar*, and although his contemporaries were lavish in their praise, few recorded concrete details of its appearance. Planché says that Kemble consulted Francis Douce for antiquarian advice, but insisted, against Douce's objections, upon drawing his information 'from the columns and arches of the emperors, and not from the contemporaneous republican authorities'.[9] Kemble was less concerned with achieving minute antiquarian accuracy than with the creation of a generally authentic atmosphere; and this fact may well account for the absence of descriptive reports. For the most part critics lauded the *mise en scène* as splendid and accurate, but focussed their attention upon the acting. Julian Charles Young alone makes anything like a specific statement. In III.i and III.ii, 'it was, really, difficult', he writes, 'to believe, that one had not been transported, while in a state of unconsciousness, from the purlieus of Bow Street . . . to the glories of the Capitol, and the very heart of the Julian Forum; so complete, in all its parts, was the illusion of the scene'.[10] Perhaps the best proof of its quality is the fact that it remained in use down to the Covent Garden revival of William Charles Macready in 1836 with little loss of popularity.[11]

With more than eighty-five supernumeraries to provide for, to say nothing of about twenty speaking characters, costuming became a major undertaking; that Kemble managed to dress this large cast with some semblance of uniformity and historic propriety constitutes no small achievement. No specific account exists of dress for *Caesar*, but it probably differed little from the costume used for *Cato*, described by John Finlay as 'the picture of accuracy'.[12] It consisted basically of the toga or robe, which was white in colour with a red border[13] and was made of heavy material which would drape gracefully. Beneath the toga went the tunic, 'a close dress something like a modern shirt, reaching in front a little below the knees, and descending behind the calves of the legs'.[14] As for footwear, Haslewood tells us that Kemble was the first to introduce 'the exact sandal, which leaves the toes at liberty'.[15] It would appear that most of the characters in the play wore this costume, or some adaptation of it; the slaves, however, wore only the tunic of white and purple.[16] The female characters were probably arrayed in Mrs Siddons' drapery derived from her study of classical sculpture.[17]

The action and grouping of these toga-clad figures are detailed in half-a-dozen promptbooks associated with the 1812 production. The fullest and most authoritative is Kemble's personal book written in his own hand in an 1812 edition.[18] Although I rely mainly upon this book,[19] all extant versions have been consulted.

Act I

As in the eighteenth century, I.i was played on the apron. Across the front of the stage, probably in the first grooves, was placed a backshutter described only as 'Rome. A Street'. Following 'a great Tumult without', Casca and Trebonius enter right. At the centre of the apron they meet some thirty plebeians[20] who enter left. The First Plebeian stations himself on Casca's left and the Second stands between Casca and Trebonius for the exchange which follows. On 'That needs must light on this ingratitude' (1.i.55), Casca crosses to the left, and the plebeians pass behind him to the right. On Trebonius' 'Go, go, good countrymen' (1.i.56), he crosses left to Casca where they stand together L for the last lines as the plebeians exit R. At the end of the scene Casca exits left and Trebonius right, while Mr Ware's music is played in the orchestra 'before the scene changes'.

This first scene with its augmented mob, its calculated movement, and general spaciousness clearly marks the beginning of a new era.

To continued music, the front scene is drawn back to discover the 'Publick Place' of 1.ii, a full set-scene with a 'Triumphal Arch', located, it seems, just right of centre stage, somewhere above the third grooves.

On the opposite side, at about the same distance upstage, the Soothsayer is 'discovered at an Altar' on which a fire is burning. Gradually the orchestra music gives way to 'Drums, Trumpets', and 'Three shouts'. Caesar's triumphal procession enters L,[21] and groups itself as directed (Illustration 4). This elaborate display with its SPQR (Senatus Populusque Romanus) banners, priests, senators, lictors, virgins, matrons, gold and silver eagles, and star is intended to establish visually the glory of Julian Rome and focus attention upon its central figure. A greater contrast could hardly be imagined than that between Kemble's splendid Caesar, flanked on either side by Lepidus and Antony and surrounded by white-draped figures and uniformed state officers, and his eighteenth-century counterpart, the carelessly-dressed audience-scapegoat accompanied by a few ragged attendants. Here, too, Kemble's pictorial sense is seen to advantage in his carefully-balanced masses of background figures and the spatial isolation of the main subject in the foreground.

At well down centre-stage, Caesar halts briefly to speak to Antony, and then begins to move off R, but is stopped by the Soothsayer's cry from LUE. Caesar looks in his direction, but his vision of the Soothsayer is blocked by the mass of lictors and guards. On Cassius' 'Fellow, come from the throng; look upon Caesar' (1.ii.21), 'the Lictors & Guards divide, and the Sooth-sayer advances quickly between them', accompanied by a 'Great bustle and appearance of surprize in every body'.

After the Soothsayer's warning, the procession exits diagonally (to allow the audience a longer view) 'through the Arch to R', unobtrusively reform-ing to allow Brutus and Cassius to go off last. The Soothsayer remains upstage throughout the remainder of the scene – a silent reminder during the conference of Brutus and Cassius of Caesar's impending doom. Brutus is about to exit at the end of the procession when Cassius stops him R. They now position themselves well forward on the apron for the discussion which follows, allowing the audience to observe the play's chief figures at close range.

L. - Cæsar's Entry.

xx} Musick in Orchestra.
x } Drums, Trumpets, & Three Shouts.

1 — 2 S.P. 2.R. - Go up to Arch.
2 — 4 Priests. - Go up to S.P. 2.R.
3 — 6 Senators. - Go up to Priests.
4 — Decius & Metellus. - x to R. — 3d Ent.
5 — Cinna & Popilius. - x to R. — 2d Ent.
6 — Cassius. ———— x to R. - Stage-door.
7 — Trebonius & Casca. - x to R. - 1st Ent.
'8 — Clitus & Servius. — x to R. - near the Altar.
9 — Strato & Pindarus. - x to R. - next to Dec & Met.
10 — Titinius & Flavius. x M. - a little towards L.
11 — Brutus. ———— x R. to Cassius - L.
12 — Lucius & Varro. — x R. - in front of Stra & Pind.
13 - 6 Virgins. }
14 - Calpurnia. } M. towards R.
15 - 4 Matrons }

xx} Drums, Trumpets, & Three Shouts.
x }
16 - 12 Lictors - Go up L. of Arch.
    } Lepidus.
17 } Julius Cæsar.
    } Antony.
18 - Star.
19 - 2 Golden Eagles.
20 - 2 Silver Eagles.
21 - 12 Guards. - Go up L. of Lictors.

4. Promptbook plan for Caesar's Procession (I.ii). John Philip Kemble's production
at Covent Garden, 1812

The reappearance of the procession is as carefully arranged as its first entrance. Slowly they re-enter through the arch UER and group themselves as follows:

Casca	6 Senators
Trebonius	12 Guards
Popilius	2 Silver Eagles
Cinna	2 Golden Eagles
Metellus	Star
Decius	12 Lictors
Brutus	2 SPQR

R   Cassius   Caesar   Antony   Lepidus   L

Here Kemble's grouping is not primarily pictorial, although that aspect is important, but functional. He clearly intends at this very early stage to array the opposing groups in two clearly-defined stage areas. On the one side stand the conspirators and Popilius, and on the other, Caesar, backed by the splendour and might of the Rome which he created. At the very outset, the audience is made aware of the enormity of the conspirators' intention and the grandeur of the figure Cassius proposes to rid the world of. In this telling moment, Kemble's use of living scenery is seen at its best.

The procession now exits left, leaving Casca standing between Brutus and Cassius at downstage right for the discussion which follows. At the end of the scene, Casca exits L, Brutus exits R, and Cassius, after his final lines, goes off L. The playing-time for act I is forty minutes.

Act II

With 'Lamps down & Turned off', the Street shutter comes on again for II.i, probably in Groove I, to allow Brutus' Garden to be set behind. Cassius enters right and meets Casca coming from the left. Thunder and lightning punctuate the conversation throughout. Without the lines in which the assassination of Caesar is linked with a violation of the natural order, the scene loses much of its original significance. Kemble employs it mainly as a transitional sequence to occupy the audience while a set-scene is readied behind.

After the exit of Cassius and Casca, the Street shutter is drawn back to reveal Brutus' garden. It was apparently a full scene, but no descriptive details survive. To the accompaniment of thunder and lightning, Brutus enters RUE and calls Lucius who enters R2E and exits R. The lamps are raised a little, and in the eerie gloom[22] Brutus begins his soliloquy.

He is standing well downstage, just to the right of centre, when the conspirators enter L, 'all with their faces muffled in their Gowns, except Cassius. They remain a little behind, while Cassius advances to Brutus.' Each man in turn then crosses R to be presented. During the introductions

'Trebonius & Decius unmuffles each his face, when Cassius presents him to
Brutus: – Casca, Cinna, and Metellus unmuffle themselves all together,
when Cassius says – "This Casca".' Powerful as this slow and sinister
revelation was, Kemble was wise enough not to prolong it unduly. Cassius
and Brutus then withdraw upstage for their consultation and the conspirators close ranks in front of them.

Brutus goes L to watch the exit of the conspirators ('muffling their faces in
their gowns again'), and turns to find Portia entering at RUE. She stops well
upstage and Brutus remains down L. Portia's lines of entreaty are apparently
delivered from upstage, thus emphasizing by spatial separation the
emotional gap between them; moreover, since Brutus is nearer the audience, his perturbation is the more readily perceptible. During Portia's
speeches Brutus moves from right to left in some agitation until she comes
downstage to kneel to him at II.i.278. They remain downstage together until
Lucius announces Ligarius' arrival. Portia exits R and Brutus follows
Lucius off L to the accompaniment of thunder and lightning.

'An Apartment in Caesar's Palace', merely a pair of shutters with an arch
in the middle, slides on probably in the second grooves. Caesar enters
through the arch[23] and calls Flavius who enters and exits R. Calphurnia
shortly follows Caesar on and sees him standing down R after dismissing
Flavius. Like Portia, she does not immediately move downstage to her
husband, but speaks to him from near the arch. Caesar crosses to her on
'The face of Caesar, they are vanished' (II.ii.12).

The conspirators and Antony enter at intervals, take up their positions,
and move little thereafter. Upon their departure Brutus remains alone at
centre-stage to declaim his

> That every like is not the same, O Caesar,
> The heart of Brutus earns to think upon! (II.ii.128–9)

A final direction for this scene in the Jones copy reads 'Begin Musick in
orchestra to play Brutus off', and he exits L, slowly, to a melancholy tune.
The playing-time for act II is forty-five minutes.

Act III

Street shutters now appear again, probably in the first grooves, to allow the
deep setting for the assassination to be readied behind. The Soothsayer
enters R and reads his 'scroll'. On 'If not, the fates with traitors do contrive'
(II.iii.16), 'He retires a little' to M. Upon seeing Portia and Lucius enter R,
he 'advances, going L' when Portia catches sight of him. At her 'Come
hither, fellow' (II.iv.21), he returns to M where their conversation takes
place.

Contrary to eighteenth-century practice, Kemble does not break the

Capitol scene into two parts; he forgoes the opportunity for a procession[24] and stages the whole scene as a discovery. Immediately after the exit of Portia and Lucius, 'A Flourish of Instruments' is heard and the shutters are withdrawn to reveal the Capitol. Apart from Julian Charles Young's brief mention of this scene, no record of its appearance has come to light. That it was an accurate and elaborate piece of work is certain.

Once again, although the scenery was obviously striking, Kemble relies heavily on supernumeraries to provide period atmosphere and formal pictorial effects. At extreme upstage stand twelve guards arranged in semicircular formation; in front are grouped twelve lictors and the man bearing the star. To right and left are officers holding SPQR standards, and slightly further forward, although still well upstage, sits the Dictator enthroned, backed by the gold and silver eagles and flanked on either side by priests. Immediately in front again sit six senators, three on either side. Finally, from about centre to well downstage are placed the conspirators (probably seated) in groups to right and left, with Antony and Lepidus among the group at R. It is worth noting that Casca, Cassius and Brutus enjoy a splendid isolation at L. Pompey's statua is placed down R.

Once the street flat is withdrawn and 'the Instruments cease', the Soothsayer enters R, hails Caesar from downstage, and 'advances as far as to Decius' where he is stopped and kneels. On III.i.10, 'Sirrah, give place', Decius 'rises, and angrily drives out the Soothsayer R'. Popilius now enters R (again he has a separate entrance as in previous productions) and 'x to Cassius' where he wishes that Cassius' enterprise may thrive, and then advances to Caesar's left. Casca now 'comes earnestly forward to Cassius R and Decius eagerly crosses over to Casca's R', clearly indicating their trepidation. Brutus says, 'Cassius, be constant' (III.i.22), pauses and watches Popilius as he 'kisses Caesar's hand', and then continues with the rest of his speech – 'for look he smiles, and Caesar doth not change' (III.i.24). At this point 'Trebonius invites Antony to withdraw with him' and they exit LUE behind Caesar's state chair.

Metellus now 'goes up to Caesar and kneels R' and proceeds to make his suit. Each of the conspirators, one at a time, seconds his plea, kneeling briefly and rising, forming two converging lines which meet at Caesar himself. Casca positions himself slightly to Caesar's left.

When Decius kneels, the group around Caesar is complete and in position. The directions for the business of the assassination are detailed and explicit:

When Caesar says '*Doth not Decius bootless kneel?*' – Metellus lays hold on his Robe; then Casca exclaims – '*Speak hands for me*' – and stabs Caesar over the left shoulder – Caesar starts up, and, turning round to Casca, wounds him with his Style, at which moment Metellus plunges his Dagger in Caesar's right side – Caesar rushes from his place aiming a stroke at Metellus with his Style – Metellus avoids him by slipping behind him (with a repetition of his blow) to Casca's L, who, still striking, has followed Caesar close from his Seat – Caesar, having missed Metellus, strikes widely at Decius, whom he next falls upon – Decius hits him full in the breast, as Cinna at the same time does – Caesar drops his Style, and staggering back towards the middle of the stage meets a most furious blow from Cassius, who at the same instant passes behind to Caesar's R, with his arm raised ready to strike again – Caesar with this last blow reels towards L – and Brutus gives him his last wound. – Caesar falls M a little towards R.

Ludwig Tieck, who saw a performance in 1817, found the spectacle of the mortally wounded Dictator 'staggering across the stage five or six times, so as to be stabbed by the conspirators, who remain quietly standing' extraordinary and unnatural. 'This scene,' he recalls, 'arranged like the most formal ballet, lost all dignity; and it was rendered outrageous by its pretentious solemnity.'[25] But naturalism of setting or action were not Kemble's object; his purpose was to elevate and improve upon nature, and to present his vision in a heightened pictorial manner. In each scene attention is focussed upon one major individual or action, and everything else is reduced to a purely secondary and complementary status. Here it is the death of Caesar that is important; supernumeraries remain where they are as a backdrop, and the conspirators move as little as possible to avoid throwing the major figures out of perspective.

By our more naturalistic standards, Kemble's techniques appear exaggerated and artificial; yet, by his very extravagance he managed to establish for all future productions the importance of the Assassination as the play's focal point. Thereafter the eighteenth-century 'stab me in the dark' impression disappears for good.

Following the death of Caesar, the senators and attendants retire 'in great confusion'. On Brutus' ejaculation, 'Let's all cry, "Peace, freedom, and liberty!"' (III.i.109), 'A general and violent movement of triumph and congratulation' breaks out among the conspirators, and they re-position themselves so that on Antony's entrance they are in a semi-circular formation upstage of Caesar's body which remains well downstage and slightly to the right.

Antony arrives L accompanied by Strato and Servius. His companions retire up left and Antony remains not far from LIE for his 'O mighty Caesar! dost thou lie so low?' speech. During the hand-shaking sequence, he works his way from left to right and 'then goes behind the body' to speak his lines beginning 'That I did love thee, Caesar' (III.i.194), addressing the audience across Caesar's corpse with the conspirators behind him. As Brutus says, 'Or else this were a savage spectacle' (III.i.223), he moves past Cassius to centre-stage where he remains beside Antony while making the funeral arrangements. After Brutus' 'Prepare the body, then, and follow us', the conspirators 'x behind Antony towards L' and exit.

Antony now commands the stage for his 'O, pardon me, thou bleeding piece of earth' speech which he pronounces from a position slightly to the left of the body. On the cue 'With carrion men, groaning for burial' (III.i.275), Flavius and Clitus enter, accompanied by the '4 Guards' introduced in the eighteenth century. With 'Come, bring the body on',[26] Antony exits L followed by '4 Guards with the Body, Strato & Servius, Flavius & Clitus'.

To allow time for the Forum scene to be set in the upstage area previously occupied by the Capitol, Kemble makes the first ten lines of the modern III.ii a separate scene. A pair of Street backshutters is pushed on in the first grooves and Cinna enters R bearing the Cap of Liberty and followed by 'a Throng of Plebeians' who utter 'repeated shouts . . . before they enter'. Behind them come Brutus, Cassius, Casca, Trebonius, Decius, and Metellus 'with their Swords drawn', and 'another Throng of Plebeians' brings up the rear. On

> *Several Ple.*   We will hear Brutus speak.
> *Several Ple.*   We will hear Cassius.[27]

Cinna and Brutus exit L 'with the greater part of the Plebeians', and Cassius follows them off with the other conspirators and the rest of the plebeians.

The front shutters now draw back to reveal the Forum setting. Like the Capitol, no record of its appearance survives apart from Young's brief mention of its effectiveness. It probably consisted basically of shutters painted to represent the Julian Forum with perhaps the temple of Venus Genetrix in the background. At centre-stage stood the all-important rostrum, the shape of which drew a reproof from *The Times* on 2 March 1812. 'In a stage which professes a strict adherence to classic models,' their critic wrote, 'we cannot in the first instance pass over the form of the rostrum without some disapprobation. It appeared to us merely made for the exhibition of the actor, and quite unlike the form of the ancient rostrum as it appears on bas-reliefs and medals.'

At the beginning of the scene the plebeians enter from the left and divide into two groups. 'One half of the Plebeians, at the head of whom are the 1st & 2nd Plebeians' crosses right to Brutus. 'The other half of the Plebeians at the head of whom are the 3rd and 4th Plebeians' remains at the left. Brutus then ascends the rostrum amid an 'uproar, and bawling of *"Silence! Silence!"*' which continues until 'Brutus lays down his Dagger.' Then, with quiet established, the oration begins. On 'Here comes his body mourn'd by Mark Antony' (III.ii.41), the four guards enter L 'with Caesar's Body on a Bier' with Antony, Servius, Strato, and Clitus following.

As Brutus exits R after completing his oration, 'a few of the Plebeians follow' him, but they 'return, when the 1st Plebeian cries – *Stay, ho! & let us* &c'. The bier is now placed in front of the rostrum; Mark Antony heeds the command to 'go up'. 'Dismissing his attendants, & the Guards', he begins the oration.

Details of business for the mob are conspicuously lacking in an otherwise carefully-marked book, and it seems likely that little business was intended. In the traditional manner, Kemble apparently regarded the oration itself as the important thing and studiously avoided anything that might distract from it; consequently, the interaction of Antony and the citizens seems to have been largely overlooked. This impression is further borne out by Kemble's drastic cutting of the citizen's interjections.

Kemble's direction at the beginning of the scene indicates that the citizens on the left were reserved as a kind of stage dressing and that only those on the right took any active part in the proceedings. Moreover, it is doubtful if the full complement of plebeians was even present. Otherwise, how can one explain the comment of the *Bell's Weekly Messenger* critic on 8 March that the mob was too small? He writes:

> The Roman populace, so finely conceived by Shakespeare, were not so well represented on the Stage – How was this? If the theatre had not sufficient numbers on its lists, could it not have borrowed some of the voluntary exhibitors of the neighbouring spouting clubs . . . It is really a pity . . . that Mr. Kemble should want a mob of orators and vagabonds.

This scarcely sounds like the complaint of a man who had seen twenty-five or thirty plebeians on stage, even if all were not active.

When the oration has ended, the plebeians exeunt R 'bearing CAESAR's Body, with great noise and tumult' as Flavius 'hastily' enters L. After the announcement of Octavius' arrival, Antony and Flavius go off left together. The playing-time for this act is fifty-five minutes.

Act IV

The setting for IV.i is described only as 'A Plain near Sardis. The Camp of Brutus', and was probably a pair of shutters drawn across in the first or second grooves to mask the upstage area in which the tent scene is now being set. The processional element is once more strong, although the atmosphere is now military rather than civil. 'A Flourish of Trumpets' marks the beginning of the scene, and Brutus enters L accompanied by Varro, Lucius, silver eagle, and 6 fasces. Metellus and Pindarus enter R and the ensuing conversation takes place on or near the apron.

Cassius then enters R, followed by Trebonius, Titinius, silver eagle, and 6 fasces. The appearance of the two generals establishes the tone of the second half of the play, and the apron positioning allows the audience a close view of the mounting tension between them before they withdraw within the proscenium area for the quarrel. On Brutus' order to 'let no man / Come to our tent till we have done our conference' (IV.ii.50–1), Brutus' forces exit L, while Cassius' following go off R. Brutus and Cassius apparently exit left and position themselves at LUE while the front shutters are drawn off.

Act IV.ii. opens with 'A Flourish of Trumpets' sounding 'till Brutus and Cassius re-enter' LUE and come downstage. The tent setting was placed above the uppermost grooves which suggests that it was not a shutter, but a drop or drapery with, perhaps, a ceiling. At centre-stage are arranged a table and five chairs. Cushions are placed at the 'back of the Tent. LUE'. Directions for the business of the quarrel are few. The only note of interest is one which states that Cassius, on 'I an itching palm!' (IV.iii.12), 'Half draws his Sword' – a return to pre-Restoration tradition discussed earlier.

Before the conference begins, Lucius enters on IV.iii.157 with a taper, and Varro carries on a 'Jar of Wine and a Goblet'. Titinius and Trebonius enter R and Metellus enters L. They seat themselves about the table with Brutus and Cassius on the side nearest the audience. As the scene proceeds the lights are gradually dimmed. Brutus apparently comes well down R for his farewells, and remains standing in the semi-darkness as Lucius enters RUE with the book. At Brutus' request Lucius goes to fetch his lute from a table at RUE. Brutus 'sits down L' and Lucius 'sits down R touching the Strings', but soon falls asleep. After Brutus has taken the lute from the sleeping boy he sits by him at R. The ghost of Caesar then enters L, crosses the full width of the stage to R, speaks to Brutus, and apparently vanishes by means of a trap. Brutus awakens his companions, questions them briefly, and gives the order for Cassius to 'set on his powers'. 'The moment Brutus has done speaking', according to the Jones copy, the orchestra is directed to 'play a strain' as Metellus exits R and Brutus, Varro, and Lucius exeunt LUE. The playing-time for this act is thirty-five minutes.

Act V

'The Plains of Philippi' setting is now run on in the second grooves. Once it is in position, Antony's party enters R2E in the following order: Antony, Octavius, Flavius, Clitus, Strato, SPQR, 2 golden eagles, 6 fasces, and 6 guards. Trumpets and drums sound from the right and left of the stage as they come into view. Servius then enters L to warn Antony of the approach of the enemy, and Brutus and Cassius arrive with much display from L2E. The leaders of each group stand face to face at centre-stage for their defiant exchanges.

After the departure of Antony's entourage R (presumably by counter-marching), 'The Attendants on Brutus & Cassius move into the Centre.' Brutus and Cassius make their farewells well downstage, and on Brutus' 'Come ho, away!' the company exits R.

The scene now changes to 'Another Part of the Field', a fresh shutter. Cassius, accompanied by Trebonius, enters R 'with an Eagle in his hand'. Pindarus then enters L, warning Cassius to 'Fly Further off'. He 'takes the Eagle, & X behind R2E' and waits for further orders. Trebonius exits R on Cassius' reconnaissance mission and Pindarus goes off R2E to act as Cassius' observer. On Cassius' 'To see my best friend ta'en before my face' (V.iii.35), Pindarus re-enters R2E and advances left to his general. As Cassius orders, 'PINDARUS takes the Sword, and CASSIUS runs upon it.' He falls near L2E. After Cassius' death, Pindarus 'Throws away the Sword' and exits L2E.

Trebonius, accompanied by Titinius, now enters R 'with a Laurel-Crown on his head'. He comes to Cassius, and 'takes off the Laurel-Crown, and lays it on the Body'. Brutus now enters R, crosses to the left of Cassius, and his company forms a rather splendid tableau for the eulogy which follows. On 'We shall try fortune in a second fight' (V.iii.110), Brutus exits L with Trebonius, Titinius, Metellus, Lucius, and Varro. A new scene 'closes on the rest' with almost the effect of a cinematic 'fade' as the 'Soldiers prepare to bear away the Body.'

The scene which made such an effective appearance depicted 'Another Part of the Field', and must have been placed in the first grooves.[28] The ensuing action demands little attention. Flavius and Servius enter L with Titinius as their prisoner. Antony enters with a procession from the opposite side, speaks his lines of commendation to Titinius, and each group exits from the direction it entered.

It is worth noting that neither here nor elsewhere does Kemble make much attempt to create a realistic impression of warfare. Several pictorial processions and a few trumpet-calls serve to establish a vaguely military atmosphere, but this aspect of the play is by no means insisted upon.

After Antony's exit the front shutters apparently drew back to reveal the full stage. Brutus enters L, accompanied now only by Metellus, Varro, and Lucius. His phrase 'Come, poor remains of friends' gains in poignancy from the contrast with the processions and pageantry of earlier scenes. Brutus moves directly to the apron.[29] Lucius and Metellus advance in turn while Brutus makes his 'ill request'. At the sound of alarums at R, Lucius urges him to fly. When Brutus asks them to retire, they 'withdraw to a little distance M'. On Metellus' 'Now is that noble vessel full of grief, / That it runs over even at his eyes' (V.v.13–14), 'they look from Brutus' and he begins his death speech, undoubtedly well forward, and finally stabs himself.

'Hearing his Sword fall they look towards Brutus, & run to support him. He sinks on the ground.' To a 'Flourish of Trumpets' Antony now enters in full procession, and his entourage group themselves picturesquely over the full depth of the stage. Antony's triumph is thus fully realized visually as well as verbally. Antony 'Advances and x towards L' and Titinius 'x to Met.' Thus with Octavius, Antony, and Titinius well downstage, the closing lines of the play are spoken, and to a 'Flourish of Martial Instruments' all exit.

The actors

Kemble's Brutus was an exemplary product of beau idéal acting theory. In Kemble's view, the dominant quality in Brutus' personality was his adherence to the stoic discipline. While Kemble would have admitted that 'the temperament of Brutus . . . is naturally warm, as appears in his quarrel with Cassius; naturally affectionate, as is displayed in his scene with Portia', he contended that 'his stoic mien, arising out of rules of thought and conduct long since adopted draws a veil over both feelings; and his affections are subdued, though not hidden, by sufferance enjoined by his philosophy'.[30] Every line of text which seemed inconsistent with this impression, no matter how natural in itself, Kemble ruthlessly excised as we have seen. Likewise in his acting Kemble disdained all tricks, starts, and transitions which, however effective, would be foreign to the stoic character. 'For him,' writes Joseph, 'the tragic conception was essentially one of consistent intensity: the character must be developed undeviatingly in one straight line of progressive intensity: everything must point to the same end.'[31]

Physically, at the age of 55, Kemble looked to one critic 'like such a man as we may naturally suppose Brutus to have been'.[32] 'His person is large and well formed,' noted *The Theatrical Inquisitor* for May 1815, 'his features are strongly marked, and capable of expressing all the higher passions with facility and precision; his eyes are dark and sparkling, and beaming with intelligence. His countenance is in the highest degree heroic, and the cold habits of his mind give to his deportment an involuntary air of grandeur.' Finally, he was gifted with a 'perfectly distinct and impressive voice',[33] capable of almost infinite modulation, although he was frequently obliged to use it sparingly due to an asthmatic condition.

With such eminent natural advantages, Kemble was obviously capable of providing a wealth of brilliant and striking moments. Such effects, however, were precluded by his artistic method. At the risk of being charged with dullness by an audience avid for flashy applause points, he sculpted a study in granite grandeur of 'the towering, the abstractedly-patriotic, the contemplative, philosophical and determined "Roman" that made country, the first consideration, and self, the second object of concern'.[34] Kemble's Brutus seemed to one reviewer

to have devoted himself like Codrus to his Country, and to have stifled every thing which interposed with his duty. There was nothing, however, or at least very little, of reluctance or remorse. He considered himself as having to do, or as having done an act of virtue and duty. His performance of it therefore, was an act of pride and glory, rather than one of self-accusation.[35]

In the Assassination scene Brutus manifested the 'calm dignity, combined with the settled purpose and determined spirit'[36] which his rule of life demanded. When he 'addressed himself to the populace from the *rostrum*, his eloquence and his demeanour were those of a Roman Senator, and that at a time when a Roman Senator would have deemed himself degraded by being put into comparison with any King upon the face of the earth'.[37] But it was in the Quarrel scene that his stoic control was seen in the strongest light. Here Kemble made it abundantly clear that 'it was the pride of that school to regard anger as a short madness; to view the ebullition of passion with contempt, and to subjugate even their most virtuous emotions to the control of a stern wisdom.'[38] His 'speaking countenance and majestic port',[39] the 'calm sarcasm with which he comported himself through most of the scene'[40] were well calculated to demonstrate 'the ascendancy of calmness over passion'.

Apparently at only one point in the entire performance did Kemble permit Brutus' emotion to approach the surface – in his announcement of the death of Portia. Immediately after Cassius said, 'I did not think you could have been so angry' (IV.iii.143), Kemble slowly turned to face Young

in a melancholy tone uttering – 'Oh Cassius, I am sick of many griefs!' and then slowly approaching him, taking one hand within his own and resting the other on *Cassius*'s shoulder and pausing a little and fixing his gaze upon the face of *Cassius*, and then with a faltering voice, and a suffused eye and choking utterance, which seemed to ... indicate that he was nerving himself in order to impart without emotion a heart-rending fact to one whose sympathies would be strongly moved and his shock would else *re-act* upon *himself* and shake his own fortitude before he added – '*Portia – is* – dead!' and closed his eyes.[41]

Kemble's success in this scene was largely due to the rigorous restraint he imposed upon emotion throughout the rest of the performance.

While Kemble's beau idéal Brutus elicited volleys of praise from both critics and audiences, there were some who found it unsatisfying. *The News* (8 March 1812) reviewer considered his gestures in the Forum scene 'fraught with eloquence', but found him lacking in the 'energies which are indispensable to the illustration of a popular harangue'. Leigh Hunt, too, although he approved of Kemble's 'philosophic appearance and manner', thought his slow and meticulous delivery seriously marred the total impression. '*Brutus*', he writes,

who affected pithiness of speech, never thought of recommending it by a drawling preachment; and really this artificial actor does so dole out his words, and so drop his syllables one by one upon the ear, as if he were measuring out laudanum for us, that a reasonable auditor, who is not to be imposed upon with the multitude in general, has no alternative between laughing or being disgusted.[42]

Tieck found the part declaimed with intelligence, but insisted that Brutus was not acted.

These objections, however, scratch only the skin of the part and fail to probe beneath the technique to the conception. Among the many who praised and the few who blamed, seldom did any stop to ask themselves if, in fact, Kemble's Brutus was Shakespeare's character. The only critic to discuss this issue at any length was Hazlitt. 'It has been suggested', he writes,

that Mr. Kemble chiefly excelled in his Roman characters, and, among others, in Brutus. If it be meant that he excelled in those which imply a certain stoicism of feeling and energy of will, this we have already granted; but Brutus is not a character of this kind, and Mr. Kemble failed in it for that reason. Brutus is not a stoic, but a humane enthusiast. There is a tenderness of nature under the garb of assumed severity; an inward current of generous feelings, which burst out, in spite of circumstances, with bleeding freshness; a secret struggle of mind, and disagreement between his situation and his intentions; a lofty inflexibility of purpose, mingled with an effeminate abstractedness of thought, which Mr. Kemble did not give.[43]

Those facets of Brutus which he did explore, however, were presented with a grandeur and truth of conception which became the aim, if seldom the realization, of every actor for decades afterwards. Later performers, it is true, came closer to presenting Brutus, the man; but Brutus, the stoic philosopher, and Brutus, the public figure, have probably never since come so vividly across the footlights.

While Kemble clearly considered Brutus the focal point of the play, he realized that the part could not achieve maximum dramatic impact without fully competent supporting actors. On the opening night he was supported by his two ablest disciples – Charles Mayne Young as Cassius and Kemble's younger brother, Charles, as Antony.

Young's Cassius was doubtless the best the stage had seen since the age of Betterton. Leigh Hunt, in fact, considered this role 'the most prominent attraction of the performance',[44] and the Bell's Weekly Messenger reviewer described it as 'only inferior to Kemble's Brutus'.

At the age of 35, Young looked the Roman he represented. He 'had a full, compact, and well-proportioned figure, a little above the medium height', and 'an intellectual cast of countenance'[45] which Cole found 'commanding'.[46] 'His voice was full and of great compass' and his 'articulation and declamation were good', although 'a slight lisp could occasionally be detected in his speech. His action was described as 'easy and graceful'.[47]

Like Kemble, Young sought for the central essence of his character and developed it, as did his master, in straight-line fashion. Even as Kemble saw

Brutus as the man of reason, Young considered Cassius the man of emotion. Although in appearance his Cassius was 'pale, wan, austere', his 'quick and nervous *pace*' immediately indicated the 'irritability and restless impetuosity'[48] which figured so largely in his temperament.

At his first encounter with Brutus he set out to point firmly the contrast between his own animated personality and the stoical, dignified, unbending nature of the man he wished to influence. 'His speech, depreciating the god-like qualities of *Caesar*', wrote one reviewer, 'was marked by all those sudden starts of passion and feeling which rendered it so adapted to attract the attention and rouse the sleeping energies of the "last of all the Romans".'[49] His speech beginning 'I know that virtue to be in you, Brutus' (I.ii.90) was described by Leigh Hunt as 'a string of varieties from the commonest colloquial familiarity to the loftiest burst of passion'. 'Mr. Young', he writes,

passes from one to another with the happiest instantaneousness of impression – from an air of indifference to one of resentment, from anecdote to indignant comment, from the subdued tone of sarcastic mimicry to the loud and impatient climax of a jealousy wrought up into rage. The transition in particular from the repetition of *Caesar*'s sick words to the contemptuous simile they occasion, and from that again to the concluding burst of astonishment accompanied by a start forward and a vehement clasp of the hands, is exceedingly striking.[50]

His handling of the long speeches was apparently never monotonous; throughout, we are told, he 'preserved a level tone of voice and delivery nicely steering between declamation and frigid repetition'.[51] His major triumph, his 'sudden starts of passion and feeling'[52] formed an exquisite counterpoint to Kemble's stoic restraint. 'This scene as acted by him and YOUNG, is really one of those exhibitions which would be injured by description', exclaimed *The Morning Post* (5 February 1814). 'We hardly know of an expression of praise to which it may not lay claim.'

Almost equally applauded was the performance of Charles Kemble as Mark Antony. Although he was 37 years of age when he first played the role, his impact was so immediate and enduring that his Antony remained for more than two decades thereafter, in spite of advancing years, the undisputed favourite of the public.

Physically, according to *Blackwood's Magazine*, Charles was 'not so fine a man as John, but then he has a noble natural air, and has studied successfully the art or the science of manner, demeanour, carriage, so as to make the most of his figure, which is cast in almost Herculean mould. His face, though far inferior in heroic expression to John's, is yet noble; and he has a voice mellow and manly, and of much compass.'[53]

Like John's Brutus, Charles's Antony was a much methodized and regularized character. Thanks to the drastic textual cutting mentioned earlier, he is no longer the calculating *arriviste*, but the noble young man motivated by a sense of friendship and justice to avenge the death of his benefactor. In the first scene of the tragedy, Charles carried immediate conviction as the athletic nobleman. According to Hunt, he looked Antony 'to perfection'.[54] Julian Charles Young recalls vividly 'the handsome, joyous face', the 'graceful tread', and the 'pliant body bending forward in courtly adulation of "Great Caesar"'.[55]

Like his predecessor, Wilks, Kemble was capable of impressively mingling nobility and intense grief. His 'O pardon me, thou bleeding piece of earth' speech 'was delivered with a tenderness and earnestness of tone that at once spoke the grief of the attached friend'.[56] But it was in the Forum scene that he achieved his most telling effects. Here he moved through a series of emotional stages from 'the youthful and feeling anxiety about Caesar' to the 'ridiculing tones in which the Conspirators are mentioned' to 'the chuckling delight evinced when he artfully roused the Roman citizens to something like a counter-revolt against the party of Brutus'.[57] Throughout the first part of the speech he admirably represented the sensitive, sincere, grief-stricken youth. He may even have taken his distress a little too far. One critic observed that his sensibility sometimes degenerated into 'effeminate lamentation' and 'his energy into rant'. Moreover, according to the same reviewer, he frequently wept audibly in a rather womanish fashion, drawing upon himself the reminder that 'men may weep only, and this too very rarely – but must never cry – above all, must never cry after the manner which sailors contemptuously call "blubbering"'.[58] Later in the scene, the way in which he 'drew the attention of the people to the will of the deceased' delighted one reviewer 'with varieties of excellence'.[59] Wrote another:

Nothing could be finer than the burst of exultation with which he concluded his speech, when he had inflamed the minds of the auditors against the conspirators, and the animation with which he uttered the words –
> – Now let it work
> Mischief, thou art a foot

excited the most unbounded applause.[60]

There were, of course, rumblings of critical disapproval, but objection was generally taken to the rendering of specific lines rather than the overall truth of conception. One critic was displeased by his manner of speaking

> Brutus says he was ambitious,
> And Brutus is an honourable man;
> So are they all, all honourable men.

According to this reviewer, he 'uttered the sentiment with all the gravity of an entire acquiescence in its force' when the implication should have been 'quite the opposite of serious admission'.[61] It is doubtful if Kemble went so far as this writer suggests, but it is clear that he did not strongly accentuate the ironic quality of the lines. In the view of another observer, the meaning would 'have been apparent to an intelligent assemblage, as it was delivered', but for a mob such as he was addressing 'the sarcasm must have a more decided feature'.[62] Tieck, on the other hand, considered that the oration was 'well spoken' and delivered with 'great energy', but found 'there was too much malignant bitterness in his laugh at its close, when he saw the people roused'.

His military scenes were no doubt successful thanks to his commanding presence and forceful declamation, but they excited little critical comment. His final eulogy over the dead Brutus, however, was described as 'particularly beautiful'.[63]

After such a roster of splendid performers one is disappointed to discover a distinctly inferior Caesar. Daniel Egerton, who played the Dictator, was a second-rate actor at best, totally dissimilar to Caesar in appearance and incapable of tragic dignity. To an audience familiar with the face and figure of Caesar from coins and busts, Egerton's 'full face and corpulent person' were such as 'wholly to disenchant the character of all probability'.[64]

Not only did Egerton's Caesar suffer from an unconvincing physique, but he also laboured under too heavy an acting style. Even as Kemble sought to lend *Caesar* a touch of imperial glory by elaborate processions and striking scenery, so did Egerton attempt to elevate the character to a proper tragic majesty. Both these intentions were admirable, but the second went too far. The fault of Egerton's Caesar was not that he lacked dignity, but that he had too much and it was of the wrong sort. According to Hunt, 'Every action is lofty, every look tragic, every turn of step and of feature imperial and bluff. When Caesar, upon a representation of Anthony's that *Cassius* was not a dangerous man, pleasantly wishes that "he were fatter"', Hunt continues, 'Mr. Egerton takes it in the light of a serious and impassioned desire, and mouths out the words like a stage-tyrant who wishes a man in his grave.' Again, when Antony 'is familiarly requested to step to the other side of him, because the ear at which he is standing is deaf, he delivers the request with as much dignity, and motions him round with as much mysterious solemnity, as if he were asking him to defend his other side from an assassin'.[65]

To such a character as Caesar the beau idéal method was not in the least congenial. Brutus and Antony might be shorn of their inconsistencies and still remain stageworthy; but to cut the lines of Caesar mentioned above would be to destroy the very core of the man; his credibility is inseparable from his human frailty. Kemble was apparently wise enough to recognize this fact and allowed the lines to stand; but when the grand style was superimposed upon Shakespeare's very natural figure, what should have been an impressive blend of dignity and humanity became but an empty and ridiculous turgidity.

To the twentieth-century theatre-goer, accustomed as we are to a comparatively full text and naturalistic acting, Kemble's beau idéal *Caesar* may well seem static and artificial; yet it remains one of the most significant revivals in the play's history. For the first time a presentation may be properly called a production – a unit moulded to form by one controlling hand to produce a predetermined artistic effect – rather than a series of virtuoso pieces for one or two star actors. For the first time, too, artist and antiquary begin to make their contribution to the play's dramatic effect. Moreover, from this point onwards, the play owes its popularity to its dramatic quality rather than its consonance with popular political sentiment.

Not since the age of Betterton had three such competent actors undertaken the leading roles; and if they did not provide well-rounded interpretations, at least they demonstrated the potential within the facets they chose to explore. Caesar, all too long a poor relation in the drama, begins to come into his own with some emphasis on his external trappings and careful management of the assassination. The interpretation of the character itself, however, still left much to be desired.

Throughout the next eighty years audiences saw no production which did not owe a direct and profound debt to the 1812 revival.

4

From Young to Phelps (1819–65)

Thanks to the impetus of the Kemble revivals, *Julius Caesar* enjoyed half a century of public favour reminiscent of the period which followed the retirement of Betterton. Most productions were associated with Charles Mayne Young, William Charles Macready, and Samuel Phelps. Young assumed the role of Brutus in 1819, two years after Kemble's last appearance, and played it in London and the provinces until 1832. William Charles Macready, who appeared as Cassius to Young's Brutus in 1819 and 1822, succeeded him in 1836 and played 'the noblest Roman of them all' with great applause for the next fifteen years in England and America. He also staged three revivals during his management at Covent Garden (1837–9) and Drury Lane (1841–3). In 1846, five years before Macready's retirement, Samuel Phelps launched the play at Sadler's Wells, with himself as Brutus; and during the next sixteen years all noteworthy *Caesar* productions, apart from Macready's farewell performances, were staged at this house. Phelps last appeared as Brutus during a brief revival at Drury Lane in 1865.

Charles Mayne Young

Throughout his career Young preferred engagements as itinerant star to the perils of management; and consequently he left little or no mark on *Julius Caesar*'s text or stagecraft. An admirer of Kemble almost to the point of idolatry, he was content to play the Kemble script[1] with the Kemble business; questions of mounting fell within the province of the stage manager.

The Kemble settings remained in use at Covent Garden throughout Young's era and afterwards. Processions and pageantry were the staple visual interest; in fact, one reviewer considered 'the attraction of military parade' as one of the major reasons for staging the play at all.[2] Effective processions necessitated authentic and picturesque costumes, and these became a much-discussed feature of productions. Thanks to the researches of Planché and his fellow antiquaries Roman dress was becoming daily more accurate. When Talma's 'senatorial robes' were proved to be more correct than Kemble's, 'they were', Cole tells us, 'transported to the London boards, and the Kemble garments were deposed'.[3] Young was the first English player to adopt the Talma toga and learned to wear it under the direction of the great actor himself.

Young's physical appearance, like that of Kemble, made him from the first a convincing representative of Roman characters and the classic features and graceful walk which earlier lent credibility to his Cassius, now, in maturer form, stood him in good stead as Brutus. With the passing years his face became more classically severe, and his movement, once more flexible than Kemble's, took on the latter's statue-like formality. His voice, rich in quality and beautifully-modulated in contrast to Kemble's weak and asthmatic utterance, did full justice to the poetry of the part which, we are told, 'like TITIAN's sunshine, diffuses itself all over his performances'.[4]

Like Kemble, Young conceived of Brutus in straight-line terms with stoicism as the governing factor in his personality. Although the beau idéal style had fallen into some disfavour amid the growing enthusiasm for the more flashy effects of Edmund Kean, Young's restrained and artificial manner was generally considered more of an asset than a liability to his Brutus. 'His defects in other characters are requisites in this', wrote the *Morning Herald* critic. 'What then might have been called tameness becomes philosophy *now*; and that, which, in other parts, we designated apathy, in *this* we justly term a property of stoicism.'[5]

In spite of his advantages, natural and acquired, Young never approached Kemble's realization of the role. His Brutus lacked the underlying consistency of Kemble's creation, born of an intellectual understanding of stoic philosophy, an innate sense of classic grandeur, and a temperamental affinity between the actor and the character he represented. 'The deep, steady, and God-like hero, the really philosophical Roman . . . [Young] may now and then put on, but cannot steadily maintain',[6] one reviewer concluded; and he spoke for many.

Although Antony was well played by Charles Kemble in all of Young's revivals save those of 1829 (when James Wallack gave two unremarkable performances), the Cassiuses, apart from Macready's in 1819 and 1822 which we shall notice later, were as far below Young's standard as Young was below Kemble's. John Cooper (1823, 1825, 1829) and James Warde (1826, 1827) were both censured for presenting Cassiuses whose Roman decorum vanished in unbecoming uproar. In the Quarrel scene Cooper's outraged general 'was like an angry urchin "kicking up a rumpus" with his school-mate for stealing his marbles'. 'Instead of arguing with *him*', wrote one reviewer, 'Brutus would have pulverised him.'[7] Warde's interpretation was little better.

Julius Caesar was played almost exclusively by the persevering, if inept,

Daniel Egerton. Thompson and H. Wallack each attempted the part once in 1829, but their appearances evoked hardly a flicker of critical interest.

Between 1819 and 1832, Young's monopoly of the role of Brutus was challenged but twice – by James Wallack in 1820 at Drury Lane and by Warde in 1825 at Covent Garden. Neither enjoyed any success.

Between the retirement of Young in 1832 and the first appearance of Macready as Brutus in 1836, public interest in *Julius Caesar* slackened. Only five revivals are recorded at the patent theatres (see *chronological handlist*). Warde, Wallack, Vandenhoff, Knowles, and Paumier, all to a greater or lesser degree adherents to the Kemble school, successively attempted Brutus and signally failed to impress. The older generation of theatre-goers had seen Kemble, and their offspring had witnessed the fitfully powerful performances of Young. How could mere copies hope to please?

But *Julius Caesar*'s theatrical decline need not be charged entirely to the actors. Equally important was the fact that Kemble's classical conception of the play was falling from critical favour. In a perceptive article on 1 November, 1829, the *Examiner* critic succinctly articulated the unease of many of his contemporaries. Beneath the artificiality of contemporary stage-Romans, he argued, lay a fundamental confusion between the popular conception of Romans, arrived at by archaeological research, and the Roman products of Shakespeare's imagination. 'The ancient Romans', he wrote, 'have become to us, in personal identity, a "dead language". We know them only from coins, medals, bas reliefs, and other sculpture, and all these impress upon the mind the idea of their being a stern, formal, severe, and unbending people.' Shakespeare, on the other hand, was not hampered by archaeology. He looked upon his Romans

as men acting from the same impulses as himself, and swayed by the same casualties . . . [Caesar's deaf ear and Cassius' thick sight] are not consonant with the general notion of 'classicality' in either high or tragic writings; but Shakespeare thought that such familiarities were consonant with *nature*, and he aimed neither higher nor lower than that standard.

Contemporary performers, faithful to the Kemble myth, were more statues than men. 'You never by any chance detect one of them in a little act of natural familiarity incident to our common humanity and to the routine of every-day life – it would appear to them derogatory from the dignity and pedestal-like station of the characters they undertake to impersonate.' Clearly the time had come for a change – for a shift from archaeology to Shakespeare and from the beau idéal style to something closer to realism.

The implications of the *Examiner* article were not only aesthetic but economic. Audiences for Roman dramas were falling off. Theatre-goers demanded not heroic, but domestic tragedy; they wanted to identify rather than admire. Sheridan Knowles astutely sniffed change in the wind as early as 1820; and although he chose in *Virginius* to dramatize Roman history, he followed Shakespeare in making the humanity of his characters more important than the Roman setting or situation. 'In what consists the interest and force of his popular play *Virginius*?' demanded Horne. 'The domestic feeling. The costume, the setting, the decorations are heroic. We have Roman tunics, but a modern English heart, – the scene is the Forum, but the sentiments those of the "Bedford Arms".'[8] Unless *Julius Caesar*'s characters could also become more than abstract glorifications of Roman virtues, lifeless copies of classic busts, its theatrical future was bleak indeed. Luckily, in 1836, just as the Kemble interpretation was breathing its last after four years of decline, William Charles Macready played Brutus for the first time.

William Charles Macready

Macready's association with *Julius Caesar* spans a period of almost four decades. He first appeared in the play in Glasgow in 1813 as Mark Antony under his father's management.[9] In 1819 and 1822 he played Cassius to Charles Young's Brutus in a number of successful performances at Covent Garden, and thereafter made the part a staple of his provincial tours until 1836.[10] Finally, at Covent Garden on 14 November 1836, he made his début as Brutus, and with this performance established himself as the leading representative of Shakespeare's noble Roman, a position he retained until his retirement in 1851. Not long before his departure from the stage he revived his old part of Cassius and sometimes alternated the two roles in his farewell performances.

Throughout most of his career Macready preferred to appear as a guest star; but for two brief periods he tried his hand at management. From 1837 to 1839 he presided over the theatrical affairs of Covent Garden, and from 1841 to 1843 he rendered a similar service to Drury Lane. During these years he presented three *Julius Caesar* revivals: the first two took place at Covent Garden in 1838 and 1839, and the third at Drury Lane in 1843. It is in these productions that the totality of his contribution to *Julius Caesar* may be best appreciated.

Macready made no claim to be a managerial innovator; he offered no revolutionary approach and founded no school, although his acting and production were not without influence.[11] He aimed to speak texts which were at least free from corruptions, to introduce settings which were both splendid and historically correct, and to provide outstanding performances of the major roles and competent playing of the minor ones.

While both Kemble and Macready devoted much attention to settings and supers, their conceptions of the function of *mise en scène* differed considerably. Where Kemble's scenes were intended to provide pictorial interest, Macready attempted realistic representation.

Macready also relied heavily on supers, and was considerably more lavish than Kemble; but he employed them differently. Where Kemble used his extras passively, merely to dress the stage and throw the major actors into relief, Macready used his actively, 'by giving purpose and action to the various members of our groups', to lend complementary interest to the major movement of any given scene. Working on an observation of Sir Thomas Lawrence that 'Every part of a picture required equal care and pains', Macready attempted 'to spread over the entire scene some portion of that energy and interest which, heretofore, the leading actor exclusively and jealously appropriated'.[12]

His impressive ensemble theory was, however, only incompletely realized in practice. In scenes in which he did not himself appear, he succeeded admirably in 'subduing that tendency to undue prominence in one figure by giving adventitious aids to the rest';[13] but when he took the stage, Vandenhoff tells us, 'actors were expected ... to lose all thought of giving prominence to their own parts'.[14]

In the space of a few pages it is, of course, impossible to treat all three *Julius Caesar* revivals in detail; but perhaps an adequate enough notion of Macready's methods and achievement may be gained from an examination of the last – at Drury Lane in 1843 – which, besides being the best documented, took place when his acting powers were at their height and his stagecraft had reached maturity. Fortunately a transcript of the 1843 promptbook, made by George Ellis (*JC* 13),[15] is still extant. This book contains a cast-list for the 1843 revival, ten manuscript pages of historical facts relevant to the play's characters and events, a ground plan (21 × 13 inches) of the Senate scene, a list of wings, scenes, and groove numbers, a nine-page book of calls, and a cast-list for an undated performance at the City Theatre.

Ellis's basic text is the Oxberry edition of 1822; and Macready may well have used the same version for the original book. Most of the Kemble notes incorporated by Oxberry, Ellis left standing; and where changes were necessary he simply crossed out the printed direction and wrote in a fresh one.

Ellis's book clearly suggests that, apart from the restoration of a few lines and the alteration of a word here and there, Macready played the Kemble text. Among his most noteworthy restorations are Brutus' idealistic outburst beginning 'what other bond / Than secret Romans, that have spoke the word' (II.i.124–8), and the hand-washing sequence in the Assassination scene.

Although placing the play somewhat further upstage than Kemble had done, Macready retained Kemble's arrangement of alternating shallow and deep scenes and most of the business set down for the major characters. Once more Brutus moved to music amidst weighty flats, splendid costumes, and swarms of supers. A scene-by-scene analysis of Macready's production would be redundant after the detailed treatment of Kemble's methods undertaken earlier. One ought, however, to mark several major differences between the two productions and to examine in detail two scenes – the Assassination and the Forum – where Macready not only carried on tradition, but went some way toward creating it.

Macready's *Julius Caesar* settings, unlike those of Kemble, were not painted for this particular revival; rather they were borrowings from other Roman plays for which, presumably, he had special scenery prepared. Most settings consisted basically of painted shutters supplemented, when necessary, by set pieces. All the street scenes were performed before the flat described as 'Faustus Street', set in the first or second grooves as occasion required, and flanked by 'Roman Street' wings. For i.ii (A Public Place), Macready used a 'Roman Street' flat mounted in the sixth grooves and fronted by a 'Roman Arch' at centre-stage in the fourth grooves. On either side were placed 'Roman Street' wings. Brutus' soliloquy was spoken in front of 'Tomkin's Garden' (doubtless a multi-purpose stock piece) to which was added a 'side arch' at R2E. Caesar's house was, quite inexplicably, a 'Modern Anti-Chamber' with 'Andrew's 2 doors' as wings.

Passing over the Assassination and Forum scenes for the moment, we come to the Quarrel scene. Brutus and Cassius have their first stormy encounter before a flat described as 'Virginius Camp' which was drawn across in the first grooves with 'Wood' wings to right and left. The quarrel itself took place in 'Pizarro's Tent' which was set in the third grooves and 'back'd by Back of Portia's Chamber' in the fourth. All of the act v settings are forest scenes of one kind or another. The opposing armies meet before 'Marshall's Wood'; Cassius dies in front of 'Tomkin's Wood'; Titinius is taken prisoner in the 'Depths of Forest'; and Brutus dies against a background of 'Pine Tree Flats'.

In terms of scenic realism, as it was understood at the time (the illusion created by painted flats and free-standing pieces), *Caesar*'s décor seems to have been judged both adequate and convincing, if not quite of the spectacular and uniform design of *Coriolanus*. The *Morning Herald* considered that 'all its scenic and stage arrangements were provided for with an unprecedented approach to completeness'.[16]

If some exceptionally demanding theatre-goer felt that Macready had shortchanged him somewhat where scenes were concerned, he no doubt found himself adequately compensated by the generous numbers of supers. According to the cast-list at the beginning of his promptbook, Macready provided no less than a hundred and seven, compared with a possible eighty used by Kemble. Moreover, the extras each played several parts, where

Kemble's played only one; thus, Macready could put on about a hundred supers at any given time, provided no costume change was required for the scene immediately following. A mob of thirty plebians appeared in the first scene; the full complement was brought on to add to Caesar's splendour in the second; Brutus and Antony were each supplied with forty guards, besides other attendants, for their confrontation at the beginning of act v (compared with Kemble's six), and no less than seventy military figures appeared in tableau arrangement for Antony's eulogy over Brutus at the end of the play.

While the mere increase in numbers lent a greater air of realism to the play, Macready's attempt to give 'purpose and action to the various members of our groups' accomplished even more. After the citizens create their lively tumult in the opening scene, they are directed to 'get round to RUE, ready to be disc^d Next Sc' where they are seen milling about the left of the stage as Caesar's procession enters. Before and during the entrance of the procession, the citizens are directed to 'look off L & shout L'. Similarly, they are expected to block the Soothsayer's way, forcing him to make a realistic struggle to 'come from the crowd'. It is surprising, however, that Macready missed the opportunity to use them actively in the battle scenes; here, like Kemble's supers, they served merely to decorate the stage.

Apart from the innovations mentioned above, Macready introduces little business not previously used by Kemble.

The conspirators, after entering Brutus' garden 'with their faces muffled in their gowns', all uncover their faces together rather than separately as Kemble intended. Brutus and Portia play their scene downstage rather than well up as in previous performances. And, most interestingly, at the end of the quarrel Macready has the drop fall 'When Brut gets to table', rather than allowing him to exit to 'a strain' as in Kemble's production.

Macready's handling of the Assassination and Forum scenes, however, shows him much more capable of creative direction than his ultra-conservative treatment of the rest of the play would indicate. Here, although he uses the Kemble arrangement as his starting point, he achieves a degree of visual splendour and realistic action which, however insignificant by comparison, establishes him as the legitimate ancestor of the Meiningen Court Company and Herbert Beerbohm Tree.

The Assassination scene

Even as early as his first performance of Brutus in 1836, under Osbaldiston's management, Macready felt strongly that the Assassination scene ought to be made the focal point of the play. Somehow he managed to convince Osbaldiston, perhaps by appealing to his sense of showmanship, and was permitted to arrange this one scene. A few days after the opening he confided to his diary with obvious relish, 'I am very pleased to hear that every paper noticed the Senate scene, which I induced Mr. Osbaldiston to have.'[17] In fact, the papers did more than notice it; they praised it very warmly indeed.

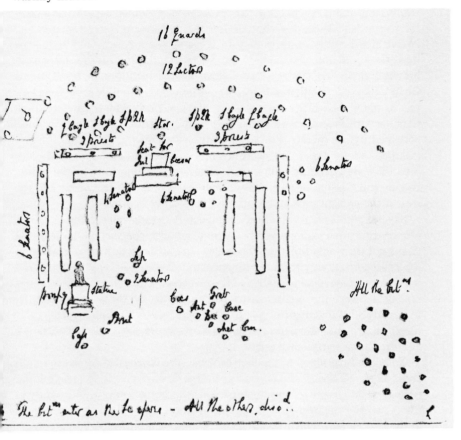

5. William Charles Macready's Ground Plan for the Capitol scene (III.i) at Drury Lane, 1843

It is hardly surprising that when he came to revive the play himself, Macready made the scene a highlight of his production. Bound in the front of his promptbook is a large ground plan, and, interleaved with the appropriate section of text, is a smaller version in somewhat more detail (see Illustration 5). With the help of these diagrams and fairly full directions, Macready's arrangement is not difficult to reconstruct.

Once Portia, the Soothsayer, and Lucius were clear of the stage, the front 'Street' flats drew back to reveal the Capitol. The basic flats, placed in the fourth grooves, are described only as 'Shakespeare Hall and Back' with wings 'to match'. No doubt this was some sort of vaguely classical stock interior, but its exact appearance is a matter of little importance; it was upon his supers that Macready relied for most of his visual effects.

As the scene opened the audience was treated to a splendid static tableau comprising about seventy-five figures arrayed in Roman costume and carefully grouped. Massed at the back of the stage were sixteen guards and twelve lictors, and, immediately in front of them to left and right, the bearers of gold and silver eagles and SPQR standards with the star-carrier between them. At centre stage Caesar sat in splendour in his 'Currule Chair', flanked on either side by three priests occupying 'Marble Benches' placed parallel with the back wall. Somewhat farther forward were three tiers of marble benches on either side of the stage at right angles to those occupied by the priests. Pompey's statue stood downstage right. Finally, grouped about the stage were twenty-four senators (compared with Kemble's six), lending colour and an air of verisimilitude to the scene. Brutus and Cassius stood aloof by Pompey's statue, while Antony and the rest of the conspirators were grouped downstage centre.

Several points about Macready's stagecraft already call for notice. While Macready's supers are obviously meant to provide spectacle, it is clear that this is not their only function. They also lend an air of numerical realism to the proceedings, an effect only imperfectly realized by Kemble; and, even more important, serve partially to fill a vast stage which, if left empty, could seriously dwarf the scene's crucial action. Part of the same scheme is Macready's arrangement of the marble benches in a roughly rectangular frame, narrowing the centre stage to a workable size and concentrating attention on a fairly small space.

To add a final touch to the *mise en scène*, the citizens, forty-seven in all, enter 'as the Sc opens' and take up positions downstage left. Besides adding further weight to the setting, their presence accentuates the public nature of the event. For the first time the people of Rome begin to take an active part in the play, a part which was to grow in importance in succeeding years.

Immediately the citizens are in place the Soothsayer makes his entry, 'pushing his way through the Citizens' with refreshing realism, and moves upstage toward Caesar 'presenting a scroll of paper'. Decius blocks his way at c and, on 'Sirrah, give place' (III.i.10), 'thrusts the Sooth among the Cit[ns]' who no doubt received him with some horseplay. Brutus and Cassius now cross 'in conversation, to L' where they meet Popilius who is just entering. After speaking to Cassius, he advances to the left of Caesar. Casca then moves to Cassius' right, and Decius to Casca's left. While Brutus calms Cassius' fears with 'For look, he smiles, and Caesar doth not change' (III.i.24), 'Treb & Ant are x'ing in conver[n], up to LUE', and make a 'leisurely exit'.

Metellus then approaches Caesar to present his petition, kneels on 'humble heart', and rises again on Caesar's 'I spurn thee like a cur out of my way' (III.i.46). As he says, 'Is there no voice more worthy than my own' (III.i.49), Metullus 'turns to the other Senators' in feigned appeal. The conspirators are not slow to respond. One by one they advance to Caesar, kneel, and when repulsed, rise and arrange themselves in the open area much as in Kemble's production.

No manuscript instructions are provided for the stabbing itself; Macready merely leaves the Oxberry directions standing:

Metellus lays hold on Caesar's robe: – Casca stabs Caesar in the neck: – Caesar catches hold of his arm: – he is then stabbed by the other Conspirators, and at last by Marcus Brutus.

It is quite likely that after the initial moves of Metellus and Casca, the rest of the conspirators leapt upon the Dictator in a body. He then seems to have staggered under their blows down the central open space to fall at the foot of Pompey's statue. A manuscript note opposite this section – 'All over quickly' – suggests that Macready had in mind something much more realistic than Kemble's ballet-like posturing.

As Caesar falls, Macready calls for

A violent movement of terror and confusion amongst Senators, priests, Soldiers, Citizens, &c. & clasping their hands they variously exclaim, 'Horror! Horror! He is dead! He is slain! – Murder! Treason! Oh Brutus! Where is Antony! Metellus! Decius! Popilius Lenas!'

Here is indeed an important innovation. Not only does Macready provide something close to a realistic murder, but he contrives a more or less natural reaction to it. No longer is the scene merely a statuesque historical pageant for an audience who admire the heroics but remain emotionally remote from what is going on; Macready attempts for the first time to offer convincing action, to pass an ethical judgement, and to involve the audience in the horror felt, not only by such alien personages as priests and senators, but by people like themselves. If this is not an overt concession to the demands of domestic tragedy, it comes very close to being so.

But to return to the scene. Paying no heed to Brutus' appeal to 'Fly not; stand still', 'All' make their way 'off during Brut speech except Consp^s'. Popilius and Lepidus linger a little longer than the rest, but exit R on 'Do so'.

Trebonius now re-enters L and the scene proceeds. Macready restores Brutus' fanatical 'Stoop, Romans, stoop, / And let us bathe our hands in Caesar's blood' (III.i.105–6) and Cassius' 'Stoop then, and wash', although the latter speech is now taken by Casca. As Casca speaks, 'They gather round the body of Caesar & place their hands on it.' On Decius' 'What, shall we forth?' (III.i.119), 'they move forw^d' into a semicircular formation for

Antony's arrival. Antony then enters L with Servius and Strato who retire upstage. His 'O mighty Caesar' lament, the hand-shaking sequence, and the discussion related to Caesar's funeral are handled much as in Kemble's production. On 'Prepare the body then, and follow us' (III.i.253), 'the conspirators X behind Antony towards L' and exit.

'Ant now kneels to Caesar's body' and begins his 'O, pardon me' speech in a kneeling position, but on 'A curse shall light upon the limbs of men' (III.i.262), he rises. Flavius once more enters with '4 Attend^{ts}' to carry off the dead Dictator, but they do not actually do so. As Antony says, 'Come, bring the body on', 'The attend^{ts} advance to Caesar's body', and the scene closes on them with a tableau effect.

The Forum scene

Although Macready's arrangement of the assassination may have had a greater immediate impact upon contemporary play-goers, his experimental treatment of the Forum scene is infinitely more important to the stage historian. Here, for the first time, Shakespeare's crowd becomes a vital force in the scene and some measure of ensemble playing between orators and mob is achieved. Almost forty years later, the Meiningen Court Company, expanding and improving upon the same design, established the Forum scene as equal, if not superior, in dramatic interest to the long-popular Assassination and Quarrel sequences.

When the 'Street' flats were drawn off, after the brief transition scene inserted by Kemble to allow the Assassination set to be replaced, 'Marshall's Set Forum' was revealed in the fifth grooves, backed by a 'Moonlight Street' in the sixth grooves, and flanked on either side by 'Roman Street Vestibule' wings. This scene was no doubt more elaborate than that used for the Assassination, since the drab costumes of the plebeians would, by themselves, provide scant visual interest. Whether the setting was especially designed for this revival is uncertain, but it is likely to have previously served other Roman plays. However, since it was prepared by a leading scene-painter and authority on classical architecture, its attractiveness need not have ended with one or two appearances.

As the scene draws, 'Brutus is disc^d on the steps of the rost^m' with 'All the Consp^{rs}, except Cassius', and the full complement of forty-seven plebeians grouped to the right and left of him. At the beginning of his speech, Brutus is obliged, realistically enough, to compete with 'A low murmuring among the Citizens' until, with the voice of authority, he says, 'be silent that you may hear'. Opposite this line is the direction 'All quiet here'. Although the noise ceases at this point, the plebeians do not become unresponsive as in Kemble's production. Macready now introduces the first recorded instance of mime for this scene. As the oration proceeds the citizens' interest increases noticeably; at specified places during the address they 'turn to one another as though quietly obtaining each other's sentiments'. It is worth noting that all these points coincide with emotionally-loaded phrases – e.g. 'To live all free men', 'would be a bondman', 'not be a Roman', 'not love his country'. Gradually the mob's antagonism wanes until enthusiastic uproar succeeds mimed interest on 'nor his offences enforc'd, for which he suffered death' (III.ii.39–40). Brutus now 'leaves Rost^m', and 'the Tumult is kept up, until he is in front'. It ceases only when he 'holds up his hand' on 'My countrymen'.[18]

On 'Here comes his body, mourned by Mark Antony', the '4 Attend^{ts}' enter L with the bier, 'followed by Antony and Servius'. Strato and Clitus, who appeared in Kemble's production, are now eliminated; no doubt Macready felt that an entourage of any size would have detracted from Antony's vulnerability. While Brutus continues his address, 'They proceed slowly, & deposit the body beneath the rostrum.' 'This is timed', reads the direction, 'so as to be done, at Brutus Exit.' As he says, 'By our permission, is allow'd to make', Brutus 'x'es RIE.' amid the 'Noise, Shouts etc.' of the adoring mob who prepare to follow him off. Brutus stops at the exit, exhorts the crowd to remain behind, and departs, dagger in hand, on 'I have the same dagger for myself, when it shall please my country to need my death' (III.ii.45–7) (see Illustration 6).[19] The other conspirators follow.

Macready restores the third Plebeian's lines:

> Let him go up into the public chair.
> We'll hear him. Noble Antony, go up.

The last words, however, are altered to 'Go up – go up – noble Antony', and are spoken by 'All'. After dismissing Servius and the attendants L, Antony accedes to their request and 'goes into the Rostrum'. As he begins his address, the citizens are at R and RC where they have remained since the departure of Brutus. On 'Peace, ho! let us hear him' (III.ii.72), 'Half the Citizens X to L'.

Again, throughout Antony's speech, 'the Citizens turn & speak to each other . . . as before' when telling points are made. The phrases thus designated are 'Brutus is an honourable man', 'presented him a kingly crown', and 'I must pause till it come back to me'. While Antony weeps, a lively discussion takes place between the speaking plebeians who are still at stage right and the majority of the mob who are now at stage left. On the fourth Plebeian's 'He would not take the crown' (III.ii.112), all shout 'No, no, no'. On the third Plebeian's 'There's not a nobler man in Rome than Antony', '8 or 10 Cit^{ns}', but not all, shout 'No, no, no'.

More mime is introduced during the will sequence. As Antony says, 'Let but the commons hear this testament' (III.ii.130), 'Several of the Citizens extend their hands to Antony, & press forw^d towards him', and on ''Tis

Mr MACREADY as BRUTUS.

BRU: With this I depart: that, as I slew my best lover for
the good of Rome, I have the same dagger for
myself, when it shall please my country to need
my death.

JULIUS CAESAR. Act 3, Sc. 2.

6. William Charles Macready as Brutus in the Forum scene (III.ii)

good you know not that you are his heirs', there is a 'movement of surprise & joy by all'. When Antony descends to read the will 'They all gather closer round the rostrum', and Antony stands just left of the bier. As he says, 'Then I, and you and all of us fell down', 'Some of the Cit^{ns} here incline their heads sorrowfully, then put their hands to their eyes.' Sorrow quickly changes to frenzied rage as Antony, 'Tearing off the mantle' which covers Caesar's body, commands 'Look you here!' Screaming 'We will be revenged', 'The mob break up & X the stage R & L as going off', but Antony's 'Stay, countrymen' causes them to 'stop suddenly and return'. He now proceeds to work them up to an even higher pitch of frenzy, subtly linking the name of Brutus with Caesar's wounds, until the citizens exclaim 'We'll mutiny.' All the plebeians now 'turn as going R & L & move a pace or two', but on 'Yet hear me speak', they 'return to Antony' to listen with growing hysteria to the reading of the will. On 'seventy-five drachmas', Macready calls for 'a general movement of surprise [among the] Cit^{ns}', and on 'Never, never', 'all the Cit^{ns}' show 'Great excitement'. At the cue 'Take up the body', 'They raise the hearse on which Caesar's body lies', and, 'All vociferating together', 'they X R & L & exit at the diff^t ent^s as rapidly as possible'. Their 'Tumult is heard dying away in the distance, until the Act Drop falls'. To the accompaniment of the fading uproar, Antony moves down R for his 'Now let it work. Mischief, thou art afoot' (III.ii.260). Flavius enters L 'hastily', and the remainder of the scene is 'All spoken very quickly!' Both then exeunt L.

To attempt further comment upon these scenes would be to labour the self-evident. Suffice it to say that the note of realism had been struck, if feebly; and Macready, even in his most visionary flights, could hardly have foreseen how far it would carry. In its heyday, half a century later, wholesale realism proved to be not an unmixed blessing. Yet, in spite of their multitudinous sins of commission and omission, the realists made a vital contribution to the play's stage development through their exploration of the dramatic potential of the Forum scene. As the initiator of this trend, Macready deserves no small measure of credit.

The actors

Although Macready's innovations in stagecraft are of considerable long-term importance, his major contribution to *Julius Caesar*'s stage history was his interpretation of Brutus. Here was not merely the initiation of a trend, but a full-blown realization of the part – a rendering unsurpassed, perhaps, by any actor since his time.

Any study of the acting in *Julius Caesar* revivals in which Macready participated during his starring years, and to a lesser degree during his period of management, is essentially a study of his Brutus and Cassius. In the provinces he was partnered by a series of players who were at best mediocre, or at worst, wholly incompetent; in London, where he was generally provided with reasonably good second-rate supporters, the fear that they might steal his thunder led him to adopt fair means and foul to keep the secondary roles as inconspicuous as possible. George Vandenhoff recalls with some bitterness, 'Whatever was his part for the night, whether it was ... Brutus or Cassius ... that part must be the feature of the play; and this was to be effected not by his own towering and surpassing excellence in the character, but by such an arrangement of the scene, and such a position of every other person on the stage, as must make all others subordinate.'[20]

Two performers, by weight of sheer ability, achieved recognition in spite of Macready's tactics – Samuel Phelps, who played Cassius in all *Julius Caesar* revivals under Macready's management, and James Anderson who, in the 1843 revival, gave probably the best performance of Antony since the retirement of Charles Kemble.

When Phelps first assumed the role of Cassius in the revival of 1838, 'he made', in his nephew's words, 'a great hit, so much so that it was only played two nights'[21] lest Macready's star-status should suffer. Macready seems, however, to have conquered his fears, and Phelps went on to partner him for five years thereafter.

Physically Phelps was an admirable representative of Shakespeare's lean and soldierly Roman. 'In person', writes Towse, 'he presented a vigorous, military figure, of medium height, broad, spare, and athletic.' His face, 'powerful and peculiar rather than pleasing', was 'set in hard lines, although remarkably mobile and flexible when he was acting.'[22] To enhance his natural advantages he added 'a dark beard and a bald wig, in which he looked a man of fifty five',[23] although at the time he was a youthful 37. His voice was strong, flexible, and rich in tone colour. He spoke Shakespeare's verse intelligently if a little laboriously.

Where Charles Young pursued a straight-line interpretation of Cassius, with fire and impetuosity the dominating quality in his personality, Phelps discovered a more complex individuality. Both his temperament and histrionic style were ideally suited to 'irritable and sensitive characters';[24] and in Cassius' fiery moods 'his nervous, rugged acting told amazingly, particularly in the quarrel scene with Brutus'.[25] But Phelps was not content merely to create a temperamental contrast with Brutus' stoic calm; he attempted also to suggest the forces which moulded the man and which would in time destroy him. 'In the expression of discontent and injury as Cassius', writes Marston, 'there was mingled with his caustic, fretful tone an impetuosity which indicated "that rash humour which his mother gave him" – made one see that his faults were largely those of impulse, and prepared one for his repentance'.[26] However adept Phelps was at portraying roughness and irritability, he was still more successful in expressing tenderness and rugged pathos; and this gift brought a new dimension to Cassius, a quality of softness which stood out in dynamic contrast to his habitual asperity. Thus in the latter part of the Quarrel scene, the farewell to Brutus before the battle, and the death scene, Phelps's Cassius achieved a signal success where others had comparatively failed. His delivery of the lines beginning 'Come, Antony, and young Octavius, come' (IV.iii.93) was particularly praised for its pathos and depth of feeling.

Although Phelps's Roman no doubt lacked something of Young's classic dignity, the deficiency was seldom noticed. On only two points was he adversely criticized: sometimes, especially in the Quarrel scene, he tended to overcolour the weakness of the character, and now and again his action was rather too fidgety.

James Anderson undertook Antony when a comparative newcomer to the London stage; and it is no small tribute to his talents that he revealed an originality of interpretation which won him considerable applause and even challenged comparison with Charles Kemble.

Anderson attempted to do for Antony what Phelps had done for Cassius – to lead him out of Kemble's beau idéal isolation toward a more complex and credible humanity. Without the Proscription scene he was unable to compass the political ruthlessness and corruption of Shakespeare's opportunist, but he did manage to find beneath Kemble's statuesque young nobleman 'a mixture of the *roué* and the warrior, full of careless swagger to the crowd', but touchingly sincere in his 'deep devotion and love to his friend and patron Caesar'.[27] Reviewers were effusive in their admiration of his performance, but niggardly of descriptive details. We know only that his Senate and Forum speeches were remarkable for their sustained declamatory effects. In the latter 'the gradual manner in which he stirs up the passions of the populace, his affected bluntness and sincerity when speaking of the "honourable conspirators", and the final look of triumph when he is once more alone' constituted 'a masterly piece of acting'.[28] The only adverse criticism I have seen comes from the *Morning Chronicle* (2 May, 1843) critic who found 'a little too much violence and noise in his concluding lines over the dead body of Caesar in the senate-house' and 'a certain degree of affectation' here and there throughout.

And so to the performance of Macready himself, 'the one mark for all eyes to look at, the one voice for all ears to listen to, and the one name for all mouths to repeat and eulogize', to use Vandenhoff's not over-kind, but apt, description.

The particulars of Macready's acting style have been much discussed from his time down to our own; but most theatre historians, however differently they may vary the proportions, are in general agreement with Vandenhoff's contention that it was an amalgam of John Kemble's and

Edmund Kean's. Yet, while this assessment is essentially accurate, it cannot
be too much stressed that Macready was no mere copyist of mannerisms,
but an original actor in his own right; and what he took from his contemporaries he transformed into something uniquely his own.

In spite of great and obvious affinities with the Kemble school, Macready
differed with them strongly on certain crucial issues. Whereas beau idéal
performers meant by 'consistency' the straight-line insistence upon a single
quality which is made to dominate every aspect of a character, Macready
considered it to be the fusion of varied qualities into a coherent unity. Nor
did he hold with the Kemble view that the actor must isolate universal
emotions and heighten these to an ideal form; although he did this to some
degree when necessary, he laid much more emphasis upon depicting the
individual traits which set off one character from another. Neither did he
attempt to enlarge and improve upon nature in the Reynolds manner, but
came closer to Garrick's method of representing nature as she is, with the
ugly alongside the beautiful. In Macready's style the heroic and domestic
emotions blended, and the latter type, more often than not, predominated.

Moreover, within any given performance he was fond of changing from
emotion to emotion by abrupt transitions – often somewhat artificial – from
the sublime to the pathetic, from the terrifying to the tender, from the
formal to the colloquial. Consequently, his realistic, as opposed to ideal,
approach and his breadth of emotional range inclined his contemporaries to
view him as a natural[29] rather than a classical actor, a closer adherent of
Kean than of Kemble.

In physical appearance, Hackett tells us, Macready was 'above the middle
height' with a 'port rather stiffly erect'. His face, continues Hackett,
'though occasionally lighted up by a pleasing smile, can hardly have beauty
predicated of it'. His action was 'generally formal and sometimes more
angular than graceful'.[30]

His voice is described by Lewes as 'powerful, extensive in compass,
capable of delicate modulation in quiet passages . . . and having tones that
thrilled and tones that stirred tears'. However, in his attempt to fit his
declamation to his natural acting style, he tended to overlook the fact that he
was speaking verse. Sometimes he delivered it in a flat colloquial manner,
and, more frequently, sacrificed the musical flow in order to make the sense
as clear as possible.

In view of the dissimilarity between Kemble and Macready in physical
appearance, vocal technique, and acting style, it is only to be expected that
their interpretations of Brutus would differ greatly. One of the most striking
initial contrasts lies in the fact that Kemble's rendering seems to have
sprung full-blown from the first and changed little thereafter, while Macready agonized over his Brutus for fifteen years. His histrionic progress, or
lack of it, is recorded in frequent entries in his diaries. After his first

performance at Covent Garden in 1836 he wrote in bitter self-reproach, 'Acted Brutus in *Julius Caesar* very, very feebly – crudely – badly – I was not prepared for it.'[31] Obviously, identification had not yet come. Almost a month later (10 December, 1836), however, he exulted, 'Acted Brutus particularly well . . . I felt the part; I think I may say "J'étois le personnage".' Five days later, he played the part but 'moderately', and 'was weak enough to retort on Mr. Vandenhoff the tricks to which he has nightly resorted . . . to deprive my effects of their applause'. In the 1843 revival he rendered Brutus 'for the most part very well', and five years later (5 April, 1848) credited himself with playing the role 'in a very masterly manner'. 'I do not think', he wrote on that occasion, 'I ever acted it with the same feeling, force, and reality.' From then on, identification was to come more easily. On 1 February, 1850, he 'acted Brutus in a style of reality and earnest naturalness', and in November of the same year offered a rendering which he judged to be 'far beyond any performance I ever gave of the character'. Yet his triumph was his final appearance (24 January 1851), after which he wrote:

Acted Brutus as I never – no, never – acted it before, in regard to dignified familiarity of dialogue, or enthusiastic inspiration of lofty purpose. The tenderness, the reluctance to deeds of violence, the instinctive abhorrence of tyranny, the open simplicity of heart, and natural grandeur of soul, I never so perfectly, so consciously, portrayed before.[32]

Physically, Macready was incapable of capturing 'that indescribable dignity with which KEMBLE alone could invest his heroic characters',[33] but he offered much by way of compensation. 'Macready's *Brutus*', wrote the *Morning Chronicle* (2 May 1843) reviewer, 'whilst it lacked more of that great daring and firmness which are so peculiarly associated with the very name of this great Roman, was particularly beautiful in the delicacy with which the redeeming graces of the more amiable features of the character were thrown in.' 'If he failed where KEMBLE most succeeded', remarked *John Bull* (20 November 1836), 'in impressing us with the solitary grandeur of the old Roman, he did that which KEMBLE did not do – he enlisted our sympathies in his cause, and carried our hearts with him.'

To say this is not to say that the Macready Brutus lacked grandeur; but it was of the spiritual rather than the physical variety. 'By his intellectual feeling', Macready elevated the character 'to a moral dignity'[34] where it was the 'never-swerving purpose and great *moral* [italics mine] grandeur of the pure patriot'[35] which made Brutus a leader of men. So far as his abilities permitted, Macready depicted Brutus' stoic severity, but he stressed even more strongly the qualities which made him human and contemporary. 'For the first time', wrote one critic, 'we felt the Brutus of the closet.'[36] Macready 'designed', wrote another, 'to pourtray a man of ordinary passions, but with an elevated soul'. His Brutus, the critic continues, 'was the representative of the high and philosophic mind in action – action however unsuited to his genius; for he perpetually wavers in between the necessity to act and his natural unfitness for "horrid deeds"'.[37] Wrote the *John Bull* reviewer on 16 April 1837:

The natural and the artificial individualities of the Roman patriot are finely blended, yet the elements of each distinctly marked. His feelings are warm, his heart sensitive, and both are icicled over by an evenness of demeanour, become habitual by the cast of his philosophy. The result is, as Antony describes it, 'a gentle life'; one of impulses schooled by principle.

In the early scenes of the play 'every line was a comment' on the sincerity of Brutus' assertion that Caesar's assassination proved 'not that I loved Caesar less, but that I loved Rome more'. Throughout there was 'a quiet earnestness . . . a subdued consciousness of the motive that pushed him on',[38] even against his natural inclination. His soliloquy in the garden, finely conveyed 'the mental conflict that unfits the philosopher for the life he is about to enter', while his 'gentleness with *Portia*' a few moments later pointed up his temperamental unfitness for the act of violence he is about to commit. In the scenes 'of tumultuous excitement' which follow, his is 'the only form that remains quiet, undisturbed, serene',[39] secure in the knowledge that he is acting for the best. Likewise in his oration he made no attempt to appeal unfairly to the emotions of his audience, or to justify by rhetorical fireworks what had obviously been the only right course of action. Here the simple earnestness of his delivery achieved an impressive effect.

The mastery of intellect over infirmity of temper has perhaps never been better demonstrated than in his rendering of the Quarrel scene. *The Theatrical Journal* (20 May 1843) pronounced it 'a magnificent illustration of the moral superiority of a well trained mind over a bold but irritable spirit. By his quiet dignity of bearing he reduced the storming Cassius to a point of humiliation which it was almost painful to witness; but then his generous advance toward reconciliation came like a healing balm, and rendered the character as amiable as it was admirable'.

Whatever success Macready enjoyed throughout the rest of *Julius Caesar*, it was his rendering of the last scenes – from the end of the quarrel to his death – which gained him most applause. Suddenly new moments, hitherto quickly passed over by other actors, sprang into vivid reality. 'In the scene where the lute . . . is taken from the jaded boy', one critic found him 'exquisitely tender, yet still lofty',[40] while another considered the 'air of pathos' with which he spoke 'the beautiful apostrophe' to Lucius as 'truly worthy of Shakespeare'.[41] A few moments later, when the ghost of Caesar entered, 'the momentary terror which overcomes the Roman so as to make "his blood run cold, his hair to stare" was depicted with thrilling earnestness'. No less effective was the swift transition which followed, when, 'in an instant he is "himself again", and has "taken heart"'.[42] It goes almost without saying that Brutus' death was 'thoroughly pathetic and impressive'.[43]

As mid-nineteenth-century audiences watched Brutus' final sword thrust, they were neither smitten with patriotic ecstasy like their eighteenth-century predecessors, nor awestruck by heroic grandeur as Kemble's auditors had been. Macready's audience had seen a murder committed by an essentially admirable fellow-human who had been led into error and punished by death. In effect, they watched not so much heroic as domestic tragedy. Brutus had somehow become one of themselves; and if they felt obliged to register appropriate moral censure of his crime, they felt keenly with and for him in his fall. 'We sympathise with the failure of Brutus', one reviewer considered, 'more deeply than we would have sympathised with the success of Cassius; and this impression produced by the melancholy, profound sensibility, and eager yearning for the just and good, makes a profounder impression on us than the sword with which he strikes at Caesar.'[44] Macready could hardly have wished for higher praise than that.

Macready's Cassius was not nearly so well known, nor so often reviewed as his Brutus, since he played it, apart from provincial revivals, in only four London seasons. The first two revivals took place in 1819 and 1822 when, as a comparative newcomer, he played Cassius to Young's Brutus at Covent Garden. Again, in 1836, shortly before undertaking Brutus, he partnered Sheridan Knowles at Covent Garden. He did not attempt the role again until his farewell performances at the Haymarket in 1850–1.

Since Brutus was generally considered to be the hero-role, Macready assumed it by right of his position as leading actor; but many critics considered it to be an unwise choice. According to Lewes, Macready's best parts were not 'characters of grandeur, physical or moral. They were domestic rather than ideal, and made but slight appeals to the larger passions which give strength to heroes.'[45] His portrayals of the irritability and injured pride of Werner, the scornful malignity of Spinola, and the super-subtlety and vaulting ambition of Richelieu were unrivalled.[46] It is not surprising, then, that the Tallis's reviewer felt he could detect at moments beneath the exterior calm of Macready's Brutus, 'something like a petty impatience, a volcanic struggling against the restraint imposed by the nature of the part'.[47] The restless and unrestrained Cassius posed him no such difficulties; his 'fiery impatience', according to Lewes, 'was just the kind of passion he could best express'.[48]

The role, described by Macready as 'one of my most real personations', was one with which he had a natural affinity. From the first, he tells us, he entered 'con amore into the study of Cassius', identifying himself readily 'with the eager ambition, the keen penetration, and the restless envy of the determined conspirator'.[49]

The dominant personality trait in Macready's Cassius was an 'irritable temper ... sensitive to a degree of morbidity'. 'In the first dialogue with Brutus', the Critic reviewer tells us, 'he shows you plainly that he does not hate the elevation of Caesar from a mere abstract principle, but that it is personally distasteful to him; that it sours his temper.'[50] 'As he stood while Caesar spoke of him', writes another, 'one felt how natural was all the dislike and distrust he inspired. With irrepressible hatred of every man above him he seemed tingling to his finger's ends. The foam of personal bitterness was on his lips when he spoke of freedom to Brutus.' Later, in the Assassination scene, 'when he stabbed at Caesar he struck him not once, or twice, but plunged his dagger many times in his breast'.[51]

In the second half of the play he displayed 'the frank, yet fierce bon homme of the soldier – quick to resent, and as quick to accuse – but with a vehemence almost exaggerated, quicker to confess his faults'.[52]

In the Quarrel scene, we learn, 'the terrible temperament is developed into open rage. Self-control is all but lost (the "all but" being finely maintained), yet still the naturally affectionate foundation is constantly kept in view, and seems ever on the point of bursting into utterance, till at last all anger vanishes in the hearty reconciliation.'[53] Throughout these moments of nigh-uncontrollable fury, Macready conveyed 'a seeming sense of outraged friendship so intense that the heart could not but be moved for him'. 'When at the close of the quarrel scene his too sensitive nature broke down into weakness and he fell weeping into his friend's arms', one critic maintained that 'all must have recognised the profound art displayed, and felt the better for what had been conveyed with such touching truth.'[54] But there was more to come.

When Brutus announced the death of Portia, Cassius' 'surprised shock of sorrow ... completed this exquisite picture'.[55] 'The heart of the Roman wept for the terrible strife of agony he gave the audience to feel had been gnawing at the heart of Brutus – he knew better than any, of the strangling sobs swallowed by the Stoic, and could well comprehend the forbearance he could not exercise himself.'[56] One of his 'most delicate strokes' was 'the manner in which he turned aside on the entrance of Lucilius and Titinius,[57] and with a voice in which the tears were still lingering, but with assumed indifference amid his grief, instructed them – "And come yourselves, and bring Messala with you, / Immediately to us".'[58] Finally, in the drinking sequence, his 'almost gigantic heartiness – the (still impetuous in all things) vast gladness with which he responds to the greeting and the full cup of Brutus',[59] completed a display of emotional variety probably unequalled in the previous history of the play.

Samuel Phelps

When Macready resigned from the management of Drury Lane after the 1843 season, Phelps recalls, 'many ladies and gentlemen who had been members of his company, were left without a stage on which their talents could be employed'. 'Having been given to understand', he continues, 'that the then managers of ... [Sadler's Wells] were about to abandon it, an arrangement was made, and myself and Mrs. Warner assumed its director-ship.'[60] Thus, by a happy conjunction of chance and necessity, Phelps embarked upon his now almost legendary era of Shakespeare production. During his eighteen-year period of management Phelps staged the only significant English *Julius Caesar* revivals to take place in London between the retirement of Macready in 1851 and the Beerbohm Tree spectacular of 1898.

Located in the unfashionable suburb of Islington, Phelps was unable to attract the throngs of fashionable and wealthy theatre-goers who frequented the city centre; consequently, he had not the financial resources which made possible the visually splendid productions of Charles Kean at the Princess's. He was obliged instead to devote his attention to the play itself, to compensate by integrity of text and all-round competence of acting for what he lacked in scenery. 'Shakespeare's plays', Henry Morley remarks, 'are always poems as performed at Sadler's Wells.' The scenery, he continues, 'is always beautiful, but it is not allowed to draw attention from the poet, with whose whole conception it is made to blend with most perfect harmony'. Likewise, 'the actors are content also to be subordinate to the play', taking care 'to subdue excesses of expression that by giving undue force to one part would destroy the balance of the whole'. Moreover, although Phelps took the leading role, unlike Macready 'he never by his acting drags it out of its place in the drama'. Thus, 'with actors, many of whom are anything but stars', Morley concludes, 'the result most to be desired is really obtained'.[61]

Such, then, one presumes, was the treatment which *Julius Caesar* received in Phelps's revivals of 1846, 1850, 1856, 1859, 1861, and 1862. For the most part, we must take Morley's statement on trust, for Phelps, Forbes-Robertson tells us, 'was never known to court the Press in any way',[62] and his productions were consequently but little reviewed, particularly in his early years of management.

Our chief source of information for the conduct of Phelps's *Julius Caesar* is his promptbook for the 1846 production (*JC* 16).[63] The basic text used is the 1814 Kemble edition in the front of which, opposite the 'Persons Represented', are written in manuscript the names of the cast for the 1846 revival. Later in the book, Caesar's procession to the games is headed 'Procession 1846'.[64] In the margins of the text and on interleaved pages are the manager's notes, some of which are in the hand of Phelps's prompter, Pepper Williams.

In the main Phelps uses the Macready text, adding to Kemble's version Macready's restorations and making two more of his own. He brings back Cassius' highly rhetorical lines to Casca beginning, 'Therein, ye gods . . .' (I.iii.91–5) and Brutus' assertion, 'For Antony is but a limb of Caesar' (II.i.165).

The book contains no record of settings, but we may assume, as Morley suggests, that they were at least adequate, if not particularly striking. Beyond this we have only the statement of the *Athenaeum* (8 August 1846) reviewer that 'Shakespeare's tragedy of "Julius Caesar" has been . . . placed on the stage with all that attention to the proprieties of the drama for which this theatre has at length become celebrated.'

However much Phelps might emphasize the poetry of the play and subordinate the sets, he was not prepared to dispense with the long-popular living scenery. On a very modest budget he provides a surprising number of supernumeraries, and uses them processionally, as Kemble and Macready did before him, to secure visual effects. His super-list calls for 32 plebeians, 6 boys, 4 priests, 6 senators, 1 star, 2 SPQR standards, 2 golden eagles, 12 guards with spears, 12 guards with fasces, and 7 ladies.

'As a manager and producer of plays', Phelps's nephew tells us, 'he undoubtedly followed in the footsteps of Mr. Macready',[65] and one could hardly wish for better proof of his assertion than the 1846 promptbook. In the main, it is a careful copy of Macready's book for the 1843 revival with some minor adaptation to suit Phelps's more meagre resources. At a few points, however, he attempts to refine upon Macready's stagecraft, and even introduces several innovations which, although hardly revolutionary, call for brief mention.

Phelps apparently shared Macready's interest in using crowds actively to lend realism and dramatic interest to certain scenes. Besides participating in Caesar's procession and the Forum and Assassination scenes, Phelps's citizens take a more energetic part in the opening confrontation with Casca and Trebonius. On 'a mender of bad soles', the citizens burst into laughter, and 'Why, sir, cobble you' is received with a similar display of mirth. Again, on 'to rejoice in his triumph', the citizens are directed to indicate their agreement by shouting 'Ay! Ay!'.

Like Kemble and Macready, Phelps places great stress on Caesar's procession to the games, and once more the citizens are brought on to help fill the stage and provide complementary action. Oddly enough, however, Phelps uses only eighteen of a possible thirty-eight plebeians which he has available. The major departure from Macready's treatment of this scene lies in the grouping for Caesar's comment upon Cassius at his second entry. Here Phelps's arrangement is studiously formal, more typical of Kemble than Macready. As in Kemble's arrangement, the opposing forces are spatially juxtaposed, with Caesar and the might of Rome on the one side, and the menacing conspirators on the other.

In the Assassination scene, Caesar is not discovered as in previous productions, but is honoured with a separate entrance. As the front flats are drawn back, the senators, priests, and soldiers are revealed standing in a semicircle to the right and left of Caesar's seat. 'At opening of Scene' a crowd of citizens enters L2E, and then, to a flourish of trumpets, Caesar comes on from R, accompanied by the conspirators. The rest of the scene closely follows the Macready pattern. One interesting piece of business, however, is provided for Antony's 'O mighty Caesar' speech. As he mourns the death of the Dictator, 'A movement of suspicious conference amongst the conspirators' is called for.

At the end of the Quarrel scene, Phelps alters his curtain slightly. Metellus now exits R while Brutus, Lucius, and Varro go into the tent. The direction reads 'Ring down when Brutus is seated' – a rather more prosaic ending than Macready's where the curtain fell as Brutus was halfway across the stage, preparing to leave for battle.

The sacrifice of visual effect to budgetary limitations is most apparent in the smallness of the forces provided for the confrontation of the two armies in v.i. Where Macready allotted 40 guards and 12 lictors to each side, Phelps musters but 6 lictors and 6 guards for each party. Little attempt is made to stage the battle scenes with any degree of realism; once more the odd procession, offstage trumpets and drums, and an occasional shout provide the bulk of the military atmosphere. It is clear, however, that Phelps was aware of the deficiency, to some degree at least; and his direction to have '8 Troops rush across in dismay from L to LH' at the start of v.ii marks an unpretentious beginning to the elaborate mime Beerbohm Tree was to introduce half a century later. Brutus' death scene is handled much as in previous revivals, although the final tableau is rather smaller. His corpse is graced with only 12 guards and 12 lictors, compared with the 40 guards and 12 lictors provided by Macready.

Only two other points call for notice. As Brutus says, 'I shall find a [sic] time' (which Phelps restores), standing by the body of Cassius, he is directed to shake the hand of his dead friend. In his own death scene, Brutus no longer asks Lucius to kill him, but makes his request of Metellus and Varro – a very great improvement.

On the whole, then, Phelps's revivals contributed little new to *Julius Caesar*'s stagecraft. Beyond making a few minor alterations, he seems to have been more concerned to hold the ground gained by Macready than to make any fresh advances of his own.

If the staging of *Julius Caesar* at Sadler's Wells offered little for the novelty-seeker, the acting provided him with even less. Over the years

Phelps was partnered by a wide variety of second-rate players in transit from
one theatre to another, and by complete tyros for whom Sadler's Wells was a
kind of nursery. Strikingly original interpretations were unlikely to come
from either sort of actor, even had Phelps's system encouraged
individualism, which it did not. It is no small tribute to Phelps's abilities,
however, that he welded such unpromising material into an ensemble of
very high calibre indeed. So successful was he, in fact, that reviewers have
left us few accounts of individual performances, although they are unanimous in praise of the high standard of the whole. There are, however, a
number of references to Phelps's Brutus which seems to have obtruded
upon the critics' notice more by his natural superiority than by any studied
contrivance.

Of Phelps's physical qualifications we have spoken earlier at some length;
it is sufficient to say at this point that the same military figure, the commanding, if not handsome, countenance, and his excellent elocution were no
small asset to his Brutus. In fact, from a physical point of view, he was a
more convincing representative of the Roman hero than was Macready. 'All
kingly and soldierly qualities he could manifest in his matchless bearing',
Phelps and Forbes-Robertson tell us, 'and, above all, he threw into such
characters a pathos which was unapproachably manly and grand.'[66] The
Sunday Times (9 April 1865) concluded, not unreasonably, that there were
'few characters in serious drama . . . in which he would be more completely
in place'.

In general, his nobly calm, firm, and tender Brutus seems to have
resembled that of Macready without being of such a consistently superlative
calibre. In some respects, however, he seems to have surpassed Macready,
particularly in his depiction of Brutus' heroic qualities. In fact, the recur-
rence of such phrases as 'his stately and impressive manner', 'the suavity
and grandeur of his declamation',[67] 'quiet feeling and calm heroism',[68] and
'repose so carefully preserved throughout',[69] would suggest that his Brutus
was more remarkable for its heroic elevation than its domestic pathos,
although the latter quality was by no means neglected.

Perhaps Phelps's best scene was the one in which Brutus joins the
conspiracy. Here 'his rejection of the oath was characterised by spirit and
energy, and his appeal to Cassius against the proposition for sacrificing Marc
Antony . . . was given in a tone so touching, and with an air so persuasive,
that Cassius must have been callous, indeed, could he have withstood it'. In
the Assassination scene, his 'burst of exultation' after the death of Caesar
was much commended, while in the quarrel he 'discovered an intimate
acquaintance not only with the author, but with the passions of the human
mind'.[70] Finally, his words to the slumbering Lucius were lauded as
'inimitable' for their 'gentleness and tenderness'.[71]

However favourably or unfavourably Phelps's interpretation may have compared with that of Macready, there can be no doubt that audiences who watched his final performance of the role at Drury Lane in 1865 witnessed the last great English Brutus of the nineteenth century and the end of a method of presentation which had lasted more than five decades. When next they saw the play more than thirty years later, the text would be vastly altered, settings would be on a scale beyond their wildest imaginings, and Brutus would no longer dominate the action as he had done for at least two centuries. Meanwhile, *Julius Caesar*'s career on the American stage awaits exploration.

5

American productions (1770–1870)

As a work of literature, *Julius Caesar* was much read and admired by eighteenth-century American intellectuals. During the Revolutionary War Abigail Adams in a letter to her husband, John, quoted the passage beginning 'There is a tide in the affairs of men' (IV.iii.218ff) and other extracts. Sometimes she even signed herself 'Portia'. Thomas Jefferson's commonplace book, into which he copied lines from his favourite poets, begins with six selections from *Caesar* on the life–honour–death theme.[1] Their contemporary, 'Theatricus', one of the earliest American drama critics, judged the play 'unrivalled in the dramatic world', and admirably suited to the temper of the times. 'Whether we consider the growing spirit of liberty it breathes, or the elegant and sublime language the author has made use of, we are equally surprised and delighted', he maintained.[2]

The play's libertarian sentiment no doubt motivated the American Company to add it to their repertory just as revolutionary fervour was approaching its meridian. Their advertisement for the first performance, at Philadelphia's Southwark Theatre on 1 June 1770, promised native patriots an exhibition of 'The noble struggles for Liberty by that renowned patriot Marcus Brutus' together with the 'remarkable orations of Brutus and Antony . . . the first shewing the necessity of his [Caesar's] death, to give Freedom to the Roman People; the latter to enflame their minds, and excite them to a commotion, in which the orator succeeds, and is the cause of the civil wars'.[3] The not so subtle link between oratorical skill and political power was finely calculated to attract a community ever more inclined to regard the eloquent man as an object of public worship.[4]

In theory *Caesar* was ideally suited to the classical tastes and republican sympathies of late eighteenth-century America; yet, curiously enough, the American Company staged only six recorded performances between 1770 and 1802. Charleston saw one (1774); Philadelphia was offered two (1770, 1791); and New York witnessed three (1788, 1791, 1802). Even with allowances made for the fragmentary nature of our records, its insignificant position in the Company's repertory is manifest. Seilhamer lists only three revivals of *Caesar* for the period 1785–97 as compared with more than thirty of *Richard III* and *Romeo and Juliet*, twenty-eight of *Hamlet*, thirteen of *Othello*, and fifteen of *Macbeth*.[5]

Whether the Company's reluctance to revive the play is attributable to any lack of enthusiasm on the part of audiences or performers cannot be determined. The first Boston revival of the play (1803) attracted the most crowded house of the season, according to the *New-England Palladium*; and there is no reason to suppose that theatre-goers elsewhere viewed it with greater disfavour. More likely the Company could muster only infrequently enough male actors of sufficient strength to make the play theatrically viable. Or perhaps Lewis Hallam, like Garrick, preferred the one-man plays in which he could shine alone.

No prompt-copy survives, but in all likelihood the text spoken broadly resembled one or another of the London versions discussed earlier. Advertisements for the 1770 and 1791 performances, announcing the play as 'JULIUS CAESAR, with the Deaths of Brutus and Cassius'[6] recall the title of the Dryden–Davenant text and the style of English newspaper playbills half a century earlier. A comparatively full cast-list for the 1794 performance, the earliest extant, sorts better with Bell's edition of 1773.[7] Roles seem to be eliminated and merged in virtually identical fashion. Artemidorus, who had been dropped from the Dryden–Davenant text, reappears here as in Bell's script. Two anomalies, however, forbid the conclusion that Bell's edition was slavishly followed. Lucilius, a feature of the 1719 script eliminated in Bell's arrangement, re-emerges. Even more curious is the presence of a character named Marcellus (perhaps a printer's misreading of the handwritten 'Marullus'), played by Mr Bisset. Marullus, it will be recalled, vanished from the boards some time prior to the 1684 acting edition.

The invaluable advertisement for the 1794 production, under the management of Lewis Hallam and John Henry, shows the play performed by sixteen men and two women, exclusive of plebeians, guards, and attendants – a cast roughly comparable in size to those of London revivals in the third quarter of the century. The leading roles, naturally enough, were assumed by the managers: Lewis Hallam appears as Brutus and John Henry as Cassius. Both had probably taken the same parts throughout the previous quarter-century, since Hallam had been the Company's leading man for at least thirty years, and Henry had played supporting roles for almost as long. Moreover, all production dates coincide with periods when both were Company members; and three revivals occur under their joint management (1788, 1791, 1794). The 1794 performance seems to have been their last appearance in these roles. Henry died a year later, and the ageing Hallam's next and final recorded attempt at the play (1802) saw him demoted to Cassius by the ambitious Hodgkinson who took Brutus for himself.

In America Brutus and Cassius were considered the plum parts, while

Antony fell to some junior member of the company with athletic good looks and a pleasant voice. In 1770 he was played by 'a young gentleman', one Richard Goodman, a law student who became a permanent company member not long after. Goodman may also have played the role in 1774. In 1792 Henry recruited 25-year-old John Hodgkinson to the ranks, and his youth and junior status guaranteed him the part in 1794. By 1802 his now-corpulent frame was better suited to Brutus, and the youthful Thomas Abthorpe Cooper inherited the subordinate character, which gained in status forthwith.

Lewis Hallam[8] was of average height, slim, and graceful in movement. His acting was modelled after Quin rather than Garrick, and was more remarkable for rhetorical virtuosity than depth of feeling. No doubt his Brutus was as much an oratorical exercise as a piece of characterization; but given the contemporary fondness for elocution, it could hardly have failed to please. Hodgkinson's[9] Brutus, at the age of 29, was five feet ten inches in height and inclining to stoutness. Burly, vigorous, and richly rhetorical, he was less graceful than Hallam's Roman, but probably a more credible personality thanks to Hodgkinson's superior acting talent.

Henry's Cassius was physically impressive and convincingly military. Dunlap recalls him as 'full six feet in height and . . . uncommonly handsome'.[10] According to Durang, 'he was at one time an officer in the British army, and you would allways discover the deport of a soldier in him, erect and firm'.[11] A protégé of Thomas Sheridan, he was an accomplished elocutionist, although his classical pronunciation may have been somewhat neglected. Alexander Macrabie in 1770 found him 'so deficient in his Latin as to call Publius Puppy-lies'.[12] Nevertheless, he apparently satisfied American audiences, and appeared in the part with some success at Drury Lane on 24 January 1780. He repeated the character the following day, and was announced again for 2 February, but illness supervened.[13]

The names of only two representatives of Caesar survive – those of Mr Richards (1794) and Joseph Tyler (1802).

Thomas Abthorpe Cooper (1802–37)

What amounted to a fashionable interest in classical culture prior to and immediately after the Revolution assumed the dimensions of a passion in the early nineteenth century. Rome, ancient and modern, its art and architecture, its history, and its literature were a subject of compelling curiosity to citizens of the fledgling republic. A flood of periodical articles on classical subjects, tales of tours to the Eternal City, and plays featuring the heroic individualists of antiquity such as Virginius and Junius Brutus found an eager audience. The related fondness for oratory, already noted in the immediate post-Revolution era, intensified with the publication of textbooks on the subject, the introduction of elocution into the school curriculum, and the popular models of pulpit and bar rhetoric provided by Webster, Calhoun, and Clay. In such a climate *Caesar*'s Roman theme and oratorical splendour could hardly languish unregarded.

Although the odd critic felt obliged to stress *Caesar*'s merits as a political homily in which 'the pabulum necessary to the sustenance of a *republic* is dealt out',[14] most theatre-goers were drawn by its rhetoric. 'The tragedy of *Julius Caesar* possesses little or no attraction', contended a typical reviewer, 'but what arises from the pleasure of hearing good speaking'.[15]

No actor was better equipped to capitalize upon *Caesar*'s attractions than the handsome, golden-voiced Thomas Abthorpe Cooper. Although his first performance as Antony in 1802 was less his own choice than Hodgkinson's, his assumption of the role in 1808, when manager and lessee of the Park Theatre at the age of 32, reflected a shrewd assessment of the tastes of his age and his own ability to cater for them.

A year after his first appearance as Antony at his own theatre, he played the role on tour for the first time during an engagement in Philadelphia; and thereafter it became a feature of his repertory in New York and elsewhere. Following his retirement from management in 1815, he played the role with considerable frequency in starring jaunts up and down the Union. In 1818, according to Ireland, his Antony 'proved to be a most admired performance in all the northern cities'.[16] In Boston, the *Boston Weekly Magazine* (7 March 1818) reported, he drew 'the most crowded audience we have seen at the theatre since the days of Cooke', while the next year at the Charleston Theatre Antony was greeted by a record turn-out, including President James Munroe. It is significant that he chose this role for his farewell New York performance at the Bowery in 1835.

The only extant *Caesar* script used in a Cooper performance is a sparsely-marked copy (*JC* 9) prepared for his appearance at Philadelphia's Chestnut Street Theatre on 14 February 1817 under William B. Wood's management.[17] This text, probably similar to those used by him elsewhere, is Kemble's edition of 1814, an obvious choice since Cooper knew Kemble and kept in close touch with the London theatres. Until Kemble's version appeared he probably played the script utilized by the American Company.

The Wood text, checked for Casca and marked only with a few light and music cues, tells us next to nothing about the performance. Three alterations in Antony's speeches, however, are worth noting. The peremptory 'Peace, ho! Caesar speaks' (I.ii.1) and the later 'Bid every noise be still; peace yet again' (I.ii.14), which Kemble gave Antony to call attention to his first entrance, are restored to Casca from whom they come more appropriately. The Forum scene ends with 'Take thou what course thou wilt' (III.ii.261) to permit Antony a stronger exit. For the same reason Cooper cuts Octavius' lines at the end of the play, and the curtain falls on Antony's

'This was a man!' (v.v.75). The two latter innovations were adopted by Booth, Benson, and Tree half a century afterwards.

Settings for New York revivals, although still of the stock sort, seem to have been qualitatively better than those provided in other cities. If they were not always entirely appropriate, at least they were seldom downright disturbing. The Forum rostrum used for Payne's *Brutus* at the Park Theatre, described by *The New-York Mirror* (15 October 1823) as a 'dark looking, little, unadorned box of pasteboard', probably did service for *Caesar* as well. In 1826 the Quarrel scene appears to have been granted a specially-created piece of décor, painted by a Mr Brunet, consisting of 'a tent-scene, painted on the *flat* . . . and the *wings*'. Gushed *The New-York Mirror* (16 December 1826), 'A more magnificent spectacle has not been exhibited in this city. It looked like the thing itself, and drew down thunders of applause from the audience.'

Outside New York, less appropriate settings gave cause for concern, especially as word of Kemble's historical correctness spread across the Atlantic. In Boston Theatre productions, audiences saw Brutus and Cassius discoursing before a drop scene which represented 'one of the most celebrated streets in *modern* Rome', in the centre of which stood 'a famous fountain, designed by an artist of the fifteenth century'. The Senate House flat was a much-used 'palace scene', the design of which formed 'a heterogeneous piece of patchwork in which it would puzzle an Italian *virtuoso* to discover what taste, what school, what architectural order, or what saints, heroes or heathen gods predominate in the motley. composition'. Caesar apparently sat upon 'an old time and finger worn *sopha* covered with a strip of crimson bombazet', which appeared in a variety of productions. 'It would be difficult', a critic comments caustically, 'for the managers to persuade us that *Banquo*, *Alexander*, or *Julius Caesar*, ever saw a Windsor chair in their lives, although they were all great travellers.[18] Costumes were hardly more apt than scenery. Leading players provided their own wardrobe, and lesser lights made do with whatever came to hand in the theatre hampers.

Critics were also mildly disappointed to find that Cooper had not 'introduced into his performance all the stage business which has been recently invented in England',[19] but he doubtless recognized that Kemble's resources were not his, and wisely kept his demands upon the stagehands to a minimum. When performing at the Park in 1824, for example, he ignored the atmospheric innovations which attended Caesar's ghost at Covent Garden; according to James G. Brooks, the unearthly visitant merely walked on 'in the front of the stage, in the full glare of light . . . very politely, like a gentleman making a morning call'.[20]

Cooper's contemporaries describe him as tallish, slender, and uncommonly graceful, with handsome and expressive features.[21] Declared one, 'Had our celebrated and much lamented countryman [Benjamin] West, attempted to centre in one figure all that we have read and all that we can conceive of Roman greatness and magnanimity, he could not have chosen a better model than the person of Cooper.'[22] His voice was of superb quality, resonant, extensive in compass, and highly musical. His elocution was singularly unaffected and effortless.

Cooper's acting style was of the Kemble school, although somewhat more impulsive in passionate scenes. Like Kemble, he excelled in scenes of heroic grandeur featuring idealized straight-line figures who relied for their impact more upon declamation than dramatic action. Unfortunately Cooper lacked Kemble's intellectual gifts and educational advantages, with the result that the subtler side of Shakespeare's creations frequently eluded him. Mark Antony, however, particularly in Kemble's version, posed no problem. 'As the passions of this character are more simple in their nature, and uniform in their operation than many other of Shakespeare's principal heroes', one writer remarked, 'it [Cooper's interpretation] has none of the occasional improprieties in recitation and partial misconceptions of character, that lessen [the] excellence of some of his more arduous and complicated personations.'[23]

At his first entrance, *en route* to the games and with little to do but display his fine figure in some striking position, Cooper's 'elegant person' and 'insinuating manners' suggested 'all the requisites, both natural and acquired for the representative of the Epicurean paramour of *Cleopatra*'.[24] But it was in the Senate scene, after Caesar's assassination, that Cooper came into his own. His forte lay in parts 'where there is a strong passion tearing the heart, that is too haughty to show its power – where two different emotions are striving for mastery'.[25] A better opportunity to display his talents could hardly be found than this scene, witnessed in Philadelphia in 1810 by Stephen Cullen Carpenter.

On his entry, the sight of Caesar's body evoked an overwhelming grief which momentarily drove everything else from Antony's mind. When, 'dropping on one knee, [he] hung over the mangled body', 'his attitude surpassed all powers of description'. 'After gazing for a time in horror at the corpse, with his hands clasped in speechless agony, he looked to heaven, as if appealing to its justice.' His eyes drawn back once more to his dead patron, he launched into the apostrophe 'O mighty Caesar', during which 'All the conflicting passions, and excruciating feelings which Antony can be supposed to have felt on that awful occasion – astonishment, fear, suspicion, grief, tender affection, indignation, and horror seem rising in tumultuous confusion in his face, and glared and flashed in his eyes.' Although sometimes accused of an inability to fully convey pathos, Cooper showed no such weakness here. Carpenter declares, 'We have rarely known the feelings of an audience so forcibly or successively appealed to, as by him in the last words: "Fare thee well".' A moment later, his rising thirst for revenge began to struggle with his sorrow until, 'like a consummate, artful politician' he 'postpones the indulgence of his grief and indignation for the accomplishment of a higher purpose' and proceeded to shake the assassins' hands and make the pact. In this sequence, Carpenter maintains, 'he was not excelled by Barry himself'.[26] His final speech ('O pardon me, thou bleeding piece of earth') brought the scene to a breathtaking conclusion. Here, 'when the feelings become too strong for longer reserve – when passion, like a mighty flood, breaking down all obstacles, will have way, and goes forth in its fury, scorning every opposition', Cooper's art was at its best.[27]

His Forum speech was almost equally celebrated. 'In majesty and symmetry of person, power of voice, eloquence of delivery', pronounced Boston's *Columbian Centinel* (2 November 1822) 'this actor conveys as faithful an idea of the Roman Orator as can be required by man.' His mob, doubtless like Luke Usher's a few years earlier, must have been less satisfying to lovers of stage realism. 'It is difficult for me to conceive', complained a member of Usher's audience, 'how some nine or ten people (all but *two* of whom were mutes,) standing in a semi-circle to hear Antony's oration, could have "aught the least similitude" to a Roman rabble.'[28] But proponents of stage realism were few. The bulk of the audience came to enjoy declamation, and were rewarded with 'one of the most chaste, pathetic and elegant displays of elocution we ever witnessed on any stage'. 'It came up',. thought one reviewer,

in our imagination, to all the blandishments of manner, as well as the 'happy eloquence' of words attributed to the voluptuous Antony. – The friendly sorrow and subdued humility of the slaughtered Caesar's advocate, who spoke but 'by permission,' – his sophistical extenuation of Caesar's faults, and insinuative enumeration of his merits; the crafty implication of the conspirators and gradual exposure of their 'bloody treason'; with the assumed forbearance by which he affects to allay the very inflammation he had artfully excited; all these master-strokes of cunning ... were successfully delineated by Cooper with such delicate and characteristic touches, as it is not in our power to point out any parallel to among all his preceding displays of elocution.[29]

On rare occasions Cooper appeared as Brutus, and once or twice as Cassius. Nothing is known of the latter role, but the former rivalled, or even surpassed, his Antony. Although he disliked playing the 'noblest Roman', he gave him a majesty unmatched by any other American performer of his time. The rugged sublimity of Cooper's Stoic struck a New England reviewer as 'the most splendid exhibition of dramatic power that a Boston audience has ever witnessed'. This Brutus, who he claimed dug the grave of all his rivals, was characterized by 'the stateliness, pride, and dignity of the patrician, softened, subdued, and mingled with the uprightness of the patriot, and the affection of the man'.[30] The vibrant emotional colours with which he painted his Antony were exchanged for more sombre, subtler hues. In a splendidly controlled performance reviewers noted that he 'never throws out a show of passion, to catch applause . . . but touches the more attenuated threads which lead to the mazes of the soul, by endeavouring to suppress and subdue not only the effervescence, but the "very motive and the cue for passion"'.[31]

The nature of Cooper's performances was ill-calculated to foster outstanding supporting roles. Most of the stock company residents drafted into the auxiliary parts achieved at most a bare competence. The best Brutus to partner Cooper was the English provincial star, William Augustus Conway, who appeared with him in joint engagements fairly often between 1824 and 1826. In 1824, in the interests of novelty, they alternated the roles of Brutus and Antony in several theatrical centres.

As tradition demanded, Conway was of heroic physical proportions, 'He is rising six feet in height', relates one reviewer, 'and his form so exquisite that it might serve as a model for an Apollo.' 'His countenance is expressive', he continues, 'and his eye penetrating. He carries his person erect, and his step is firm and majestic.'[32] In 1814 Kemble had invited Conway to Covent Garden to play Antony to his Brutus, and liked the result well enough to offer him return engagements for the 1815 and 1816 revivals. Akin to Kemble in physique and mind, it is not surprising that Conway took his manager's Brutus as a model.

In the early scenes of the play audiences were agreeably startled by Brutus' elegant and impressive appearance; but in the Assassination scene patrician grace was transcended in the severe grandeur of the priest–king. Conway's Brutus, like Kemble's, saw Caesar's assassination as, not butchery, but an inevitable sacrifice to be undertaken with clear-eyed resolution. As he struck the dagger in Caesar's bosom, we are told, 'his face glowed with all the godlike majesty of the old Roman: there was no hatred, no wrath, no hurry in his expression, but he wore a look of stern necessity'.[33] Although his majesty in the Quarrel scene was impressive, he outdid himself 'in depicting those warm and generous feelings with which [the part] abounds'.[34] His reconciliation with Cassius and his later consideration for Lucius were singled out for special praise.

The Cassiuses who supported Cooper were even more mediocre than the Brutuses; and only Junius Brutus Booth's performance need detain us. Booth's Cassius, if not so consistently fine as the Antony and Brutus of Cooper and Conway, was by moments worthy of comparison with their best efforts, and in toto superior to any other American interpretation between John Henry and Lawrence Barrett. Booth's 'Gothic' conspirator made his début at Drury Lane in 1820 (with James Wallack as Brutus), and first appeared in New York (with Thomas Hamblin as Brutus) in 1826. In 1831 he played Cassius to Cooper's Antony with some success, and continued to co-star with him at intervals until Cooper's retirement. He retained Cassius in his repertory for some years thereafter, and frequently partnered Thomas Hamblin and other lesser lights.

When he assumed the role, Booth, as a small man, flouted the tradition of heroically-proportioned Cassiuses dating from the Restoration. Doubtless he calculated that 'a head and face of antique beauty; dark hair; blue eyes; a neck and chest of ample but symmetrical mould', combined with 'a step and movement elastic, assured, kingly',[35] would go far to compensate; and he was not mistaken. But it was Booth's voice, 'deep, massive, resonant, many-stringed, changeful, vast in volume, of marvellous flexibility and range',[36] which put him beyond the reach of most of his competitors. What better qualification could be desired in the representative of Cassius whose fiery and passionate rhetoric is his trademark?

His acting style, a curiously effective amalgam of the styles of Kemble, Kean, and Cooke, was eminently suited to the character. Like Kemble, his action, though graceful, was restrained; and much of his impact derived from his skilled elocution.[37] Not for him, however, the carefully-rehearsed and polished effects of the beau idéal performer; like Kean he tended to rely for inspiration upon the impulse of the moment and varied his inflections, movement, and business from night to night.

Booth's Cassius, with his 'subtle mind, restless spirit, and splenetic humor', suggested to Gould the modern Italian. In the first two acts Booth played easily and spoke colloquially; and thanks to his originality the street scenes lived as in no previous performance. 'His description of himself and Caesar swimming in the Tiber . . . and of Caesar's sickness "when he was in Spain", were especially noteworthy', we are told. Here 'Booth's vivid portraiture recreated the event. He touched the arm of Brutus; leaned, without undue familiarity, upon his shoulder.' As he spoke the line 'His coward lips did from their color fly' (I.ii.122), Cassius 'illustrated the meaning by a momentary gesture, as if carrying a standard'.[38]

With fewer vocal opportunities in the Assassination scene, he was obliged to rely upon the eloquence of his features and a few well-chosen actions. 'After Caesar had been encompassed and stabbed by the conspirators, and lay extended on the floor of the Senate-house', Gould tells us, 'Booth strode right across the dead body, and out of the scene, in silent and disdainful triumph.'[39] It is difficult to imagine a movement more suggestive of Cassius' ruthlessness, or more finely contrasted with the formalized, sacrificial ritual in which Brutus sees himself engaged.

Unfortunately, Booth's spontaneity and originality proved to be the weakness as well as the strength of the role. When at his best, his Cassius was a remarkable creation; but when low in energy or short on inspiration his reading was inconsistent if not downright inept. On one occasion a critic found him 'too flippant and easy for Cassius';[40] on another, a reviewer judged him unable 'to successfully invest the long speeches . . . with that continuous interest which alone tells with an audience'.[41] M. M. Noah and others repeatedly warned that 'He should not disgust by his indifference in one scene, and astonish by his powers in another';[42] but their admonitions went unheeded.

In addition to Cooper's reading, early nineteenth-century audiences saw two other outstanding Antonys. Conway undertook the character with critical acclaim a number of times in 1824, and the young Edwin Forrest played the role on several occasions while *en route* to stardom. Forrest made his début as Antony at Albany's South Pearl Street Theatre with Conway's Brutus in October of 1825; and they repeated the characters at the Bowery a year later. In 1828 Forrest seconded Cooper's Brutus at the Chestnut Street Theatre, Philadelphia; and over the next few years they appeared in the same roles in New York and perhaps elsewhere. Their last co-operative attempt took place at the Bowery in 1834. After Cooper's retirement, Forrest seems to have dropped Antony from his repertory. Only one New York performance is recorded – with Hamblin's Brutus at the Bowery in 1840.

At the age of nineteen or twenty, Forrest was splendidly convincing as the Roman athlete. According to Henry Wikoff, 'He seemed intended by nature as the representative of classic heroes: tall, massive, and admirably proportioned.'[43] Like Bangs, who followed Forrest in the part fifty years later, he was gifted with extraordinary strength of limb, and missed no opportunity of displaying his muscular charms. Descriptive details of Forrest's interpretation are frustratingly few, but we learn that the dominant feature was highly-coloured rhetoric rendered intelligible by a degree of study unusual in actors of his age. The accompanying action demonstrated striking animal strength and vitality, if not always perfect classic grace. He followed Cooper in making the Senate scene the summit of his performance and 'electrified' his audience.[44]

It would be pleasant to record a Caesar comparable in stature to the Antony of Cooper or the Cassius of Booth, but none presents itself. The character was frequently considered too insignificant for inclusion in newspaper cast-lists, and critics usually ignored the role altogether. One can only hope that all Dictators were not as abysmal as the gentleman who companioned Hamblin, Booth, and Cooper in 1831. 'We were perfectly delighted with the death of Caesar', a disillusioned reviewer sniffed, 'not because of any particular elegance with which the ceremony was executed, but from the reflection that when the necessity of the piece should produce the actor again upon the stage during the evening, he would be compelled to lie still and hold his tongue.'[45]

With Cooper's retirement Antony effectively disappeared from public notice. Booth's Cassius titillated playgoers occasionally during the fourth and fifth decades of the century. But it was chiefly Thomas Hamblin's Brutus which accounted for *Caesar*'s steady if unspectacular presence on the boards for seventeen years after Cooper's departure.

Thomas Hamblin (1826–52)

Thomas Hamblin's association with *Julius Caesar* virtually spanned his acting lifetime. During his apprenticeship in the English provincial theatres he arrayed his Cassius against Conway's Brutus at Birmingham (1820) at the age of 20, and in Bath partnered Young (1821) and Warde (1825). In 1826, a year after his arrival in New York, he played Brutus for the first time – at Henry Wallack's Chatham Garden – with Booth as Cassius. Conway's death two years later left him the leading American representative of the character. In 1830, upon his assumption of the Bowery management, he invited Cooper to play Antony to his Brutus; and their collaboration met with considerable success. Between this first venture under his own regime and his last in 1852, he mounted thirty-one Bowery revivals of *Caesar*, and starred as Brutus in three-quarters of them. Only nine productions were staged elsewhere in New York during the period, and none was of any historical significance.

During the golden age of the Bowery in the 1830's, when 'pack'd from ceiling to pit with its audience mainly of alert, well dress'd, full blooded young and middle-aged men',[46] *Caesar*'s heroic masculine sentiment full-throatedly declaimed by Cooper, Booth, and Forrest aroused unconfined enthusiasm. In the 1840s, however, the growing taste for melodrama and extravaganza diminished the popular appeal of classical pieces. Such audiences as still frequented Shakespearian productions found the characters increasingly smothered by 'the rhodomontade of acting, its unnatural conventional chant of delivery, its stilted pomposity, and the whole host of excrescences that now degrade and deform it'.[47] Hampered by public indifference and a dearth of competent tragedians, it is much to the credit of Hamblin's Brutus, although a feeble heir to a virile tradition, that Caesar retained some attraction, enough presumably to pay its way.

Like all American stage Romans (with the exception of Booth), Hamblin was of heroic mould. According to his one-time partner, James Hackett, he 'was in height above the ordinary stature of men, and his frame was more bony than fleshy'. 'His head', he recalls, 'was remarkable for its covering by a shock of thick and curly dark-brown hair; his nose was high and thick, and long like his visage'.[48] With his tall figure costumed to advantage and skilled in 'such artificial bearing as has become consonant with our modern ideas of the manner of ancient Romans,' Hackett grudgingly conceded that he made 'a respectable stand'.[49] Allston Brown more generously described him as 'a study for a painter'.[50] The straight-line interpretation of the Roman Stoic inherited from Kemble rendered his facial inflexibility less of a drawback than in other parts, while Brutus' comtemplative character justified the slow and stately elocution in which he excelled. Reviewers of Hamblin's performances, while generally commendatory, are chary of concrete description. 'The philosophic Brutus was ably sustained',[51] writes a typical commentator; and his unadorned conclusion is echoed by most of his confrères. The sentiment was doubtless more gratifying to Hamblin than to the theatre historian.

Throughout the era of Hamblin's Bowery management Booth frequently appeared as Cassius; and while other actors attempted the role none (see chronological handlist) approached his excellence. The Antonys of Cooper and Forrest found no worthy successors during the Bowery era, although a series of handsome elocutionists contrived to do the part some justice (see chronological handlist). A host of mediocre Caesars went unheralded in Hamblin's advertisements and unnoticed by the critics.

Although Hamblin was widely recognized as the best Brutus of his day, his primacy did not go unchallenged, John Vandenhoff (National, 1837), Thomas Cline (Chatham, 1840), William Hield (Chatham, 1842), George Vandenhoff (Chatham, 1843), James Wallack (Park, 1843), Wyzeman Marshall (Bowery, 1848), and Richard L. Graham (Bowery, 1850) all took the field, but managed to eke out only a night or two.

E. L. Davenport (1853–70)

With the death of Booth in 1852 and Hamblin in 1853, *Caesar* lost its best exponents, but retained nonetheless a toehold on the New York stage. Throughout the next eighteen years it survived a succession of onslaughts by the dimmest of stars and their attendant crews of comedians, pillars of the melodrama, and fair to medium stock tragedians (see chronological handlist).

The tedium was occasionally relieved, however, by Edward Loomis Davenport, destined to rival Edwin Booth as the greatest Brutus of the second half of the century. He first appeared in the part at the Bowery on 11 November 1845 under Hamblin's management, with the Cassius of C. W. Clarke and the Antony of J. R. Scott. Hamblin must have pronounced himself satisfied for Davenport repeated the role for him the following spring with the same supporting cast. In 1850 Davenport alternated Brutus and Cassius with the thankless Macready during the latter's farewell performances in London, after which he seems to have dropped the play from his repertory for seven years. In 1857 he undertook Brutus at the Broadway Theatre, and two years later played him at Niblo's Garden. He appeared in the role at the New Bowery in 1861 and at Niblo's Garden in 1862; and then seems to have again discarded the play – this time for eight years. All these revivals were of the stock sort, and his support, although good by the standards of the time, falls short when measured by any other yardstick.

Most productions held the stage for only a performance or two and offered few visual delights at a time when scenic splendour was becoming *de rigeueur*. The 1862 Niblo's Garden effort, under the management of Jarrett and Palmer, did arouse a flicker of critical interest since the scenery was 'nearly all new, the forum and market place being exact representations of those old Roman localities';[52] but most of the time reviewers betook themselves elsewhere on *Caesar* nights. As a result the Brutus of Davenport's early and middle years went largely unchronicled.

On 5 September 1870, the enterprising Jarrett and Palmer again revived the play at Niblo's Garden – along with *Othello* – as part of a week of Shakespeare. They dressed the production appropriately if not lavishly, and secured performers for the leading roles superior to any seen since the Hamblin–Booth–Cooper combination of 1835. Davenport offered his now mature, if not slightly ageing, Brutus. Young Lawrence Barrett, freshly returned from California, played Cassius with such success that he monopolized the role for two decades thereafter. As Antony, audiences saw the brilliant but ill-fated Walter Montgomery and cheered him to the echo. Years later, even after seeing the more lavish productions at Booth's Theatre in 1871 and 1875, Henry Goddard considered this 'the most finished production of *Julius Caesar*, if not the most thoroughly satisfactory Shakespearian revival, yet seen upon the American stage'.[53] Davenport himself contended near the end of his life that 'the play was never so well cast in this country as during that brief season at Niblo's'.[54] The managers found to their delight that the public thronged the theatre in near record numbers.

The New York Times and *The Sun* attributed public enthusiasm to the play's political subject. Only the day before (1 September) the French Caesar, Napoleon III, had been deposed. 'The name of JULIUS CAESAR is just now, portentous', claimed the *Times* reviewer on 6 September. 'At a moment when the greatest modern system which that name typifies is crashing to its ruin, at a moment when the breezes that blow over the fairest champaigne of France are thick with battle-smoke, and heavy with the scent of blood, humanity hears the very title of CAESAR with a shudder.' The *World* critic (8 September) dismissed such speculation as pure fancy. More likely the managers had simply discovered 'that of all novelties just now, that of a first-class play, with a first-class company, is the greatest'.

After a quarter century of critical neglect, Davenport's Brutus was recognized as a superlative creation. Although statuesque and grand, like his predecessors of the Kemble and Macready school, his quiet dignity and natural delivery struck a new note. This Brutus immediately declared himself the legitimate successor of Macready's Roman. Endowed with the heroic physique Macready lacked, Davenport was able to allow Brutus a more natural behaviour without sacrificing the classic aura that audiences demanded. In so doing he set the course of the role for the next century. Detailed examination of his portrayal must await the next chapter and the fuller documentation available for his celebrated performances in 1875.

The unquestioned sensation of the 1870 revival was the Cassius of Lawrence Barrett. 'The actor grasped the part with a grip of gold', exulted William Winter, 'and he moved his sympathetic auditors to literal tears of delight.'[55] His two thousand performances of the part over the next twenty years left a generation of American theatre-goers unable to conceive of any other interpretation. Further treatment of his reading, at its best perhaps in the 1871 and 1875 revivals, more properly belongs to the next chapter.

The Antony of Walter Montgomery, however, demands immediate attention, for he essayed the part only a few times before his suicide the next year. His portrayal quickly became something of a legend. William Winter considered his interpretation second only to Edwin Booth's, while Davenport thought it 'by far the best of the many that he had seen'.[56]

Born in America, Montgomery served his theatrical apprenticeship in England and gained some reputation there. His appearance as Antony marked his New York début. 'To Roman characters Mr. Montgomery is particularly well suited', we are told, 'by reason of his stalwart yet compact frame. He can look the Roman, and he wears his toga well.'[57] According to Towse, 'his voice was strong, his carriage gallant, and his gesture bold and free'. Moreover, 'Nature had bestowed upon him a striking and virile personality, high ambition, energy, and keen dramatic intelligence.'[58] It is hardly surprising, then, that he carried the house with him from the outset. In the early scenes 'he was quiet . . . and seemed content to satisfy the eye'.[59] Moving with a grace more suggestive of social ease than athletic skill, wearing make-up vaguely oriental, he represented the bland courtier and complacent voluptuary with utter conviction, his 'careless good-fellowship . . . giving him a power over men that rendered it easy for him to play the demagogue'.[60]

The easy-going self-indulgence of the opening episodes rendered all the more striking his transformation after the assassination into the resolute and dangerous man of action. His lament over Caesar's corpse was declaimed 'with fervent emotion', Winter tells us, 'and he vociferated the prophecy of calamitous war with all the requisite imaginative perception of impending horrors and sufferings'.[61] In his Forum speech, 'he was specious, various, and impassioned',[62] although his voice was somewhat hoarse from over-strain. Montgomery's Antony was decidedly the best audiences had seen since the days of Cooper and Forrest; and his emphasis upon Antony's voluptuous and pleasure-seeking sentiment was highly unusual if not unique. Its absence from the character of later Antonys was a frequent disappointment to reviewers.

The Caesar of Theodore Hamilton regrettably did not share the excellence of its companion portraits. 'Mr. Theodore Hamilton has an imperfect notion, we fear, of the historical lineaments of CAESAR, whether physical or intellectual', remarked *The New York Times* (6 September 1870), 'and although he reads the lines with accuracy and a due sense of responsibility, fails either to set forth the contrast intended by SHAKESPEARE, or to meet the ideal expected by a historical student.' Few critical voices were raised in disagreement.

In its way, the 1870 revival was as much a landmark in *Julius Caesar*'s American stage history as the first American Company performance exactly a century earlier. Whatever Caesar's weaknesses, audiences at least saw splendid interpretations of the other main roles simultaneously, and were able to perceive their inter-relationships. More important still, the play ceased to function solely as a star-vehicle, and demonstrated an artistic character of its own.

'"Julius Caesar" ought to be played a long time, and there is no need of a change', urged Winter.[63] But Jarrett and Palmer were unable or unwilling to extend the season. Edwin Booth, however, desperately in need of a legitimate drama with money-making potential for Booth's Theatre, took Winter at his word; and sixteen months later *Caesar* began its first long-run in America.

6

The Booth–Barrett–Davenport era

Between 1871 and 1891 in the United States, *Julius Caesar* enjoyed a degree of popular favour unmatched in its history. Of the thousands of performances staged, the most satisfying and significant were two New York long-runs. Easily the more important is Edwin Booth's eighty-five-night revival at Booth's Theatre on 25 December 1871, featuring himself as Brutus, Barrett as Cassius, and Frank Bangs as Antony. After Booth's bankruptcy, Jarrett and Palmer, now lessees of his theatre, launched a flamboyant revival on 27 December 1875. The old Niblo's Garden favourites, Davenport and Barrett, once more appeared as Brutus and Cassius, and Frank Bangs undertook Antony. The spectacle enjoyed an unprecedented run of 103 nights.

Edwin Booth (1871)

Edwin Booth first encountered *Julius Caesar* in a schoolboy production of the Quarrel scene in which he appeared with his future partner and brother-in-law, John Sleeper Clarke.[1] In early adolescence, as he followed his drunken, half-deranged father from town to town, he must often have witnessed the flawed splendour of the elder Booth's Cassius;[2] and made his professional début in the play in the same role – at the Howard Athenaeum, Boston, in 1861, with Davenport as Brutus. He first appeared as Brutus in 1864 at New York's Winter Garden, when he staged a revival in support of the Shakespeare Monument Fund.[3] The mounting of the production was unremarkable, but the promise that 'the three sons of the great Booth' would take the leading roles was sufficient to attract an overflowing house. Edwin played Brutus; John Wilkes, destined a few months later to assassinate President Lincoln, represented Antony; and Junius Brutus Jr appeared as Cassius.

The following evening Booth launched his 'Hundred Nights *Hamlet*', and *Caesar* faded from memory. Over the next six years, at vast expenditure of energy and fortune, first at the Winter Garden and later at his ultramodern Booth's Theatre, he established himself as the leading producer of

Shakespeare in America. The advent of *Caesar* at Niblo's Garden in 1870, and Winter's warm reaction, re-awakened his interest.[4] Within two months plans for a production were firmly under way, his most lavish to date.

None of Booth's biographers contends that he was a deep or original thinker. His early education was haphazard at best; and although in later life he made a number of intellectual friends, their concerns left him largely untouched. Only his first wife, Mollie Devlin, and Adam Badeau, young man-about-the-arts and a close friend during his early years in New York, had any demonstrable influence.[5] Mollie, captivated by the philosophical idealism of Victor Cousin, encouraged in him a belief in art as a means of improving human conduct; Badeau criticized his acting, guided his reading, much of it in theatrical history, and nourished his appreciation for painting and sculpture.

Perhaps in reaction to his Bohemian upbringing, Booth adopted a strongly conservative stance in both his life and art. He had little sympathy with the growing moral tolerance of his time, nor for its reflection in the contemporary drama. For him most that was good lay in the past. Theatre was the classical repertory, and Shakespeare the supreme playwright. His task, as he saw it, was to elevate public taste above the decadence and materialism which characterized the Gilded Age; and thereby perhaps to ameliorate public and private conduct.

One of the chief glories of his Shakespeare revivals was, he maintained, the fullness and accuracy of the scripts; but his notions of textual integrity were hardly those of a Granville-Barker or a Bridges-Adams. To his credit be it said, however, that he reconsidered the texts with some care if no great expertise, and that if he cut with too liberal a hand, at least he did not add anything.

Although the archaeological accuracy and spectacular nature of his *mise en scène* ally him with the tradition of Charles Kean, his art smacks more of the chapel than the museum. His goal was not photographic naturalism for its own sake, but rather the use of visual splendour to enhance the spiritual and emotional impact of the acting. The soul, he hoped, might be reached through the senses. His settings, much lauded for correctness, often achieved a poetic dimension which went beyond their surface realism and commanded attention as painterly compositions in their own right. His accuracy of detail, muted colours, complex chiaroscuro, picturesque groupings, and fluid line are broadly evocative of the art of the Romantic Realists; but individual components of his living paintings – poses, groupings, or lighting effects – or sometimes whole scenes, were appropriated with wonderful catholicity from any canvas which caught his eye. The brilliance of his conceptions was matched by the skills of first-rate scenic artists, among whom Charles Witham, the set-painter for *Julius Caesar*, was outstanding.

Whatever the imagined scholarship of Booth's texts, or the genuine artistry of his settings, it was the acting which charmed critics and audiences. Unfortunately, however, superlative performances rarely extended beyond the leading roles. Booth made it clear to all comers that he was the star in his own theatre, and gave himself first choice of roles and top billing; but he never resorted to Macready's textual tampering and egocentric stagecraft to monopolize the limelight. On the contrary, he sought out the best supporting players available, paid them all he could afford, and allowed them whatever prominence the script warranted. Thanks to Booth's skilled direction and the co-ordinated gifts of the principals, scenes and speeches long-neglected emerged with fresh vitality; and if his textual cutting obscured the full richness of the plays, audiences saw strong, well-balanced ensemble performances of what remained.

Booth's moral and aesthetic views go far to explain his choice of *Julius Caesar*. Apart from its demonstrated popular appeal, Shakespeare's lofty subject awakened his romantic nostalgia for a noble past which shamed a decadent present. Moreover, the sensational nature of *Caesar*'s events and the picturesqueness of its background offered unlimited opportunity to point the message with visual magnificence. True, the play offered no starring role equal to Hamlet or Richelieu, and Booth's figure fell short of the heroic majesty expected of stage Romans. Nevertheless, perhaps he could remake Brutus in his own image, and give him another kind of grandeur. And when the novelty of that wore off, the roles of Cassius and Antony were waiting.

The theatrical shape Booth's ideals assumed in his 1871 *Caesar* is richly documented. Apart from two of Witham's designs and a mass of newspaper and periodical reviews, there exists a treasure-trove of promptbooks[6] including the one used for the original production (*JC* 32) and a number of derivative versions employed by Booth and Barrett on tours. I have relied as far as possible upon the 1871 book, and have added occasional supplemental information from the road copies where indicated. Since Barrett's interpretation of Cassius varied little from his first to his last performance, I have fleshed out the somewhat sketchy accounts of his 1871 portrayal with material drawn from Leon John Vincent's transcription of the prompt-copy for the Jarrett–Palmer revival of 1875 (*JC* 38) when he repeated the role. Further light is shed on his interpretation by the richly descriptive memorial book of the Jarrett–Palmer production prepared by George Becks (*JC* 39) and Edward Tuckerman Mason's helpful record of the stage business of Davenport and Barrett made about the same time (*JC* 43). Information drawn from the latter three sources is identified as it occurs by (V) for Vincent's book, (B) for Becks's, and (M) for Mason's.

Despite Booth's sweeping claims for the fullness and scholarly correctness of his acting texts,[7] his version of *Julius Caesar* was only marginally better than that of his predecessors. For his promptbook he used not a critical edition, but French's Standard Drama text, virtually a reprint of Kemble's arrangement. His decision to follow Kemble derived, it appears, from his temperamental and aesthetic affinity with the Covent Garden manager whose work he must have known well from oral tradition and his studies in theatre history.

Although he found Kemble's version apt in the main for his purposes, Booth did not accept it wholesale. His promptbook reveals a close comparison of Kemble's text with others, and a fair number of alterations result. Many of them seem trivial, but some are significant. We are spared this once a fresh juggling of characters. Kemble's list of *dramatis personae* is retained in full with the addition of Caius Ligarius since his scene reappears. And instances of speech-redistribution are refreshingly few. In all he cuts close to one hundred and twenty-five of the lines left standing by Kemble, and restores about eighty.

He begins by dividing the play into six acts in contrast to the traditional five. His playbill 'SYNOPSIS OF SCENERY AND INCIDENTS' provides an excellent overview of the structural features of the production:

Act 1

GRAND SQUARE IN ROME. The procession of Caesar on its way to the Sports of the Lupercal. The Prediction. 'BEWARE OF [sic] THE IDES OF MARCH.'

Act 2

Scene 1 – Street in Rome. NIGHT AND STORM. Scene 2 – BRUTUS' GARDEN. Meeting of the Conspirators. Scene 3. Apartment in Caesar's House.

Act 3

Scene, THE ROMAN SENATE. 'THE IDES OF MARCH ARE COME.' The Prediction Fulfilled. The Assassination of Caesar.

Act 4

Scene, PUBLIC SQUARE IN ROME. THE FORUM. Brutus' Oration over Caesar's Body. Marc Antony's Peroration. Its Result.

Act 5

Scene, THE TENT OF BRUTUS. THE APPARITION.

Act 6

The Scenes of this Act comprise the Battle Field near and the PLAINS OF PHILLIPPI [sic]. DEATH OF BRUTUS.

Booth's prospectus suggests that he viewed the play largely as a series of more or less independent historical events, each opening with a striking picture and closing with a strong curtain. It went without saying that scenes should follow each other as closely as possible. Kemble had gone a fair distance in this direction, but Booth managed to press on well beyond him.

In act I, to allow Caesar's procession to enter hard on the heels of the citizens' discomfiture, he permits Casca (Shakespeare–Flavius) to observe only 'See where their basest mettle be not moved: / They vanish tongue-tied in their guiltiness' (I.i.61–2) before the spectacle gets under way. Later, in order to speed the action directly from Caesar's House to the Senate, the sequence in which Artemidorus reads his letter (II.iii) and the scene between Portia, Lucius, and the Soothsayer (II.iv) are sacrificed. The latter cut is one of Booth's most insensitive; for with it the Assassination scene lost preparatory suspense, and the audience was deprived of an encounter with Portia which would presently render her suicide both comprehensible and pathetic. With similar disregard of organic dramatic structure, he elimi-nates the entire colloquy between Antony and the servant at the end of the Assassination scene, and rings down the curtain on Antony's

> That this foul deed shall smell above the earth
> With carrion men, groaning for burial. (III.i.274–5).

At the conclusion of the Forum scene, to secure a showy if unsubtle climax, he adopts Cooper's innovation and terminates the action with Antony's defiant 'Take thou what course thou wilt' (III.ii.261). The ghost of Cooper is once more invoked in the final moments of the play when Octavius' com-ments over the dead Brutus are cut, and Antony's more florid 'This was a man' (V.v.75) sends the audience homeward.

Booth's concern for taut dramatic action was matched by his determina-tion to highlight Brutus wherever possible. In the main he was satisfied with the thoroughgoing moral paragon delineated in the Kemble text, but mod-ified a couple of his comings and goings to secure a more ostentatious theatrical effect. In the first act Booth provides a becomingly stellar entrance for Brutus and Cassius by bringing them on after the procession moves off, rather than with the parade as in previous versions. In the Forum scene he went to considerable pains to strengthen Brutus' exit. Several of Brutus' remarks spoken on the entrance of Antony with Caesar's corpse (III.ii.41–7) are transposed to inflate his unpretentious leave-taking. The resultant patchwork inserted in the promptbook runs as follows:

Let me depart alone, an [sic] for my sake stay here with Antony – who – though – he had no hand in *Caesar*'s death shall enjoy the benefit of his dying – a place in the Commonwealth as which of you shall not (*Shouts*) Do grace to *Caesar*'s Corpse & grace his speech tending to *Caesar*'s glories which Antony by our permission is allowed to make with this I depart etc.

The rhetorical fervour of 'I have the same dagger for myself, when it shall please my country to need my death' has undeniable gallery appeal, but clashes utterly with Brutus' altruistic objectives at this point. Moreover, from a directorial point of view, the actor playing Antony is left with the tempo of the scene marred if not destroyed. In the last act, as an overt concession to textual integrity, Booth restores Brutus' six-line scene beginning 'Ride, ride, Messala' (v.ii); and gained an extra appearance for his pains.

It is gratifying to discover, however, that Brutus' death scene is closer to Shakespeare than Kemble. Downstage properties were no problem in Booth's superbly equipped plant, so Brutus invites his companions to 'rest on this rock' (v.v.1), perhaps for the first time since the Restoration. Lucius is not asked to kill his master. The request is more fittingly made of Metellus and Trebonius. Metellus' (Shakespeare–Clitus) lines 'Now is that noble vessel full of grief, / That it runs over even at his eyes' (v.v.13–14) are no longer spoken just before Brutus' sword-thrust, but return to their original position. The Dryden–Davenant–Kemble death speech disappears, and most of the lines Shakespeare gives Brutus are retained. There is, however, no appeal for Strato to hold the sword. Booth's Brutus stabbed himself in the manner of his tragic forbears.

Booth's feats of blatant textual self-service should not be allowed to obscure his rehabilitation of several of Brutus' best moments. In the conspiracy sequence the patriot is again permitted his emphatic 'And what other oath' speech (II.i.126–31). His misguided assessment of Antony as 'but a limb of Caesar' (II.i.165) is also restored. The moving apostrophe to Lucius after the departure of the conspirators (II.i.229–33) returns, and the Caius Ligarius sequence reappears after an absence of at least a century. The lines to Lucius were as crucial to Booth's interpretation of Brutus as they were inconsistent with Kemble's; and the Caius Ligarius scene, even if it slowed dramatic action somewhat, justified itself by its potent illustration of Brutus' political and moral stature. Curiously enough, although Booth fails to restore Brutus' poignant promise to his dead comrade, 'I shall find time, Cassius, I shall find time' (v.iii.103), he reinstates his instructions for Cassius' funeral (v.iii.104–6).

Booth's remaining deletions and restorations, most fairly minor and idiosyncratic, do not warrant extensive comment. The encounter of Cicero and Casca is partially restored to the Storm scene, with Cicero's speeches taken by Trebonius. But Trebonius was not permitted to enquire whether Casca had seen 'anything more wonderful', and the latter did not expand his account of the supernatural visitations unbidden. A few lines of Caesar's braggadocio (II.ii.44–8), cut in 1812 at Covent Garden, find their way back. In the Assassination scene, Cinna's 'Liberty! Freedom! Tyranny is dead!' (III.i.78), given by Kemble to Brutus, is reallocated to Cassius from whom it comes more appropriately. Brutus' and Cassius' prescient allusion to future theatrical enactments (III.i.111–18) is removed with one hand, and with the other, Brutus' casuistic 'So are we Caesar's friends, that have abridged / His time of fearing death' (III.i.104–5) is restored. In the final act, Trebonius

(Shakespeare–Titinius) is again allowed to garland Cassius' body (v.iii.85–7), but does not kill himself. Finally, to cleanse the text of the faintest vestige of impropriety, Booth has Portia describe herself as Brutus' mistress rather than his harlot, and expunges the mention of her thigh wound altogether.

Stagecraft

In Booth's aesthetic credo, archaeological accuracy, however desirable, yielded pride of place to pictorial effect. Like Kemble, he found the Republican period too drab, and followed his canny predecessor in setting the action in the resplendent Augustan era. But his Imperial Rome was more the creation of an artist than the re-creation of an archaeologist:[8] only the most picturesque features were preserved, albeit with minute correctness, and these were re-worked into a carefully-contrived artistic composition.

The setting for act I, described in the playbill as 'Grand Square in Rome', was designed as a breathtaking introduction to an age in which architectural splendour reflected the grandeur of human ideals. In contrast to the drab and inappropriate Street drops which long had graced American re-creations of this scene, audiences revelled in a splendid vista of Roman buildings surrounding three sides of an open plaza bisected horizontally at centre-stage by a flight of steps (Illustration 7). Immediately upstage lay the Roman Forum, and in the background rose the Capitoline Hill. Although the ensemble was not a precise representation of any specific area in Augustan Rome, individual buildings were accurately re-created. Witham's watercolour sketch of this scene (in the Museum of the City of New York) provides an invaluable key to Booth's colour scheme for the entire production. Instead of the stark marmoreal whiteness of later revivals, his marble is a warm tan, complemented by crimson columns, and brightened by friezes painted in rich blues, greens, and reds. Above, the blue sky is delicately clouded.

As the curtain rises 'groups of Plebians male & Female & children' are discovered standing about, and the Soothsayer occupies himself up left at the altar originally introduced by Kemble. For the first time women and children appear in the crowd; and their presence represents both a concession to the demands of realism and an opportunity to capitalize upon the visual interest afforded by their vivid costumes. As the curtain rises the crowd provides 'Loud murmurs', but the promptbook gives them little else to do. Unlike Macready, Booth seems to have seen them as mainly a pictorial adjunct to the setting, and left them to invent whatever business they pleased. They probably numbered about fifteen at the first performance,[9] and were judged too few and too maladroit to suit the stately

7. 'Grand Square in Rome' (I.i). Edwin Booth's production at Booth's Theatre,
New York, 1871. Designed by Charles Witham

surroundings. In a few moments, Casca and Trebonius come down the
steep flight of steps on stage right and confront the merrymakers. After
Casca's harangue, as the crowd shrinks away, lictors enter in advance of the
procession '& drive citizens up steps at back, & form across the back of
stage' (*JC* 48). Here the line of lictors restraining the crowd lends a note of
realism, while their uniforms and the costumes of the citizens splash
colourfully against the soft tans of the marble façades behind them. The
procession now enters down the stairs at the right, and consists of the usual
named characters meagrely companioned by only about forty of the familiar
guards, standard-bearers, lictors, soldiers, and the like. The spectacle, not
surprisingly, passed almost unnoticed by reviewers.

Although Booth's artistic intuition dictated the modest number of supers
in the opening scene, critical disapproval of his mob and neglect of his
procession soon overcame his aesthetic sensibilities; and on 31 December
The Star was able to report that 'in the procession ... there are nearly two
hundred persons on the stage', some of whom doubtless augmented the
citizens while the rest swelled the parade. Soon the mob was judged better
drilled as well.

The Storm scene (II.i) was, as always, a rudimentary affair, consisting of
merely a street drop, with perhaps a free-standing arch, at about the
position of the first or second grooves to allow the 'Public Square' setting to

be struck behind. The meeting between Casca and Trebonius occurs in a grotesque twilight.

In Brutus' garden (II.ii) a combination of 'stone seats' backed by 'cut (sections) wood on to break up sc. [ene]' was artfully lighted to secure 'a weird night effect showing the terrace and distant foliage'.[10] In contrast to the splendour and bustle of the first scene and the celestial pyrotechnics of the second, the simple interplay of light and shade evoked an eerie tranquillity. Touched by sinister shadows Brutus spoke his soliloquy, and the conspirators conferred in oppressive gloom. A tableau effect preceded the striking of the clock. Years later Winter recalled 'as one of the most perfectly poetical illusions of reality ever created on the stage the picture of that shadowy garden and the sinister forms of the conspirators when all action was suddenly arrested by the admonition, "Peace! count the clock," and far away the bell struck three.'[11] 'The audience', according to the *Guardian* (3 February, 1872), 'listened spell-bound in awe, and gazed on the gloomy stage and the ghastly conspirators with suppressed breathing.' This tension was created and sustained by constant understatement; from the moment Brutus says, 'Give me your hands' (II.i.112), performers are reminded 'This scene to be played quiet and suppressed.' (*JC* 48).

The set for the 'Apartment in Caesar's House' was merely a chamber wall raised from the cellar at the position traditionally occupied by the second grooves; and a ceiling border was lowered from the flies to meet it. The scene was played quite straightforwardly, and was followed by a twenty-four minute intermission to allow the elaborate Senate scene to be readied.

The centre of gravity in *Julius Caesar* was for Booth, as for Macready, the assassination. The setting is based on Jean-Louis Gérôme's celebrated work, *La Mort de César*, painted four years earlier.[12] (Illustration 8.) Witham's design is happily preserved although regrettably uncoloured (Illustration 9), and obviates the necessity of detailed description. It will be noted that Booth's setting is an adaptation, and not a copy, of Gérôme. The foreground arrangement of the painting is retained with the curving rows of senatorial benches on stage left backed by a colonnade, and Caesar's curile chair more or less opposite the seats farthest downstage. To the severe architectural features of Gérôme's conception, Witham adds a hefty amount of ornamentation.

This scene, a typical piece of historical realism with romantic overtones, was designed, as was the Grand Square in Rome, to underline visually the spiritual grandeur of the action. Like Gérôme's painting, it derived its power not so much from its historical fidelity, although that was patent, as from its compositional strength. Booth was particularly taken with Gérôme's placement of Caesar relative to the conspirators. The side focus

8. 'La Mort de César' by Jean-Louis Gérôme

9. 'The Roman Senate' (III.i). Edwin Booth's production at Booth's Theatre, New York, 1871. Designed by Charles Witham

and asymmetry of the arrangement offered endless opportunities for fluid and natural movement and picturesque groupings when contrasted with the rigid and artificial action necessitated by Kemble's location of Caesar at upstage centre with the conspirators in parallel lines from upstage to downstage on either side of the throne.

The 1871 promptbook contains few directions for the conduct of the assassination, but since the Jarrett–Palmer production employed the same basic set and their promptbook notes tally closely with newspaper accounts of the conduct of this scene in 1871, we may not err seriously by accepting the arrangement outlined by Vincent and Becks as broadly representative of Booth's original staging.

As the curtain rose to 'March in Orchestra', the audience was greeted by a literal 'moving picture'. Between thirty-nine and forty-six senators[13] stood at their places. Thirteen 'Ladies & Citizens' were 'discovered at Back' behind the colonnade on the first night, but their sparse numbers were soon augmented. Although male citizens had been introduced into this scene by Macready, the appearance of ladies was a novelty. In the foreground, Caesar stands near his throne and the Soothsayer kneels RC slightly on the diagonal with arms extended holding his schedule. Antony, Trebonius, and Decius are grouped at centre stage, with Metellus, Casca, and Cinna on the steps DL. As applause breaks out, Brutus and Cassius once more make a star entrance. 'Brut enters at back comes down C to Cass who enters L. They meet – Shake' (B). The business of the scene can now go forward.

From this moment onwards, the action moves with relentless precision to its inevitable conclusion. As the Soothsayer says, 'Read this schedule' (III.i.3), Decius intervenes forcefully on behalf of Trebonius, 'placing his paper directly over the soothsayers' (V). Once rejected, the Soothsayer withdraws and reappears a moment later in the colourful mob at the back, his dark figure a potent reminder of approaching disaster. With the Soothsayer gone, Decius relaxes and joins Brutus and Cassius at LC. Popilius now enters L2E '& Xs beh^d Brutus & Casca to R of Cassius' (V). He touches Cassius casually on the shoulder, wishes well to his enterprise, and enigmatically passes on. After Antony's departure, the conspirators, with chilling precision and disarming naturalness, take their positions for the Dance of Death to follow.

Metellus advances to Caesar and kneels; and when his petition is denied, he appeals, still kneeling, to the other senators who kneel in turn. The directions for the stabbing suggest a degree of realism, but imply at the same time a certain picturesque stylization. 'When Cassius kneels', runs Vincent's book, 'Casca rises a little later & Xs to RH beh^d the Throne, at his cue he springs upon steps & stabs Caesar, the other conspirators rise & rush upon Caesar excepting Cassius & Brutus. Cassius pulls Caesar from throne, stabs & throws him over to Brutus, who then stabs him.' Becks records that

'Caesar retreats with a look of horror' after Brutus' sword-thrust, and on '*Et tu, Brute?*' (III.i.77) he 'throws Mantle over his head & falls Centre.' 'As soon as Brutus has stabbed Caesar, he averts his face, raises hands in sorrow, and goes left.'[14] The moment is splendidly recorded for us in Witham's design. Meanwhile, 'The citizens are in great Excitement crying "Murder etc.–" rushing up & down at Back. stopping when Cassius is astride of Caesars body' (V) for his exultant shout, 'Liberty! Freedom! Tyranny is dead!' (III.i.78). As all the conspirators echo 'Liberty, Freedom & Enfranchisement', Booth halts the action for a tableau. 'When the tragedy occurs, when the conspirators strike at "mighty Caesar", and the vast concourse breaks up in wild confusion, the act loses the customary stage prettiness, and expands in the imagination of the spectator to the dignity of a great historical incident', claimed *Appleton's Journal* (20 January 1872). Which was just what Booth had in mind.

It is worth noting that for the first time Brutus and Cassius are given characteristic and contrasting action as each confronts the Dictator at the scene's climax. Cassius, imperious and vicious, savours his conquest by pulling Caesar from the throne before he strikes him; then, lest Brutus weaken, he thrusts the dying figure at him. Brutus, on the contrary, has no stomach for violence. Trapped by Cassius' manoeuvre, he stabs with manifest reluctance and turns away in revulsion. Booth's treatment of the citizens is also of some interest. While allowing them to react realistically to the murder, he keeps them well upstage behind the colonnade, employing them primarily as pictorial background in the manner of Kemble and Macready.

Soon after the tableau, the citizens and extraneous senators melt away, leaving the conspirators to confront Antony. The spectacle is over for the moment; only the acting of the principals matters. At the conclusion of Antony's imprecation, he 'Throws himself over body of C [aesar]' in an appropriately graphic attitude, and a quick curtain ends the scene. An intermission of twenty-six minutes follows to permit the Forum to be arranged.

While the assassination was the undeniable highlight of the production, the Forum scene was not far behind it. The rise of the curtain revealed another eye-catching Roman plaza surrounded, like the Grand Square in act I, by striking recreations of classical architecture, with a Grecian temple in the centre upstage as a prominent feature. In front of it stood the rostrum. On the first night a thin crowd of forty or fifty drew the complaint that the scene lacked 'life and fullness, and suggests that Rome is deserted'.[15] But ere long the same two hundred bodies who graced the Grand Square and the Senate chamber appeared here as well.

In the Forum, as elsewhere, the function of Booth's supers seems more pictorial than histrionic. Under no circumstances, whatever the demands of realism, were they permitted to attract undue attention to themselves or mask the star.

To judge from the 1871 promptbook, the crowd did little beyond what Shakespeare's text explicitly demands, save perhaps for a few additional shouts of 'Aye, aye' and similar ejaculations. At the close of the action, Antony executes a spectacular leap from the six-foot-high rostrum, and rushes off right. As in Kemble's and Macready's productions the curtain falls as the bearers stoop to take up Caesar's body. The audience now endures another interval, probably not a long one, while the tent setting is put in place.

Brutus' tent consisted of draperies hung at either side of the stage and joined by a gauze wall at the back. Behind the gauze was a landscape drop. Borders were let down near the curtain line to mask the tops of the draperies and suggest a roof. All the traditional furnishings were provided, supplemented by animal skins on the floor. The visual highlight of the scene was predictably the appearance of Caesar's ghost; and once again audiences marvelled at Booth's capacity to create imaginative and romantic atmosphere by visual means. Again, as in Brutus' garden, Booth relies upon the subtle use of chiaroscuro. When the scene begins the lighting is '¼ down' and is arranged to 'Work Down During the Act'. As the quarrel nears its end the 'Stage Grows Gradually Dark'. The conference with Trebonius and Metellus takes place round the taper in a soft gloom which somehow becomes more melancholy and ominous when Brutus finds himself alone. As he turns to adjust the guttering lamp, the dead Dictator floats into view, arms outstretched and eyes fixed on his assassin. The sudden radiance of the apparition must have offered an astonishing contrast to the shadowed foreground, and could hardly have failed to amaze the audience almost as much as Brutus. Throughout the rest of the scene, the lights are gradually raised as reality returns, day breaks, and the battle beckons. Lost in thought in the final moments, 'Brutus turns to C looking off. Lucius touches him, he turns startled, & sight of Lucius reassures him' (*JC* 48). A 'Quick Curtain' falls on this picture.

Few details of settings for the battle scenes survive. No doubt some simple arrangement of drops, wings, and set pieces was used, with minor variations to suit each of the four scenes in act IV. The only contemporary comment to come to light is faintly critical. 'The scene is beautiful', remarks the *Albion* reviewer, 'but it is an old friend, which has been seen many times before in various plays; and . . . is wholly inconsistent with the situation, representing, as it does, vegetable growth wholly foreign to Rome.'[16] No reviewer describes the action of the final episodes; and the promptbook is only lightly marked. In the absence of contrary evidence, one must assume that there was no excessive military panoply.

The actors

Booth's Brutus, while less satisfying on the whole than Barrett's Cassius, received the lion's share of attention because of its novelty. When the five-feet-seven-inch, slightly built Brutus made his first entrance, it was immediately apparent that the Kemble tradition of majestic patriots had been violated. 'It must be owned that Mr. BOOTH lacks figure and port for the character', complained *The New York Times* the next day. 'Brutus is one of our most clearly defined ideals of classic manliness and dignity . . . His is a figure cast in the very antique mold – large, massive, calm and evenly balanced.' Worse still, the heroic stride and the majestic poses were missing. 'These men of antiquity, with their countless statues, their practical worship of the body . . . their flowing garments, their exalted conception of personal and national dignity must infallibly have carried themselves . . . in a manner different from the manner of today; and this is what Mr. BOOTH does not do.'[17]

Booth was fully aware of his physical unfitness for heroic Roman characters; and he rejected Coriolanus for just this reason. 'With my physique', he wrote, '*Coriolanus* would appear more of a boaster than a man of deeds, I fear.'[18] But Brutus was for him not a man of deeds, but a man of exalted ideals and exquisite sensibility, one who attracts by what he is and not by what he does. His claims to heroic stature derive not from his physical size and patriotic enterprise, but from his beauty of soul and purity of motive.

This Brutus, as romantically beau idéal as Kemble's was classically so, was a predictable product of Booth's own introspective, idealistic, and refined sensibility. 'His essential spirit', according to Winter, found ideal expression 'in characters which rest on spiritualized intellect, or on sensibility to fragile loveliness, the joy that is unattainable, the glory that fades, and the beauty that perishes.'[19] To romanticize Brutus in this way was to warp his personality in one direction as seriously as Kemble had done in the other; but Booth seems not to have fretted unduly. He emphasized those facets of the character which flattered his own talents and gratified the sentiments of his audience. Discordant elements were casually eliminated or repressed.

Given the sentimentalized aestheticism of Booth's notion of Brutus, the deliberate, understated sincerity of his acting style suited the conception admirably. But to suggest that Booth's interpretation was quietly sincere is not to imply that it was a mere exercise in prosaic realism, any more than Booth's settings were. Like all Booth's roles, Brutus was given a poetic dimension which lifted him as far above literal realism as Millet's peasants are above grime and sweat. He was in favour of a certain naturalness in acting, Winter tells us, but maintained 'that an actor can be natural without being literal'. As he saw it, 'art is romantic, and . . . the moment romance is sacrificed to reality acting becomes worse than useless'.[20]

The Roman philosopher seen by audiences on the first night of *Caesar*, if not large, was well proportioned, and graceful. About 38 years of age, with long black hair, large and luminous dark eyes, and strong mouth, Brutus was a remarkably poetic figure. Booth's voice, richly melodic, clear, and mellow, with superb articulation, was fully capable of conveying subtly and variously the emotional complexity of Brutus' temperament without resort to unbecomingly flamboyant vocal effects.[21]

As Brutus enters, with the tumult of the procession receding in the distance, 'a gentle melancholy, a sad abstraction, an autumnal pensiveness' seems to hang over him. Already he is troubled, 'impelled to an act which he believes imperative for the public good, yet as to the rectitude of which he is unsure'.[22] As Cassius speaks there is a coldness and seriousness in Brutus' reaction which reflects the gravity of the act they contemplate. At the same time he is fraught with an underlying tension, anxious and over-solicitous for the thoughts and deeds of others. 'The trouble of his mind was shown in his care-worn face, and the cause of it was told in his simple utterance of the words "I fear the people choose Caesar for their king!"'[23] The strength of his friendship for Caesar, however, almost paralyses his sense of public duty.

Tortured irresolution terminates in the Garden scene, and here Booth achieved some of his finest moments. The soliloquy showed Brutus to be, like Hamlet, 'quick to suffer but slow to act'. Wrapped in shadow, his tortured '"It *must* be by his *death*"' – expressed afflicting mental perturbation, and his embodiment, then and thenceforward was suffused by a lofty, pathetic solemnity.'[24] His authority and gravity in the conversation with the conspirators were profoundly impressive. At the moment of his commitment to the plot, as he turned to ask, 'Give me your hands all over, one by one' (II.i.112), he broke away from Cassius with a degree of violence considered by one reviewer 'abrupt and unnatural',[25] but appropriate enough to a man who knows that if he does not summon all his forces this instant, he may never manage to do so. Caught up for the moment in the lofty idealism of his vision, his appeal for sacrifice not butchery saw him 'aroused from his sombre, stoical mood, and kindled into deepest earnestness, and these words dropped from his lips in tones of glorious, thrilling eloquence'.[26] With the departure of the conspirators, as Brutus apostrophizes the sleeping Lucius, a touch of almost feminine grace and tenderness softened the masculine gravity which characterized the previous sequence. His conversation with Portia was marked by a 'lofty and lovely chivalry'.[27]

Throughout the early part of the Assassination scene, he manifested the same nervous excitement, intense though suppressed, observable in his first interview with Cassius. Moved by the contending claims of private love and public duty, he waits to stab Caesar until the last possible moment, and does so then with reluctance and horror only when Cassius pushes the bleeding dictator into his arms. The moment the deed is done, Brutus realizes that, whatever the justice or injustice of his cause, retribution is inevitable; and from this point on, 'his mind is darkly overshadowed with a sense of impending doom – so keen is his spiritual perception of nature's inexorable vigilance to punish the shedder of human blood'.[28] Whatever nemesis awaits, Brutus is determined that his crime will not be compounded by further violence. Two pieces of business in one of the Booth–Barrett promptbooks underline his humane concern. As Servius enters with Antony's message, 'Cassius draws his sword & rushes at him. Servius darts under his arm, & kneels to & is protected by Brutus' (*JC* 48). Again, near the end of the scene, after Brutus tells Antony 'Prepare the body, then; and follow us' (III.i.253), 'As Brutus & Cassius retire back of Antony, Cassius quickly turns & is about to stab Antony, but Brutus prevents him, & appears to pacify him as they ex [it] LUE.' (*JC* 48).

Unlike the traditional interpretation of the Forum speech, Booth's reading was more a conversation than a harangue. 'It is the dignity of Brutus', one critic remarked, 'his sincerity, his earnestness, that tells upon the people. Booth's is an explanation; his honest patriotism does not need encore.'[29] Winter felt the tame and ineffective delivery was one more proof of Brutus' half-hearted belief in the rightness of his action.

By the time the Quarrel scene was reached, ethical uncertainty had been succeeded by weary disillusion; yet even now his self-control did not waver. His supreme tolerance of Cassius' animosity testified to a 'poise of an almost stoical nature. He never acts with the impetuosity of impulse, but always with the deliberation of reason. . . . His range of mental vision is so wide that he can sympathise with the view of his antagonist as well as with his own view.'[30] Yet patience did not imply weakness; and when pushed too far, 'the predominating look of authority in his eyes inspired awe'[31] as the penitent Cassius dropped to his knee. A moment later, with passion spent, his 'soul-sickness' was 'so pregnant . . . as to make one doubt that it was wholly counterfeited. The theatre was hushed, and heavy tear-drops welled in the actor's eyes as he sighed with a melody simple, penetrating, and melting the words, "Portia is dead!"'[32] When Cassius' murmured 'Portia, art thou gone?' (IV.iii.4) threatens Brutus' precarious self-discipline during the military conference, 'the grief-laden meaning he [gave] to the short phrase, "speak no more of her," so indifferent in word, so affecting in delivery'[33] struck Laura Keene as masterful. In his confrontation with the apparition, Winter found him 'one of the few actors ever seen in our time who could, in the presence of an imagined spirit, make the spectator see and feel the supernatural quality of the visitation'.[34]

The military scenes attracted little attention. These final moments were for Brutus merely the working out of a retributive justice he had long accepted and expected. His absence of martial bearing and unconvincing belligerence were a pathetic confirmation of his temperamental unfitness for the role of man of action. His simple farewell to Cassius 'was spoken with a manly pathos which was specially beautiful and touching'.[35] His death, like his life, was unpretentious. As he dies, he hears a 'Shrill trumpet call'. 'At the sound Brutus half raises himself' (*JC* 48) in a poignantly ineffective attempt to return to what he sees as his duty; then he falls.

Booth's oversimplified, sentimentalized Brutus proved eminently palatable to his audiences; but reviewers were less easily pleased. 'All the philosophy of Brutus, and the good emanating from that philosophy, are drawn with a loving hand', conceded one of several dissatisfied critics, 'but the sterner qualities are made to recede too much to make the picture altogether harmonious. It is instinct with a pure and mellow light of a pure and noble inspiration, in which the shadows are but half shadows, and all is blended into a symmetric whole which lacks but one element – strength.'[36]

If Booth's offstage personality was demonstrably akin to his Brutus, Lawrence Barrett in private life was the complete Cassius. Otis Skinner, who knew him well, found him 'many-sided, frequently wrong, subject to suspicion and jealousy, sensitive and hot headed. His egotism was stupendous but his sense of right was not always out of joint; unjust, but often, when his errors were shown to him, ready to acknowledge himself in the wrong.' 'No one could play Cassius', concludes Skinner, '. . . better than he. It was his outstanding impersonation – he was born for the part.'[37]

Like Booth, he 'was not above the middle height, but his inherent dignity of demeanor invested him with peculiar distinction. His head was finely formed; his features were regular; his face was pale; his eyes, dark, lurid, and deeply sunken, were brilliant with intense lustre. His figure was thin . . . His glance was quick, eager and comprehensive.'[38] His physical qualifications for the role could hardly be bettered.

Barrett's acting was particularly praised for its vitality, energy, and 'nervous momentum'. His talents were best exploited, Winter considered, in 'a part in which, after long repression, the torrent of passion can break loose in a tumult of frenzy and a wild strain of eloquent words'.[39] At such times audiences were swept into near hysteria by the splendour of his declamation.

Barrett's Cassius, while not as simplistically conceived as Booth's Brutus, was presented in quite the most favourable light the text would permit. He took Brutus' assessment of Cassius as 'The last of all the Romans' to be the literal objective truth, and not merely a testimony to Brutus' friendly feelings towards a dead comrade. Without cutting the text, Barrett sought, with immense ingenuity, to wrest every line to Cassius' moral advantage.

One is tempted to conjecture that he brought to Shakespeare's character the kind of sensitive understanding he coveted for his own conduct. His Cassius was at the core an 'intellectual ascetic', but withal a man of action. While 'his nature may have been embittered by disappointed ambition and by saddening study of the qualities and deeds of men',[40] he is no Iago. His decision to assassinate Caesar is motivated by a passionate hatred of despotism rather than a personal hostility to Caesar. 'His purpose is a good purpose to him; and if, as he considers, the means by which he pursues it have an ignoble aspect, they are the only means that can succeed.'[41] He sees his manipulation of Brutus as 'using right means to a good end, and embarking his friend upon a glorious enterprise'.[42] When the venture fails, he accepts his responsibility without question, and meets his death with decision and courage.

On Cassius' first entrance, his picturesque appearance alone kindled excitement. 'His drapery and costume is a sight to see', enthused a reviewer. 'Since Rachel, we have never beheld anything like its classical grace and exquisite management ... His thin wiry figure is displayed to perfection beneath the folds and pleats of his toga.'[43] But the compelling feature was his 'pale and haggard' face in which 'the dark eyes, stern and gloomy in expression, seemed ablaze with inward light'. His 'voice was clear, copious, penetrating, instinct with fervent emotion; the demeanor was that of enforced self-control at a high pitch of excitement; the action was at times vigilantly deliberate, at other times nervous and rapid; the passion was ever intense, but the intellect predominant'.[44] He seemed 'the perfect image of the fiery spirit that preys upon itself in its intellectual isolation, its scorn of human weakness, and its passionate hatred of tyranny'.[45]

The opening lines of his colloquy with Brutus revealed 'a glacier beneath which volcanic fires are burning',[46] and the flames broke forth with terrifying vehemence as the scene proceeded. His movement throughout was unremittingly restless; now moving left, then moving right, shaking his head, advancing to Brutus one moment and withdrawing the next, 'lashed into anger and impatience' (M) by the fervid shouts of the mob. Dissimulation was unthinkable; Cassius believed implicitly in what he was saying. Although his speech beginning 'I know that virtue to be in you, Brutus' (I.ii.90) was to some extent a declamatory set-piece, it retained a fair degree of naturalness. After his remark about the capacity of Brutus and himself to withstand the winter weather as well as Caesar, he paused; then, 'as if suddenly remembering a fact illustrating and proving his former statement' (M), he began the anecdote about the swimming match. His passionate contempt for weakness of any sort was vividly underlined by 'drawing in his breath, audibly, between his clenched teeth' (M) before he said 'tired Caesar'. In another unaffected touch, reminiscent of the elder Booth, he 'comes close to Brutus, lays his hand upon his shoulder ... and, after a brief pause, says, in a low expressive tone: 'Men at some time &c.' (M). Although Cassius put his case forcefully, it was abundantly evident that Brutus was prevailed upon not by any duplicity, but by Cassius' transcendent earnestness and the conviction that he was unquestionably a patriot and a noble one.

As the procession re-enters, Cassius' icy demeanour gives Caesar ample cause for concern. With a splendid disregard of social propriety, he 'crosses left, with a cold salutation to Caesar. He unrolls the parchment, as he crosses, reading it for a short time; then, folding his arms, he stands meditating, left, near front, during the dialogue between Caesar and Antony' (M). Already his intuitive dislike of Antony is apparent in his pointed refusal to greet him.[47] Alone on stage at the conclusion of the act, as 'his eye naturally followed the retiring form of . . . Brutus', he remarked,

> Well, Brutus, thou art noble; yet I see
> Thy honourable mettle may be wrought
> From that it is disposed . . . . (I.ii.308–18)

This was not a piece of Iago-type gloating, but merely the 'passing evanescent comment' of an intellectual 'on the weakness of a mind that will take advice from anybody'.[48]

In the conspiracy sequence, he revealed himself as a 'natural leader, a born soldier, with a soldier's willingness to make the ends justify the means'.[49] His insistence upon Antony's murder derived not from casual bloodthirstiness, but from a shrewd assessment of Antony's capacity to cause mischief. 'His advisement of the killing of Antony – "Let Antony and Caesar fall together"', we are told, 'was spoken with such deadly earnestness as caused a shudder.'[50]

At the beginning of the Assassination scene Cassius was unwontedly quiet. 'Stern in countenance, calm and implacable in purpose', he stood 'eyeing his victim and his fellow-conspirators with keen sagacity, in silence watching the development of the conspiracy.'[51] When Casca initiates the attack, all his concentrated energy explodes as he 'rushes instantly into the midst of the conspirators, eager to strike' (M). He drags Caesar from the throne, thrusts his dagger with 'awful energy', and, ever alert to human frailty, forces the reeling dictator on Brutus. As Caesar falls, with a 'wild, half-joyous, half-frenzied outburst of triumph'[52] he 'strides over Caesar's body. He stands over it as he says: "Liberty, freedom &c."' (M). His exaltation seemed motivated not so much by personal satisfaction as by 'the sincerity of political fanaticism'.[53] His jubilation is short-lived, however; almost immediately his gnawing distrust of Antony reawakens. He 'goes quickly to Trebonius, seizing his arm, and coming rapidly down the stage with him, asking, in high excitement, about Antony' (M).

All of Cassius' strategic instincts insist that Antony must be killed. After

Antony's entry, when Brutus and the other conspirators sheathe their swords, 'Cassius is the last to sheathe his sword, and does so very slowly, and with marked reluctance' (M). When the placatory Brutus affirms, 'To you our swords have leaden points, Mark Antony' (III.i.173), 'Cassius turns away, shaking his head, negatively. He folds his arms, and takes a step, left' (M), firmly dissociating himself from such ill-advised benevolence. As Antony approaches to shake his hand, he 'does not turn toward Antony, who advances to him. He keeps Antony waiting with outstretched hand. He then, very slowly, stretches out his own hand to Antony, without looking at him. He makes no response, and after Antony has grasped his hand, he puts it again into his bosom' (M). On several later occasions, he threatens to rush on Antony, but allows his better judgment to be overridden by Brutus. 'At the very last, Cassius shows his strong desire to go back to kill Antony, and expresses his discontent as Brutus persuades him to go' (M).

In Brutus' tent Cassius' patience with Brutus' misguided ideals reaches exhaustion; and his pent-up fury is at last set free. He enters 'with a short, rapid gait. He carries a spear, which he hands to a soldier. He goes to Brutus at centre. Brutus holds out his hand, which Cassius repels with his truncheon, as he says: "Most noble &c."' (M). In the first stages of the argument he replies to Brutus' calm observations 'loudly and excitedly', and 'paces, angrily and rapidly, up and down' (M). His performance at this point was censured as 'restless and pettish',[54] but this rather feminine display of temperament was precisely what Cassius refers to later as 'that rash humour which my mother gave me'. As the altercation proceeds, Cassius' rage grows more masculine and uncontrollable. Beside himself at Brutus' suggestion that Cassius 'durst not so have tempted' Caesar, he draws his sword and threatens Brutus, but suddenly horrified by his violence, 'He then resheathes it, and staggers backward up the stage, before saying: "Do not presume &c."' (M).

His reconciliation with Brutus when it came was as wholehearted as his anger had been. At first, nearly hysterical with resentment and frustration, he flings his dagger before Brutus and falls on his knees with breast bared to receive the blow. Disarmed by Brutus' amiability his passion gradually subsides; and Brutus' confession of ill-temper brings him rushing enthusiastically with hand outstretched. A hitherto unsuspected 'sweet, pathetic current of feeling ... beneath the gnarled exterior of austerity'[55] revealed itself at the announcement of the death of Portia; and for some time afterwards he remained unusually subdued. At the table during the military conference, he 'maintained a sad aspect – sense of death heavy on him & intensified by hearing of Cicero's death' (B). He 'does not regain composure till Bru says "Well to our work"', when 'with effort [he] throws off depression [and] turns full to table' (B). During the goodnights which end the act, Cassius, appropriately enough, salutes Brutus with the same truncheon with which he repulsed him earlier. In a telling final touch, his sensitive response to the smallest act of kindness once more betrays itself. When Brutus says, 'Good night, good brother', Cassius, deeply touched by his warm-heartedness, 'returns quickly, and they again embrace' (M).

In the confrontation with Antony and Octavius at the start of the final act, he was once more his choleric and testy self. 'In the exchange of farewells', according to Winter, 'Barrett manifested the more acute sensibility. In Booth's manner and voice there was great solemnity; in those of Barrett great sorrow; he spoke as if possessed by dark presentiment – like a man who intuitively knows that his life is drawing to an end.'[56]

As Cassius enters for his final scene, 'he confronts a retreating standard-bearer, stabs him, and takes the ensign from his hand' (M). When he learns of the capture of Trebonius, with typical rashness he 'attempts to kill himself with the sword which he has not replaced in its sheath after killing the standard-bearer' (M); but discovers 'His resolution is not strong enough, and he turns impetuously to Pindarus' (M). As Pindarus takes the sword, Cassius 'raises the mantle, slowly and tremblingly' (M), and, 'After a momentary pause, he throws himself upon the sword, falling upon one knee as the sword enters his breast. Still kneeling, he withdraws the sword, which falls upon the stage. He rises, convulsively, staggers to centre, from left, and is caught by Pindarus, who lowers the body to the ground' (M).

Although generally admired, Barrett's Cassius disturbed some reviewers by its idealization of the crafty assassin. 'He has too open a way at times', contended a representative of this viewpoint; 'he shows a loyal manhood not understood of Cassius; he is not fox enough'.[57] But audiences did not question Barrett's Cassius any more than they did Booth's Brutus. In 'the fervor of his eloquence ... the glittering simplicity of his action, the splendour of his sanguinary and guilty triumph, and the lonely and solemn magnificence of his death',[58] they found cosy reassurance of the basic goodness of the human heart and gratifying confirmation that crime does not pay. Moral and psychological ambiguities were an unwelcome distraction.

Frank Bangs was not Booth's first choice for Antony. He had originally hoped to recruit Edwin Adams, and failed to do so.[59] But as it turned out, Bangs was probably as well suited to the pictorial idealism of Booth's production style as any performer of his time. Although Bangs was a second-rate actor, he possessed a first-rate physique; and Booth shamelessly exploited his virile glamour to enliven his stage pictures. Nevertheless, Booth and Barrett were the undisputed stars, and he was firmly kept in a subordinate position.[60]

There was little opportunity, with the Proscription scene removed, to depict the seamier side of Antony's character; and Bangs followed his superiors in repressing any traces of moral weakness elsewhere. Reviewers looked in vain for that 'voluptuous and pleasure-seeking sentiment which informed poor Walter Montgomery's impersonation';[61] and found precious little opportunism either. Bangs's interpretation was distinctly calculated to make 'the manly and resolute side of the character prevalent over the crafty and politic elements'; and, within its strictly limited compass, his execution was 'fierce, strong, and deeply effective'.[62]

In the Assassination scene his performance was so upstaged by Barrett's Cassius that critics tended to overlook it. 'His tenderness and grief over the body of *Caesar*' were considered 'admirable' by the *World* critic who noticed it *en passant*, although Bunce found him vocally defective.[63]

Few complained, however, of his treatment of the Forum speech in which his striking appearance and flamboyant delivery brought down the house. His costume, flattering but historically inaccurate, was black from head to foot. Nym Crinkle (A. C. Wheeler) persuaded himself that he was gazing on some Athenian statue. 'When it appears on the pedestal of the Forum', he wrote, 'we want to keep it there to feast the eye with flowing lines and curves of beauty. Nothing more sumptuous, more virile, more elegant in the exquisite mingling of manly strength with manly grace comes to me out of the classic atelier of the theatre.'[64] Leaping athletically from the six-foot rostrum to the stage floor and back up again, Bangs captured with great vigour the more violent passions. And although his delivery was highly emotional, it was singularly untainted by oratorical trickery. 'Mr. Bangs unlocks his lines, as it were', reports Bunce, 'and gives them play, and ease, and unction, evolving the meaning, touching with color, varying with light and shade – giving the whole range of expression the speech calls for; now calm, now tumultuous, now ironical – swaying his hearers, taking possession of them, moulding them, filling them with his own suppressed fury.'[65]

Caesar was played by D. W. Waller, a competent stock performer and long-time friend of Booth. Waller's interpretation broke no new ground, nor was it expected to. One critic thought he 'faithfully reproduced the well-known historic figure of *Caesar* – the tall, thin, bald-headed, black-eyed warrior';[66] and another credited him with delivering his lines 'with just self-possession and grace' and dying as becomingly as he lived.[67] No one felt moved to ask for more.

In mid-February, Barrett left the company to fulfil commitments else-where, and on 19 February 1872 Junius Brutus Booth replaced him as Cassius; but, according to most of the critical fraternity, he could neither look the part nor act it. On 4 March Edwin Booth undertook Cassius, partnered by the wooden and ponderous Brutus of William Creswick.[68] The arrangement lasted a week and constituted a substantial theatrical novelty.

Booth's Cassius, while not quite the equal of Barrett's, was judged to be better than his Brutus, and an original and sensitive interpretation in its own right.

The lack of heroic physique that so troubled critics when Booth played Brutus was considered no drawback to his Cassius. His make-up, more elaborate apparently than for Brutus, included a close-fitting wig of curly, grey hair, which framed a 'pale, student-like face, the sunken cheek furrowed by care, [and] eyes that were never at rest'.[69]

This Cassius, although 'remarkable for beauty and nobility of aspect and demeanor', laid no claim to moral elevation. Booth's conspirator was 'wild, impetuous, violent, vindictive, as if inspired more by loathing of the tyrant than by hatred of tyranny'.[70] Nevertheless, whatever his faults, he was not entirely to be despised. 'Disappointed and ambitious he surely was', wrote one critic, 'but at the same time he was fully as honest, in his way, in the assassination of Caesar, as was his more philosophical comrade, Brutus . . . Hot and impetuous he might have been, but still he must have been a man of culture, intelligence, and a thorough knowledge of mankind to have gathered around him the men he did.'[71]

'When he plays upon the feelings of *Brutus* in the first act, dealing simply in innuendo, he looks as he does in *Iago*, when he has fretted the *Moor*', we are told. 'His eye expresses, instead of frankness, exultation at the prospect of success. The lips are compressed and the mouth set hard, while the whole contour of the face betokens that of a man bent on the commission of a hellish, not a noble deed – to take a life for revenge, not for the good of Rome.'[72] His ardent and nervous temperament, spare figure, quick gesture, and rapid speech and action suggested a spirit that was 'comet-like, rushing, and terrible – not lacking, neither, in human emotion, but colored through-out with something sinister'.[73] This sinister quality was compounded mainly of inveterate pride and selfishness laced with a terrifying streak of viciousness.

In an abandon of vindictiveness at the moment of the assassination, one observer recorded, 'he breaks all bounds, and slashes and cuts at *Caesar* as if he would indeed hack his limbs'.[74] When Caesar fell he strode across the body, not in the unthinking callousness of patriotic frenzy, but in an unbridled display of imperiousness and scorn of danger. His 'scarce-restrained impatience at the words of Mark Antony'[75] spoke of a malevol-ence thirsting for expression in further violence.

In the last two acts, with 'the hunger of a jealousy appeased, and the imminence of the crisis calling forth all his energies, *Cassius* [was] another and a better man'.[76] The transformation came, predictably enough, with the Quarrel scene. 'The passionate entry, the dashing of his shield and helmet on the floor, and the quick, broken utterance, all betray the anger and agitation of the hour. Then, when he learns of the death of Portia, all the good, the true and noble in the man comes out, and he stands before his friend, grieved and abashed, sueing for pardon.'[77] At this point, 'the blank, stony look, the dejected mien, and his repetition of the lines, "How 'scaped I killing" was given with a depth of feeling that went far to gloss the memory of previous errors.'[78] The battlefield sequences, however, may have suffered from an excess of the same soft-heartedness. At least one reviewer found that at the moment of Cassius' suicide Booth's portrayal 'lacked the manhood and stern resolve that actuated Cassius, exhibiting more of the woman than the Roman'.[79]

On 11 March Booth made his début as Antony, and became the first actor ever to play all three roles during a single run. Partnered by the unlikely Brutus of Bangs and the undistinguished Cassius of Creswick, his Antony was the cynosure of all eyes for the final week of the production. While Brutus' melancholy idealism and Cassius' vital malice were obviously well adapted to Booth's talents, Antony's athletic sensuality at first sight seemed outside his range. But Booth's success was as complete as it was unexpected.

Booth brought to the role little in the way of fresh interpretation; as one might expect, the idealized young nobleman of the Kemble tradition gratified his moral sensibilities to a nicety. 'To the lighter and more winning qualities, to the patrician nobility and refinement of *Antony*, Mr. Booth rendered the utmost justice', Winter concluded. 'The darker shades of the character were judiciously repressed.'[80]

Although lacking the muscular glamour of Bangs, Booth's person, features, and bearing were well suited to the urbane courtier. His manner towards Caesar in the first scene struck Winter as 'that of perfect suavity commingled not with servile homage, but profound respect. The tone in which he said, referring to *Cassius*, "Fear him not, Caesar; he's not dangerous", was exceedingly gentle.'[81] Others detected a cringing sycophancy in his demeanor. To the *Weekly Review* critic Antony seemed 'to follow at Caesar's heels like a sleek and well-fed spaniel'.[82]

With the death of Caesar Antony revealed, in the traditional manner, resources hitherto unsuspected: instantly he became 'a person of politic, restless, and somewhat treacherous nature, yet manly, resolute, strong, and fierce'.[83] Without the overt nods and winks at the audience affected by his predecessors in the role, he made clear 'his instantaneous determination to avenge the murder' and 'his rapid apprehension of the political consequences impending from so tremendous an act'.[84] He was genuinely grieved; but with a degree of craft unknown to Bangs's Antony, he denied his sorrow its full indulgence until he could be alone. For the moment, dissimulation was all-important if he was to live and achieve his objective. His pretended commitment to the fortunes of the conspirators was portrayed with such conviction that Brutus' misconception was entirely credible. At the conspirators' exit, he followed them with a baleful look, wonderful 'in its flashing and concentrated intensity of hate, animosity and vengeful fire'.[85] He then turned to the body and begged pardon with a tenderness breathtakingly contrasted with the malignant vehemence of a moment past; and his grief at last found untrammelled release. The terrible prophecy that follows he launched 'with an inspiration that no pythoness could have surpassed', we are told, and he rose 'to the acme of lurid sublimity which electrified the house'.[86] As he threw his body across the corpse in a picturesque attitude for the final curtain, he topped even the excitement of the assassination itself; and for 'the glowing passion of the effort, at this point, the actor was twice called out'.[87]

His success in the Senate scene was but a prelude to the adulation which greeted his Forum speech. To allow him to look at the face of the corpse without turning away from the mob, he arranged the body with its head towards the auditorium rather than in the traditional cross-stage position. While his reading was undeniably declamatory and poetic, it was not without naturalness. 'His manner at first was deferential to the people. He spoke in a low tone, and as if struggling to curb emotion. He watched, without seeming to watch, the effect of every sentence. He did not assume success. The advance was gradual, the feeling cumulative. The acted grief seemed real.'[88] Particularly impressive was the spectacular conclusion of the speech 'with the quicker and quicker delivery, till it swelled to a torrent of words; finally, the leap from the tribune (a trick, but a clever trick), and his thunderous denunciation of the conspirators'. 'The house was swept away in an irresistible rush of enthusiastic sympathy', Laura Keene recalls, 'and there was no room to doubt that we had seen and heard a great actor.'[89]

The Jarrett and Palmer revival (1875)

With Booth's bankruptcy in 1874, the management of his theatre passed into the hands of Henry C. Jarrett and Henry D. Palmer, who for six years previously had made Niblo's Garden a Mecca for lovers of spectacle. Jarrett and Palmer were businessmen, not actors; their care was to discover what the public wanted, and to give it to them. Show-business instinct told them that a spectacular production of *Julius Caesar* at Booth's Theatre might not come amiss on the centenary of American independence; and their judgement was once more vindicated.

Scrutiny of the Booth's Theatre stock established that the settings from the 1871 revival were still usable, and the scenic artist, William Voigtlin, was set to refurbish them. New costumes and properties were also prepared. Barrett and Davenport were invited to repeat their 1870 Niblo's triumph, and Bangs was brought in to fill the place of Walter Montgomery. The production opened on 27 December 1875, and ran for a total of 103 performances.

The Jarrett–Palmer revival, while undeniably well acted, lacked overall artistic unity and taste, not to mention the spiritual idealism, which informed Booth's production. Although Voigtlin retained the major components of the 1871 décor, he added arches, painted new backdrops, and altered perspective with abandon.[90] And as a meretricious flourish, Jarrett and Palmer introduced at the end of act VI a lurid tableau featuring the cremation of Brutus. 'The scene is night', Bunce tells us.

The lights of the distant city glitter on the hillside, and the army, marshalled in the foreground, looks strange and weird with its many torches and the reflected lights on helmets, shields, and spears. In the centre of the stage is the funeral-pyre, which is presently lighted; and then, amid music, a wild confusion of lights and mysterious shadows, warlike ranks with banners and glittering arms, and a leaping blaze in the centre, the curtain falls.[91]

The singular increase in scenic scale was reflected in a sharper emphasis upon the visual effect of supers. While the production employed roughly the same numbers as did Booth, all males were required to be at least six feet in height, and costumes and properties were more garish and elaborate.[92] The procession in act I, with its lictors, magistrates, captured barbarians, brawny soldiers bearing the spoils of war, trumpeters, flute players, dancing girls, standard bearers, Calphurnia borne aloft in a palanquin surrounded by attendant virgins, and a host of red- and green-garbed guards fore and aft, constituted not so much an adjunct to the dramatic action as an attraction in its own right.[93]

The six-act textual arrangement was basically Booth's; but while most of Booth's cuts were preserved, many of his restorations were not. The major alterations seem to have been made to accommodate Davenport who played the Kemble version all his life, and was not about to recast the part now. Thus the Caius Ligarius scene was once more removed, as were the lines to Lucius after the exit of the conspirators. And Brutus killed himself in the time-honoured Kemble manner with the Kemble death-speech on his lips.

The performances of Barrett and Bangs were much the same as four years earlier; and the major acting novelty proved to be the Brutus of Davenport. After years of makeshift stock appearances, his Brutus was now presented under highly favourable, if not ideal, conditions. Unfortunately, opportunity knocked so late that the brilliance of his intention sometimes exceeded the energy available for its execution. But audiences were slow to criticize. They applauded the nobility of Davenport's conception, overlooked the occasional want of energy and vocal weakness, and pronounced his Brutus one of the century's finest.[94]

At the age of 60, Davenport was a much older Brutus than most of his predecessors; but, according to Winter, his realization of the character was 'grandeur incarnate'.[95] Unlike Booth, his physique was admirably suited to the popular conception of the classic Roman. 'His figure was massive, without being ponderous', we are told. 'His head was noble ... He was unusually handsome, in the grand style. His features were regular, his eyes blue, and very eager and sweet in expression. His movements were marked by the involuntary ease that is an attribute of strength. His gestures were broad and fine.'[96] His voice in earlier years 'was copious, flexible, and, at moments of excitement, characterized by a ringing quality which was singularly affecting';[97] but by the time of the Jarrett–Palmer revival it betrayed a certain huskiness.

Davenport's acting style derived from the Kemble–Macready tradition, but was less artificial than Macready's if less natural than Booth's. His fondness for declamation recalled a more formal age, while the realism of his gestures and by-play lent his performance a remarkable modernity. Davenport's charm was of the intellectual, rather than the emotional or spiritual variety.

His deliberate approach was well adapted to the notion of Brutus he presented. His Roman had none of the twilight spirituality of Booth's tortured idealist of 38; instead, audiences found a warm, sunset portrait of a Roman patrician of late middle age, a magnanimous elder statesman, courteous, intellectually-inclined, loyal to his friends, and deeply conscious of his civic responsibility. He does what he thinks is for the best, discovers he has erred, and atones for his misjudgement with grace and courage.

On his first entrance 'the solidity and perfect mental poise which are the main constituents of *Brutus* were signified ... simply by his presence', Winter recalls. 'There was a certain melancholy abstraction in his demeanour, when listening to *Cassius*, which at once enlisted sympathy. He seemed then the authentic image of heroic virtue foredoomed to ruin.'[98] The source of his concern is revealed with the first shout of the mob, at which he 'turns, and goes up left, looking off as he says: "I do fear &c"' (M). Throughout Cassius' tirade he 'remains c with bowed head' (B), while Cassius paces feverishly. Even when Cassius 'lays his hand upon his shoulder' (M) to urge, 'Men at some time are masters of their fates' (I.ii.139), Brutus seems not to notice, engrossed in his reflections to the exclusion of all else. But Cassius' fervid 'Brutus will start a spirit as soon as Caesar' (I.ii.147) penetrates his reverie, and Brutus 'nods slightly' (M). The decision is being made.

Davenport's Brutus, although self-absorbed, remains warmly solicitous for Cassius' feelings. To assuage Cassius' concern he moves close to him, 'takes the hand of Cassius, and holds it until the end of the speech' (M) in which he explains his unaccustomed behaviour. 'Into the manner of *Brutus* toward *Cassius*', Winter remarks, 'he infused a beautiful spirit of comradeship, gentle and loving, without insipidity or any trace of ebullience.'[99] When Cassius finishes his appeal, Brutus 'Shakes Cassius' hand emphatically' (B) as he promises to consider his point of view. Brutus is not unaware, however, of the dangers inherent in Cassius' temperamental rashness. When Cassius draws Casca aside in search of information, Brutus throws 'a look of suspicion to Cas[sius]' lest he act unwisely. Later, when Cassius brashly asserts that 'we have the falling sickness', 'Brutus restrains him' (B) in case he speaks too frankly.

In this opening scene, Davenport was also at pains to establish Brutus' friendship with Caesar and Calphurnia, the strength of which intensifies further his conflict between private sentiment and public duty. When the procession entered, Brutus went up C and in a 'deferential manner ... saluted Calphurnia, and carried on a dumb-show conversation with her during the entire time that Caesar and his retinue remained upon the stage'.[100] Later, as Caesar moves off, 'Brutus comes down, and crosses him with a friendly bow' (M).

In the Garden scene Brutus was discovered 'en tableau hooded' (B), 'sitting upon a garden-seat' (M) in a darkness sporadically relieved by lightning flashes. During his 'It must be by his death' speech (II.i.10ff.), he moves about with deliberation, pausing at intervals to work out the implications of a thought. He takes the letter from Lucius and reads it 'in a calm meditative tone' (M). Although firmly in command of himself, the strain of decision-making has taken its toll. Alone for a moment as Lucius goes to answer the conspirators' knock, he 'wearily raises his hands to his head' (M) and admits, 'Since Cassius first did whet me against Caesar, / I have not slept' (II.i.61–62). Throughout the rest of the scene, Brutus undertakes with calm resolution to do what he must. At the exit of the conspirators, he 'stands left, in deep thought. Portia surprises him, coming behind him, and laying her hand upon his shoulder' (M). His concentration disrupted by his wife's reproaches, he urges her to go to bed, 'not ungently but with manifest desire to be alone' (B). Her importunity overcomes his impatience, however, and 'Just before the knocking is heard, Brutus seems to be about to tell all to Portia, but is interrupted by the knocking' (M). He 'Leads Portia to House Kissing her on forehead & she leaves him' (V). His tender concern for Portia's feelings tellingly highlights the incompatibility between Brutus' gentle nature and the callous deed he contemplates.

At Caesar's house, Brutus has little to say; but his manner towards Caesar was 'touchingly expressive of mental struggle between fervour of friendship and sense of imperative duty'.[101]

In the Assassination scene, Brutus' innate aversion to violence is confronted and momentarily overcome. As the conspirators rush upon Caesar, 'Brutus crosses left, drawing his sword, as if reluctant to take part, but resolved to do so' (M). 'As soon as Brutus has stabbed Caesar, he averts his face, raises his hands in sorrow, and goes left' (M). During Cassius' triumphant outburst he stands apart, shaken by the enormity of his act; but the horrified cries and shouts of citizens and senators recall him from self-indulgence to public obligation. Here 'he was magnificent in his stately bearing, dominant over all the elements of fear and horror, and his voice, exclaiming "People and Senators, be not affrighted", rang like a clarion'.[102]

Once the bloodshed is past, his guilt and revulsion seek relief in unconfined magnanimity. As Antony enters, he warmly extends his hand only to have it disdained. When Antony offers himself to the conspirators as a further sacrifice, 'Brutus, by gesture and facial expression, shows his horror at the idea of killing Antony' (M). Even when sorely provoked by Antony's apostrophe to Caesar, he 'holds himself in check by a determination that no harm shall befall Antony' (B). When Cassius 'rushes toward him in a fury', 'He is met and restrained by Brutus, who takes his hand and lays his left hand on Cassius' shoulder' (M). Cassius' shrewd warnings are overborne again and again by the flood-tide of Brutus' goodwill.

In the Forum Brutus exercised more of the quiet, yet potent, command he demonstrated in the Senate sequence; but by the Quarrel scene, although ever gracious and considerate, he seemed on the verge of exhaustion. Nevertheless, his self-discipline remained unshaken. On Cassius' arrival he offers his hand, and only 'slightly shrugs his shoulders' (B) when he is repulsed. Throughout the altercation Davenport's Brutus conducts himself with less wooden grandeur and more natural action and reaction than most of his predecessors. Entering the tent, 'Brutus seats himself at the council-table, facing front. He quietly takes off his helmet, and lays it upon the table, carelessly passing his hand through his hair. His whole bearing denotes calm self-possession' (M). During the first part of the quarrel, Brutus remains seated, while Cassius ramps up and down. Brutus rises, however, to demand, 'What, shall one of us ...' (IV.iii.21), and stands quietly 'right centre, partially turned away from Cassius' (M) while the latter threatens. As Brutus remarks, 'You say you are a better soldier' (IV.iii.51), he 'returns to the table, and again sits, rather wearily' (M). With singular realism, in response to Cassius' half-apologetic 'Did I say better?' (IV.iii.57), 'Brutus, still seated at the table, carelessly takes up a paper, at which he glances, as he says: "If you did &c." He expresses contempt, and weariness of the dispute' (M).

Brutus' sympathy for Cassius' wounded feelings at last transcends both anger and fatigue. As Cassius throws his dagger before Brutus and falls on his knees, 'Brutus gently lifts up dagger & places hilt of it in Cassius' hand & rises, Cassius doing same' (V). The emotive force of his lines beginning 'Be angry when you will' (IV.iii.108ff.) moved Becks to write opposite them 'How full of love & soft-kindly feeling was this speech!' A few moments later, relaxation allows his weariness and sorrow to reassert themselves; and he 'clasps his hands – raises them (fingers locked –) across his eyes – palms outward' (B) as he announces Portia's death. Just before he sits for the military conference, Cassius murmurs 'Portia, art thou gone?' (IV.iii.164) and threatens Brutus' precarious self-control; immediately 'Brutus goes to him and says with strong emotion: "No more"; then, after an instant's pause, laying his hand upon Cassius' shoulder: "I pray you"' (M). At parting, Brutus underscored their brotherly affection by 'raising his arm, and laying his hand familiarly and very emphatically upon Cassius' shoulder' (M) as he said, 'Everything is well' (IV.iii.236).

During the first bars of Lucius' music, 'Brutus paces about'; but soon he 'seats himself, meditating' (M). When Lucius falls asleep, 'He gently composes the boy's head and arms in an easy posture; lightly caresses his head; takes the gown from his own shoulders, and covers Lucius with it' (M). Davenport's 'inexpressible tenderness of manner' at this point Goddard described as 'never to be forgotten'.[103] 'In the Ghost Scene', Winter tells us, 'at "How ill this taper burns", his sense of the awe and dread that come upon *Brutus* was so completely assumed that it conveyed itself to his audience. No actor within my long observation has played that difficult scene more fitly or so as to cause a more thrilling effect.'[104] As the curtain falls, calmly prepared to face the worst, 'Brutus remains upon the stage, Lucius kneeling at his feet, and clasping him around the waist' (M).

The battle scenes, which passed unremarked in Booth's performance, were among Davenport's best. 'In the last acts, when he wears the glittering accoutrements of an ancient warrior', according to *Spirit of the Times* (1 January), 'he looked every inch a Roman hero. He might have been the statue of old Brutus himself.' Beside Cassius' body,

Brutus kneels and takes Cassius's hand . . . The line 'I shall find time, Cassius, I shall find time', is restored. As Brutus speaks that line, he rises, and goes right. Brutus stands right as the soldiers raise the body upon their shoulders. Then, as they bear it off, left, Brutus raises his hand to his lips and waves a last salute to his dead friend. Then, following the body, he lays his hand upon Cassius's head, and after going forward a few steps, he pauses, and allows his hand to drop from the head as the soldiers carry the corpse away. He stands wistfully gazing after them until they disappear. He covers his face with his hand. He is recalled to himself by Trebonius, who touches his arm, and points off, right, to the field. He starts, brushes the tears from his eyes, looks off, right, following Trebonius's gesture, and then rapidly exits, right (M).

In the final scene, Brutus and his friends are discovered upstage. Brutus moves down to ask Lucius (as in Kemble's version) to kill him. When Lucius refuses, 'Brutus does not look at Lucius, but grasps his hand, presses it earnestly, and turns away his head, so that Lucius may not see his emotion' (M). After Metellus denies his request, Brutus 'comes down to front, and stands, weeping, his face covered by his hand' (M). As he says, 'This was the justest cause that ever men / Did draw their swords for' he moves upstage towards his friends, and then abruptly turns downstage.

He stabs himself violently, raising the sword with both hands above his head. He stands for an instant, plucking the sword from his breast (the sword standing upright, as though it had entered just below the throat, being driven in from above), and casting it away from him. He then staggers, and is caught by Lucius and Metellus, who uphold him. Resting upon their shoulders, after a momentary pause, he says, in a low, languid tone, 'Caesar, now be still, &c.' His head droops upon his breast. He rests in their arms a moment, with relaxed limbs and drooping eyes. A trumpet-call sounds without and he suddenly rouses himself, springs away full of martial ardour and animation, as about to rush into battle. At the height of this action, he is seized by the death-tremor. He shudders, reels, clutches his mantle, and with one last convulsive effort throws it over his face, and falls dead in the arms of his friends, who lower the body to the ground (M).

The heroic struggle of Davenport's patriot at the moment of death when contrasted with the melancholy and passive demise of Booth's conscience-stricken philosopher discovers a pivotal point in the interpretation of the role. Davenport's patrician, albeit somewhat softened and sentimentalized, looked back on six decades of tragic grandeur; Booth's poetic idealist looked towards a new century, and its resolute, even wayward, attempts to plumb Brutus' unheroic and all-too-fallible humanity.

John McCullough (1878–84)

In the year of Davenport's death (1878), John McCullough[105] appeared as Brutus for the first time in New York. Over the next six years he perpetuated, albeit in weakened form, the Kemble–Macready–Davenport tradition. A disciple of Edwin Forrest and his frequent second on tours, McCullough had a fine physique, a robust voice, and an heroic presence as good or better than Forrest's. A memorable touch in the Assassination scene was 'the slight shudder, instantly repressed, with which Brutus shrank from touching the hand of *Caesar*, and his horror of it when he struck the fatal blow'. In the Quarrel scene 'there was suggestion of a continuous presentiment of impending calamity . . . His face was worn and haggard, exhibiting the ravages of care and sorrow.' Among his best effects were 'the bleak grief of his voice when he said "Portia is dead", and the tender, protective act of covering with his mantle the sleeping boy, *Lucius*, and, later, the tremor of apprehension, just before the entrance of the *Ghost of Caesar* – as if he were vaguely conscious of something awful at hand'.[106]

Most of McCullough's appearances took place on the road, and settings and costumes were seldom of much artistic interest.[107] An exception, however, was the first Dramatic Festival in Cincinnati in 1883 when he played Brutus to the Cassius of Lawrence Barrett and the Antony of 71-year-old James Murdoch.[108] This revival, staged in the Music Hall, accommodating about five thousand persons, was one of the most grandiose in the play's stage history. A joint effort by several theatre companies, including Barrett's and McCullough's, it featured some six hundred people on the stage, five hundred of whom were specially-recruited supers. The settings were opulent to the point of absurdity: the statue of Pompey alone cost one thousand dollars. Brutus' orchard, described by Winter as 'of great extent and weird beauty', was 'closed by a hedge of cedar shrubbery, displaying the name *Brutus*, deftly carved in the foliage'.[109] Unlike the traditional arrangement of the Quarrel scene, in which the tent occupied the whole of the stage, the Cincinnati production made it 'only a part of the picture and placed at one side. In the distance could be seen other tents of the army, and soldiers in little groups huddled about burning fires, while the noise of preparation heard in the distance made the scene startlingly realistic.'[110] The comparatively sparse Plains of Philippi settings familiar in previous productions were replaced by an elaborate tableau showing the battlefield after the fight had ended, 'a wide plain, strewn with chariot wheels, broken weapons and standards, dead men and horses; a medley of ruins; in its realism excessive; in its suggestiveness terrible to contemplate.'[111]

An attempt to emulate the effects of the Meiningen company (see chapter 7) in the Forum scene came to nothing in spite of the presence and goodwill of a multitude of supers. At rehearsal, as the plebeians 'worked with a will in vast rivalry to outdo one another in maniacal yells in response to Antony's appeals', a very worried Murdoch, accustomed to the half dozen more or less mute souls of fifty years earlier, protested, 'If you do that to-night, you will knock every line out of my head.' 'Our populace of Rome', Otis Skinner remembers, 'for Mr. Murdoch's sake, remained as passive as gate posts, receiving Antony's stinging sarcasm and the news of Caesar's munificence ... in dead silence.'[112]

With the death of McCullough in 1885, Barrett and Booth attained a virtual monopoly of *Julius Caesar* performances. Over the next few years singly and jointly, and often with poor supporting players, they took the play to every corner of the country. Probably the best road productions were provided by the Booth–Barrett tours between 1887 and 1891 when Booth appeared under Barrett's management. After Barrett's death in 1891, Booth attempted the play no more; and *Julius Caesar*'s American salad days ended. Never since has the play enjoyed such sustained popularity in the United States, nor have any pair of leading actors so closely identified themselves with its major roles. The two facts may not be unrelated.

7

The Meiningen Court Company (1881) and Beerbohm Tree (1898)

Beerbohm Tree's revival of *Julius Caesar* at Her Majesty's on 22 January 1898 triumphantly returned the play to the London stage amid salvoes of critical acclaim after more than a thirty-year absence. The public roared its approval through a run of over a hundred performances in the first season and a series of highly successful repetitions during the next eighteen years. Practically all reviewers took pains, however, to make it clear that they were lauding not a great acting revival, but a striking pictorial display. Performances were in no way comparable to those of Kemble, Macready, Phelps, or Booth and Barrett; but viewed as an exercise in spectacular realism, Tree's realization has probably never been surpassed.

The influence of theatrical precedent being stronger then than now, it seems likely that Tree cast his eye back over recent English dramatic history to learn what he could from previous revivals; and of course he found next to none. The only noteworthy performance he could have seen was by the Meiningen Court Company at Drury Lane in 1881;[1] and it was here that he found his inspiration. Before turning to details of Tree's revival, it is well to mark its salient features.

The governing principle behind Saxe-Meiningen productions was the strictest attention to ensemble. No role was supposed to dominate to the detriment of another; even the lowliest super had his contribution to make and was intensively coached to make it in the most effective manner. The advantages of this approach were particularly evident in their management of crowd scenes, an aspect of production heretofore neglected. The same minute attention paid to acting extended also to settings and costumes. Meticulous historical accuracy and utmost splendour were of the essence.

The performance was given in German in the translation of Tieck and Schlegel,[2] but how much of the text was spoken cannot be ascertained. To judge from the cast-list,[3] very little, if anything, was cut. The only character absent is the Camp Poet. The fact that Cinna the Poet and Young Cato appear would suggest that the version was fuller than the English stage had seen for almost two centuries.

The mounting of the play, 'designed especially by the Duke himself, aided by Visconti, the eminent art critic, from exact Roman studies',[4] fully lived up to expectations. 'The two different aspects of the Forum, the one with a view on the Capitol, the other with that on Mount Palatine, the interior of the Capitol, and the battle-field of Philippi' were described by *The Era* (4 June 1881) as 'triumphs of stage painting'.

Reviewers found themselves agreeably impressed with the overall acting standard, but voiced two major complaints: the subordination of the leading roles to the overall effect meant a certain mediocrity of individual performance, and the increased attention to minor roles seriously detracted from the legitimate dominance of the major ones. Nesper's Brutus and Teller's Cassius were relegated to second-class status while Antony and the crowd shamelessly usurped the limelight.

The Meiningen mob was larger than for any previous revival of the play, perhaps even the most sizeable stage crowd ever seen in London. The Duke brought with him a company of eighty, of which a fair proportion provided the nucleus of the group. To these he added 'hundreds of supernumeraries',[5] recruited and trained in London by the stage manager, Herr Chronegk. The crowd's dramatic impact was made, however, not by its size, but its function. In contrast to the inert, living scenery of Kemble's revival or the infrequently-employed supers of Macready, the Meiningen Romans were an integral part of the play, representing by meaningful and realistic activity, 'a thoroughly Shakespearean "rabblement", an entirely Roman "common herd", an entirely Italian "tag-rag people", as liable to be moved by Cicero 40 B.C. as they were by Ciceroacchio A.D. 1848'.[6] Like Macready, the Duke introduced his crowd on two occasions when their presence is uninvited by Shakespeare – during Caesar's procession to the games and at the assassination. In the latter scene their behaviour was marked by quiet dignity within a severe grouping, almost columnar in character; nevertheless, the *Saturday Review* critic found they masked the conspirators and were, in any case, out of place. 'None but senators should have seen the deed', he protested. 'Loafers, women, and children were not allowed to cover the floor of a Roman Curia.'[7]

However critics might cavil at the presence and deportment of the crowd in other scenes, none was prepared to deny its effectiveness in the Forum; but before turning to this sequence, its second component, Mark Antony, warrants some attention.

Unlike the crowd, it appears that Ludwig Barnay's Antony predominated more by accident than design. Barnay was not a regular company member, but a star in his own right, engaged especially for the London performances; consequently, it was not easy for him to subordinate his acting in the required fashion. Moreover, he was a player of considerably higher calibre than his fellows. Finally, the colourful nature of his role, and the fact that he appeared with the eye-catching crowd, tended to give him a marked advantage over the less sensational, although richer, characters of Brutus and Cassius. Whatever the underlying reasons, he received more critical attention than all of the other actors combined.

'Handsome, graceful, intelligent and a born impersonator of orators',[8] Barnay seemed to the *Queen* reviewer 'the most perfect picture of a noble Roman that it is possible to imagine'.[9] If Barnay's Antony was all of this, he was at the same time a far more complex figure than Charles Kemble's straight-line athlete and grief-stricken young noble. Here was the rising opportunist, the master diplomatist as well. When he joined the conspirators in the Capitol, Barnay's bearing 'was that of a man who knows himself in the lion's den, and is conscious that nothing but perfect tact and self-possession can save his life'.[10] Suppressed grief characterized his reading in the early moments of the scene, but rising excitement overshadowed it as his plan took shape. Barnay was, however, careful to avoid giving the impression that Antony's grief was feigned; on the contrary, the simulated sincerity displayed towards the conspirators only served to point more poignantly his emotional abandonment after their departure.

In the Forum when he joined forces with the crowd, the strongest elements in the production came together like musician and instrument. Brander Matthews, who saw the production two years later in New York, leaves us a sensitive re-creation of the scene which may be quoted *in extenso* in preference to a wider sampling from less perceptive critics. 'When Brutus has gone, Mark Antony is bidden to the rostrum', he recalls,

and a moment later he begins to speak . . . He made us believe that he did not know in the least what he was going to say, even if he had clearly in mind the goal to which he hoped to arrive; and as he spoke he conveyed the impression that he was 'making it up as he went along', that his address was spontaneous, unpremeditated, absolutely impromptu.

Those to whom he was speaking were not only hostile, they were hopelessly indifferent, broken into little groups, talking over the speech of Brutus, and caring nothing at all either for the dead Caesar or the living Antony. Scarce half a score at the foot of the rostrum were even pretending to listen to him. Therefore, Mark Antony begins by soliciting their attention:

Friends – Romans – countrymen – lend me your *ears*.

and Barnay waited until these words had enticed a group or two to break off their chatter and to draw nearer to the rostrum. His praise of Caesar was deprecatory and his praise of Brutus not yet ironical. His manner was modest, not to call it timorous; and it slowly began to win more and more of the mob to hear what he had to say. At the end of every sentence, Barnay paused to let his meaning sink in; and his glance searched for one little knot of men after another who might be attracted by the appeal of his voice and his eye. In time the murmur was vanquished, and the throng slowly compacted itself about the rostrum . . .

When Mark Antony pretended that he did not mean to read the will, Barnay thrust back the parchment into his bosom. He had awakened the curiosity of his listeners and he had aroused their sympathy. He adroitly tested the extent of his conquest over their passions by the frankly ironic suggestion,

> I fear I wrong the honorable men
> Whose daggers have stabbed Caesar.

The outcries of the excited citizens assured him of his victory; and then he yielded to their clamor for the will. Thereafter he held the mob in the hollow of his hand, swaying it to his purpose . . . . The words poured from him, fiery, burning, heated by his overmastering emotion, and always, as they tumbled after one another they seemed unstudied, indisputably spontaneous, born of the passion of the moment.[11]

Here, then, was the attainment of the goal towards which Macready had taken the first tentative steps forty years earlier. With the Meiningen performance the scene established itself as a naturalistic study in demagoguery calling for co-ordinated performance between orator and mob, with the latter no less essential than, although subservient to, the former.

The pity was that the Meininger made their valid point too strongly; and the play reached its climax at the halfway mark. The final scenes were left to limp to a conclusion as best they could. With this shift in emphasis vanished the longstanding popularity of Brutus and Cassius and the perennial charm of their quarrel. The critical neglect they suffered was but the beginning of two decades of disfavour. Antony's star was in the ascendant.

Tree left the Meiningen production impressed with *Caesar*'s adaptability to spectacular settings, confident that Antony, supported by a well-trained mob, could be the starring role, and convinced that the second half of the play was anti-climactic. The influence of these views on his production was to be profound.

If modern audiences were to be impressed by Shakespeare as Tree felt they should be, the desired result could only be obtained by presenting him in a production style with which they were familiar. Theatre-goers had come to expect a very high standard of scenic realism in contemporary plays, and would tolerate nothing less in Shakespeare. Surely it would be 'better to draw multitudes by doing Shakespeare in the way the public prefers than to keep the theatre empty by only presenting him "adequately"'.[12] Of course, argue as he might that scenery did not distract from, but in fact enhanced, the plays, Tree could not deny that its lavish use prevented him from playing the poet's full text. In justification he argued from the *Hamlet* quartos that the plays were probably cut in Shakespeare's own time, and must be even more drastically curtailed in ours to suit altered theatre conditions.

In the reconstruction of Tree's *Caesar* we are much aided, if somewhat overwhelmed, by the wealth of documentation available in the Beerbohm

Tree Collection.[13] Included are the rehearsal-book, signed by Arthur Coe
(*JC* 56), and replete with stage directions, maps, and sketches, a similar
book, signed by Alfred Wigley (*JC* 57), costume, super, and property
plots, and a special printed super plot for the management of the Forum
scene (*JC* 63). The most useful item for our purposes, however, is a very
full promptbook, signed also by Arthur Coe (*JC* 58), which, when supplemented by a second, bound in white vellum and containing printed
sketches of all the scenes (*JC* 59), and Coe's stage manager's book (*JC* 60),
offers almost as complete a picture of the production as we could wish.

   Like his predecessors, Tree found himself unhappy with the large
number of speaking parts, and reduced them by fifteen, Lepidus, Cicero,
Cinna the Poet, the Camp Poet, and young Cato were eliminated and their
lines cut. A further reduction of three was effected by reallocating the
speeches of Flavius and Marullus to Trebonius and Metellus respectively,
and those of Artemidorus to the Soothsayer. Titinius and Messala also
vanished. In the conference sequence (IV.iii) and Cassius' death scene (V.iii)
they are replaced by Metellus and Trebonius. Elsewhere their speeches are
cut. Lucilius likewise disappears, together with most of his lines, save for
those previous to Cassius' entry at IV.ii which are taken by Metellus.
Volumnius, Clitus, Strato, and Dardanius no longer companion Brutus'
final moments; Trebonius, Claudius, and Metellus replace them, and Trebonius speaks the few lines retained.

   From the era of Charles Kean onwards, it was an accepted principle in the
theatre that whenever Shakespeare was staged, his texts must be played in
their purity, free from interpolations and re-writings. At the same time,
however, the vogue for realistic presentation gave rise to depredations of a
different kind; and while indeed managers presented the Bard unimproved,
they were obliged to offer far less of him than formerly to accommodate the
scene-shifters.[14] The choice of what was to be cut, and how much, was
largely determined by the nature of Tree's own role. Had he chosen to play
Brutus rather than Antony, he might have cut a similar amount, but he
would have cut differently.

   Fifty years earlier Tree would have appropriated Brutus without question; but the Meiningen performance had altered both critical opinion and
public taste. The character of Antony and the situation in which he found
himself drew him irresistibly. 'For the scholar Brutus, for the actor Cassius,
for the public Antony', he scribbled revealingly in his notebook.[15] Again, he
wrote to his wife in the summer of 1896, 'I like Brutus best – he is so much
deeper – but I still feel that Antony has the colour – the glamour of the play,
don't you?'[16] Where Barnay triumphed by sheer superior ability, Tree
usurped precedence by cutting and rearrangement of text.

   His first task was to render Antony's character more palatable to the tastes
of the contemporary play-goer. For Antony to be something of a *bon viveur*

was permissible, but to be a liar and a ruthless opportunist was quite another matter. In order to clear him of the charge of untruthfulness, Tree excised Antony's purely tactical promise to 'follow / The fortunes and affairs of noble Brutus / Thorough the hazards of this untrod state, / With all true faith' (III.i.134–7). Needless to say, the entire Proscription scene (IV.i.) had also to be omitted. Finally, he blue-pencilled three of Brutus' death lines:

> I shall have glory by this losing day
> More than Octavius and Mark Antony
> By this vile conquest shall attain unto. (V.v.36–8)

in order to avoid any denigration of the hero-role so near the end of the play.

But even with a vastly improved character, Antony could hardly dominate the play as it stood. Clearly, the Assassination and Forum scenes must be heightened to become the focal point of the action. Tree well realized, however, that if the Forum sequence were staged in spectacular fashion, as it must be if Antony is to emerge as the dominant personality, the tragedy would reach its climax at this point; moreover, to have the star off the stage for the better part of two whole acts was unthinkable. The obvious solution would have been to cut the final acts altogether; but this Tree hardly dared do. He arrived instead at a compromise where he included only as much as was necessary to tie up the loose ends of the plot – the quarrel, the confrontation of the rival armies, and the deaths of Brutus and Cassius – thus hurrying the play to its close while Antony's impact was still fresh. The Cinna the Poet scene (III.iii) was excised altogether and the Tent sequence (IV.ii) severely abridged. In the latter episode the entire discussion among Lucilius, Pindarus, and Brutus concerning Cassius' untoward behaviour (IV.ii.4–29) is omitted, and Cassius enters for the quarrel almost at the rise of the curtain. The quarrel itself is left untouched, but the conversation between Brutus and Messala regarding the contents of their letters and the second announcement of Portia's death (IV.iii.166–95) are removed.

The Confrontation scene (V.i) is played in its entirety so long as Antony is on the stage, but after his departure, Brutus and Cassius are hurried out of the limelight with just time to make their farewells. The whole of Cassius' birthday speech (V.i.69–92) is omitted. Again, as in the Kemble version, the 'Ride, ride, Messala' episode is cut.

Scene iii of act V escapes relatively unscathed until Cassius' death, but undergoes drastic abridgement afterwards. The sequence in which Trebonius and Metellus (Shakespeare – Titinius and Messala) discover Cassius' body is reduced from forty lines to ten. Titinius' lament and Messala's apostrophe to Error disappear. Trebonius' (Shakespeare–Titinius) speech after the exit of Messala is shortened by nine lines: he neither crowns Cassius nor takes his own life. Brutus' eulogy is left intact, but much of the remainder of the scene (V.iii.92–3, 96–7, 106–9) is cut.

To permit the action to move directly from the death of Cassius to the demise of Brutus, the whole of v.iv (thirty-two lines) in which young Cato dies and Lucilius is captured, is deleted. In Tree's version, Brutus has hardly issued the instructions for Cassius' burial when he returns to die himself.

From Brutus' death scene (v.v) all the preliminaries (v.v.2–14), in which he asks Clitus and Dardanius to kill him, disappear. He enters with 'Come, poor remains of friends, rest on this rock', and calls Trebonius (Shakespeare–Volumnius) to him immediately. He makes no mention of the visits of Caesar's ghost, but proceeds straightway to his 'ill request'. When Trebonius refuses, Brutus takes his own life, without, however, speaking the interpolated Kemble death-speech. No sooner has Brutus fallen than Antony arrives and speaks the eulogy with which Tree concludes the play.

Most of Tree's deletions prior to the Forum scene, except for a few propriety-cuts, were designed to quicken the pace. The entire colloquy between Cicero and Casca (i.iii.1–40) is removed, as is the discussion between Casca and Cassius about the significance of the omens (i.iii.46–71) and the incident in which Cassius gives the papers to Cinna (i.iii.131–52). From the Garden scene, Tree removes fifteen lines of Brutus' rejection of the oath (ii.i.126–40) and the exclusion of Cicero as a conspirator (ii.i.141–53).

The Street scenes (ii.iii. iv) are both curtailed and revised. Sixteen lines of Portia's conversation with the Soothsayer (ii.iv.21–3, 25–38) are omitted. Her 'I must go in' speech (ii.iv.39–46) is transposed to come after Lucius' 'Sooth, madam, I hear nothing' (ii.iv.20), while the Soothsayer (Shakespeare–Artemidorus) reads his paper after Portia's exit rather than before her arrival. As in Booth's text, the citizens in i.i exit on 'That needs must light on this ingratitude', and in the Forum scene the curtain falls on Antony's triumphant 'Mischief, thou art afoot, / Take thou what course thou wilt!'

The text, now some five hundred and fifty lines lighter, he divided into three acts which might be titled Antony Introduced, Antony Contriving, and Antony Triumphant. The first long act embraced everything up to and including the death of Caesar. The second comprised only the Forum sequence, much expanded by extra-Shakespearian business. The third consisted of the surviving disjointed incidents of the last two acts – the Quarrel scene, the confrontation of the opposing armies, and the deaths of Brutus and Cassius. At the end of each act, Antony had a tableau curtain to himself – Antony breathing vengeance in act I, Antony grimly exultant in act II, and Antony victorious beside the dead Brutus in act III.

Before leaving the text, a brief word must be said about Tree's scenic division within the acts. By eliminating the Cinna the Poet scene, Antony's

House, the 'Ride, ride, Messala' sequence, and the capture of Lucilius, Tree decreased the number initially by four. He then staged the modern I.i, I.ii, and I.iii all in the 'Public Place' setting, compressed II.iii and II.iv into one street scene, played IV.ii and IV.iii in a continuous Tent setting, and ran the remaining three scenes of act V into one. His scene-plan then stood as follows:

Act I

Scene 1	A Public Place	Scene 2	Brutus' Orchard
Scene 3	Caesar's House	Scene 4	A Public Street
Scene 5	The Senate House		

Act II
The Forum

Act III

| Scene 1 | Brutus' Tent, near Sardis | Scene 2 | The Plains of Philippi |

Stagecraft

Tree's decision to revive *Julius Caesar* was born of a conviction that the play was particularly susceptible to realistic treatment. Rome, he contended, was an integral part of the play, and as such must be convincingly presented. 'At Her Majesty's', a 1898 Souvenir Programme note informs us, 'it is not the historic band of conspirators that strikes the key note of the play. It is not even the mighty figure of *Caesar* treacherously brought low. It is the feverish pulsing life of the imperial city.'

The re-creation was entrusted to the eminent Academic painter, Lawrence Alma-Tadema.[17] Throughout most of the play his Republican settings were eminently accurate, but in the Public Place and Forum scenes his love of the ornate took precedence over strict archaeology. The result was that certain buildings belonged architecturally to the period of the Emperors, bearing evidence of 'those Greek and Eastern ornamentations which so decisively transformed it [Rome] when "the Orontes flowed into the Tiber"'.[18] When chided by critics for sacrificing historical truth to picturesqueness, the theatre issued an official apologia for Alma-Tadema's design in which it contended that the pieces of Eastern-style architecture, although admittedly anachronistic, in no way violated the luxury-loving spirit of Julian Rome; indeed, the Eastern influence was felt in Roman manners, if not in architecture, long before the death of Caesar.

The exquisite grace of Alma-Tadema's costumes may be readily appreciated by an examination of the accompanying plates. The conspirators and senators all wore crimson robes and white woollen togas with crimson borders, suggestive of affluence without ostentation. Caesar's costume, on the other hand, was a robe of 'claret-red silk, shot with violet', over which went a 'long, winding cloak ... of vivid amethyst-hued brocade'.

Mark Antony was swathed in soft silk of two shades of red which he modified slightly in the Forum scene by adding a scarf of black crepe twisted about the shoulders. The plebeians' costumes were all in period, but of less delicate materials than those of the principals. Calphurnia wore a 'clinging gown of pale electric blue "soie ondulée"' with 'rich drapery . . . of sapphire blue, brocaded with upright clusters of gold lilies, rather after the Morris style';[19] while Portia appeared 'clad from head to foot in pearly white draperies of some soft, cloudy substance', with the only spot of colour in her costume 'a rare old turquoise and silver clasp, with a pendant attached to it, worn on the left breast'.[20] Morris, himself, could hardly have done better.

Act I, scene i

A Public Place

To music composed by Raymond Roze the curtain went up on the first act to reveal the Public Place setting. 'Temple and palace, street and forum were revealed aglow with Italian colour . . . .' we are told. 'It was the forum of Julius with the Temple of Venus Genetrix seen through a vast arch of triumph spanning the front of the stage . . . In the centre of the Forum stood a bronze statue of Caesar "decked with ceremony" and flanked by trees. In the background the roof of the Temple of Jupiter Capitolinus rose against the sky.'[21] One needs only add that almost the whole of the setting was built on a raised platform reached by a flight of steps. To the left of the platform, well downstage, was placed a fountain, and at centre stage were two curved seats facing each other.

Everywhere are clusters of 'laughing and talking' citizens. At centre-stage a group of girls dance to the music of a blind piper who stands L by the fountain, surrounded by small boys at play. To the right of centre-stage, near the seat, more children are diverting themselves. Cone-sellers and fruit-sellers move through the crowds plying their wares. At RIE a girl enters with a pitcher which she fills at the fountain. '4 Runners' enter LIE, run quickly up C, and exit LUE to the fervid applause of the onlookers. Twelve lictors march on from RIE and exit LUE, the citizens making way for them as they pass. Finally, a 'Patrician lady with child (boy), and negro servant following her, enters RUE, and crosses down C to exit LIE.' Tree envisioned 'a generally bright and lively scene'.

'There is a constant noise of murmurs, applause, etc.; when the noise is at its height, enter Trebonius and Metullus.' Just before they come on, however, another touch of realism is added as 'Two boys [are] sent off LIE by citizen who cuffs them as they pass.' From RUE Trebonius bursts upon the revellers with 'Hence! home, you idle creatures'; the 'citizens turn to look at him and murmurs die down'. The pair then begins to move about the crowd, pausing now to demand of the carpenter, 'Speak, what trade art thou?' and again of the cobbler, 'You, sir, what trade are you?' On the cobbler's 'we make holiday to see Caesar, and to rejoice in his triumph', the citizens break into loud cries of 'Ave Caesar' and 'Caesar'. 'General cheering and movement' continue 'until Metellus stops it with gesture of hand and commences to speak' his 'Wherefore rejoice?' lines. He now stands on one of the seats at c, and the 'Cits surround seat & listen' with interest. As he asks, 'Knew you not Pompey?' the 'Citizens repeat "Pompey", and whisper'. On 'That needs must light on this ingratitude', the shamefaced merrymakers 'exit slowly and silently' RUE and LUE. Briefly, now, the holiday mood is broken. Metellus exits R I E and Trebonius, RUE, the latter 'Tearing garlands from house R' as he goes. A neat touch of realism has 'Trebonius about to tear garlands off statue c when he hears music and shouts of approaching procession', and quickly exits.

The procession now enters LUE replete with senators, patricians, patrician's wives and children, and runners. 'Great excitement' is called for at this point, with the 'Citizens cheering and crying, "Ave Caesar", etc.' as Caesar himself appears.

Casca carries a wand and acts as Caesar's spokesman. When Caesar reaches c, he calls, 'Calphurnia', and motions to Casca as he does so. The latter with 'back to audience', holds up his wand for silence, and 'All shouts and murmurs stop'. After the instructions to Antony, as Caesar is about to exit, the Soothsayer, from the 'Base of Statue c', warns, 'Beware the Ides of March', at which the 'Cits whisper'. Once the Soothsayer has been curtly dismissed, Caesar 'x's to R', and, as he passes, a patrician lady 'at window R throws rose leaves [petals] which fall at Caesar's feet (they are red)'. Caesar 'starts Then looks round at soothsayer & Exits followed by Antony, ladies & others'. The Soothsayer stands for a moment on the steps of the platform watching the procession depart, 'raises his hands as tho' invoking the Gods', and exits LUE.

It is difficult to deny the dramatic effectiveness of Tree's stagecraft. The first moments establish the Roman locale and introduce the Roman people who figure so largely later, while the pageantry accentuates the grandeur of Rome incarnate in Caesar. At the end of the sequence, triumphal enthusiasm yields to sombre foreboding as the blood-red petals flutter downwards and the Soothsayer's hands rise in supplication.

The Brutus–Cassius conversation proceeds unremarkably; and Caesar's procession re-enters. As the boys appear RIE, 'Brutus moves up to R of statue c standing there.' The 'Cits & plebeian women' next arrive accompanied by

Antony laughing & talking with women followed by slave with cloak. They x L to fountain – Antony drinks laughingly toasting Cassius – who stands c watching him. One woman takes cloak from slave & puts it on Antony's shoulders.

Antony now begins to make his presence felt. Without a word spoken, his popularity with the people, and with women in particular, is pointed; and the striking juxtaposition with the sour and conniving Cassius is noted.

Caesar enters and 'Xs C looking at Cassius (C)' as he does so. Cassius bows and 'Xs slowly in front of Caesar to R'. Caesar stands for a moment, looking after him with distrust. When commanded to 'Come on my right hand', 'Antony stands L of Caesar who turns back to audience, so that Antony speaks in his R ear – They both turn and look at Cassius then laugh.' The business is repeated as they go up the steps to exit. Antony has changed Caesar's view of Cassius; no longer is he a menace, but merely an object of scorn. Cassius' dislike of Antony is clearly not unjustified.

The Brutus–Cassius–Casca colloquy is treated naturalistically – Casca even takes time to drink at the fountain on one occasion – but little else calls for notice.

The Storm episode is played in the same setting. The curtain is simply lowered and raised to mark the passage of time and the stage is darkened. Buffeted by a spectacular tempest, 'Cits X stage R to L – L to R – running – shouting – women screaming then pause.' After a moment Cassius appears on the platform, braving the elements; and the ensuing action takes place straightforwardly.

Act I, scene ii

Brutus' Orchard

At the rear of the stage was placed a backing, depicting 'a lovely glimpse of garden', fronted by a 'Gawsed cut cloth' suggestive of 'the end of a pillared court'. On the right of the cut cloth stood a 'Stage wing', and to the left, a 'Wood wing'. At centre stage was a 'Stone seat' before which hung a 'Frame Cloth'. Between the frame cloth and the proscenium were placed four tiger-skin rugs, two on either side of the stage. Over the whole hung 'a dark blue canopy and twinkling stars'.[22]

As the curtain rises, Brutus enters L2E and crosses to R and then C in considerable agitation. From C he calls Lucius. After Lucius' exit, he begins his 'It must be by his death' speech, sitting on the stone bench at C. According to Simpson, however, 'he rose as he continued it and leaned meditatively against a pillar'.[23] A few moments later the conspirators enter R2E with Cassius at their head. Perhaps the most interesting feature of this section is Tree's attempt to contrast the temperamental mildness of Brutus with the violence of the rest. Cassius' demand for radical bloodletting is greeted with enthusiastic support, while Brutus' appeals for restraint are met with significant silence. When the clock strikes, 'Luc enters R1E and lays down on rugs R' as the conspirators prepare to leave.

A moment before Cassius' departure, Portia 'enters LIE and sees Br. & Cas.' and 'hesitates'. 'Then as Cas. exits', she 'xs quickly up to behind seat C'. Brutus moves downstage to where the sleeping Lucius lies, and Portia, who has been listening, advances from behind the seat to inquire the source of her husband's anxiety. Throughout their encounter, Brutus moves about in agitation, now approaching Portia with affection, now repulsing her, fearing to reveal what he knows.

Ligarius enters RIE, supported by Lucius. On his 'Boy, stand aside', Brutus 'takes Caius from Lucius and leads him to seat. Caius sits'. When Caius asserts, 'I here discard my sickness', he rises, rashly 'Throwing down stick' as he does so; but before their exit Brutus tactfully 'picks up stick' and returns it to him. The scene ends with one of Tree's familiar mimed sequences. As Brutus thoughtlessly says, 'Follow me then', 'Caius attempts to follow but after a step or two falters.' Brutus then 'moves back' and 'takes his arm as they move R' while the curtain falls.

Act I, scene iii

Caesar's House

The luxury of Caesar's House contrasted sharply with the severe simplicity of Brutus' Orchard. Here Alma-Tadema provided 'a gorgeous restoration of a Roman atrium' where 'Garlanded busts of the Hermes type (carved heads on square pedestals) stood against the pillared walls'. 'In the centre was the impluvium or basin below the opening in the pannelled ceiling which served as a smoke-vent and drained off the rain-water from the roof', and beyond could be seen 'the trinclinium or dining room, and the peristyle or pillared court'.[24]

At the beginning of the scene Caesar enters LIE, calls the servant, and dispatches him to the augurers. A moment later Calphurnia joins him. In the action which follows, Calphurnia assumes a prominence far greater than she received in previous productions, and considerably more than the text warrants. No longer is she merely Caesar's wife, but almost a tragic character in her own right – a Cassandra-like figure who clearly foresees approaching disaster, but is powerless to prevent it. Throughout the scene she engages in a constant flow of business, calling attention to herself at Caesar's expense.

When the servant announces that the augurers 'could not find a heart within the beast', Calphurnia exclaims aloud. In an agony of concern she kneels to her husband on 'Let me, upon my knee prevail'; and when Caesar grants her request, she 'kisses Cae robe' in grateful relief. With the entry of Decius, however, she instinctively senses approaching danger, and moves protectively to the back of Caesar's chair. She is far less convinced by

Decius' explanation than is her husband, and indicates her dissent at intervals throughout his speech. When Decius challenges, 'If Caesar hide himself, shall they not whisper, / "Lo, Caesar is afraid"?' she 'turns and looks at Dec' with growing suspicion. When, to her horror, Caesar demands his robe, Calphurnia 'kneels protesting', but to no avail. For the remainder of the scene she sits in the chair at LC, a terrified witness to her husband's folly. As Antony enters RIE he 'removes hood of toga and takes Cae hand' and then 'xs to behind chair LC and speaks to Calp', apparently to reassure her. The party now moves off into the house; Brutus, however, touched by remorse at the warmth of Caesar's greeting, remains behind. His 'That every like' lines are spoken well down R. As Caesar is about to exit, he turns round and sees Brutus standing alone. 'Caesar holds out his hand to him', and Brutus moves upstage. Caesar then places his 'R hand on Br. L shoulder' and they exit together. Calphurnia is left 'sitting on chair LC' and 'looking into auditorium', alone now with her fears. Tree allows for a pause; then music begins as the curtain falls.

Act I, scene iv

A Public Street

Unlike the sliding shutters of previous productions, the 'Public Street' of Tree's revival was a full set-scene. In the foreground were 'Pillared buildings'; 'then a row of shops with lowered sun-blinds led to a distant archway with Ionic pilasters and massive entablature. Across the street ran a line of those curious stepping-stones still to be seen at Pompeii, to enable passengers to cross in bad weather.'[25]

Portia, accompanied by Lucius, enters immediately from LIE. On 'O, I grow faint', she 'catches Luc. hand swaying then slowly recovers'. Little need detain us until a flourish in the orchestra heralds the approach of Caesar – the first time he had processed to the Capitol since the eighteenth century. First enter '12 Lictors in double file', followed by Casca, Caesar, Cassius and Decius Brutus, Trebonius, Caius Ligarius, Publius, and '4 or 5 super senators'. They slowly make their way from LIE to RIE.

When Caesar is about to exit, he catches sight of the Soothsayer and reminds him that 'The ides of March are come.' The latter moves up to Caesar holding out 'a scrip'; but at the same moment Decius presents one as well. 'Cae stretches out his hand as though to take parchment of Sooth then alters his mind and takes the scrip Decius holds out.' The Soothsayer, in desperation, 'turns and makes imploring gesture to Cae. – with his L hand out behind him'. Cassius seizes the outstretched hand and 'swings Sooth round to LC' as he says, 'What, urge you your petitions in the street?' When Caesar has gone, the Soothsayer, alone now, once more 'lifts his arms as though to the Gods' as the curtain falls.

Act I, scene v

The Senate House

The visual splendour of Alma-Tadema's Senate House may be appreciated
from the accompanying photograph (Illustration 10). The rigid symmetry
of the setting, derived from Kemble and Macready, is the very antithesis of
Booth's studiedly informal composition. The scene opens with the senators
seated, engaged in casual conversation as they await the arrival of Caesar.
The Roman people, who disturbed critics at the Jarrett–Palmer and
Meiningen revivals, are excluded.

To a flourish of trumpets in the orchestra, twelve lictors enter RIE in
double file and arrange themselves on either side of the stage. Caesar himself
then enters, in company with Brutus, Cassius, and Casca, crosses to the seat
at C, and sits. Casca, who stands down R with Brutus and Cassius, 'signals
Lictors to Exit, by raising wand'. Caesar then beckons Antony who ascends
the steps and stands on Caesar's left. Popilius now approaches Cassius, who
is invoking the statue of Pompey, and wishes success to his enterprise.
Meanwhile Antony is seen 'talking to senators – taking a scrip and laughing
etc'. Once more Antony's essentially amiable nature, his closeness to
Caesar, and his popularity with his colleagues is underlined. Trebonius now
takes Antony's arm and leads him toward LC, whispering in his ear as they
go. 'They stop and both laugh slightly' before they exit LC.

On Cassius' 'Casca, you are the first that rears your hand', 'Casca gets
up R onto platform and stands behind Caesar' while Cassius moves to
Caesar's left on floor level. Metellus presents his suit, kneeling on the steps
leading to Caesar's state chair; and one by one conspirators and super
senators kneel in his support. At the appropriate moment, Casca stabs
Caesar from behind.

When Casca stabs Caesar rises – all consp. and senators rise. The consp. all close
round Cae – and stab him. Br. alone standing down LC Caesar forces his way through
Consp. – and falls on one knee then rises with difficulty and goes to Br with arms out
– Br stabs him. While the consp. stab Cae they cry 'Kill Kill' etc – other senators give
cries of horror & terror – which cease when Cae falls on one knee.

When Caesar falls (down RC by Pompey's statue), the direction instructs the
actors to 'count six' to allow for a picture effect. Casca then cries 'Liberty!'
from Caesar's seat, whereupon 'all senators who are not consp. exit RC & LC
respectively with cries of terror'.

Moments later Brutus calls for the ceremonial hand-washing, and the
'Consp stoop round the body'. As Cassius rises on 'The men that gave their
country liberty', he 'raises sword' and 'All consp. raise swords to a "bush"
and repeat "Liberty"'. Then, on 'Brutus shall lead', the power-drunk
assassins rush toward the LC entrance with 'Br. leading them'. At this

10. The Assassination of Caesar (III.i). Herbert Beerbohm Tree's production at Her Majesty's Theatre, 1898. Designed by Sir Lawrence Alma-Tadema

moment Antony's servant confronts them at LC, and Brutus returns to C to hear him. After his exit, the conspirators and sympathetic senators gather close round Brutus to await the arrival of Antony.

Two important points emerge from the conduct of the scene thus far: first, that the assassination and hand-washing episodes are staged quickly, so quickly in fact as to be almost underplayed, and, second, that the brutal side of the conspirators' behaviour is distinctly emphasized – witness the boorish rush for the exit before the entry of Antony's servant. Consequently, the emotional response evoked is quite the reverse of that prompted by the dignified handling of the Kemble and Macready revivals. Caesar's death becomes not so much a sacrifice to the cause of liberty as an act of sadistic butchery. Tree's motives are not difficult to understand; he wants to get Antony back on stage with utmost rapidity, and to throw his future action into as favourable a light as possible. With his re-appearance, the scene moves much more deliberately.

Antony now enters quickly LC, then 'stands (with hood over his head) holding curtains of opening behind him'. At this point Tree calls for a 'picture' to accentuate the turn in the action. Antony folds his arms, pauses once more, and slowly descends the steps to the body, 'looking through' the conspirators, who cross immediately to R. On 'O mighty Caesar!' he stretches his arms out to the corpse in high tragic fashion, and at 'Fare thee well' covers Caesar's face with the mantle. A pause ensues before he turns his attention to the conspirators.

At the end of his appeal for death, Brutus comes to him at LC to urge, 'O Antony, beg not your death of us.' Throughout Brutus' apology Antony 'looks at audience motionless', and at the end of Brutus' appeal there is another pause. Cassius then approaches to promise him a voice in 'the disposing of new dignities'; but his overture meets with no response. Antony merely 'looks at him and folds his arms' while another pause ensues. Antony attempts to gain the upper hand by simple impassivity, using his silence to place the conspirators on the defensive, to oblige them to cajole and concede.

To Brutus he speaks, 'I doubt not of your wisdom', and gives him his right hand. To Cassius he offers his left, and as he withdraws it he looks at the blood upon it. On 'my valiant Casca, yours', 'Cas[ca] starts X to Antony LC looks him in face and smears his arm with blood then shakes hands.' On 'Gentlemen all', Antony moves down RC, 'smells blood on his hands', and makes 'a gesture of revenge'. The brutality of the conspirators could hardly be more strongly emphasized.

Antony now begins his 'That I did love thee, Caesar' speech, successively raising his eyes, touching the body, and bowing his head 'as though overcome by emotion' in a desperate effort to arouse Brutus' sympathies. When Cassius interrupts him, Antony rises and approaches Brutus to make his request. Brutus' agreement causes a 'General movement of consp'. As Cassius says, 'Brutus, a word with you', he 'steps over body and Xs to Br L' – another act of callousness which is not lost on Antony who makes a 'mov. of anger'. When the conspirators exit, all of Cassius' pent-up resentment and suspicion of Antony break loose in an elaborate bit of mime. On Brutus' 'Prepare the body then, and follow us' comes a piece of business used by Barrett but no doubt derived from an earlier source.

Consp. mov. up to and exit at LC murmuring among themselves. Cas makes mov. to Br. expressing desire to kill Ant. Br. by gesture refuses. Cas moves up LC followed by Br. Cas suddenly turns and moves quickly toward Ant with drawn sword – as if about to kill him. Br. seizes him by the arm – and points off LC.

When Brutus, who exits last, is in the doorway LC, he raises his sword and shouts, 'Peace, Freedom & Liberty'. All the conspirators, who are now off L, take up the cry. As their shouts are dying, 'Ant throws himself on body', then raising himself 'on one knee', he 'uncovers Caesar's face'. Putting his 'L hand on Cae hand which is on his breast', he begins his 'O pardon me' speech. His imprecation beginning 'A curse shall light' is delivered directly to the audience.

The servant now enters LIE, crosses to LC, and kneels. 'Ant. rushes on servant with "murder" in face. Then with gesture across eyes recovers himself.' As Antony says, 'Here is a mourning Rome', the murmurs of the angry populace are heard. On 'Hie hence, and tell him so', Antony 'hears horn' offstage, and a 'look of possibility comes over his face'. The horn sounds a second time; and Antony, 'with gesture and look of revenge', comes to the head of the body RC for 'Lend me your hand'.

The servant 'xs to below body' to assist him, and as he does so 'Calp. enters LC gets slowly down to feet of body and kneels'; then, as 'Ant & serv. lean over body to raise it', she extends both arms to heaven in an abandon of grief. Tree orders a slow curtain which catches two tableaux – 'ist. Picture. Ant raises Cae head. 2nd. Ant & serv. half raise body.'

To comment at length upon Tree's slanted emotionalism would be to labour the obvious. The scene is indisputably Antony's. The avenger of callous murder we have seen before; the champion of the widow is a novel, even unique, variant.

Act II

The Forum

The Forum scene, the most elaborate of the production, featured massive reconstructions of the Temple of Saturn, the Temple of Jupiter, and the Temple of Concord. In front of the latter, at stage left, stood the all-important rostrum and gallery. Adding to the visual impressiveness was a crowd of some two hundred and fifty supers, all attired in multi-coloured costumes. According to Simpson, 'The towering height of the buildings and the vast surging crowd gave the impression of enormous space.'[26]

As the curtain rises, groups of citizens are discovered about the stage 'angrily discussing'. Six guards enter and 'clear space for Brutus R & L'. As Cassius leads off some of the citizens LIE, Brutus ascends the rostrum, leaving Casca and seven senators lingering about the base. Throughout Brutus' speech the crowd is constantly active in the Meiningen manner – repeating significant words of Brutus' address, standing in 'Dead Silence', pausing, 'growl [ing] slightly', or demonstrating 'general approval'. On the whole, however, the mob-handling for Brutus' oration is not nearly so carefully contrived as for Antony's; clearly Tree was bent on avoiding any possibility of anti-climax.

As Brutus says, 'his death is enrolled in the Capitol', a 'Distant horn' sounds; and shortly after, Caesar's cortège enters. Approbation for Brutus' speech is abruptly succeeded by a moment of 'Dead silence, while bearers put body in front of rostrum.' 'Two Distant Horns' are heard. Antony remains at the head of the body for a moment before moving 'to base of rostrum' where he stands 'looking at cits'. Meanwhile, Brutus continues his appeal to the people to remain for Antony's speech, and descends amid wild enthusiasm.

While Brutus remained, the crowd's respect for him forbade any display of their real feelings toward Antony; but as Brutus disappears, they begin to 'hiss & hoot' Antony, keeping up a noisy discussion which makes speech impossible. The First Citizen 'raises sledge hammer as though about to strike Ant. Ant walks up to him and looks at him. 1st Cit. shrinks away L.' Unable to see any hope of gaining a hearing, 'Antony looks at cits with despair'; but at this moment a 'Woman xs from R down stage', one of those who appeared with Antony in the first scene. He approaches her, urges her by gesture to influence the populace on his behalf, then half-pushes her toward the group of citizens at RC. He repeats the business with another woman who is crossing from R, and propels her toward the plebeians at L. The first woman persuades the Second Citizen to listen, and then mingles with others. At last, over the angry muttering, a few cries of 'We'll hear him' are heard. Antony seizes the opportunity to say, 'For Brutus' sake, I am beholding to you', and begins to move toward the rostrum. As he passes, 'A woman laughs at him'; and when the Third Citizen parrots, 'He finds himself beholden', all join in derisive murmurs and laughter. While they are thus occupied, Antony mounts the rostrum, goes to a 'chalice of incense', and 'lifts arms as though in prayer'. He then turns to say, 'You gentle Romans', but cannot make himself heard above the uproar. He tries again, speaking 'Friends' to the citizens down L, 'Romans' to those up R, 'Countrymen' to those down R, and 'lend me your ears' in the direction of the audience. He then pauses abruptly 'With commanding gesture – arms out' and 'orders as it were, silence'. A 'DEAD SILENCE' ensues. Leaning forward to 'cits at base of rostrum' he assures them, 'I come to bury Caesar, not to praise him'. A 'slight murmur' follows. During the next few lines, the plebeians who left with Brutus 'slowly straggle on'; and with their return, Antony proceeds to business.

It is worth noting at this point that even at the risk of slowing the scene intolerably, Tree takes infinite pains to render Antony's task as difficult as possible in order to render his ultimate triumph the greater.

To Antony's assertion, 'The noble Brutus / Hath told you Caesar was ambitious', the citizens reply, 'Ay Brutus said he – was ambitious.' 'If it were so, it was a grievous fault', continues Antony, 'soothing cits with gesture' to forestall an outburst at his 'If'. He puts the first 'For Brutus is an honourable man' as a straightforward statement, at which 'Omnes FF murmur "Ay" "He is" "True, True."' He speaks 'So are they all' in a soothing tone, gesturing his agreement and 'looking all round'. His second assertion of Brutus' honourableness is met with further shouts of approbation, rising now to 'FFF' volume. Above the enthusiasm of the upstage citizens, Antony, almost casually, remarks, 'He hath brought many captives home to Rome.' When, a moment later, he mentions that their ransoms filled the general coffers, he 'holds his arms out to audience – looking round'. The slightly-shaken citizens turn to each other to reassure themselves. Meanwhile, Antony, 'with hand to face as though thinking to himself', asks quietly, 'Did this in Caesar seem ambitious?' A 'General whisper and uneasy movement' follow. Once again he tests the atmosphere with 'Brutus is an honourable man', but is met with strong murmurs of assent as before. Clearly the time is not yet ripe.

He now begins to move about the rostrum. More confident after a line or two, he tries another reference to Brutus' honourableness, this time with 'slight sarcasm'. The result is an outbreak of 'General strong murmurs', and the citizens begin to advance upon him. Two threateningly 'mount steps of rostrum', necessitating the hurried explanation, 'I speak not to disprove what Brutus spoke', which he makes with 'Arms out to cits advance as though protesting.' He now realizes that he has over-stepped himself; a change of tactics is in order. As he says, 'But here I am to speak what I do know', there is 'Slight murmur. General movement – then attention and *dead* Silence.'

Antony now shifts his attention from the living Brutus to the dead Caesar, from a reasonable appeal to an emotional one. As he says, 'You all did love him once', he spreads his 'arms out as though to the world', and angrily demands, 'What cause withholds you then to mourn for him?' When he asserts that 'men have lost their reason', he pauses with 'both hands to head'; and the citizens 'turn and look at each other' with a 'General movement of anger and surprise'. Conveniently, at this point, Antony 'covers his head with mourning drapery and turns away' to weep. Overcome by Antony's grief, the citizens' resistance gives way. As one says, 'If it be found so, some will dear abide it', the wily demagogue uncovers his head and returns to the front of the rostrum.

Before he speaks, he makes a 'Gesture . . . as though about to pour forth some piece of eloquence', holding up his right hand for attention. Having caught the interest of the audience, he lets his hand fall and speaks simply. Confidentially, he leans forward on 'O masters, if I were disposed', and the 'Cits commence to take great interest.' When he mentions 'mutiny and rage', 'he makes a gesture with R. hand as though inspiring cits', who 'sway to & fro' in great excitement. Once more he ventures to mention the 'honourable men', this time receiving a vastly different response – 'Great dissent – hooting etc.'

'I will not do them wrong', he continues, amid murmurs of disapproval;
'I rather choose / To wrong the dead', pointing to Caesar's body, 'to wrong
myself', placing his 'hands on breast', 'and you', holding both hands
outwards towards the citizens. This line is greeted with 'Great uproar and
murmurs'. 'Than I will wrong such honourable men' is received with even
fiercer uproar, during which 'Ant looks as though judging the humour of
cits', determined not to be taken in again.

The furore persists until Antony produces the will from his breast. As he
shows the seal, 'General excitement and curiosity' are apparent, and the
principals repeat 'Seal of Caesar'. On ''tis his will', Antony holds up the
parchment, and 'Omnes repeat "his will"'. 'Tapping will with hand', he
urges, 'Let but the commons hear this testament', at which a 'murmur of
greed' runs through the group. When he puts the will away again, 'General
disappointment' is evident. Throughout the next lines, the citizens' curiosity builds to a crescendo: in their eagerness, they press about the rostrum
with hands outstretched. Turning to the citizens up C, Antony says, 'You
are not wood', and proceeds to tease them beyond endurance. Finally, as the
mob, 'holding out hands', repeats 'the Will, the Will', Antony moves to the
left side of the rostrum. Tree now calls for a picture. Antony then moves
back to the centre of the rostrum, 'looks at all the hands up', and 'sees the
moment has come'. Above the roars of the crowd, he shouts, 'You will
compel me then to read the will?' to which all reply 'We will.' Antony slowly
descends the steps.

When Antony reaches the bottom he gets down to LC. Citizens crowd round Antony
trying to touch or kiss his toga. Ant with gesture of disgust motions citizens to
stand away. [On 'Room for Antony, most noble Antony!'] 1st cit swings 2nd cit,
who is kissing Ant. gown, round to L then brushes Ant. gown with the greatest
reverence.

Antony 'gets up C to head of Body. buries his face in his hands for a moment.
then gets on base of rostrum C.' As he does so, there is 'Dead silence –
expectation' among the citizens.

'Taking hold of Caesar's mantle', he says, 'If you have tears'. 'Lifting the
mantle a little and looking all round', he urges, 'You all do know this
mantle.' The citizens 'crane forward – 1st cit Xs from R to L in front of the
body'. 'Half raising the mantle as though to the Gods', Antony calls on
Heaven to judge Caesar's love for Brutus, at which the citizens appear
greatly moved. Throughout the next lines emotional tension mounts until a
'wave of sorrow' runs through the crowd on 'quite vanquished him'.
Sorrow, however, changes to fury as Antony drives home the fact that
'bloody treason' has flourished over them, and a 'shout of execration
follows'. 'Then women sob and wail. All cits bend their heads – many
weeping. Sobs throughout.' 'Patting some of the cits heads' indulgently,

Antony remarks, 'I perceive you feel / The dint of pity.' He now uncovers the body with 'great attention of cits', and as he commands, 'Look you here', the sobs cease. When the corpse is revealed, 'Great shudder and wailing' are renewed, and continue for some time. At the second citizen's shout, 'We will be revenged!' 'Omnes repeat Revenge.' 'Cits rush up C as though about to exit' after 'Revenge! – About! – Seek! – Burn! – Fire! – Kill! –' Antony 'looks at cits. then gets down from base of rostrum – appealing by gesture to cits to stay, he then rushes up C then onto steps R'. From the steps he orders, 'Stay, countrymen', amid a general uproar. During the next few lines Antony moves about the crowd, standing up LC and on the base of the rostrum. When hysteria is at fever pitch, he raises both hands and allows it to break loose. As the maddened horde screams, 'We'll mutiny', the audience is meant to observe the 'Look of triumph on Antony's face'. Antony now calls his servant who is down LC and 'X's with him R'. He 'points off R directing him', then returns to the mob as the third citizen presses, 'Come, seek the conspirators.' From the base of the statue R Antony demands, 'Wherein hath Caesar thus deserv'd your loves?'; and the citizens look at each other perplexed. The will is soon read, and at an acme of frenzy the citizens exit.

On 'Now let it work', Antony makes a 'triumphal gesture', and 'holds his head with L hand' as he says, 'Take thou what course thou wilt!' At this point the 'Great Distant shout' of an enraged populace is heard; and the scene ends with a series of three tableaux. The direction reads:

1st. Picture. Ant Xs to head of body and kneels. Cits with torches and weapons X from RUE to LIE and from LIE to R and LUE. 2nd Picture. Body of cits X from LIE dragging Senator with them and exit RUE. Ant. rises sees senator being dragged across and makes gesture of revenge. 3rd Picture. Antony standing at Head of body with arms extended as though praying – then slowly places hands on the forehead of Caesar.

The curtain falls.

In this scene, Tree not only equalled the success of the Meiningen revival – he surpassed it; but to the same degree that the Forum scene gained in effectiveness, the interest in the second half of the play declined. Even Tree's drastic cutting did little to alter the impression of anti-climax. The best solution, in the opinion of many reviewers, would have been to end the play with the Forum speech. After all, argued one critic, 'The quarrels of Brutus and Cassius, their defeat and suicide after the customary futile Shakespearian battle at Philippi, tell us nothing that we need to know.'[27] The very fact that such a statement could be made indicates how thoroughly Tree had demolished the traditional supremacy of Brutus and Cassius and the perennial popularity of their quarrel. If Tree was aware of the problem, he never satisfactorily solved it; he neither cut the play further, nor subordinated the Forum scene in any way. Consequently, the latter part of *Julius Caesar* was obliged to limp pathetically throughout the next two decades.

Act III, scene i

Brutus' Tent

In contrast with the splendour which preceded, the setting for Brutus' Tent was strikingly simple. Above centre-stage were placed two rock pieces, one on either side. Between them were draped curtains 'of blue cloth striped with crimson', suggesting the back wall of the tent. These were hung in such a way as to leave an ample open exit through which one caught 'a glimpse of peaceful valleys lying beyond'.[28] To enhance the tent effect, two cut cloths were placed at either side of the proscenium. The only furnishings were a torch-holder at the left, a table and stools at centre stage, and skin rugs slightly farther forward to right and left.

As the curtain rises, Brutus is 'discovered seated L of table C' with Lucius at R and Claudius RC. Cassius then enters upstage (outside the tent) with Pindarus and ten soldiers. Brutus rises and goes out to meet him. The confrontation takes place just above the open exit. As the quarrel itself begins, the generals come downstage into the tent, and Lucius closes the curtains on them.

Brutus sits to the right of the table and Cassius places himself down left. There are few directions provided for the conduct of the quarrel, apart from basic instructions as to when to sit, stand, and cross. On 'For your life you durst not', the direction calls for a 'quick mov. of Cas up to Br with his hand on dagger – then as if with control Cas moves away LC'. As Cassius says, 'O, I could weep / My spirit from mine eyes!' he sobs. When he challenges Brutus with 'There is my dagger', he 'throws dagger at the feet of Brutus RC', kneels, and bares his breast. 'Br. slowly picks up dagger and puts it in Cas hands.' A pause follows. On 'Hath Cassius lived', he slowly rises; and Lucius enters with a torch which he places in the bracket up L. Brutus then proceeds to announce Portia's death, at which Cassius 'falls back as though astounded'. On 'O insupportable and touching loss!' Cassius 'slowly gets to Br. R puts his arm half round Br.'. The drinking episode is handled much as in previous productions.

Trebonius and Metellus now enter, and the conference gets under way. Shortly after, Lucius comes in and lies down on the rugs at L. The only point worthy of note in this part of the scene is Tree's emphasis on Cassius' eagerness to please and his determined exercise of self-control. He tries to make himself heard on 'Hear me, good brother', but when Brutus interrupts with 'Under your pardon', Cassius resolutely 'gets slowly down L', leaving Brutus to address his strategy to Metellus and Trebonius. As Cassius reluctantly gives his consent to 'meet them at Philippi', he stands by the curtain absently looking out, resigned to inevitable defeat. After the exit of Trebonius and Metellus, Cassius moves 'to Br. taking his hand'. On 'Good night, my lord', he servilely 'tries to kiss Br. hand', but 'Br. stops him'. A pause ensues, then 'they embrace', and Cassius exits c. Distant trumpets are heard three times during their last lines.

Lucius now brings Brutus' gown and places it over his shoulders; he then calls Varro and Claudius who 'lie down on rugs R' as Brutus instructs. Lucius crosses to the rugs at L, takes up his lute, and tunes it as he says, 'It is my duty, sir.' As Brutus promises to do him good if he lives, he crosses and touches the boy's head; then, lest sentiment should be lacking, Lucius kisses his hand. Brutus now sits L of table and Lucius sings 'Orpheus with his Lute', falling asleep, conveniently enough, when the song ends. Brutus then rises, takes the lute from him, and places it by the table. 'Luc shivers as if cold. Br. seeing this takes cloak from his own shoulders and lays it over Luc.' Having put out the torch at LC, he returns to the table, and the lights are lowered.

The Ghost then enters 'behind gauze RC' (probably outside the tent), speaks his lines, and then vanishes. The paucity of directions in the promptbook would suggest that very little was made of this scene. On 'Now I have taken heart', he rises and moves 'up to where the Ghost has disappeared'. A moment after, as Claudius and Varro exit, 'Br. mov. as though to see if Ghost is there then sits L of table.' Music now begins in the orchestra. 'Br tries to read book but keeps looking where Ghost appeared as though unable to concentrate his attention on book. The Book falls and Br buries his face in his arms and sobs on table.' On this tableau the curtain falls.

Act III, scene ii

The Plains of Philippi

The setting for the final scene comprised a seascape backcloth, set well upstage, with two ground rows in front and wings on either side. Immediately in front again were 'Rock Rostrums' to right and left.

Antony, Octavius, a standard-bearer, trumpeters, and a captain are discovered on the rocks at R. At the base of the rocks stand two groups of four soldiers each, located at RC and down R. Another standard-bearer is stationed near the latter group. Antony looks off L with 'shield raised to protect eyes from sun' (a neat realistic touch), while the trumpeter sounds a flourish and 'Distant flourish answers him'. A messenger enters running from LUE and exits RUE. Brutus, Cassius, Lucius, Metellus, Trebonius, and three captains shortly appear on the rocks at L, and the parley begins.

After the farewells Cassius 'gets up C, gives signal off LUE and *Exits* RUE followed by all except Br. Luc. and one Capt. When Cas exits 4 Bodies of Soldiers commence crossing from LUE to RUE in double file. Lucius gets down LC and gives Brutus his helmet and shield.' Brutus then 'gives signal off L and Exits R2E followed by Luc and Capt. 2 Bodies of soldiers X from L2E in double file.' The direction continues:

When soldiers have finished Xing – Alarums and sounds of battle are heard off R. Then body of soldiers enter RUE and run across to LUE. These men are in flight and some have no weapons. Cassius enters RUE after them he carries a standard. Trebonius enters R2E gets up to Cas who is up C.

Cassius' death is not prolonged. After delivering the fatal news, Pindarus comes down to Cassius and kneels at C. As he says, 'Come now, keep thine oath', Cassius 'takes off armour aided by Pind who puts it down L'. On 'take thou the hilts', 'Pind takes sword', and Cassius 'covers face with cloak'. 'Pind goes to him with sword pointed – but hesitates then Cas pulls Pind to him so that the sword runs through him.' Before Cassius falls he uncovers his face and points to the standard. Pindarus then exits above the body R2E.

Trebonius and Metellus now appear 'on rocks L', and descend on seeing the body. Metellus exits and quickly returns with Brutus, Lucius, two captains and four soldiers. Brutus' 'Come therefore, and to Thasos send his body' is spoken to the four soldiers who 'get down to body and raise it on their shoulders – and Exit LIE'. As they exit, 'all salute'.

When the stage is again clear, Tree provides a Battle Tableau reminiscent of, but vastly more elaborate than, Phelps's seven or eight soldiers who ran across the stage in flight. To 'Music in orchestra',

Soldiers enter R and L – they fight. Brutus gets on rocks L. Ant enters – cuts down one soldier and follows Br. up on rocks. They fight but drives Br. off L. During this Cʒt Caesar has entered R and fought with Trebonius and driven him off L. The general spirit of the scene is that of a mêlée – but those soldiers (Ant army) who have entered R drive off those who have entered L. After their exit a body of swordsmen and spearmen enter RUE and run across and exit LUE as though in pursuit of enemy. pause –

Tree becomes the first producer in the play's history to attempt anything like a realistic re-creation of the military mood; nevertheless, despite his efforts, the scenes remained unconvincing.

At the finish of the battle tableau, Brutus enters with Trebonius, Metellus, and Lucius. From LC he says, 'Thou seest the world, Trebonius', and when his request is refused, he begins his farewells. 'Ist farewell to Lucius who kneels. Br. lays his hand on Luc. head, then Luc rises and gets up C. 2nd farewell to Metellus who is R – Br. gives him his right hand and L hand to Trebonius.' At this moment a soldier 'descends rocks and exits running', warning Brutus to fly as he goes. Brutus commands 'Hence', and his companions exit RUE. He then 'draws his sword', and stabs himself. As he says, 'Caesar now be still', he is seen 'pointing as though seeing the Ghost of Caesar'. He falls C.

In the distance soldiers are heard singing 'Ave Caesar', and shortly they enter R and L and form lines from up L to down L and from LC to down R. 'Luc enters C and gets down to body of Br. kneeling by it. Octavius enters C and gets down RC.' When Antony arrives, 'all shout "Ave Antony" raising swords and spears as in salute'. As Antony raises his sword, all fall silent; and the eulogy begins. On 'This was a man', 'Antony lowers sword, all lower swords or spears to the ground, as for a mourning salute to the body of Brutus.' As the final curtain falls, Tree calls for two pictures – 'First Picture – All Supers remain as before. Second Picture – All Supers at attention.'

The actors

The passion for realism which inspired *Caesar*'s *mise en scène* was not without its impact on the acting style as well. Although the conspirators might be toga-draped, Tree was bent on proving that they were 'wrapped around also with that imagination of the poet which makes them of today – actual as though the Curia were at Westminster, the Forum no farther than Trafalgar Square, and, Caesar's murder the sensation of the hour'.[29] The presentation of Shakespeare in a more natural and contemporary manner had for some years been standard practice for the other plays;[30] now, somewhat belatedly applied to *Caesar*, it met with immense success. The *Daily Mail* critic (24 January 1898) rejoiced to discover that Tree's Romans had 'no cousinship' with those of previous years who 'bated not a jot of oratorical sonority or laborious majesty of carriage'. In reality, however, oratory was only muted, not eradicated; and Tree, to judge from a recording of his 'O, pardon me, thou bleeding piece of earth' speech,[31] was a prime example of the ponderous declamation he claimed to eschew. Nevertheless, his Antony, if not the most natural Roman of them all, was easily the most discussed.

Even in his own time Tree was not regarded as an actor of the stature of Kemble, Macready, Phelps, or even Irving. In Desmond MacCarthy's opinion, and few of his contemporaries disagreed, Tree was essentially a character actor. His gift for graphic detail and picturesque by-play was more suited to creating memorable people than sustaining a dramatic situation. Within the range of character parts, MacCarthy considered Tree temperamentally best fitted for characters 'who, in varying degrees, were the play-actors of their own emotions'. 'He understood', says MacCarthy, 'the orator, the actor, the artist whose emotions are his own material, and the half-sincere advocate.'[32]

Tree's choice of Antony, with his real and simulated emotion, was a wise one. His considerable height was no drawback; in fact, it enabled him to dominate the crowd as a less physically impressive actor could not have done. He also lacked the verse-speaking skill so long considered essential; but his novel interpretation, especially in the Forum scene, rendered his deficiencies less obvious.

In Tree's view, the beau idéal conception of Antony was a serious over-simplification. 'Marc Antony has the complex nature of a man', he asserted, 'and is not merely a stage figure';[33] consequently, his Antony, even without the Proscription scene, was a more vivid, less consistent, and altogether richer characterization than that of Charles Kemble or Edwin Booth.

In the early scenes of the play, where he had little to say, Tree seized the opportunity, as we observed earlier, to depict by dumb-show the 'careless, dissipated Roman noble, easy, good-tempered, and a trifle complaisant',[34] not so much Kemble's admirable athlete as the 'gay voluptuary, with a ribald joke for Caesar's ear, and a wanton eye for every pretty face'.[35] 'Even his costume for the Lupercalian race', wrote one reviewer, 'suggests a certain luxury and dandyism.'[36] With sometimes delicate, sometimes over-obvious, by-play, he constantly threw himself into contrast with the sour, unbending Cassius, establishing an image against which his future volte-face could be judged.

From the moment of Caesar's murder, a new Antony gradually came into being – a figure 'haggard, desperate, a prey to grief and passion'.[37] Here all of Tree's powers of character creation were called into play. Lady Tree vividly recalls the moment of his entry into the Senate House: first, 'the terrible uplifting of their [the conspirators'] dripping swords, as they cried in dreadful unison, "Peace, Freedom and Liberty!"'

Then the silent, breathless, fearsome falling apart as the great figure of Marc Antony appeared, like a grim question silencing the heroics that died on guilty lips ...

There stands Marc Antony among the murderers, searching their eyes with his own scorching, agonized gaze, as each man renders him his bloody hand, while Casca with rude intent and purposeful cruelty smirches with a crimson stain the arm of butchered Caesar's friend. One actually saw a new soul grow in careless, light-hearted Antony who revels late o' nights; one saw grey purpose blotting out the gay colour of his life; one saw doubt, fear and foreboding spread like a pall over the confronters of this new Antony, this changed man come to judge the cruel issue of these bloody men. This scene was not acted – it was *lived* by all concerned. Herbert towered above them ... like an avenging angel: albeit an angel with no less of Lucifer than of Gabriel in his attitude.[38]

From the moment of his entry until the end of the scene, Antony conveyed the impression 'that the dead man's defender was playing his own game throughout'.³⁹ His 'O mighty Caesar!' lament was at least partly theatrical, a calculated attempt to awaken Brutus' sympathies and make him more amenable to his request. In the next few minutes 'he followed it up skilfully by the crafty manner in which . . . [he] wins concessions from the conspirators', 'while every now and then his horror and rage break through'⁴⁰ to inform the audience of the true state of his feelings. The *Westminster Gazette* critic thought his simulation of grief was 'perhaps a little excessive', but Tree cleverly redressed the balance by his eminently plausible 'look of horror and passion when Cassius hastily stepped over the body'.⁴¹

From the moment of his entry Tree stuck 'quite clearly and forcibly the note of Antony's affectionate and almost sentimental devotion to Caesar',⁴² but it was not until he was left alone that he allowed his grief full rein in the 'O, pardon me' speech. Here, however, most critics found him less successful. In Richard Dickins' opinion, Tree was incomparably better in passages where he was acting emotion than in those in which he was supposed to feel it. In this final speech, Dickins found him 'wholly ineffective' in conveying Antony's genuine sorrow.⁴³ William Archer thought his action 'lacking in dignity' and his speech 'far too loud', particularly the 'Cry "Havoc!"' where his tone was 'not one of reflection . . . but frenzied exhortation'.⁴⁴

It was in the Forum scene, however, that Tree triumphed. By handling the episode as naturalistically as possible he threw his own role into greater prominence and deflected attention from his declamatory weakness. Since he could not 'strike the true high note which might have been struck', he concentrated instead on Antony's consummate 'art and craftiness'.⁴⁵ 'In the Forum scene . . . where Antony is acting', wrote Dickins, 'where there is no deep feeling, but where he is playing on the emotions of the crowd, the actor could not well have been better – every line was carefully considered and every intonation effective – he was never monotonous, and the scene was supremely fine and successful from Antony's opening words to its frenzied close'.⁴⁶ Most critics were equally generous.

In Tree's third act, Antony makes his impact more by dumb-show than by speech, and apparently his performance was at least satisfactory, although critics seldom remarked upon it. In any case, he took pains to make a strong visual impression by decking himself 'in all the gorgeous array of a general, with scarlet toga above his steel lorica', and wearing on his head 'a steel helmet with white plume'.⁴⁷ The words of the final eulogy 'sounded clear and true in their loyal manliness and ungrudging appreciation'.⁴⁸

Lewis Waller, who played Brutus, had, like his manager, small claim to greatness, but was a competent performer by the standards of the time. In fact, he appears to have been a better tragedian than Tree. Endowed with a fine physique, classical features, and a good voice, he looked a Roman patrician and spoke the verse with a feeling for its music.

His Brutus, although somewhat less formal in speech and action, claimed close kinship with the cold and reserved philosopher-patriot of Kemble. The dominant note of the character, as Gordon Crosse saw it, was 'a calm and dignified, rather self-conscious superiority'.[49] Where Kemble had emphasized the contemplative side of Brutus' nature, Waller's Roman 'did not seem to convey the idea of the philosopher and thought-lover so much as of a naturally taciturn, hard man, lofty in idea and conduct',[50] with, as someone said, 'plenty of art, but no heart'.

In the early scenes of the play Waller worked for a rigid stillness, somewhat reminiscent of Kemble's statuesque presence, but met with slight approval. Audience tastes had changed; and Brutus seemed 'a trifle hard and cold' and 'needlessly reserved'.[51] From the death of Caesar onward, Shaw considered him better. Thanks to Waller's splendid bearing, Brutus' authoritative appeal immediately after the murder was highly effective, and his apt gestures, sensitive intonation, and clear enunciation won his Forum speech widespread praise. In the Quarrel scene, his stoical dignity supplied a worthy foil to the mercurial Cassius, although one critic, at least, thought it 'unnecessary to appear so coldly argumentative or so priggishly superior'.[52] In the early part of the scene, he rendered Brutus' wrath 'terrible from its very calmness', with only one emotional outburst to contrast with his former stillness.[53] His death-scene received almost no critical comment apart from an assertion or two that it was 'well rendered'. Whatever its shortcomings, Waller's interpretation served well enough to throw Antony into relief, which, to judge from the promptbook, was its prime function.

Cassius was Franklyn McLeay, a promising, but short-lived actor, whose performance came close to rivalling Tree's in popularity. McLeay conceived his Roman mainly in terms of febrile energy, and, accordingly, 'he acted from a tension of nerves, which gave his words their immediate effect'.[54] In the first scenes he depicted the highly-strung, 'stern, uncompromising soldier, who sees the liberty of his caste threatened by Caesar's growing power' with an 'intensity, truth, and absence of conventionality' which seemed to one reviewer 'little short of perfect'.[55] 'With hawklike glances of the eye, with pale, haggard features', he seemed the very man 'so justly dreaded by Caesar'.[56] The *Star* critic described this scene as a 'fine piece of impulsive, red-hot acting',[57] and even the hyper-critical Shaw praised its 'deliberate staginess and imposing assumptiveness', although he was less than happy with the verse-speaking.[58] From the Quarrel scene onward his impersonation got rather out of hand. Here, according to *The Illustrated London News* (29 January), he was 'betrayed into extravagant and melodramatic violence'. His suicide passed almost unnoticed save for Shaw's assertion that his Cassius 'died the death of an incorrigible poseur, not of a noble Roman'.[59]

After a somewhat dismal account of an Antony, a Brutus, and a Cassius who were all to some extent unsatisfactory, it is pleasant to record a Caesar who was undoubtedly one of the century's best. Not only were Charles Fulton's features peculiarly suited to a convincing portrayal of the Dictator, but his considerable insight and discrimination led him to discover an inner dimension. This Caesar was neither a travesty of Shakespeare's figure like the interpretations of the eighteenth century, nor was he the absurdly pompous puppet depicted by Egerton at the beginning of the nineteenth. 'The Caesar of Mr. Charles Fulton is dignified, and dignity is all important', wrote the *Times* reviewer;[60] but without sacrificing his essential stateliness, Fulton did 'laudable justice to the gentleness and affability',[61] the genial humanity, of Caesar as well. Even Caesar's egoistic flights, which often seem mere braggadocio, Fulton managed to convey with 'a resolute coolness and reserved force'[62] which left Caesar's distinction unmarred. 'Though measured by the number of words which it contains . . . [the part] is short', wrote the *Era* critic, 'Mr. Fulton's performance is distinctly engraven on our memories.' Such a compliment could be paid to few Caesars who preceded him.

If Tree can be said to have presented Shakespeare at all, his was a pictorial, rather than a dramatic, representation. Viewed through Poel–Granville–Barker spectacles, it appears as a wilful distortion of the playwright's form to please the star actor and the pageant-lover, containing much to condemn and little to admire. However, even out of distortion can come a kind of truth. Although Tree admittedly aggrandized Antony beyond any conceivable intention of Shakespeare, and inevitably mangled the play in so doing, this very concentration upon one facet, hitherto much neglected, revealed unsuspected dramatic resources. Never again could Antony be simply a fervid young orator, nor the crowd a negligible factor in the performance.

8

F. R. Benson at Stratford (1892–1915)

Beerbohm Tree was not the only young actor to fall under the Meiningen company spell during their London visit. Present also was F. R. Benson, then only 23 and fresh from a triumphant amateur production of the *Agamemnon* at Oxford. Two years later when he launched his own company, his programmes bravely announced that it would be 'conducted on the Meiningen system';[1] but within a short time he realized that the sophisticated German methods were ill-suited to the needs of an impoverished touring group, and the phrase was dropped. His admiration for the Meiningen, however, remained unaltered; and his *Julius Caesar* was indelibly impressed with their stamp.

Benson's first embryonic *Caesar* was staged in 1890, in evening dress, before the forbidding Miss Beale and her charges at Cheltenham Ladies' College; and shortly after, more appropriately mounted, it assumed an important place in the Bensonian repertoire. Between 1890 and 1933 he staged scores of performances throughout the British Isles, and, in 1921, toured the play in South Africa. In 1892 he brought it to the Memorial Theatre, Stratford-upon-Avon,[2] and repeated it with considerable success at the Shakespeare Festivals of 1896, 1898, 1904, 1906, 1908, 1909, 1910, 1911, 1914, and 1915.

Benson's only formal theatrical training was a year spent in London beginning in the autumn of 1881 where he haunted the Lyceum, and studied privately with the veteran mid-nineteenth-century stagers Walter Lacy, William Creswick, and Hermann Vezin. Their tuition in heroic deportment, traditional business, and verse-speaking convinced him that the older school of tragic acting had been unjustly denigrated. Naturalistic interpretation, epitomized in the Robertsonian comedians, was a greater threat to the future of Shakespeare in Britain; although the 'cuff-and-collar brigade' at its best had its points. 'I conceived it my job', he tells us, 'to preserve what was best in the old and blend it with the constructive forces of the new.'[3]

In 1883, now 25 and with only a year of undistinguished professional engagements behind him, he took over the bankrupt Walter Bentley Company, made Shakespeare the staple of his repertory, and assumed the leading roles himself.[4] Over the next fifty years he recruited young actors, trained them in classical technique, and toured them indefatigably throughout the provincial hinterland. In all he revived thirty-five of the thirty-seven plays, a record unrivalled until the Old Vic staged the complete works in recent times.

Convinced that the built-up settings of the ultra-realists were smothering Shakespeare and distracting attention from the actor, he returned to the simple and flexible scenery employed by Phelps – painted drops, a few flats, and matching wings. While the nature of his company and a restricted budget demanded that backgrounds be cheap and portable, this did not mean tawdry or unapt. Insofar as he could afford it, his scenery was painted by the best artists and aimed at a union of picturesqueness and simplicity. He also approved of graphic business and eye-catching tableaux, but usually employed them at points when they would not impede the flow of the language.

Benson preached that 'no play should be adapted . . . so as to give greater prominence than the text invites to any single role';[5] but he blue-pencilled with abandon for other reasons, and the structure of the plays inevitably suffered. Moreover, his assumption of the 'leads', supported by actors with less mature technique and judgement than his own, caused his characters to obtrude unduly. Nevertheless, audiences saw swift-paced Shakespeare, constantly and in variety, if not invariably in fullness and balance. Benson heroic tragedy, muscular and full-throated, shaped the tastes of more than two generations of theatre-goers; and the tragic tradition perpetuated by his actors continued to enrich Shakespeare performances world-wide until the onset of the Second World War.

To observe Benson's work at its best, one must look to the Stratford Shakespeare Festivals. At the Memorial Theatre he had a stage superior to those on which he usually worked; he was provided with a grant which freed him from undue financial strain; and his productions were frequented by an audience with a genuine appreciation for what he was trying to do.

Our reconstruction of these revivals is greatly aided by the only known promptbook, now preserved in the Shakespeare Centre Library (*JC* 77). Identified on the first page as belonging to 'SIR FRANK BENSON'S COMPANY', it was probably prepared sometime between 1916 and 1920. Although dating from Benson's post-Stratford era, it doubtless represents an accurate copy of one used much earlier.[6] The Benson 'Catalogue of Wardrobe', compiled in the summer of 1906, and the 'Benson Company Music Book'[7] are valuable supplements. Where the promptbook notes have been incomplete or confusing, Mr Dennis Roberts, stage manager and actor with Benson from 1922 to 1933, has generously offered clarification.

Like managers for two centuries before him, Benson found that *Caesar*'s thirty-five named characters overtaxed his company's resources. Worse still, they threatened to blur the clarity of dramatic outline he sought to create. His solution was the time-honoured one – mass elimination of minor characters with omission or redistribution of their speeches.

Flavius and Marullus disappear as usual; and Trebonius and Metellus harangue the holiday-makers. Cicero's ominous prognostications are enunciated by Metellus. Cinna, the conspirator, vanishes, and his speeches are either cut or allocated elsewhere. Caius Ligarius and Publius are eliminated; and, again, the Soothsayer and Artemidorus are merged. Once more, Cinna the Poet, Lepidus, and the Camp Poet are consigned to limbo, followed by Lucilius. The latter's lines in the Quarrel scene are taken by Metellus, and the account of his capture is excised altogether. Metellus and Claudius do duty for Titinius and Messala in the Quarrel episode and in Cassius' death scene, although, as usual, there is no suicide by Cassius' body. Young Cato, Clitus, Voluminius, Dardanius, and Strato do not appear in the final moments; Brutus is accompanied by Claudius and Varro. In all Benson reduces Shakespeare's dramatis personae from thirty-five to a compact seventeen, exclusive of servants and supers.

Although Benson's production notions were quite different from those of Tree, he cut the play just as heavily – a total of almost five hundred and fifty lines in all. This abridgement was not dictated, as in Tree's case, by the demands of realistic-spectacular stagecraft, but by Benson's own view of Shakespearian dramatic structure, a view which was strongly conditioned by his study with Lacy, Creswick, and Vezin and his profound admiration for Greek tragedy.

His first concern, like Kemble's, was the preparation of a suitably heroic text; and, as usual, Brutus receives the lion's share of attention. Most of the traditional propriety-cuts are preserved, and one or two new ones are added. Brutus does not weaken to the point of promising to reveal his guilty secret to Portia (II.i. 305–8); and does not risk his dignity by appearing in the Confrontation scene. His blustering retorts, when they are left standing, are taken by Cassius, to whom Benson considered them more appropriate. The first twenty-one lines of his death scene are also cut: the audience does not hear his fruitless appeals to Clitus and Dardanius, nor does Clitus note his tears. Benson's conception of Brutus, like Kemble's, was that of the disciplined Stoic walking clear-eyed to his death; there was no room for emotion, nor for much human frailty either. In the end Brutus once more takes his own life in high tragic fashion, but without Kemble's interpolation.

Benson apparently found Cassius satisfactory enough as Shakespeare left him, and contented himself with just two attempts at improvement. He excises his bombastic 'Therein, ye gods, you make the weak most strong' lines (I.iii.91–5) and his superstitious and somewhat fearful birthday speech (V.i.69–92). Apart from serious cuts in the speeches of Antony, to which we shall return, Benson left the other major characters comparatively untouched.

Not only did Benson share with his eighteenth- and nineteenth-century counterparts a common interest in casting Shakespeare in the heroic mould, but his view of Shakespearian structure was not unlike theirs. He judged Shakespeare, as they did, by the standards of classical tragedy and found him wanting. When he produced the *Agamemnon* while still an undergraduate he was powerfully aided, according to his brother, 'in the expression of dramatic unity ... by the strongly defined structure of Aeschylus'.[8] In Shakespeare he found the design less obvious, and concluded that Shakespeare's art was defective. Rashly he decided that the Bard could be recast in the Greek mould and gain in power by being so treated. 'The Agamemnon company', he writes, 'had succeeded by their simple sincerity in a Greek play. Why not apply the same method to Shakespeare? There I was right; I had grasped the idea of simple strength, the simple strength, the complex potentiality dominant in a Greek statue.'[9]

Benson's Shakespeare simplified differed little from Kemble's Shakespeare methodized. In both cases the procedure was to pare away everything not strictly essential to the plot in order to accentuate a single unified action, which, trim and fast-moving, would proceed straightforwardly from beginning to end. Breadth and depth of character and rise and fall of dramatic tension were of little moment; pace was all. The rush of Bensonian action was a stock joke among actors, and a constant complaint of critics; but Benson paid little heed. So late as his last Stratford *Caesar* (1915), a reviewer felt compelled to note

a neglect of certain fundamental principles of the drama in representation, which leads to monotony, dulness, and exhaustion. It never from start to finish lets up; it is on one tone from beginning to end and that tone is a shout. It was like a hydrant working at full pressure, and never extinguishing the conflagration ... Contrast was rarely thought on; and hence for the most part it was played for all that 'Caesar' is not worth.[10]

The fault, however, lay as much in Benson's text as in the speed of playing. Had the critic compared the promptbook with the original script, one reason for the exhausting pace and emotional monotony would have been clear: a number of the passages designed to ensure relaxation of tension and variety of mood were absent.

Benson's first major excision is twenty-six lines of Cassius' and Casca's discussion of the omens (I.iii.46–71). Then in order to hurry forward the action from Brutus' Orchard to Caesar's House, everything is deleted from Brutus' 'O ye gods, / Render me worthy of this noble wife!' (II.i.302–03) to the end of the Caius Ligarius scene. Immediately after the scene in Caesar's house, Benson takes the audience to the Capitol, transposing the Soothsayer's (Shakespeare–Artemidorus') letter-reading sequence (II.iii) to come just before the entrance of Caesar, and cutting entirely the transitional Street scene (II.iv) with Portia and Lucius. To speed the action from the Forum to Brutus' tent, Benson cuts, in the usual manner, both the Cinna the Poet episode (III.iii) and the Proscription scene (IV.i), eighty-nine lines in all. In act V, almost a third of the confrontation (V.i) is removed, together with the 'Ride, ride, Messala' sequence (V.ii). Although Cassius' death scene remains intact, much of the ensuing action is cut to bring the deaths of the two generals into proximity. Brutus enters within a few lines of the discovery of the body, speaks his 'O Julius Caesar, thou art mighty yet' lines, delivers his eulogy, and exits. In a moment he is back to die himself. To telescope the action thus Benson was obliged to omit the scene in which Cato dies in battle and Lucilius is taken prisoner (V.iv), a total of thirty-two lines. Immediately after his entry, Brutus calls Claudius (Shakespeare–Voluminius) to him, and when his request is denied, launches forthwith into his death speech. Octavius' final lines are omitted, and Antony's 'This was a man' brings down the curtain.

　　With Benson's cuts in the interests of heroic tone and unity of action out of the way, few significant excisions remain to be dealt with; and most relate to the character of Antony. Like the Meininger, Benson determined to make the Forum scene the highlight of the play; and in all likelihood his heavy cutting of the last two acts was designed to obviate their impression of anti-climax. But Benson differed strongly from Barnay, and from Tree, too, for that matter, in his interpretation of Antony. Rather than subscribe to Barnay's subtle reading, he turned back to the beau idéal school, and found his model in the Antony of Charles Kemble – the noble young athlete, who, grief-stricken at the murder of his friend, rouses his powers to avenge his death, and effects a revolution. Benson, in characterization as in structure, worked mainly for simplicity and clarity. Shakespeare's complex composition must be reduced to a bold outline, and his delicate interplay of light and shade replaced by vivid primary tones.

　　Benson's most telling slash came in the Assassination scene where he cut everything from the end of the hand-washing sequence to Antony's entrance (III.i.114–46). The elimination of the servant is crucial. In Tree's interpretation, Antony relied strongly on the fact that he had, through the servant, been promised safe-conduct; it was this assurance that enabled him to play-act from the beginning. Benson's Antony had no such guarantee; and was no such contriver. Impulsively, without thought for his own safety, he comes crashing into the Capitol, risking his life at the hands of the conspirators to grieve over his dead benefactor.

　　In the same scene Benson goes to considerable lengths to free Antony of any taint of opportunism, at least before his request to speak at Caesar's funeral. At his entry he has no plan for revenge in mind, nor do the conspirators suggest that he may have one. Cassius' premonitory misgivings (III.i.144–6) and his warning to Brutus of his crowd-pleasing gifts (III.i.232–5) are removed.

Brutus makes no mention of his intention to precede Antony into the pulpit and inform the citizens that he will speak by permission of the conspirators (III.i.235–41). He merely instructs, 'You shall not in your funeral speech blame us.' The scene ended on the powerful curtain line, 'Cry havoc and let slip the dogs of war', eliminating the entrance of Octavius' servant and Antony's announcement of his strategy.

In the Forum scene, in order to bring Antony into action as quickly as possible, Benson cuts the first eleven lines in which the mob is divided between Brutus and Cassius. Brutus mounts the rostrum and begins his speech immediately. Antony's oration is little altered, save for the deletion of several of the lines in which he reminds the citizens of the will (III.ii.237–40). At the end of the scene, Octavius' servant is dispensed with to secure a stronger curtain on 'Mischief, thou art afoot, / Take thou what course thou wilt!'

Benson's simplified and fast-moving text was divided into acts and scenes as follows:

Act I

Scene 1	A Public Place	Scene 2	A Street in Rome
Scene 3	Brutus' Garden		

Act II

Scene 1	Caesar's House	Scene 2	The Senate

Act III
The Forum

Act IV

Scene 1	Brutus' Tent	Scene 2	Plain near Philippi
Scene 3	Battlefield near Philippi		

The object of this arrangement was to give Antony three act-curtains out of four – Antony clamouring for vengeance in act II, Antony unleashing havoc in act III, and Antony victorious beside the corpse of Brutus in act IV. Rather more generously than Tree, Benson allows Brutus one act-curtain, although by no means as strong as any of his own – 'O ye Gods! / Render me worthy of this noble wife!' which terminates act I. To lend heightened significance to the Forum scene, Benson makes it, as did Tree, a separate act.

Stagecraft

Act I, scene i

Benson's 'Public Place' setting, inspired by his scenic principles discussed earlier, was adequate without being in any way ostentatious. In the foreground, to left and right, was arranged a series of pillars which were backed, further upstage, by wings intended to suggest buildings along a Roman street. Beyond these, near the back wall, hung a sky-cloth. Settings were kept well to the back and sides of the stage, leaving the central portion uncluttered. The only moveable pieces used were a pedestal hung with a garland, at well up centre, and a stone at RC on which Metellus stood to make his appeal to the citizens. Benson's setting was clearly localized, but realism was not allowed to hinder the action or constitute an interest in itself.

As the curtain rose, twelve supers and an indefinite number of the regular Benson company were discovered, 'all carrying Laurel branches & shouting "Ave Caesar"'. Shortly after, four lictors enter RIE and 'X up & exit RUE'. Trebonius and Metellus follow them on from RIE and come down C to where the holiday-makers are rioting near the proscenium. Although the citizens remain in a state of excitement throughout the tribunes' interrogation – shouting, laughing, and waving their laurel branches – they indulge in no extraneous business to deflect attention from the major figures.

As Metellus begins his 'wherefore rejoice?' speech, he gets 'on stone R' and the citizens gather around him. It is soon apparent that this is not the mercurial mob of previous productions, swayed without resistance from holiday mirth to shamefaced guilt by Metellus' impassioned rhetoric. Benson's plebeians are indeed the 'hard hearts' and 'cruel men of Rome' that Metellus suggests they are. When he addresses them as 'cruel men of Rome' (I.i.36), they 'slightly turn their backs' on him. To his question, 'Knew you not Pompey?' there is a consenting 'Ay! Ay!', but to his reminder of their former devotion, their only reply is a defiant 'Well?' Caesar now has all of their regard, and they refuse to be seduced from it. At last, partly pushed off by Trebonius on 'Go, go, good countrymen', they reluctantly exit R and L with 'murmurs of discontent'. As Benson saw it, Trebonius' comment about their vanishing 'tongue-tied in their guiltiness' (I.i.62) was more indicative of his own capacity for wishful thinking than of any change of heart on the part of the citizens. It is clear from the outset that in the people of Rome, Brutus will have an ugly mob to deal with; the ungrateful treatment now accorded to Pompey will soon be the reward of another well-meaning saviour of the populace. Shortly after the departure of the citizens, Metellus and Trebonius make their exit; as the latter leaves, he 'pulls garlands off' the pedestal at C.

The brass and wood sections of the orchestra now herald the approach of Caesar with appropriate music, and a moment later the crowd enters LUE backwards, once more waving their laurel branches and shouting 'Ave Caesar'. Behind them come six 'Flower girls', also walking backwards, who 'strew in front of Caesar'. Four lictors follow them on, pushing the mob across the stage and clearing a path for the procession. A 'Company of

Senators' then enters, and close behind them comes Antony, clad in leopard-skins and accompanied by two dancing-girls whom he embraces fondly. Already Benson is at work to create the impression of the *bon viveur* in preparation for his about-face in the Assassination scene. Brutus, Cassius, and the rest of the party enter in turn, and, last of all, '4 Blacks' appear 'carrying Caesar on bier'. Benson was not against colourful display; he merely disapproved of its use at the wrong times.

The conversation between Brutus and Cassius is handled very simply with a minimum of movement. Only one small piece of business is introduced. As the conspirators hear the shouts off, 'Three of the crowd rush across the stage from LUE to R shouting Ave Caesar' in a heavy-handed attempt to underline the threat posed by Caesar's popularity. A moment later Brutus says, 'I do fear the people / Choose Caesar for their king' (I.ii.79–80). At I.ii.176, the procession re-enters RUE. The only change worthy of note is in Antony's entourage. He is now escorted by '4 flower girls leading him with garlands round his neck'.

Casca is about to follow the procession off when Brutus stops him. During the ensuing conference, there is again little movement. Casca sits for most of his speeches. At I.ii.273 Benson inserts the direction 'Enter Soothsayer LUE exits RUE', a superfluous reminder of perilous times.

The setting for the Storm scene, a painted drop representing a Roman street, allowed Brutus' Garden to be readied simultaneously upstage. There is little business. Speed and simplicity are everything.

Act I, scene iii

Brutus' Garden, although visually effective, was merely a variation upon the Public Place setting. To left and right were the pillars mentioned earlier, and behind them, well upstage, was placed a low wall beyond which could be seen several free-standing cypress trees against a sky-cloth. At stage right was a pillar-type wing suggesting the entrance to Brutus' house with a functional set of steps in front. To the left, well downstage, was a garden seat, and on the opposite side a stone block. Near the block a light burned feebly on a lampstand. The stage remained fairly dark throughout the first part of the scene.

Brutus moves very little during his moral crisis; in fact, he speaks most of his soliloquy seated on the seat at L – a refreshing change from the uneasy pacing of many previous productions. Just before the entry of the conspirators, a direction reads 'blue Limes quietly on. Floats up a little.' On the sky-cloth at the back the first hints of dawn appear, throwing the cypress trees into silhouette. As the conspirators enter L2E, Brutus goes down R to receive them; Lucius lies down on the steps of the house and falls asleep.

The most noteworthy point in the conference sequence is Benson's attempt to give the impression that Brutus and Cassius were the only members of the conspiracy with firmly defined principles. The rest simply follow the leaders, shouting fervent approval to the views of both.

Typical of Benson's fondness for vivid and simple effects is his lighting for the latter part of the scene. As Brutus appeals to the conspirators to be 'sacrificers, but not butchers', Benson emphasizes the bloody nature of the contemplated action by the direction 'Put in RED and Some WHITE.' A few lines later, as Decius boasts of his influence over Caesar, a note reads 'LIGHTS gradually up to red.' In a symbolic crimson glow, the conspirators take their farewell of Brutus and exit LIE.

Brutus then walks up to the steps on which Lucius is lying and speaks his short soliloquy. Afterwards he returns to the seat at L. 'When Brutus is seated', Portia enters 'from House R'. The sequence is played simply; and they embrace as the curtain falls. Then follows an entr'acte of eight minutes while Caesar's House is put in place.

Act II, scene i

The only photograph of Caesar's House to come to light depicts a setting by Alma-Tadema for Benson's first revivals and destroyed in the Newcastle fire in 1899. Subsequent versions, however, must have differed little since the promptbook directions even twenty years later tally almost perfectly with the early design.

At about centre-stage hung a backcloth representing the interior of Caesar's house with a view of an open court and a landscape beyond. In front, on either side, went large house-interior wings, both of which had built-in curtained entrances. The only moveable pieces were two statues, immediately in front of the drop, and a seat well forward on the right.[11]

As in the previous sequence between Brutus and Portia, Benson keeps movement economical. Caesar sits on the seat during most of the interview. Calphurnia begins her account of the omens standing at LC, but, terrified by her own tale, she 'comes over L above seat' at the mention of the shrieking ghosts as if to claim her husband's protection. Later she kneels beside him.

Decius enters RIE and stands before Caesar during his seductive rhetoric. On 'How foolish do your fears seem now, Calphurnia!' Caesar rises and 'takes up robe' which lies on the back of the seat; and Benson's Calphurnia, with more self-discipline than Tree's distraught and brooding matron, moves immediately to assist him. She 'takes it [the robe] from him, fastens it on him & kisses him'. Caesar's decision must be accepted; she has done what she could. At this moment a servant enters escorting Brutus, Metellus, Casca, and Trebonius. Without more ado, Calphurnia follows him off. At the end of the scene, Caesar exits LIE with 'all but Brutus', who remains alone on stage to speak his last lines. As he turns to go in, the curtain falls.

Most of the Capitol setting was pre-set during the Caesar's House episode. Two minutes of curtain music now allow time to ready the downstage section of it.

Act II, scene ii

In keeping with tradition Benson made the Assassination a feature of his production, and staged it elaborately. Again, the only available photograph of the Capitol setting is an Alma-Tadema design for pre-1900 productions. It agrees well with the later promptbook directions, however, and no doubt represents the basic set-plan used by Benson throughout his career. The debt to Gérôme is obvious. Perhaps Benson learned from Creswick of Booth's Capitol setting, and asked Alma-Tadema to design him something similar but simpler.

As the curtain rises, Brutus, Cassius, Trebonius, Antony, Casca, and Decius are discovered fairly well upstage. Unlike the Meiningen revival, the citizens are not present. The only supers introduced are a few senators, but whether they are discovered or enter later with Caesar is not clear from the promptbook. The Soothsayer, standing down R, now reads his letter which has been transposed from II.iii. Immediately after, Caesar enters C2R without his earlier pageantry. Passing the Soothsayer, he reminds him confidently, 'The ides of March are come.'

This scene, although rather more lavishly set than the previous ones, is again characterized by swift and uncluttered action. By reducing to a minimum the number of persons present, Benson focusses attention exclusively upon the major figures – the conspirators and Caesar. The assassination is reached with all possible speed.

As Decius asks, 'Where is Metellus Cimber?' Metellus enters C2L and 'advances & kneels to Caesar' at C. One by one the rest of the conspirators kneel and rise as in previous productions. On Caesar's 'The skies are painted with unnumbered sparks', Casca 'kneels close to Caesar's chair'. When Caesar exclaims, 'Hence! Wilt thou lift up Olympus?' Casca 'rises & gets upon the steps of chair'. A moment later, Decius Brutus, standing beside the platform, suddenly 'draws Caesar's cloak tight across Caesar's body'. The stabbing itself is handled thus:

Casca stabs Caesar standing above him behind Caesar's chair. Caesar seizes Decius throwing him down. Cassius & Metellus & other conspirators fling themselves on Caesar like wolves in front[.] struggling mass[.] Caesar breaks through then staggers towards Brutus who reluctantly gives coup de grâce. Caesar falls LC.

Benson and his company, with their intense fondness for athletics, took special delight in staging realistic action whenever opportunity offered. A greater contrast could hardly be imagined than that between the savage vigor of the Benson assassination and Kemble's formal ballet.

As Caesar falls, Metellus, 'running R', places the Phrygian Cap of Liberty on the end of his sword, shouting 'Liberty! Freedom! Tyranny is dead!' The cry is taken up by the crowd offstage. Shortly after, Popilius and the super senators exit. Trebonius, having disposed of Antony temporarily, now re-enters C2R. In response to Brutus' 'Stoop, Romans, stoop', the conspirators gather round the body with their backs to the audience and hands outstretched. Trebonius proceeds to smear their arms with the blood sponge.

Before Antony appears, the citizens are heard shouting 'Ave Antony' offstage. Antony enters RUE, pauses a moment, then runs downstage and 'kneels by Caesar's body' in traditional fashion. On 'fare thee well' he covers Caesar's face with a portion of his toga. At this point there is a threatening 'movement from Casca & Met' who are still of the opinion that Antony and Caesar should fall together. Brutus, however, restrains them. Their continued malevolent by-play motivates Antony's 'I do beseech ye, if you bear me hard ... Fulfil your pleasure.' Antony is not play-acting here; he is in deadly earnest.

Brutus and Cassius now attempt to win Antony to their way of thinking, and the handshaking sequence follows. As Casca moves to take Antony's hand, he viciously 'rubs blood on to Ant arm'.[12] Apart from this calculated bit of business and the savagery of the murder itself, there is no attempt made to underline the brutality of the conspirators' act. The text is allowed to speak for itself.

The remainder of the scene is got through expeditiously. Antony's maddened 'Cry havoc' is the cue for a 'quick curtain'. An eight-minute entr'acte follows.

Act III, scene i

Benson's setting for the Forum scene was the same as that used for the Public Place in act I – a combination of columns and street-wings. Up centre was placed a two-levelled rostrum, in front of which was left plenty of space for the rioting citizens.

Benson's crowds bore small resemblance to the highly-skilled ensemble of the Meininger. His citizens were mainly recruited from local townspeople with an evening to spare; and the sum of their dramatic training was usually a scant hour or two of rehearsal under the stage manager. Depending on the strength of counter-attractions, the number ranged night by night from twenty to eighty. Although Benson attempted to use his crowd realistically rather than as stage-dressing, he could expect little of them beyond frequent shouts and the simplest of movement. The creation of a mob personality was largely the responsibility of regular members of the Benson company who took it in turn to act as mob-leaders. Made up in a highly-individualized

11. The F. R. Benson Company Rehearses the Forum scene (III.ii)

manner, it was their task to keep the townspeople in uproar and to provide occasional naturalistic touches. During the 1896 Festival a local critic called attention to four of these leaders – 'A grey-haired old woman, an eager impetuous youth . . . an aged man, a frail frantic girl.'[13]

As the curtain rises, Brutus is discovered amid this motley throng who are milling about vigorously and demanding satisfaction. On the lower level of the rostrum stands Antony, wrapped in a black mourning cloak; and immediately in front of him lies the body of Caesar on its bier with faggots piled high about it ready for lighting. (Illustration 11.)[14]

Benson's introduction of Antony at the beginning of the scene is an intriguing tactic. In the first place it permits Antony a longer time on stage than he would ordinarily have. Moreover, he provides a focal point for the citizens' insults during Brutus' speech, thus allowing Brutus' influence upon them to be more vividly demonstrated. Finally, the humiliation and abuse which Antony undergoes in the early part of this scene serve to enhance his later triumph. Such an arrangement is eminently to Antony's advantage, but Brutus' impact is inevitably weakened by such a division of the audience's attention.

Without delay, Brutus makes his way to the upper level of the rostrum on 'Be patient till the last', and launches immediately into his address. In order not to make Antony's oration anti-climactic, Benson allows Brutus an easy conquest over his audience's emotions; in fact, they seem predisposed to accept his explanation from the outset. Having expressed his willingness to die for the state, Brutus 'comes down from the pulpit' to shouts of adulation. As he moves to exit L I E, '2 girls in crowd kiss Brutus robe', and the entire crowd proceeds to follow him off. Brutus turns round to beg them to hear Antony, but they reply, 'Down with Antony.' In the end, however, they reluctantly agree to his request, contenting themselves with exclamations of 'Ave Brutus' until he is lost from sight. Antony is now left alone with the enraged citizenry who greet him with a torrent of 'murmurs and howls'.

Like Tree, Benson accentuates the antipathy to Antony; but he steers well clear of Tree's elaborate mimed effects which would retard the dramatic movement. Nor does he handle the oration in the over-slow and ultra-realistic style. When Mr Roberts reconstructed Benson's rendering of the oration for me, it became quite clear that Benson's intention was to 'speak right on' in the nineteenth-century manner, treating the speech primarily as a piece of declamation. The crowd nevertheless responds realistically, although their exclamations and business are carefully subordinated to the flow of the rhetoric.

Throughout the first part of the speech, Antony's task seems Herculean. But his despairing: 'O judgment, thou art fled to brutish beasts, / And men have lost their reason' (III.ii.104–5) marks a turning point. Benson's crowd was by no means unanimous in its reactions; the mob-leaders saw to that. Some were apparently moved by Antony's appeal; others were unconvinced. As Antony turns away, the third citizen asserts, 'There's not a nobler man in Rome than Antony', but his remark is met with 'howls'. Another shouts, 'Ave Antony' and 'is seized and pushed away'. But at least some of the citizens are on Antony's side. Since the start of the oration the lights had been gradually lowered until, by this time, the stage was almost entirely in shadow. Benson now focusses a spotlight on Antony and Caesar's corpse, throwing the screaming mob into silhouette. The lights grow in intensity as Antony's power over the citizens increases.

When Antony turns back to the plebeians, they are at least prepared to give him a hearing; and steadily the tide turns against Brutus until, by the time Antony produces the will, the citizens are firmly on his side.

To read the will, he comes down to the lower level of the rostrum. As in Tree's production, each of Antony's lines describing the assassination is met with 'shudders' and 'cries'. Frequently the crowd is directed to 'weep and moan' as the emotional build-up continues toward the display of the body. When Antony pulls back the mantle on 'Here is himself', the citizens contemplate the corpse with awed 'shudders' which soon give place to hysterical 'Shouts. cries. tumult.' The plebeians are well on their way to the exit when Antony recalls them with 'Stay, countrymen.' His ironic assertion, 'They that have done this deed are honourable,' draws cries of

'Traitors' and outraged shouts of 'honourable'. When he suggests that the conspirators may 'with reason answer' the charges, the frantic citizens reply, 'they cannot'. Antony now reads, and as he does so the mob repeats the terms of the legacy in frenzied chorus.

Amid the tumult, lictors enter and stand in front of the bier to mask the property man who comes on to light the fire. As Antony exclaims, 'Here was a Caesar! when comes such another?' he returns to the upper level of the rostrum. Simultaneously the lictors move to the left revealing the fire now mounting above the body. With the light full down, save for the spotlight on Antony, the leaping flames throw the citizens into grotesque silhouette as they riot wildly about the stage. A red glow slowly comes up on the sky-cloth at the back as if to suggest that the city is burning. In the foreground a 'Man with hammer smashes bench.' From the height of the rostrum a triumphant Antony surveys his handiwork. As he shouts, 'Mischief, thou art afoot', he throws wide the mourning cloak, revealing beneath it a suit of golden armour. On this sensational picture the curtain fell and rose again and again.

In his treatment of the Forum sequence, Benson calls to his aid both the methods of the old school and those of the new. Throughout most of the scene his objective is clearly the swift action and impressive declamation characteristic of Kemble; but with this final stroke he nods more than slightly in the direction of his realist-contemporaries. Naturally, the tableau effect was immensely popular with spectacle-lovers, but there is no denying that it seriously upsets the overall rhythm of the play. After the emotional abandon of the Forum scene, the events which follow seemed tame.

Act IV, Scene i

The Tent locale was suggested by two sets of curtains. One set, loosely draped, hung at either side of the proscenium to represent the tent front. The other set, left free-hanging, was placed at centre stage to function as the back. The latter were widely parted to reveal a ground-row and a sky-cloth behind. Between the sky-cloth and the upper set of curtains hung a gauze used during the appearance of Caesar's ghost. The only furnishings were a table with a boat-lamp, four stools, and several cushions.

As the curtain rises, Brutus is discovered within the tent. The initial confrontation takes place well upstage, outside the tent, but for the quarrel itself, Brutus and Cassius move downstage and inside. Both men pace about agitatedly during the interview, but there is no unusual business. During the conference, the stage is gradually darkened in the traditional manner. When Brutus asks, 'There is no more to say?' 'all rise & salute Brutus'. On 'Good night, my lord', Cassius 'kneels to Brutus', but 'Brutus raises him.'

A few moments later, Lucius touches his 'harp' while a 'Violin on stage' is played pizzicato. When 'his hand falls across the strings and drops by his side', Brutus takes the instrument from him and covers the sleeping boy with his cloak – one of the few softer touches Benson allows the heroic Roman. He then moves to the table, 'sits down again', and picks up his book. The ghost of Caesar enters behind the gauze,[15] speaks his warning, and quickly vanishes. After the exit of his companions, Brutus, visibly shaken, 'sits at table L & says At Philippi' as the curtain falls.

Act IV, Scene ii

The setting for the Confrontation scene, as for the previous one, comprised only the bare essentials. Well upstage hung an 'Ext[erior] cloth' fronted by tree and rock wings up right and down left with rostrums behind. 'Tree wings' masked the sides of the stage and led the eye toward the central area.

Benson establishes the military mood at the outset with an impressionistic tableau, similar to that of Phelps, where 'Men run across R to L as scene opens.' After their exit, Octavius and Antony enter with '2 standard bearers & 4 men'. Cassius, Pindarus, and Metellus, accompanied by '4 soldiers [and] I standard bearer', follow them on. The rival generals stand at opposite sides of the stage and hurl their recriminations across the open space between. When Antony and his party have gone, Brutus enters with four soldiers for the speeches of farewell. Cassius then leads his men off L2E, and a moment later Brutus and his group follow. The scene ends with a black-out.

Act IV, Scene iii

There is no scene change for Cassius' death. As trumpets sound an alarum, the lights come up on nine soldiers who enter running from RUE and 'fight Testudo' (in Roman tortoise formation), with each man shouting for his respective general. A standard-bearer enters L, 'flying across R', 'Cassius stops him & takes standard, wounds standard-bearer who staggers off L.' To Metellus, who enters LUE, Cassius says, 'O, look, Metellus, look, the villains fly.' Benson obviously recognized the need for a military atmosphere in the second half of the play and sought to create it by mimed realistic action. Had he but realized it, the poetry which he cut might well have saved him the labour.

Pindarus now enters L2E to warn Cassius to 'Fly further off.' A moment later, in response to Cassius' order, Metellus exits LUE to make his reconnaissance, and Pindarus stands 'on mound' (the rostrum behind the wing up R) to observe his movements. When ordered to 'Come down', Pindarus joins Cassius near the proscenium and kneels. The stabbing is handled quite straightforwardly with Pindarus holding the sword and Cassius running upon it. Appropriately enough, shouts of 'Ave Caesar' are heard offstage as Cassius dies. Metellus and Claudius discover the body; and not long after, Brutus, companioned by Metellus, '4 soldiers & Varro', arrives to speak the eulogy. As Brutus goes off, the '4 Soldiers lift Cassius body on their shoulders'; and Metellus advances and crowns him with the garland. These lines are transposed from the earlier part of the scene to add a little colour to Cassius' final exit.

Once the stage is clear, Brutus re-enters with Claudius and four soldiers. The death scene is handled in the Kemble manner. Brutus makes his 'ill request' of Claudius and is refused. Varro then rushes on LUE to warn Brutus to fly. Brutus sends off his party to safety and launches directly into his final soliloquy. At this point the lighting is altered to create a sunset effect. As Brutus falls, more cries of 'Ave Caesar' are heard off L.

Octavius, Antony, and their army enter immediately. Soldiers 'carrying brass standards follow Antony on L3E and remain L till curtain'. All available supers, in military garb, enter and group themselves on either side of the stage. As Antony says, 'This was a man', the entire company raise their swords in salute and a funeral march begins. On this grim pageant the curtain falls.

The actors

Benson's stagecraft made the actor the focal point of the production; but few of his young and comparatively inexperienced company could fully meet the challenge. The centrepiece of the performance was always Benson's Antony, a polished and practiced characterization, enhanced by both text and staging. The other roles, entrusted to less seasoned performers and diminished in impact by textual abridgment, constituted a purely secondary interest.

Although only five feet ten and a half inches in height, Benson was a master of the heroic majesty characteristic of Kemble and his school. Dorothy Green asserted in 1948, 'Benson had more natural dignity, both on and off the stage than any actor I have ever seen – except Irving. This commanded a unique respect, without conscious effort on his part.'[16] Benson's style offered little to lovers of contemporary naturalism; his forte was the supra-natural conduct of heroes. Even the young Hesketh Pearson, to whom Shakespeare was 'intolerably tedious at school', found him 'wonderful and mysterious'[17] as Benson played him.

In an age when the theatre attempted to make poetry sound as much as possible like prose, Benson stood almost alone in his insistence upon traditional verse-speaking. 'His voice, at its best, had a bell-like clarity', wrote one critic, 'and it had great dignity and distinction despite a certain nasal quality which, however, gave it character, and which was invaluable

for the colour it lent to some of the ringing speeches in the historical plays
... The words clanged like shields.'[18]

While the heroic tradition was the fountainhead of Benson's strengths, it
was also the source of most of his weaknesses. When he managed to embody
heroic theory satisfactorily in practice, his work was infinitely the better for
it; but when he succeeded only imperfectly, the result was grotesqueness
and extravagance. And Benson could not always tell the difference. Not
infrequently an exaggerated concern for impressive action led him into mere
staginess, and an over-attention to declamation tempted him into sing-song
and rant.

Antony accentuated his strengths and rendered his weaknesses less obvious. His clear-cut classical features lent him an air of convincing Romanness
while his 'dignity and elocutionary powers were praiseworthy in the
extreme'.[19] Occasional staginess was not obtrusive in a character so much
the histrion, and declamatory extravagance less jarring than in a less rhetorical role. Even as late as 1911, when his idiosyncrasies were becoming
uncomfortably conspicuous in other parts, The Morning Post (26 April) still
found 'Mr. Benson's methods ... not out of place in Marcus Antonius'.

Benson's Antony had nothing of Tree's super-subtlety about him. Delicate interplay of emotion and complexity of motivation interested Benson
little. He attempted instead to reduce the composite nature of his character
to a series of simple but telling impressions, linked together by startling
transitions. His interpretation comprised four distinct moods, each clearly
marked off from the others. In the first act, Antony was the masker and
reveller; in the Assassination scene, the grief-stricken and impetuous young
nobleman; in the Forum scene, the impassioned demagogue; and, in the
battle sequences, the confident and magnanimous general.

In his early performances, thanks no doubt to his own fondness for sport,
Benson's portrayal of the aristocratic athlete was highly impressive. 'When
Caesar said "Forget not in your speed, Antonius ..."', Bridges-Adams
recalls, 'one didn't want to laugh, as too often one does'.[20] Draped in
leopard skins, and playfully whipping his female companions with the tails,
he appeared 'remarkably youthful and sportive'.[21] At no time did he use this
first scene to establish an antipathy between Antony and Cassius, or even to
accentuate Antony's friendship for Caesar, as Tree did. He concentrated on
depicting Antony, the sportsman and sensualist – nothing more.

But it was quite another Antony who burst into the Capitol immediately
after the blood-rite. According to Dennis Roberts, he arrived in a state of
extreme agitation, paused for just a moment to survey the scene, and then
rushed to the body of Caesar, throwing himself upon his knees beside the
corpse in an abandon of grief. Throughout the first lines of his 'O mighty
Caesar' speech, he seemed totally oblivious of the presence of the conspirators. Pathos, at this point, was the dominant note.

Soon, however, the pathetic note changed to one of 'stern declamation'[22] as he rose to face the conspirators. On 'I know not, gentlemen', (III.i.151) he effected a Kean-like transition which struck one reviewer as having been made 'with admirable sharpness of outline'.[23] A moment later, when he challenged the conspirators to take his life, he defiantly bared his breast, in high tragic fashion, and offered it to the conspirators' swords.[24]

The sequence in which Antony makes his reluctant compact with the conspirators was played on the most obvious level. In Benson's view, Antony agrees quite genuinely, partly from an inability to resist the blandishments of the conspirators and partly from a preoccupation with his grief which prevented him from fully realizing what he is doing. Suddenly, at the moment of looking down at Caesar, his sense of horror returns; and, shortly afterward, at the moment of requesting permission to 'speak in the order of his funeral', the plan to use his oration as a tool for revenge suggests itself. Benson did not overemphasize this point, but conveyed the impression fleetingly by an eye transition – a common histrionic device a hundred years earlier. As the thought struck him, he raised his eyes excitedly; an instant later he lowered them again, afraid of giving himself away.[25] As one might expect, the 'O pardon me' speech was admirably declaimed.

By modern standards, Benson's rendering of this scene seems artificial to say the least; but few of Benson's contemporaries found it so. One critic did note that he 'rather overacted the scene at Caesar's death',[26] and another found 'the lamentations over Caesar's body were so "stagey" as to become unconvincing';[27] but such censure was rare. Most reviewers seemed to consider his reading, if not beyond praise, at least beyond criticism.

The acme of Benson's performance, however, was the Forum speech. Here his superlative declamation did the rhetoric full justice, while his heroic presence inimitably dominated the crowd. 'His action was dignified', commented one critic; 'his delivery was marked by intensity, intellectual keenness, and impressiveness, and altogether it was a fine study and a striking example of effective and impassioned oratory'.[28] Other reviewers, although they might alter the wording, had not much to add to that assessment.

In the early part of the speech, Benson focussed on Antony's craftiness, holding his passionate energy in store. These first lines Benson spoke slowly with 'significant posings', 'artfully prolonged pauses', and 'many changes of tone of voice',[29] without, however, sacrificing rhythm to realism in the manner of Tree. When he returned from his pause for tears, Benson began to unleash his forces. From 'But yesterday, the word of Caesar might / Have stood against the world' (III.ii.120–1) he contrived a gradual build-up of rhetorical vehemence which culminated only with his 'burst of wild exultation',[30] 'Mischief, thou art afoot.' Reviewers on all sides could hardly find warm enough praise for his portrayal of Antony's 'lofty eloquence', 'the blazing fire of his passion', and 'the intense subtlety of his argument'.[31]

Inevitably, after such a splendid display of virtuoso playing, Benson's succeeding scenes were bound to seem less impressive. Critics, having exhausted superlatives on the Forum oration, seldom commented on the battle sequences at all. Wanting evidence to the contrary, one can only assume that the same nobility which, in Bridges-Adams's opinion, was 'the making of his Henry V'[32] stood him in equally good stead in a similar, if less demanding role.

The respect which Benson himself possessed for early nineteenth-century technique and interpretation, he passed on to his young actors by both precept and example. It is not surprising, then, that their Brutuses, Cassiuses, and Caesars should embody many of the virtues and most of the faults characteristic of the work of their predecessors.

Once more the Kemble Brutus stalked the stage – splendidly declamatory, admirably dignified, but all too often lacking in human warmth. Among the most noteworthy were Oscar Asche (1896, 1898), B. A. Pittar (1906), E. A. Warburton (1908, 1909), and Otho Stuart (1910, 1911, 1915).

Stuart was perhaps the best of these. A gifted and accomplished performer, he had begun his career with Benson in 1885 and later became manager of the Adelphi. Approaching middle-age when he played the part at Stratford in 1910 during a guest appearance, he brought to the role 'a full sense of the nobility of the character' and set 'an example in his declamation which the younger actors might follow to advantage'.[33]

More mature than most of his predecessors and less susceptible to Benson's prejudices, Stuart managed to escape most of the limitations of beau idéal characterization without sacrificing the advantages of beau idéal acting technique. Consequently, his Brutus combined the 'calmness and dignity', the 'masterfulness and majestic power',[34] characteristic of the classical portrayals, with something approaching the human complexity of Shakespeare's design. 'He delineated with great subtlety', writes one reviewer, 'his lofty integrity and self-denial, his purity of life, his generous impulses and his noble patriotism'.[35] But at the same time his stoical patriot remained credibly 'human and sincere'.[36] 'The nobility of character that gave Brutus his epitaph . . . showed admirably in the Quarrel scene', we learn; and his sensitive grasp of Brutus' emotional depths made 'beautiful' his heartbroken announcement, 'Portia's dead.'[37]

If most Bensonian Brutuses came short of being entirely satisfactory, Bensonian Cassiuses were downright disappointing. Of a long line stretching across three decades of Stratford performances, few came near to giving anything like a competent interpretation. Some did not look the part; others caught only one facet or another of the whole man; and still others reduced Shakespeare's delicate portrait to a mere caricature.

The only outstanding readings were those of Henry Ainley and Randle Ayrton. Both men were mature players; both had been trained by Benson; and both played the role after long absences elsewhere. Ainley appeared as a guest star during the 1911 Festival, while Ayrton undertook the part in 1912 and 1914 in the course of a more lengthy Bensonian engagement.

Of the two, perhaps Ainley's Cassius was slightly the better. Thanks to his classical features and graceful movement Ainley suggested physically a 'picture of the scheming Roman of the utmost worth'.[38] Throughout he declaimed his lines 'with admirable clearness and becoming vehemence, yet never losing the sense of rhythm'.[39] Cassius' highly-strung temperament he depicted, not by unbecoming rant, but by a 'finely suggestive restlessness in all his movement'.[40] In the early scenes, one reviewer felt he was perhaps 'too much of the noble Roman soldier, and just a little lacking of the insidious conspirator'; but in the Assassination and Quarrel scenes, 'he more than recovered his little leeway'[41] and played with suitably sinister fire.

Where Ainley concentrated on the 'noble Roman' aspect of Cassius' character, Ayrton emphasized the crafty, conspiratorial side. The *Stratford-upon-Avon Herald* critic described his rendering as an 'earnest, conscientious, intelligent, virile, and passionate performance'. 'Such was his intensity in the earlier scenes', the reviewer continues, 'that sometimes he seemed to be the only one of the conspirators who was really desperately in earnest about the killing of Caesar'. Intensity, however, did not imply boisterousness. In the Quarrel scene, for example, although 'he rose to the height of passion',[42] he maintained the '"cut and thrust" dialogue' with 'great technical skill'. 'Nor did he overdo', according to one reviewer, 'the rhetoric of his first scene with Brutus'.[43] Beyond these scattered comments, descriptive details are almost totally lacking.

In Bensonian revivals, Caesar was at least certain of having an exponent who spoke and moved well; but only two actors – George Fitzgerald (1896, 1898) and Murray Carrington (1908, 1909, 1910, 1911) – brought much imagination to the role. Fitzgerald both 'looked the character and was possessed of sufficient dignity'[44] to make his reading credible. His portrait, however, was not that of the 'all-conquering general' of previous revivals, but of a Caesar 'declining in greatness, weakening in body and hastening to his death at the hands of his disaffected countrymen'[45] – an approach which was to be more fully explored in recent times.

Murray Carrington, who 'not merely looked the part, but acted with dignity',[46] presented a similar romantic portrait of Shakespeare's Colossus. Although still a 'potent and masterful personage',[47] Carrington's Caesar had become, with increasing age, 'a little lacking in strength and over-moody'. According to one critic, 'the underlying suggestion seemed to be that Caesar, at the period of his death, was losing his grip on his friends and fellow citizens by reason of the failings which herald dotage. His strength is becoming mere obstinacy, his justice, asperity, and his love of power an over-weening ambition.'[48] After at least two centuries of being a figurehead, Caesar at last begins to receive some consideration as a man.

Although Benson's savage text-cutting and adaptation delayed a full appreciation of *Julius Caesar*'s dramatic structure by three decades, his productions constitute a crucial bridge between the classical tradition and the modern neo-Elizabethan approach. His insistence upon the heroic acting style and the intelligent speaking of Shakespeare's verse stoutly defended *Julius Caesar*'s tragic stature against the inroads of naturalism until the neo-Elizabethan movement had gained sufficient influence in the commercial theatre to permit a fresh investigation of its potential. And the art and craft of the players he trained lent rare heroic radiance to the pioneering full-text revivals by William Bridges-Adams at the Memorial Theatre and Robert Atkins at the Old Vic.

9

William Bridges-Adams at Stratford
(1919–34)

In 1919, at the age of 60, Benson returned to Stratford for what proved to be his last Birthday Festival. Shortly after, it was announced that the New Shakespeare Company would succeed the Bensonians in the summer season, with William Bridges-Adams[1] as Festival Director. *Julius Caesar* was staged in August in the first full-text production at a major theatre since the Restoration;[2] and a second revival followed in 1922. When the theatre burned in 1926, Bridges-Adams made *Caesar* a feature of his initial season at the Greenhill Street cinema, where he repeated it in 1928 and 1930. In 1932, during his inaugural Festival at the new theatre, he re-staged the play with all the resources of modern technology; and in 1934 brought his mature art to a final production, just two years before his resignation. The 1919 revival saw *Caesar* shaped for the first time by the craft of the director rather than the whim of the actor-manager, an innovation crucial to the course of the play in this century.

If only 30 when he arrived in Stratford, Bridges-Adams was no theatrical novice; behind him lay ten years of acting and directing, part of it under the tutelage of William Poel and Harley Granville-Barker. His contact with Poel made him thoroughly familiar with the latter's fanatical, often cranky, crusade in favour of uncut texts,[3] swift speaking, and Elizabethan stagecraft; and he broadly sympathized with his goals. To Granville-Barker, however, he turned for a production method which adapted Poel's sometimes esoteric notions to the realities of a professional theatre.

'As a general sort of principle we are going on the lines of full text',[4] Bridges-Adams announced shortly after his appointment; and the experiment was on the whole a success. 'When mutilation was still customary', he wrote later, 'it was a good thing to pass the whole of Shakespeare under review and see what he amounted to. Certainly it restored much neglected beauty.'[5] After any play had been attempted once in its entirety, he frequently made minor deletions. The First Folio, experience convinced him, 'abounds in imperfections, even setting its seal on some unmistakeable gags'.[6]

To fit relatively full texts to normal theatre-going hours meant rapid speech and an end to tedious business. Running time was further shortened by radical alteration of the proscenium stage along Granville-Barker lines. The cramped conditions of both the old Memorial Theatre and the Greenhill Street cinema ruled out an apron, but the rest of Granville-Barker's arrangement, slightly modified, was readily reproduced.

Bridges-Adams installed a false proscenium slightly behind the main one, rather than within it as Granville-Barker had done, thus adding some depth to the forward part of the stage to compensate for want of an apron. Immediately behind the arch he flew a black curtain which dropped as necessary to separate the front of the stage from the back. Much of the action took place well forward; and the space upstage of the arch was reserved mainly for settings. This area could be subdivided by a second curtain to allow two shallow sets to be readied simultaneously. Thanks to the fluidity of the curtain technique, complemented by a brisk acting style, a play could be performed in its entirety in about three hours, even allowing for one or two intervals totalling from ten to twenty minutes. With some slight alteration from year to year, play to play, and theatre to theatre, Bridges-Adams retained the same basic format throughout his Stratford management.

Although at one with Poel and Granville-Barker on many issues, he differed from both on the question of décor. He was no lover of Poel's bare platform; nor was his scenic taste as avant-garde as Granville-Barker's. He opted instead for effects which were pictorial without being strictly representational – a compromise between traditional realism and Craig's atmospherics. As a rule scenery was lightly built, pre-set offstage on trolleys, and wheeled on as required. In the new theatre trolleys were superseded by the rolling stage.

Wherever possible he eliminated footlights, and lit the stage à la Craig from the dress circle. For the tragedies in particular he relied strongly on chiaroscuro to underline the emotional progress of the action; but he never fully mastered the technique, and many of the most crucial scenes were woefully underlighted.

Although Bridges-Adams shared his mentors' commitment to ensemble performance, its realization eluded him. Shakespearian actors were in short supply: the Bensonians were ageing and younger players lacked classical skills. Moreover, a one-week rehearsal period for each play left time for little more than a passable standard of interpretation and some semblance of overall co-ordination. 'These productions have got to bear the same relation to the sort of Shakespeare we aim at doing as an artist's first sketch will bear to the finished painting', he warned. 'That is to say, we may in many cases have to claim to be judged by what we are suggesting than by what we achieve.'[7] Whatever the shortcomings, and they were patent, audiences saw each play in its entirety with no star to come between them and the work itself; and that was a rare and novel experience. After two centuries of service as a star-vehicle, the play at last assumed an identity of its own.

To properly appreciate Bridges-Adams' contribution to *Julius Caesar* production one must look at the revivals of 1932 and 1934 when his technical facilities were for the first time other than makeshift. The 1932 revival, although well-received, was marred by the director's unfamiliarity with his stage. In 1934, however, after two years of experimentation, he re-worked the same production with greater success; and here execution most nearly matched conception. An invaluable guide to its reconstruction is the promptbook (*JC* 80) used in 1928, 1932, and 1934. Another book (*JC* 79), containing fuller directions for manipulation of scenery and probably prepared by the stage manager in 1932, helps clarify a number of perplexing technical points.[8]

Compared with the drastic cast-reduction of earlier times, Bridges-Adams's alterations in this area are minor. Publius and Young Cato are eliminated; and at Brutus' death, Claudius and Lucilius replace Dardanius and Clitus. In the main, however, doubling was preferred to speech-redistribution: one actor played Octavius and Cinna, another, Lepidus and Cicero, a third, Trebonius and Messala, a fourth, Decius Brutus and Lucilius, a fifth, the Soothsayer and Pindarus, and a sixth, Ligarius and Titinius.

The 1919 full-text production excited widespread critical comment, most of it favourable.[9] The *Stratford Herald* reviewer hastened to congratulate the director 'on the restoration to the play of various scenes and lines which in almost every case helped on the story of the tragedy';[10] while the *Daily Mail* critic went further to claim that 'in all the matter included ... there was nothing that could have been dispensed with save to the detriment of the picture as a whole'.[11] Bridges-Adams found himself satisfied in the main with the play as Shakespeare left it, but felt judicious pruning here and there would render it 'cleaner and stronger'. For later revivals he blue-pencilled vocabulary and syntax which might prove puzzling at first hearing, puns which seemed forced or inappropriate, and short passages which blurred the sense of long speeches or unduly retarded their movement. Occasionally, too, he excised minor incidents when the dramatic action seemed in danger of lagging. Among the passages cut to clarify and accelerate the longer speeches were four lines of Casca's description of the portents (I.iii.22–5) and thirteen lines of Cassius' reiteration of much the same material (I.iii.59–71). The latter part of Cassius' account of Caesar's superstition (II.i.198–201) was snipped as similarly redundant.

Six passages in all are dispensed with as inimical to dramatic flow. Brutus' disquisition on declining friendship (IV.ii.19–27), shortly before the arrival of Cassius at the tent, is the first cut of this type. From the Tent scene, the

Camp Poet, 'as unnecessary as he is intrusive',[12] is once more banished. The brief comments made within each party before they confront each other (v.i.21–6) are also marked for omission. Brutus' 'Ride, ride, Messala' speech (v.ii) is rejected as inconsequential; and the employment of Strato by Mark Antony (v.v.58–67) is dismissed as anticlimactic.

A few further cuts were made on the grounds of propriety. Since the costumes were 'orthodox, and accurate, Roman: togas, breastplates and so on',[13] references to hats, cloaks, and gowns were removed whenever possible. A curious survival of the traditional heroic cut is the exclusion of Portia's mention of Brutus' head-scratching and foot-stamping (ii.i.243–5) and Caesar's reference to Ligarius' ague (ii.ii.111–13).

In addition to scattered minor abridgements, two major excisions were made – the Cinna the Poet scene (iii.iii) and the sequence in which Lucilius is captured by Antony's forces (v.iv); but both cuts were dictated more by necessity than choice. Bridges-Adams felt the Cinna incident 'should certainly be kept in, provided the *stimmung* can be maintained', but fearing it would afford only 'a wry comment' in the hands of an inexperienced crowd of townspeople, he removed it. Similarly, he would have preferred to retain the scene in which Lucilius is taken prisoner (v.iv), but 'with six first nights in a week', he writes, 'my supers were not quite up to a convincing battle'.[14]

Apart from the two rather heavier cuts just mentioned, Bridges-Adams's alterations, if annoying to the textual purist, were hardly of serious detriment to the play's integrity.

Stagecraft

Before attempting some reconstruction of the 1934 revival, two additions to the basic stage discussed earlier must be noted. The spacious interior of the new theatre would have allowed Bridges-Adams to build a Granville-Barker-type apron over the orchestra pit had he so desired; instead he chose to place a broad flight of steps in the same area.[15] Such an arrangement meant that scenes could be played 'as it were under the feet of the stalls',[16] and, when necessary, action could take place on two levels simultaneously. Even more important, perhaps, was the installation of the rolling stage. Prior to 1932, visual splendour had frequently been sacrificed to manual mobility; now with ample bays on either side of the acting area, substantial scenes could be pre-set and rolled on electrically as required. Complexity of setting and continuity of action were no longer incompatible.

The scenery for the 1932 and 1934 revivals was designed by Aubrey Hammond who felt, as did the *Times* critic, that *Julius Caesar* seemed 'to require an architectural background suggesting the massive grandeur of Rome'.[17] Without attempting anything like a detailed re-creation of the

12. 'A Public Place' (I.i). William Bridges-Adams's production at the Shakespeare Memorial Theatre, 1934. Designed by Aubrey Hammond

city, Hammond aimed to weave, by a combination of towering columns, arches, and steps, an atmosphere convincingly Roman and sufficiently weighty and permanent to throw the frailty of the human figures into sharp relief.

Act I, scene i

To a 'Long Flourish', the curtain rises on the Public Place setting (Illustration 12), an arrangement of steps and columns backed by arches and a statue set against the skyline. The positioning of the steps[18] moves the action well forward and later allows for multi-level groupings.

The mob is already romping about the stage in holiday mood; and almost immediately Flavius and Marullus enter R2E, the former carrying a scroll. As in Benson's productions, the revellers take an active part, but are carefully subordinated to Flavius and Marullus. During the bout with the cobbler, they laugh at his retorts, but undertake no business on their own account. When the cobbler refers to himself as a 'surgeon to old shoes', 'Flavius turns to Mar. & smiles.' Bridges-Adams starts on a low note; the early moments are relaxed and amusing; only gradually is the serious theme introduced.

The steps come into play with Marullus' 'Wherefore rejoice?' speech. For this he stands well toward the top with the citizens in clusters from the steps just below him to the main stage floor. Bridges-Adams's mob is less fierce than Benson's; beyond the occasional murmur they do nothing to impede the flow of the rhetoric. From the first they are submissive to Marullus' reproaches, and exit on 'That needs must light on this ingratitude' (i.i.55), murmuring guiltily among themselves.

With the crowd and tribunes off, martial music begins in the orchestra, and Caesar's procession enters from the right at the top of the steps. The dramatic effect of the Dictator's first appearance is considerably enhanced by placing him above stage level. Most of the panoply which had accumulated over two centuries is dispensed with; Caesar's once-splendid following now comprises merely the characters named and the crowd.

The Soothsayer enters right, by a downstage entrance, and shouts to Caesar as he begins his descent of the steps. A moment later he moves upstage to repeat his admonition; and here, too, the lines profit by being spoken from above. The party then passes downstage and exits left.

Brutus, standing by the pillar at RC, is about to exit right when Cassius stops him. Their exchange of views is swift and uncluttered by business. Caesar's procession then re-enters from the left. He pauses briefly to speak to Antony, and moves off right. The remainder of the scene is played straightforwardly with only one novel touch. When Casca is asked to dinner by Cassius, the former is seen 'Taking out Tablets from Toga', which he consults like a modern appointment-book before he replies.

This scene is typical of Bridges-Adams direction throughout. Already apparent is a fine sensitivity to *Caesar*'s integral rhythm; full weight is given to the words themselves, and nothing is introduced which would hamper their flow. Action is sparse, save when it is significant, and almost all business vanishes. Although the setting has undeniable visual appeal, its form is clearly secondary to its function.

Act I, scene ii

While the curtain is down for a moment, part of the steps on the left are struck and an arch is rolled on to suggest a change of locale. The curtain rises again to the roar of thunder and wind. Cicero enters 'L from orchestra', that is up the steps covering the orchestra pit. Here the steps are used as an apron to bring the ominous rhetoric as close as possible to the audience. Thunderclaps are heard at intervals throughout. When the stage is finally clear, the post-proscenium curtain falls just long enough for the Street setting to be rolled off and replaced.

Act I, scene iii

The setting for the Orchard episode marks a radical departure from both Shakespeare and tradition. Bridges-Adams and Hammond, probably in a conscious attempt to contravene custom, moved the action from the garden to the interior of Brutus' house. The walls of a Roman room were suggested; and in the background, through an arch, a hill could be seen looming against the sky. This exterior view permits the later outdoor references to be included without impropriety. The only furnishings are a table and four chairs at centre left. Whether such a change of locale is in the interest of the play is problematical; if it does nothing worse, it tends to break the link between man and nature which gives the Storm and Orchard sequences some measure of continuity.

Brutus is 'discovered standing L of arch – looking off R'. He sits 'R of table' for his soliloquy. The speech is delivered quietly, directly, and intensely; no extraneous movement or histrionic posturing interrupts his agonized reflection. With 'Am I entreated . . .', his decision is reached; and he rises resolutely to implement it.

Shortly after, the conspirators enter R2E, and 'Each man holds his R hand up in salute as his name is called. Brutus holds salute throughout.' From this point onwards, Brutus is the recognized leader. Instead of the traditional silence during the hand-shaking sequence, Brutus begins his 'No, not an oath' speech directly, shaking hands as he speaks, and pausing by each man to deliver a few lines of his appeal. As he finishes, several of the conspirators 'move to table all murmuring'. Brutus sits, and Cassius proceeds to 'put scroll of names on Table' in front of him, asking as he does so, 'But what of Cicero?' While the question is debated, all group themselves about the table, sitting and standing. When his demand for the murder of Antony is rejected, Cassius moves to the left and ramps up and down in annoyance.

On 'The clock hath stricken three', 'all rise except Decius', who remains seated a moment longer, and begin to move to the right. At this point, Cassius' better nature triumphs; and, passing toward RC on '. . . we'll leave you Brutus' (II.i.221), he affectionately rests his 'Hand on Brutus' shoulders'. Just before leaving, he impulsively 'turns & shakes hands' warmheartedly, then exits with his companions R2E.

Unlike her nineteenth-century counterparts, Portia does not appear until the grim visitors have gone. She then enters C, standing at some distance from her husband as she says, 'Brutus, my lord'. While she recounts his strange behaviour, Brutus sits remote and unmoved; then, absently, he 'holds out his hand to her', urging, 'Good Portia, go to bed.' Portia does not take it, but persists with her inquiry kneeling. Brutus 'turns away from her'. At the mention of her self-inflicted wound, however, his reticence vanishes.

He 'Rises – raising Portia', kisses her, and agrees to construe his engagements later.

This scene is a model of swift pace and emotional intensity. Portia's distraught legato pleas counterpointed by Brutus' tortured staccato rejoinders, offer a marked contrast in rhythm and mood with the impersonal deliberation of the conspiracy sequence.

Portia exits C, and Ligarius, assisted by Lucius, enters RIE. No attempt is made to overstress the conversation which follows; it serves merely to separate the two domestic episodes.

Act II, scene i

Since two scenes had now to be pre-set for almost simultaneous use, no space was available for a deep Caesar's House setting. A full set could have been provided by allowing an interval; but Bridges-Adams was reluctant to break the rhythm at this point. Instead, the scene was played before simple grey curtains drawn just behind the black ones. No furniture was used, and the characters stood throughout.

At the beginning of the scene, Caesar enters 'thro' tabs C' and 'claps hands once', demanding 'Who's within?' After the servant's exit, Calphurnia arrives from L. She remains at a respectful distance as she hesitatingly recounts the supernatural events; then, emboldened by her fear, she comes closer and 'kneels L to him'. Like Portia, she remains thus for some time. Finally, convinced that resistance is futile, she rises; but a moment later, in a last desperate attempt, she once more kneels, pleading, 'Let me upon me knee prevail in this' (II.ii.54). Caesar then 'raises her' with the promise, 'And for thy humour I will stay at home' (II.ii.56). Here, as in the previous scene, physical movement is economical; the words themselves are Bridges-Adams's prime concern.

Decius now enters R2E and proceeds to shake Caesar's resolution. Throughout the conversation Decius does not stir. Caesar crosses to him as he enters, and they stand close together for the first part of the interview. As Caesar describes Calphurnia's fears, he moves back to her and takes her hand affectionately. By stressing the warmth of Caesar's feeling for Calphurnia, Bridges-Adams correspondingly underscores the strength of the vanity which shortly overcomes it. 'How foolish do your fears seem now, Calphurnia!' (II.ii.105) fractures the mood of domestic harmony; and on 'Give me my robe', Calphurnia exits resignedly to do as he requests.

At this point, the conspirators arrive from the right proscenium door, and Antony follows almost immediately. The remainder of the scene is briskly played; and as Brutus exits the drop falls.

Act II, scene ii

To approximate Elizabethan continuity, Bridges-Adams merged the events of the next three scenes – Artemidorus' reading of his paper, Portia's meeting with the Soothsayer, and the assassination – into one long sequence, thus allowing tension to build without interruption from Artemidorus' appearance to Caesar's death-struggle. The first part of the scene was played within a heavy architectural setting representing the exterior of Brutus' House. A back-flat with a functional door fronted by steps and pillars was placed just behind the false proscenium. Artemidorus is discovered C, reading his paper; and when he has finished, he exits L2E, and Portia and Lucius enter. Their conversation takes place well forward at C. The Soothsayer appears and is avidly questioned. Once he has gone, almost hysterical with concern, Portia 'put[s] Lucius across L' in her eagerness to have him away and back with news. Then, excitedly looking after him, she 'exits into house C'.

'When doors are shut', Artemidorus enters and stands upstage left. To music from the orchestra, Caesar's procession enters, preceded by the crowd. As Caesar comes level with Artemidorus, the latter shouts from near the pillars, 'Hail, Caesar! Read this schedule.' Decius 'Throw [s] Art. over C' and Cassius 'swings him away up C'.

The procession once more moves off, and as it does so, the rolling stage brings the Capitol setting into view. A greater contrast could hardly be imagined than that between the elegant Capitols of the realistic era and the bare, functional interior now employed. Luxurious draperies, sculptures, and friezes yield to a severe arrangement of Roman columns against the cyclorama. Immediately in front, well upstage, were stone benches for the senators. Forward and to the left stood Caesar's chair on a pedestal, and on the opposite side loomed the base of Pompey's statue.

Like Benson, Bridges-Adams realized that to admit the crowd to the stage would be to lessen somewhat the interest in Caesar. At the same time, however, he was reluctant to eliminate altogether the Roman people, on whose behalf the assassination is ostensibly perpetrated. In the end the citizens stood offstage right with lictors at the door to keep them back. The audience was thus audibly reminded without being visually distracted. Apart from a handful of extra senators, only the characters directly involved were onstage.

Popilius' approach to Cassius and Mark Antony's withdrawal with Trebonius are soon over, and the action moves swiftly toward the assassination itself. As Cassius (not Cinna) says, 'Casca, you are the first that rears your hand', Casca 'xs L below Caesar' to await his opportunity. Caesar asks, 'Are we all ready?' and Metellus kneels to present his petition. The other senators sit. When Metellus appeals, 'Is there no voice more worthy than my own', the conspirators approach one by one, kneel before Caesar, rise, and group themselves in a rough semi-circle about him. As Casca stabs, shouting, 'Speak hands for me!' 'all senators rise – Caesar staggers down steps into C of circle – then all stab – he staggers forward RC – meets Brutus – who stabs him'. He falls downstage right at the base of Pompey's statue.

Thus, in the most austere of settings, Bridges-Adams swiftly and cleanly presents the crucial action of the play. And, managed in this way, used neither to aggrandize the conspirators, as in the eighteenth century, nor Mark Antony, as in Tree's revivals, Caesar himself took on a new significance. 'Caesar's tragedy is the key to Mr. Bridges Adams' production', wrote the *Yorkshire Post* critic. 'His assassination, apparently to the public good, is made a reason for mourning, and even when mourning gives place to mutiny the spirit of the general, who thrice refused a crown, hovers always sadly near.'[19] The basic soundness of Hudson's suggestion, made half a century earlier, that 'Caesar is not only the subject but also the governing power of it [the play] throughout'[20] was clearly demonstrated in the playhouse.

In the confusion Trebonius re-enters 'with Blood sponge concealed'. From up LC, Cassius exclaims, 'Stoop then, and wash', and 'all kneel but Cassius & put blood upon arms'. As Brutus bathes, he contemplatively asks, 'How many times shall Caesar bleed in sport, / That now on Pompey's basis lies along, / No worthier than the dust!' (III.i.114–16). Almost immediately Cassius 'kneel[s] L of body', suggesting more pragmatically, 'So oft as that shall be, / So often shall the knot of us be call'd / The men that gave their country liberty' (III.i.116–18). By having each man participate in the bloodrite separately, Bridges-Adams tellingly points Shakespeare's contrasting portraits – Brutus, the humanist and philosopher, detachedly speculating about history as theatre, and Cassius, the politician, subjectively assessing his role in it.

As the conspirators prepare to exit, the servant arrives with Antony's message, and Antony himself appears shortly. Paying no attention to the conspirators, he moves immediately 'to R of body' to speak his lament. 'All swords are levelled at Antony' as Brutus says, 'Welcome, Mark Antony', thus lending a fine ironic touch to the greeting.

No attempt is made to accentuate Antony's role by intrusive business; at the same time, however, Bridges-Adams takes special care to prevent the rest of the characters from attracting attention at Antony's expense. Antony does indeed rise to dominance, but by the impact of the lines themselves, not by directorial ingenuity. Apart from Antony, the only character permitted to budge is the febrile Cassius. When Antony requests permission to produce Caesar's body in the market-place, the shrewd conspirator, deeply perturbed, 'turns to Casca'. A moment later he is protesting to Brutus, and, soon after, he 'xs R to Trebonius up C' to make his point once more. As the conspirators quit the stage, Bridges-Adams introduces one of Tree's managerial touches. Nearing the exit, Brutus triumphantly 'raises his sword' and all cry, 'Peace! Freedom! & Liberty!'

Antony kneels by the body for the first part of his 'O, pardon me, thou bleeding piece of earth' speech, but rises on 'And Caesar's spirit', emphasizing by decisive movement the impact the dead Dictator will have upon the course of future events. As he concludes the imprecation Octavius' servant enters R2E and kneels. Since Antony is standing between him and the corpse, the servant sees nothing until 'Antony holds toga back.' His horror-stricken reaction to the bleeding hulk prefigures the mass shock which will follow the same revelation in the next scene. On 'Lend me your hand' Antony 'xs to head of body & kneels' while the servant 'xs to L of body'. At this point orchestral music begins and the curtain falls.

A five-minute interval marks the end of what the programme describes as the 'First Part' of the play. After the almost unbroken concentration demanded by Bridges-Adams's continuous action, the audience could well profit from a few minutes' relaxation before the second movement begins.

Act III

During the interval, 'the rolling-stage parted in the middle and the Forum came up on bridges'.[21] This, the heaviest setting of all, consisted of a massive flight of steps[22] behind which were placed pieces suggestive of Roman architecture. Immediately in front, at the top of the steps, stood an immense black column. The brightly-lit cyclorama in the background lent an air of vast space to the whole. Antony gave his oration from what appears to have been a small rock piece placed slightly right of centre; no rostrum as such was used.[23]

As the curtain rises, some citizens are discovered milling about on the Forum steps, and more 'surge up from the orchestra pit', bringing the audience, as it were, within the scene. Brutus and Cassius follow them on and pause near the proscenium to 'part the numbers'. The latter immediately 'exits down steps to orchestra R' with his party as Brutus ascends the steps. Outlined in silhouette against the sky, Brutus begins his oration. Below him stand the citizens, spread out over the Forum steps, the proscenium area, and the steps leading to the orchestra pit.

Throughout the oration the citizens take their usual active part, repeating significant phrases, murmuring, and shouting 'Aye' at appropriate intervals. Like his predecessors, Bridges-Adams is careful to start the scene on a restrained note, allowing Brutus a fairly easy triumph over the citizens' antipathy so as not to detract from the effect of Antony's demagoguery. The only point worthy of note in the scene's early moments is the fact that the citizens shout 'Aye! aye! mournfully' to Brutus' assertion, 'but as he was ambitious, I slew him'. Although they take Brutus' word for the necessity of Caesar's death, they are none the less saddened by it. And it is this underlying mood of regret for the loss of a popular leader which Antony later plays upon to such good purpose.

As Brutus says, 'Here comes his body', he 'points off R to Caesar's procession'. Antony and his party now enter R2E and deposit the body in the centre of the proscenium area. Shortly after, to enthusiastic shouts, Brutus exits by way of the orchestra steps.

Antony now climbs to the spot Brutus has just vacated and seeks to gain a hearing; but he is met with the usual laughter, shouts, and howls. For the most part, the speech is handled in the Benson manner, spoken 'right on' with the dissenting voices coming up over it at intervals. Throughout the early part of the address, Antony struggles against strenuous opposition; but when he turns aside to weep the balance dips slightly in his favour. The citizens avidly discuss the matter among themselves. Many of them genuinely feel the grief that Antony is at such pains to simulate. Two of the more violent partisans even break into fisticuffs and are separated by their less impetuous fellows.

The scene is played in the Benson mode until the citizens demand to hear the testament. Bridges-Adams then strikes out on his own. 'You will compel me then to read the will?' demands Antony, and shouts of 'The Will!!' 'swell up and gradually die down – up again and down to silence'. To utter stillness Antony makes a long descent of the steps and stands on the floor of the main stage just behind the body. Before him the citizens mill about feverishly on the orchestra steps. By bringing the action out of the proscenium area at this point, Bridges-Adams comes close to reproducing the intimacy of the Globe stage. Massed behind the seething crowd, the audience become virtual participants in the action.

As Antony catalogues the dagger-holes, sobs run through the crowd and tension mounts steadily. Sobs in turn are succeeded by 'screams and moans' when he 'strip[s] off mantle' and the citizens catch sight of their murdered leader. Antony's ironical assertion that the conspirators are 'wise and honourable' provokes a burst of disillusioned laughter, and shrieking, 'We'll burn the house of Brutus', the mob begins to push toward L. The lights are now lowered, and in the half-dark Antony reads the will. As he exclaims, 'Here was a Caesar! when comes such another?' four frenzied citizens raise Caesar's body, carry it up the full height of the steps, and disappear. While the mob surges against the skyline, red lights, reminiscent of Benson's burning Rome, come up on the cyclorama. In the reflected glow, Antony stands posed 'with his back to the audience and his arms raised, invoking a blessing on his work'[24] while 'a beggar clutches at his legs'.[25] The servant then enters to announce Octavius' arrival. A moment later he and Antony exit together as the drop descends.

Viewed as an isolated unit, Bridges-Adams's Forum scene was regarded as highly successful; when judged as part of a larger composition, however, critics found he had staged it too well. In the earlier part of the play, he had been scrupulously attentive to *Caesar*'s overall shape; but with the Forum sequence he seems to have lost perspective. As in the Benson and Tree productions, the play reached a dramatic pitch which could neither be sustained nor surpassed; and, yet again, acts IV and V seemed somewhat dull and anti-climactic, all the more so since Bridges-Adams cut far less than did the actor-managers. The sense of let-down was hardly lessened by a fifteen-minute interval before the episode in Antony's house.

Act IV, scene i

The Proscription sequence was played before a colourful curtain hung just behind the proscenium. The only furniture was a table and three chairs. The triumvirs remain seated throughout, save for Lepidus who rises and exits on 'Fetch the will hither'. The forward setting permits the audience to watch the sordid political manoeuvres at very close range indeed; and here, as earlier, Bridges-Adams focusses attention on emotional interplay by limiting physical movement. The most noteworthy point about this scene, however, is the fact that it was played at all. The drop falls as Antony and Octavius exit to allow the furniture to be removed and the curtain withdrawn.

Act IV, scene ii

The Tent, another shallow and simple setting, was located just behind the space occupied by Antony's house. Blue or purple drapes (referred to as 'Royals') were suspended at centre-stage, fronted by grey curtains on either side. The Royals were parted, as in Benson's design, to reveal a stone row and an expanse of sky behind. Above was an awning to suggest a roof, and towards the left stood a tent-pole. Just to the right of the pole were a table and stools.

Brutus enters C and gives his helmet to Lucius who stands LC. Lucilius and Pindarus enter soon after. Cassius arrives from the right and 'Throw[s] helmet to Pindarus' as he enters. The trivial act of dispensing with headgear is used by Bridges-Adams, as by Barrett and Davenport, to point up the temperamental dissimilarity between the two men.

Once Pindarus and Lucilius are dismissed, Brutus 'sits behind the table' while Cassius, characteristically enough, 'ramp[s] up & down'. Agitatedly he picks up a chair and moves it upstage as he contemptuously echoes Brutus' 'Chastisement'. A moment later, warning, 'Urge me no more', he comes threateningly to where Brutus sits. Brutus puts down his scroll and rises decisively. During his verbal onslaught, Brutus moves but little, driving home his words with reserved force. As Cassius at last breaks under the attack, he comes abjectly to where Brutus stands, 'Kneels & offers Brutus his dagger.' Impassively Brutus takes the sword from him and returns it 'hilt foremost', raising Cassius as he does so. He finds it harder to maintain the same imperturbability a few lines later as he announces his wife's death. Turning away from Cassius, he stoops to pick up his cloak from the ground, saying quite simply, 'Portia is dead.'

The drinking and conference sequences are played without fuss. The only point worthy of note is another of Bridges-Adams's subtle character insights embodied in significant action. As Messala asks, 'Had you your letters from your wife, my lord?' Cassius impulsively 'puts his hand over Brutus'', wordlessly attempting to shield him against the reminder of his loss. This very simple gesture serves once more to emphasize Cassius' essential likeability, a point which must be firmly made if the audience is to sympathize to any degree with his suicide.

When the visitors have gone Lucius enters with the gown. Brutus seats himself at the right of the table while Lucius sings. When the latter falls asleep, Brutus 'takes instrument & puts it down against stool R'. The ghost now appears, but apparently Bridges-Adams made little of it; certainly not enough to satisfy the *Stratford Herald* critic who objected that 'the ghost of Caesar is not given much of a show'. This, he thought, was a 'factor contributing to the loss of dramatic value in the later scenes'.[26] As the ghost vanishes, Brutus abruptly 'rises – knocks over table – holds lamp'. This sudden, agitated movement assumes considerable significance when compared with the restraint which has characterized his action elsewhere. He now awakens Lucius, Claudius, and Varro and questions them fervidly. The drop falls as Varro and Claudius salute and begin to move off. Orchestral music bridges the brief wait between this scene and the next.

Act V, scene i

During the musical interlude, the curtains and stone row are drawn off and the canopy is raised into the flies, revealing the full Plains of Philippi setting behind. In order to permit quick and continuous action in the battle scenes and yet provide some visual variety, Hammond designed a special pre-set rural vista, sixty-six feet in width,[27] which could be rolled on a little at a time (Illustration 13).

13. 'The Plains of Philippi' (act v). William Bridges-Adams's production at the Shakespeare Memorial Theatre, 1934. Designed by Aubrey Hammond

Apart from the scenic novelty, there is little of interest in the Confrontation sequence. At its close the black curtain behind the false proscenium falls briefly to allow a fresh part of the setting to be rolled into view.

Act V, scene ii

The scene opens with a battle tableau in the Benson mode. As the curtain rises there is a 'general fight across'. From the left enter four soldiers who go 'over hill & exit R'. Cassius comes on in combat with the ensign bearer and 'kill [s] him behind bank'. Titinius now appears and 'takes the Ensign from Cassius & gets down R'. The orchestra provides appropriate martial music at intervals.

Cassius' death is not prolonged. Pindarus comes down from the hill, takes the sword which Cassius holds out to him, 'turns away' momentarily 'as if to refuse', then does as he is bidden. As Cassius dies, he 'staggers up stage & falls C'.

It is worth noting in passing that the sequence in which Titinius kills himself is restored. When Messala exits to inform Brutus of Cassius' death, Titinius 'move[s] down L of Cassius' and kneels. On 'By your leave, gods!' he is directed to 'undo shoulder buckle of breastplate'. He then stabs himself and 'fall[s] across Cassius face up'.

As Brutus and his party discover the bodies, a 'voice off L' is heard in a single shout of 'Caesar!' Startled, all 'look off L'. Only Brutus comprehends the meaning of the cry, and remarks, deeply moved, 'O Julius Caesar, thou art mighty yet.' Here, as the play nears its end, Bridges-Adams again underscores Caesar's central position in the tragedy. His eulogy completed, Brutus commands, 'let us to the field', and exits as the black curtain descends. The curtain here serves to indicate a time-lapse, a function normally served by the episode in which Lucilius is taken prisoner.

Act V, scene iii

Brutus now, enters L and moves slowly to the rock at R. The officers remain on the opposite side of the stage. One by one Brutus summons them to sit by him, and makes his 'ill request'. After refusing, each man moves back to his original position. Strato, meanwhile, falls asleep, but awakens as Clitus shouts, 'Fly, fly, my lord.' At this point, Brutus stands and begins his farewells, 'taking all their hands' in turn. With the command 'Hence!' the officers exit. Strato is about to follow when Brutus 'signs' to him, and he comes to sit on Brutus' left.

As the sword is drawn, both rise, and when Brutus has run upon it, Strato 'catches him & supports him till he dies – falling on rock C'. Once more the cry 'Caesar!' is heard, linking the sinister influence of the living Caesar which tempted the first dagger-thrusts with the retributive puissance of the dead Colossus which completes the cycle of violence.

Antony now enters with Messala, Octavius, and his army. The soldiers pass behind the rock and group themselves upstage. With Antony's eulogy spoken and the funeral arrangements made, the drop falls to a long flourish from the orchestra.

The actors

To say that interpretations of *Caesar*'s major roles were not of star standard during the Bridges-Adams era, or even to call them 'sketches', as he did, is not to suggest that they lacked interest. Since the play was performed in comparatively full text, facets of the characters hitherto unnoticed continually caught the eye. Freed from the domination of the actor-manager and the constraint of tradition, actors found freedom to explore and experiment. The non-Bensonians, in particular, brought a fresh and unorthodox outlook to their roles, sweeping away the long-accumulated cobwebs and exposing them to the light of modern thinking.

In contrast to the stolid, impassive Brutus familiar from the time of Kemble, Eric Maxon's Roman was 'all action and activity'.[28] George Hayes saw him as a stoic 'sufficient and vain in his virtue',[29] while the more romantic John Wyse portrayed the 'haunted and unhappy soul, movingly pathetic if not truly tragic'.[30]

Cassius, too, came in for considerable, if less radical, change. 'Not all unscrupulousness', like so many of his predecessors, Maxon's Cassius was 'a man with many better instincts, but always his envy and ambition drove him to stifle them'.[31] Baliol Holloway's more subtle portrait depicted 'the man of action tired of the political game, yet using, despite himself, the politician's wiles in a politician's world'.[32] In the hands of Hayes, however, Holloway's tired politician became 'a flaming figure of revolt, storming through scene after scene like a revivalist preacher'.[33]

Antony, predictably, underwent a shattering metamorphosis. With the Proscription scene restored, Charles Kemble's magnanimous young Roman abruptly shed his halo. If the Antonys of Bridges-Adams's revivals were less noble in bearing and less nimble of tongue than their forbears, they were, by way of compensation, more intricate personalities. Holloway captured the 'crafty and somewhat raucous demagogue, risen from the ranks and up to every trick of the trade'.[34] Wilfrid Walter created an impressive portrait of 'the cunning mind at work beneath a bluff, forthright manner',[35] and limned with special effectiveness the emotional progression 'from Caesar's pretty boy ... to the manly mourner'.[36] No doubt Charles Kemble would have been more disturbed by the Antony of Neil Porter than any other. Possessing 'none of the physical and vocal "commandingness" usually associated with the part',[37] Porter's orator was 'dark and Italianate-looking with beard, lips and gleaming teeth and glinting eyes'. 'Insidious and inscrutable', he proved 'almost Satanic in his conscious devilry'.[38]

While actors of other roles struck out in new and sometimes startling directions, Caesar's exponents kept to routes previously charted. Maxon's 'cold, impersonal Julius', with 'a fine touch of Imperial purple',[39] clove stoutly to the nineteenth-century tradition. Stanley Lathbury and Kenneth Wicksteed, however, found more to their liking the reading pioneered by the Bensonians Fitzgerald and Carrington. Lathbury's Caesar, a 'snarling, decrepit old man', seemed 'sick and weary of war and intrigue ... mind-troubled by harassing doubts and strange portents'.[40] Wicksteed's version was labelled 'more the dyspeptic than the despot'.[41] Sniffed one reviewer, 'Rome has nothing to fear from this man, and one is forced to the thought that Cassius is making a needless fuss about nothing, for, on the face of things, the Brutus remedy is like to prove far worse than the disease, which calls for a cure no sharper than a digestive biscuit.'[42] While some exploration of Caesar's mortal attributes was welcome, over-accentuation of his frailty proved even more dangerous than the reverse.

Viewed as a first attempt at a fresh approach to the play, as an attack on two centuries of mistreatment textual and scenic, Bridges-Adams's *Caesars* are of landmark stature. Restoration of the text and the rediscovery of fluid stagecraft offer ample cause for rejoicing. Yet joy must be less than unconfined. At the very moment, ironically enough, that the play won the freedom to be itself, actors who could give it tragic dimension were no longer to be found. With the end of the star era and the advent of naturalistic acting, its grandeur dimmed; and the nineteenth-century audience's sense of awe and wonder has been only fitfully ours. *Julius Caesar*'s stage history in this century is the tale of an heroic play adrift in an anti-heroic age.

10

American productions (1892–1949)

The Booth–Barrett tradition cast a long shadow; and for a decade after their last *Caesar* performance in 1891 the American stage echoed with ever-paler imitations. Robert Downing toured an uninspired production in 1892, and in 1893 the Warde–James combination initiated a series of conventional revivals which spanned the next five years. A motley effort by the Mac-Lean–Tyler–Hanford Company in 1899 occasioned more nostalgia than enthusiasm. A thorough facelift was clearly in order, and Richard Mansfield[1] was not one to shy at a challenge.

Richard Mansfield

Mansfield's revival, the first American *Caesar* production of this century and the first by a leading actor-manager since the Booth–Barrett era, premiered at the Grand Opera House, Chicago, on 14 October 1902, and transferred to the Herald Square Theatre in New York on 1 December. Although Mansfield was perhaps drawn to *Caesar* initially by Tree's success, his treatment of the play was unique. Unusual settings and a bizarre Brutus earned him a New York run of fifty performances and a profitable tour for the rest of the season.

Mansfield's scenery and at least some of his costumes were originally designed by Sir Lawrence Alma-Tadema for Irving's 1901 revival of *Coriolanus* at the Lyceum. With his usual concern for archaeological exactness, Alma-Tadema set the play in the Etruscan period, and drew much of his inspiration from carvings in Etruscan and Lycian tombs and from Vitruvius' description of an Etruscan temple.[2] Captivated by its picturesque elegance, the American manager shut his eyes to historic propriety, purchased the whole production for $3000,[3] and proceeded to rework it for *Julius Caesar*.

Mansfield's text, according to James Huneker,[4] was the Booth–Barrett version with some alterations. The entire Storm scene was cut; and the episode with Portia, Lucius, and Artemidorus was restored, as was the conversation between Antony and Octavius' servant at the end of the

Forum sequence. The play was divided into six acts,[5] but in a slightly different manner from the Booth–Barrett format. Act II was devoted entirely to the scene in Brutus' Garden. Act III comprised the scenes in Caesar's House, the Street, and the Senate. Changes were rather swifter than at Booth's Theatre. Only three short intermissions were needed – ten minutes after act II, twelve minutes after act III, and ten minutes after act IV.

The Public Place of the first act was dominated by a bronze statue of Caesar, appropriately decorated, in the foreground. Behind rose orange buildings with red-tiled roofs and square Etruscan columns etched against an Italian blue sky. Hundreds of supers in procession enlivened the static cityscape, 'the dull motley of the rabble intensifying the deep bronze of the lictors'.[6] Caesar, crowned with laurel and dressed in flowing golden robes, kept his wonted state; and Calphurnia, with uncommon indolence, reclined in a purple gown atop a litter. Brutus' Garden, as in Booth's production, received particular attention. Downstage, under the spreading branches of two massive cypresses, stood a Roman settee draped in purple; farther up, a flight of steps led to a barely visible mansion. The moon was just setting, and the scene was bathed in 'the blue-gray of night that just precedes the breaking of dawn'.[7]

Mansfield rejected Gérôme's conception of the Senate, and positioned Caesar at centre stage on a lofty throne hung with royal purple. On either side in graceful semi-circular tiers sat massed ranks of senators. Caesar wore a red robe, and a scarlet carpet flowed from his feet down the marble steps. Beyond him, in the distance, the Roman skyline could be glimpsed through elegant columns. The Forum scene, described only as a 'fine restoration of a corner of the Forum',[8] was hidden by a hyper-active mob of more than three hundred. The Plains of Philippi were framed by effectively lighted cypresses, and in Brutus' death scene, a shattered pine and a mass of rock dominated the foreground.

However intriguing the décor, it was Mansfield's Brutus which carried the day, a focus of both public adulation and critical scorn.

Mansfield was no tragedian, but like Tree was a competent character actor. His idiosyncratic portraits of Baron Chevrial (*A Parisian Romance*), Dr Jekyll, and the title roles in *Cyrano de Bergerac* and Clyde Fitch's *Beau Brummell* made his name almost a household word. At the age of 45, he was robust and stocky, with features regular but not particularly noble.[9] He strove, not always with complete success, for naturalness of speech and movement. Although his physique favoured a Brutus in the heroic tradition, Mansfield preferred Booth's romantically lyrical reading; thus from the outset there was a visual incongruity between Brutus' rugged masculinity and the ethereal air he assumed. Moreover, the tortured and subtle spirituality of Booth's Brutus lay well outside Mansfield's range. To render

Brutus a fit vehicle for his talents he was obliged to recast him in the melodramatic mould.

The Mansfield Brutus appeared to be about 35 years of age, with 'a wavy wig of brown with Byronic locks, careless and poetic rather than neatly barbered. His countenance', according to Hillary Bell, 'depends on the distance from which it is considered. Nearby it seems unwashed, but in proper perspective it is shadowed over with the gloom of care.'[10] Critics remarked a resemblance to Hamlet; and Mansfield may well have been familiar with Paul Stapfer's suggestion that Brutus was a preliminary draft of the gloomy prince.[11] Brutus was already on stage when the curtain rose, dressed, appropriately enough, in a black toga traced with silver embroidery over a tunic of dull grey. 'There was no impressive "entrance", no fanfare of trumpets', James O'Donnell Bennet recalls.

The dark sinewy figure of a man leaned against the basin of a fountain and smiled gently as he watched the freemen of Rome throw high their caps for joy at *Caesar*'s progress. His smile was sadder than tears.

Slowly the calm eyes of the silent man leaning against the fountain swept the scene again and again. Once he shifted his pose slightly to catch a glimpse of the oncoming ranks of lictors, soldiers and slaves. That was the only movement he made for quite three minutes. . .

There was in him a curious mingling of poetic ardor and physical strength. The poetry was in the pensive eyes, the thin, quivering nostrils, the tender mouth. The strength was in the majestic poise of the motionless body, in the whipcords of the arms, in the sturdy shoulders, which were raised from time to time, half in scorn, half in resignation.

The crowd dissolved at a gesture from *Antony*. The dark figure advanced from the shadowy corner, where the fountain played, and was stopped by *Cassius*'s question: 'Will you go see the order of the course?' 'I am not so [sic] gamesome', *Brutus* answered, in sharp staccato.[12]

Hillary Bell was not so stirred. 'This Brutus is a stalwart', he observed, 'with sturdy legs, the torso of an athlete, the neck of a gladiator, the arms of a wrestler in the Roman arena – a vigorous personality that ill beseems the flickering, dreamy purpose of the character.'[13]

In his conversation with Cassius, it became clear that Brutus was a man of haunted imagination, at the mercy of the 'figures and fantasies' which 'busy care draws in the brains of men'. Portia's concern about his erratic behaviour was fully justified; he was clearly on the borderline of insanity. 'He needed not the promptings of *Cassius*', notes Winter. 'He was already ripe to do the murder that he thought a sacrifice. The conflict in his soul has almost crazed him.'[14]

In the Garden soliloquy he was remarkably Hamlet-like, tortured by *folie de doute* and verging on hysteria. In this scene Huneker found him 'the very picture of a human being hallucinated by his visions of universal justice . . .

Liberty of the individual comes before all in his scheme of idealism . . . He is the true *Anarch*, the dreamer of mad dreams, the regenerator of universal ills. Loving *Caesar*, he is yet ready to kill him at a hint from *Cassius*, because of what *Caesar* may become! Here is political idealism run to crazy paradox!'[15] Throughout the scene melancholy fanaticism drives him 'as one in a semi-dream, never looking at friend or passerby, addressing them as persons without seeming to see them, and moving uncannily, as if his mind were not on things of earth.'[16] His voice, in contrast to the grave, authoritative tone of Booth or Davenport, was tremulous and distressed until near the exit of the conspirators when 'it became stern and solemn, as if with a terrible, resolution; the access of fanaticism'.[17] With the appearance of Portia, his abstraction and mania seemed to lift for a moment, and his fundamental gentleness revealed itself.

The assassination brought a similar recession of his delirium, an instant of agonized awareness.

At Casca's call the conspirators rushed in a crowd upon the tribune and, when one after another they fleshed their knives in Caesar's bosom, they fell away, revealing him face to face with Brutus whose arm was raised to strike. 'Et tu, Brute!' sighed the dying man. A shadow of infinite sorrow mantled his friend's face. A tremor shook his frame. The murder was already consummated, but his pledge had been given and the issue was met with a poet's touch. Tenderly, sorrowfully, sacrificially the patriot laid his blade on the bleeding breast of his friend, the point directed at his own heart.[18]

As Caesar falls, he recoils horror-stricken in the manner of Booth; but 'momentary remorse is soon crowded from his face by a rapt joy – the joy of a man who has fulfilled his mission. He is no mere regicide, but an arm selected by the gods to scourge the tyrannical, the unrighteous.'[19] One recognizes with a start the wild-eyed terrorist of all times and places.

The Forum speech found Brutus calm and utterly self-controlled. His earlier abstraction had vanished; and the oration was delivered straightforwardly without self-consciousness or rhetorical flourish. Loud shouts followed the words 'Hear me for my cause', and the ensuing command, 'And be silent that you may hear', was spoken as a check to the uproar. Beginning with this sequence, Mansfield built Brutus' remaining scenes into a resistless crescendo, reaching a compelling height in the Quarrel episode and concluding with triumphant splendour on the Plains of Philippi.

In line with this design, the quarrel was rendered more crudely sensational. The action opened with Brutus seated in his great tent.

The lights are dim and grotesque. His hands are upon his knees, his head bowed in thought. The impetuous Cassius, angered at seeming neglect, enters madly. Brutus does not change his position during the first part of the colloquy. He has deprecated the anger of his violent colleague, and shows none himself. Still, with his hands on his knees and head down, he answers the impatient reproaches of his friend, but his voice grows louder and clearer.[20]

When Cassius demanded, 'Must I endure all this?' (IV.iii.41), 'Brutus rose to his full height and then expanded like a genie, until he seemed eight feet tall. And out of this Titan body came a voice that grew and grew, overwhelming the audience with an avalanche of sound, backing the plaintive accents of the thoroughly affrighted Cassius into a corner.'[21] This display of vocal virtuosity, while theatrically dynamic, was utterly inconsistent with the portrait of the listless, weak-willed melancholic of the early acts, and a resounding rejection of more than two centuries of theatrical tradition. The encounter with the ghost was equally inconoclastic. Considered merely a figment of Brutus' diseased imagination, the apparition did not appear. The stage was flooded with green-blue light and a voice spoke Caesar's lines from the wings. The unconfined paroxysms of terror which seized Brutus at this point would have done more credit to Richard III.

The death scene was squeezed of every drop of melodramatic sentiment; and contemporary accounts linger with relish over its lushness. As the curtain rose, we learn,

...all was whispered awe, majesty, and silence. The hour was evening, after the day of battle, the hour when twilight beckons night. At the foot of a shattered pine on a mass of rock sat Brutus, full armoured, helmet on head, shield and sword in hand, spent and brooding, a warrior figure Michael Angelo might have carved. As one retainer after another heard his whispered appeal for death, they fled from the spot, leaving him alone. Over the sad face and dreamy eye there passed the memory of the whole tragedy in one moment of immovable silence. Then drawing his shield before his breast and face, his sword slowly searched his heart. There was the fortitude of a general in the convulsion of the whole frame as he withdrew the blade. He slowly lowered the shield, and the sword fell from his fingers as they groped straight before him, and he addressed a second vision of the friend he came to meet:

> Caesar, now be still –
> I killed not thee with half so good a will.

The head dropped upon his breast ...[22]

Antony and Octavius now arrive at the head of their troops,

a large body of men equipped with shining armor and waving their swords. Antony seeing the dead Brutus speaks the famous lines that conclude the play. The day was darkened into twilight, which is deepened under the shadow of the trees of Philippi. In the bluish hazy light the upraised swords gleam and the armor of the soldiers glistens weirdly. And just beyond the impassive face of the dead Brutus looks down from the mount, unmoved by the grief of friends or the tributes of enemies.[23]

Alongside Mansfield's idiosyncratic characterization, the supporting roles, conventionally interpreted, seemed colourless.

Mansfield's *Caesar*, it is clear, was not tragedy but melodrama. The misguided behaviour and just punishment of a half-mad political assassin were thrilling enough, but hardly a source of pity and terror. Nevertheless, the production has a curiously modern flavour, and may even be said to prefigure two major trends in twentieth-century productions: an effort to make the play relevant by novel, often bizarre, trappings, and a compulsion to pluck out the heart of Brutus' mystery by reducing his stature to that of a contemporary politician of dubious rationality and discernment. Mansfield's innovations were short-lived, however, and with his death in 1905 the Booth–Barrett tradition, in the person of Robert Bruce Mantell, reasserted itself.

Mantell staged his first New York *Caesar* on 26 November 1906. He roughly followed the Booth–Barrett text,[24] and played a Brutus which owed something to both Booth and Davenport. Unlike his exemplars, however, this Brutus was occasionally given to playing to the gallery. In Caesar's house, he clutched an attendant by the shoulder, and watched him flee in terror at his touch. At the end of the Quarrel scene, he was known to finish 'with an almost hysterical outcry to his officers, "Go and commend me to my brother Cassius", and then almost collapse, embracing *Lucius* and vociferating "My boy! my boy!"' as the curtain fell.[25] But on the whole his performance was more than respectable, and, partnered by a succession of ill-assorted auxiliaries, he starred with success throughout the country until his death in 1928.

Mantell's only serious competition appeared in 1912 when William Faversham, a matinée idol, staged a revival. Faversham himself played Antony, with Tyrone Power as Brutus, Frank Keenan as Cassius, and Fuller Mellish as Caesar. Faversham used Booth's text as published by William Winter,[26] but he restored Antony's colloquy with the servant at the end of the Assassination scene and fiddled with odd lines elsewhere.

Joseph Harker's sets took their inspiration from the vivid hues and abrupt contrasts of the Pompeiian frescoes; and the decorative motifs and overall colour scheme suggested the oriental influence so dear to the heart of Tree. The tent was more picturesque than usual, a massive drapery which filled 'the entire width and height of the stage with color that shifts with the movement of the torches from a Gobelin hue to a deep, illusive green. The effects of night, of seclusion, of a haunted place, and of a time of impending doom are created . . . by masterly painting, and the skilful, subtle, reserved manipulation of lights', James O'Donnell Bennet records.[27] Roman lamps burning with bluish flames and the gleam of burnished armour and crimson trappings lent the military conference a mood more pictorial than dramatic.

The Plains of Philippi, in keeping with the scenic wonders of the Tree and Mansfield battlefields, was a vast landscape with rugged countryside in the foreground, backed by distant mountain peaks touched with the first hints of dawn.

The acting was considerably less spectacular than the décor. Faversham's Antony was workmanlike, but untouched at any point by genius. All he did, according to Alan Dale, was 'to "orate" in mellifluous and ornate English, and to do it all easily, gracefully, and even "elegantly"'.[28] Frank Keenan, a well-known character actor, made Cassius a crack-brained, malignant, turbulent creature, with 'the mien and manner of a taxicab robber'.[29] With Tyrone Power's Brutus the line of heroic American philosopher–patriots at last ran to seed. His commanding stature, stately bearing, and resonant voice allowed him to give a fair imitation of Davenport; but its charm was that of a fossil.

Although the Mantell and Faversham revivals were the only significant ones of the second and third decades of this century, several others may be noted briefly. In 1916 a colossal *Caesar* was staged as a benefit for the Actors' Fund of America at the Beechwood Amphitheatre near Los Angeles.[30] Five thousand performers took part on multiple stages. Three hundred gladiators appeared in an extraneous arena scene; a similar number of girls danced as Caesar's captives; and a total of three thousand soldiers took part in the battle sequences. Theodore Roberts took the title role, with Tyrone Power as Brutus, Frank Keenan as Cassius, and William Farnum as Antony. In similar epic vein was a revival at the Hollywood Bowl in 1926, using costumes and settings borrowed from the MGM film *Ben-Hur*. Caesar arrived for the Lupercal in Ben-Hur's chariot, drawn by four white horses. The stage was the size of a city block and dominated by a central tower eighty feet in height. Caesar was played by James Gordon; Brutus by R. D. MacLean; Cassius by William Humphrey; and Antony by William Farnum.

On somewhat more human scale was The Players' *Caesar*, staged in 1927 as their annual classical production with Power as Brutus, Bensonian Basil Rathbone as Cassius, and James Rennie as Antony. An ill-rehearsed hodge-podge of acting styles, it smacked more of the museum than the living theatre. In 1930 and 1931 Fritz Leiber brought his repertory company to New York sponsored by the Chicago Civic Shakespeare Society. Long on scenery and short on text, the revivals lacked any semblance of imaginative interpretation.

Had the ghost of some nineteenth-century theatre-goer wandered into any of these early-1930s performances, he would have found little that was unfamiliar; marble and oratory still kept the field. So far as American *Caesar* productions were concerned, Poel, Granville-Barker, Craig, and Bridges-Adams might never have been. But the days of the marmoreal style were numbered.

Mercury Theatre Production, 1937

On 6 November 1937, at his fledgling Mercury Theatre, Orson Welles dragged *Caesar* with traumatic abruptness into the twentieth century, accompanied by a degree of controversy unknown in its history.

In the spring of 1937, as a director for the New York wing of the Federal Theatre, he rehearsed Marc Blitzstein's pro-labour musical satire, *The Cradle Will Rock*; and when its presentation was vetoed for political reasons by Washington, he promptly resigned, rented the Venice Theatre, and staged it with resounding success under the management of himself and John Houseman. A few months later, heartened by their first venture into management, Welles and Houseman leased the Comedy Theatre, renamed it the Mercury, and announced that the first production would be *Julius Caesar*. 'By the use of apron, lighting, sound devices, music, etc.', Welles informed his public, 'we hope to give this production much of the speed and violence it must have had on the Elizabethan stage. The Roman Senators when they murder the Dictator will not be clad (any more than were the Elizabethan actors) in traditional nineteenth-century togas.'[31]

Welles's reference to the Elizabethan theatre was backed up by considerable familiarity with contemporary scholarship. Like Poel and Granville-Barker he was taken with the fluidity of the Elizabethan stage; but their commitment to textual integrity had little appeal for him. Welles was not a scholar but a showman. He recognized a market for classical theatre, but felt the plays could not be trusted to speak for themselves. A gimmick was needed to lend them contemporary excitement. Having found it, he shaped both text and stagecraft to fit his eccentric vision and the result was not so much a revival of a play as a re-creation.

Welles saw *Julius Caesar*, according to Houseman, as 'a political melodrama with clear contemporary parallels. All over the Western world sophisticated democratic structures were breaking down. First in Italy, then in Germany, dictatorships had taken over; the issues of political violence and the moral duty of the individual in the face of tyranny had become urgent and inescapable.'[32] The play was accordingly sub-titled 'Death of a Dictator', and the text was viciously hacked to underline the political motif. Speed and visual interest derived not from an apron, proscenium doors, and inner stage, but from the magic of shifting light – a technique originating with Appia and Craig, but refined by Bel Geddes, Jones, and Simonson. Costumes were both simple and cheap – Fascist uniforms and street clothes. The performance lasted a total of 109 minutes without an intermission, and was greeted with adulation, derision, and puzzlement in varying proportions. Nevertheless, its New York run of 157 performances is unmatched in *Julius Caesar*'s American stage history.

Although the press labelled his production anti-Fascist, Welles denied it.

The play, he insisted, was really about the character of Brutus, 'the classical picture of the eternal, impotent, ineffectual, fumbling liberal; the reformer who wants to do something about things but doesn't know how and gets it in the neck in the end. He's dead right all the time, and dead at the final curtain. He's Shakespeare's favourite hero – the fellow who thinks the times are out of joint but who is really out of joint with his time. He's the bourgeois intellectual, who, under a modern dictatorship would be the first to be put up against a wall and shot.'[33] As Welles saw it, the menace of Caesarism which confronted Brutus was not unlike the contemporary threat posed by burgeoning Fascist dictatorships; and their instrument in ancient Rome and modern Europe was ever a mindless mob, 'the hoodlum element you find in any big city after a war, a mob that is without the stuff that makes them intelligently alive, a lynching mob, the kind of mob that gives you a Hitler or a Mussolini.'[34] The play thus reduced itself, in Welles's conception, to a fast-moving tale of a well-meaning altruist caught between Fascist authoritarianism at the top of the social scale and animal viciousness at the bottom. Unable to fight Caesarism with its own weapons, violence and demagogy, Brutus liberates by his misguided idealism the very forces which destroy him and his cause. As a political statement, Welles's production did not go much further than that. His real interest lay in the theatrical realization of his narrative; and the audience was left to deduce the moral of its choice.

Welles's promptbook (*JC* 82)[35] makes it clear that apart from scenes involving Caesar, Brutus, and the mob, virtually everything else in Shakespeare's text was expendable. Indeed, so extreme was his abridgement that for the first and only time in *Caesar*'s history it is easier to record what was played than what was deleted. The text is not divided into acts and scenes, but follows the format of a radio or film script with episodes fading one into another, punctuated only by light, darkness, and sound effects.

The play opens with Caesar's encounter with the Soothsayer (I.ii.12–24) transposed from its usual place to provide a sinister overture. After Caesar's exit, Flavius and Marullus engage in an abbreviated colloquy with the crowd, and Brutus and Cassius converse, but with fewer rhetorical flights than usual. Casca arrives before Caesar returns and tells of Antony's offer of the crown. Brutus then exits leaving Cassius and Casca together. They divide between them the lines normally spoken by Cassius as a soliloquy:

> *Cassius* (to Casca)
> Well, Brutus, thou art noble; yet I see
> Thy honorable metal may be wrought
> From that it is dispos'd . . . .
>   *Casca*
> Therefore, it is meet
> That noble minds keep ever with their likes;
> For who so firm that cannot be seduc'd?

Cassius continues with 'If I were Brutus now, and he were Cassius', but ceases abruptly on 'And after this, let Caesar seat him sure', for the Dictator and his party enter. Caesar expresses his mistrust of Cassius, and the scene ends with his defiant 'for always . . . I am Caesar'.

The Storm scene, heavily cut, is retained to trace the evolution of the conspiracy and to establish the provenance of Brutus' letters. The Orchard scene is restructured and shortened. Brutus reads his letters at the beginning of the scene, and its contents motivate his decision, 'It must be by his death.' Portia enters at the end of this soliloquy, and after her exit the conspirators arrive. Ligarius comes before they depart, and Brutus and his confederates all go out together. The scene in Caesar's house is allowed to stand; but Brutus loses his curtain-lines. Instead, Caesar invites Ligarius to be near him later in the day and moves off with his party. Ligarius turns to Trebonius and concludes the scene with the sardonic aside:

> And so near will I be,
> That your best friends shall wish I had been further.

Artemidorus is allowed to read his letter (II.iii), but the Portia–Lucius–Soothsayer episode (II.iv) is deleted. The Senate scene is played quite straightforwardly until the assassination, but is mangled afterwards. The hand-washing ritual is removed, as is the conversation with Antony's servant. Antony enters unannounced, and straightaway proceeds to make his peace with the conspirators and to negotiate the funeral oration. He does not address the corpse until he finds himself alone at the end of the scene. At this point he speaks a *mélange* of the 'O mighty Caesar!' speech and the 'O, pardon me, thou bleeding piece of earth' soliloquy. Antony's role in Welles's scheme of things is mainly that of wily demagogue. He is given his head in the Forum, but is kept firmly in check elsewhere.

The crowd in the Forum, although comparatively small, was probably the most active and best-orchestrated the American *Caesar*-goer has seen. Numerous responses are written into the text, most of which are echoes of what the orator has just said. It is worth noting that, as in Booth's production, Brutus exits on 'I have the same dagger for myself, / When it shall please my country to need my death', and the scene ends with 'Now let it work: mischief, thou art afoot, / Take thou what course thou wilt.'

Welles's fascination with mob violence as a concomitant of Fascism led him to play the Cinna the Poet scene in full for the first time in America, and even to augment it with a number of lines filched from the citizens in *Coriolanus*.

In act IV Antony is further subordinated by the omission of his Proscription scene. The action moves directly from the death of Cinna to Brutus' tent. The quarrel is played pretty well entire; but later the Camp Poet is cut,

the military conference is curtailed and, prior to the exchange of goodnights, a few lines of Cassius' farewell conversation with Brutus in V.i are
inserted to make this the last meeting between the generals:

> *Cassius*
> If we do lose this battle, then is this
> The very last time we shall speak together,
> Are you contented to be led in triumph
> Through the streets of Rome?
> *Brutus*
> No, Cassius, no: think not, thou noble Roman,
> That every Brutus will go bound to Rome;
> *Cassius*
> O my dear brother [etc.]

At the end of the scene, as a final inconoclastic flourish, the ghost sequence
disappears, and the lights go down on Lucius' song.

Almost the whole of act V is blue-pencilled, save for Brutus' death. In his
notes to a *Julius Caesar* edition prepared while still in his teens, Welles
remarked, 'I have never seen a production of *Caesar* with actual armies in
synthetic combat that was less than a little silly';[36] and perhaps his dissatisfaction with the military character of these scenes provoked his savage
cutting. More likely, however, he felt that the events of the last act had little
to do with his theme. Brutus' fate was sealed with the end of the Forum
scene; and the Cinna the Poet episode terrifyingly foreshadowed a new
order. Only Brutus' death remained to round out the tale, and he saw no
reason to delay it.

As the lights come up after the Tent scene, Brutus, Cinna, Trebonius,
and Metellus are discovered in conversation, unaware that Cassius lies dead
nearby. Cassius' query about the fire in his tents is transposed from V.iii and
given to Brutus. Trebonius has just reported the disappearance of Statilius
when Brutus' eye lights on Cassius, and the shock of the discovery motivates
his 'Slaying is the word . . .' He promises to find time to weep, and speaks
the apostrophe beginning 'O Julius Caesar, thou art mighty yet.' At this
moment his duty becomes clear. He calls Trebonius to him, and to
Trebonius' 'What says my lord?' he replies:

> Why this Trebonius.
> Thou seest the world, how it goes,
> Our enemies have beat us to the pit:
> It is more worthy, to leap in ourselves,
> Than tarry till they push us.
> I shall have glory by this losing day
> More than Octavius, and Mark Antony,
> By this vile conquest shall attain unto.

Metellus interrupts with 'Fly, my lord', and Brutus shouts, 'Hence, I will follow' as the lights fade. When they come up again, Brutus lies dead, and Antony stands ready to speak the eulogy.

Although Welles's text may be readily anatomized, the production itself cannot so easily be dealt with. Unlike the solid sets and well-defined movement and business of traditional revivals, this *Caesar* was an elusive, almost symphonic creation of light, shadow, sound, and shifting images caught in a timeless space. Much was suggested, almost nothing represented. Atmosphere was everything.

The stage was a bare platform with three levels. The main downstage playing area, about fourteen feet in depth, including an apron, was raked to meet a set of steps spanning the full width of the stage. Above these was a second platform, approximately eight feet deep, which led in turn to another set of steps topped by a third and very shallow platform about six and a half feet higher than the stage floor. A fanning ramp ran from the topmost level almost to the back wall. This brick rear-wall, carefully painted blood-red, served as a backdrop. 'That brick wall', said Welles later, 'was as important to my production as the settings of any elaborate play. I wanted to present "Julius Caesar" against a texture of brick, not of stone, and I wanted a color of red that had certain vibrations of blue.'[37]

The crucial element in the décor, however, was the lighting, now capable of apparently miraculous feats thanks to the introduction of remote control in the early 1930s. *Caesar*'s lighting was designed by Jean Rosenthal, a protégée of Abe Feder, one of Broadway's leading innovators in the field. Pouring light down from overhead and streaming it upward in stabbing columns through traps in the platforms and steps, Miss Rosenthal defined space, narrowing and widening it at will, faded scenes in and out with cinematic freedom, picked out key faces and threw them into sharpened focus as a camera might, and created atmosphere with a speed and flexibility undreamt of by conventional scenery.

Miss Rosenthal's lighting was sensitively partnered by Marc Blitzstein's score for trumpet, horn, percussion and Hammond organ, which, according to Houseman, achieved 'amazingly varied effects – from the distant bugles of a sleeping camp to the blaring brass and deep, massive, rhythmic beat which instantly evoked the pounding march of Hitler's storm troopers'.[38] Blitzstein's sounds were an ever-present textural component of the production, an auditory equivalent of Jean Rosenthal's visual effects.

The production opens with the stage in darkness, and Blitzstein's overture throbbing ominously. A voice suddenly and piercingly cries, 'Caesar', and the light come up on the arrogantly self-controlled Dictator, in the military dress affected by Mussolini and Hitler, surrounded by subordinates in dark-green uniforms. Civilians in contemporary street clothes look on admiringly. 'Up-angled shafts of light marked this Caesar well – his striding height, jutting chin, cross-belted military tunic, sleek modern breeches.'[39] He seemed to Richard Lockridge 'not real, not a puny man. He is bigger than natural and stiffer and more angular. His voice is a harsh stylization of the human voice and his salute a spare summary of the Fascist gesture.'[40] From the murky abyss beyond the shaft of light in which Caesar stands comes the warning, 'Beware the Ides of March'; but the mysterious speaker disregards orders to 'Come from the throng' and 'Look upon Caesar.' On 'He is a dreamer', the group moves off with shouts of 'Hail, Caesar' and Fascist salutes. In the distance can be heard the thunder of marching feet. Flavius and Marullus draw the Carpenter and the Cobbler from the disappearing crowd, and question them tensely. A moment later they release them and exit. This scene with its hard-edged lighting, sinister shadows, staccato 'Hails', and open-palm salutes powerfully evokes the authoritarian mood which permeates the first half of the play. Caesarism is tangible. 'Something deathless and dangerous in the world sweeps past you down the darkened aisles at the Mercury and takes possession of the proud, gaunt stage', wrote John Mason Brown. 'It is something fearful and ominous, something turbulent and to be dreaded, which distends the drama to include the life of nations as well as of men.'[41]

Brutus and Cassius now enter by way of the upstage ramp under lights more benign, and move down speaking colloquially and easily. Part of the time they sit together on the steps nearest the audience. Casca joins them later, and his tale is told straightforwardly. At intervals the roars of the besotted mob interrupt the restrained conversation; and Brutus hears with growing chagrin the death-knell of the Republic. After Brutus leaves, Caesar and his entourage make another grim appearance. His 'for always . . . I am Caesar' signals a blackout, followed by thunder, and the first stab of lightning. In intervals of darkness rain is heard; a momentary lightning-flash reveals an eerie empty stage; and the bass notes of the organ and the boom of an ancient thunder drum virtually rock the theatre on its foundations. Throughout the Storm scene, the thunder drum rolled steadily, but otherwise the episode was treated simply.

The lighting for Brutus' orchard evoked a mood of melancholy beauty by an apparently artless criss-cross of weird, broken shadows cast by a worklight in the flies through the grid and hanging lines to the stage floor.[42] Shuffling self-consciously out of the dark come the conspirators, over-coated, hats pulled well down, looking, Burns Mantle thought, 'a little like a committee of C.I.O. strikers'. The feeling was entirely that of a conspiracy in a modern city; and theatre-goers found themselves startled to hear the characters speak blank verse. Played as a clandestine meeting in a police state, there was little show of formality. The business was swiftly concluded, and the grim company left together.

The scene in Caesar's house and the prelude to the assassination were given quickly and cleanly; nor was the assassination itself lingered over. As the surly Dictator, his face mask-like in its inflexibility, repels the conspirators one by one, they gradually encircle him. At the appropriate moment, drawing knives from their coat pockets, they stab him in gangland style.

Even as the first half of the play was dominated by the soulless militarism of an authoritarian regime, the second half of the play pulsed with rampant emotionalism and the horrifying violence which attends its exploitation.

In the black-out after Antony's 'Cry "Havoc", and let slip the dogs of war', the rushing feet of the mob are heard in the darkness; and the organ and thunder drum contrive an almost unbearable tension. Meanwhile, a ten-foot rostrum draped in black velour was wheeled on, and a modern coffin deposited at the foot. The lights, when they came up, suggested with almost newsreel accuracy the aura of Hitler's night ceremonies. The faces of Brutus and Antony seemed to float in space; behind Brutus shadows formed a massive cross on the back wall, while above Antony flickered a menacing shape suggestive of crossed fasces. Below the rostrum the mob shuffled and growled in the half-dark, an imprisoned animal impatient for release. Throughout Antony's speech, delivered with every wile of the political spellbinder, the mob's superbly orchestrated whispers, murmurs, shouts, chants, and screams deftly accompanied the shifting moods and rhythms of the harangue; and the continuous shuffle and stamp of their feet on the hollow, unpadded platforms beat out a terrifying obbligato to their crescent fury. Released at last at the peak of hysteria, they roared off the stage like a cyclone, mindless and deadly.

The Cinna the Poet scene, perhaps the most celebrated feature of the production, caught the imagination of audiences by its unfamiliarity and sheer theatricality. In splendid contrast to the tumult of the Forum, the action commenced in dim light and a deceptive quiet, with Cinna, a slender, red-haired figure in a dark suit, starched collar and neutral tie, 'emerging from the basement into a ring of light, whistling a little carefree air on his wistful way to death'.[43] 'In the half-light', Sidney Whipple records, 'he is confronted by a little knot of man hunters, obviously trying to mop up the conspirators and any suspects who come in their way. There are questions.

'But I am Cinna, the poet', he says mildly, repeating over and over the words, 'Cinna the poet', and handing out his scribblings with polite bewilderment, to prove his identity.

For several moments not a hand is laid on him. He starts to move away, but out of the darkness another group of men appear to block him. He turns and turns again, and each time a new force moves in to face him.

'But I am Cinna, the poet; Cinna, the poet', he protests. The mob becomes more

14. The Cinna the Poet scene (III.iii). Orson Welles's production at the Mercury
Theatre, New York, 1937. Cinna is played by Norman Lloyd

dense. Around him is a small ring of light, and in the shadows an ever-tightening,
pincer-like mass movement. Then in one awful moment of madness the jaws of the
mob come together on him and he is swallowed up and rushed into black oblivion.
    Mr. Lloyd's gently comic bewilderment, his pathetic innocence and the crushing
climax as the human juggernaut rolls down upon him make this one of the most
dynamic scenes in today's theatre.[44]

It is doubtful if this scene has ever been better staged.
    Anti-climax was of course inevitable in spite of Welles's savage cutting;
and he made little further effort to minimize it. The Quarrel scene, so long
the high point of the play, now marked the beginning of the dénouement.
'When Brutus and Cassius quarrel', wrote Burns Mantle, 'it is as citizen
soldiers met in a field and a little fearful of awaking nearby sleepers'.[45]
Brutus' death, shorn of its alarums and excursions, seemed almost a

pathetic afterthought. Critics were more prone to recall a curtain of vertical shafts of light against which Antony spoke his eulogy – an effect inspired by photographs of the Nazi Congress at Nuremberg a few months earlier.[46]

Although the uniqueness of the production lay in its contemporary slant and avant-garde stagecraft, the acting was not without interest. Many of the players were comparatively youthful and inexperienced, but Welles achieved some remarkable ensemble effects nonetheless. There were no stars; but the major roles were respectably played, and at moments even approached brilliance.

The controversial Brutus of Welles was the undisputed pivot of the action. Dressed in a blue serge suit at his first entrance, he struck Richard Lockridge as 'a quiet, thoughtful man, rather like a liberal-minded college professor. He makes no gestures and seldom raises his voice; he is simple and rational as a letter carrier and about as dramatic. Amid all the flashing lights and stern commands of the stagecraft he muses gently, the talkative liberal of the realistic twentieth century.'[47] Although deprived of his traditional heroic paraphernalia, the essential nobility of Welles's Brutus was never in doubt. Sidney Whipple found him 'an honest man, an almost saintly man, a man ever fixed in principle and faithful to his conscience. The conspirators surrounding him, even to the lean and hungry ones, are made for a time to appear heroic in the light of the honesty that inspires his decisions.'[48]

He entered the conspiracy with reluctance and remorse, forlornly lamenting until the last that Caesar's spirit could not be come by without murder. Huddled in his overcoat in the Forum, he was 'stricken, but restrained and dignified . . . exasperatingly scrupulous and sincere in his determination not to use the execution of the dictator for his own personal or political advantage'.[49] The total lack of histrionics in Brutus' speech or behaviour was a remarkable foil to the theatricality of the production and the flamboyant rhetoric of Caesar and Antony. In the Quarrel scene, the keynote was gentleness and reserve; a philosopher had lost his way and wandered onto the battlefield. Every speech was considered, weighed with care, and delivered with firmness. In the end, his death seemed only an honest man's modest acceptance of his fate. This Brutus Archibald MacLeish considered a genuinely tragic figure, one 'familiar enough in American ideology if not in American practice'.

He belongs . . . to the admirable and tragic class of those who will defend liberty by liberty or not at all, who will oppose violence by law or not oppose it, who will overcome deceit by truthfulness or let deceit prevail . . . He is great in the sense in which these attributes are great. He is weak in the sense in which these attributes are unworldly. His tragedy is truly tragic because it is the destruction of virtuousness by the logic of its own virtue.[50]

Martin Gabel was physically the most unlikely Cassius imaginable – thick-set, bull-necked, and square-jawed – but he admirably captured the spirit of the fiery agitator. In his first encounter with Brutus, Houseman recalls, 'there was something recognizable and terrifying in the way he intruded upon Brutus, violating his privacy with his corrosive, vengeful discontent, tearing his way through that serene self-righteousness to plant the seed of murder in his ear'.[51] Shrewd and purposeful, practical to the point of callousness, this Cassius seemed to Heywood Broun less a scheming villain than 'the only man among the conspirators who stands out as realistic in his point of view'.[52] His blunt vitality captured the goodwill of the audience from the first, and his bitter humiliation in the Quarrel scene was profoundly pathetic.

Welles's script inevitably left Antony a one-dimensional figure, but that dimension George Colouris played superbly. An arch-opportunist, a schemer, and a hypocrite, Antony's Forum performance was a marvel of contemporary hucksterism. The lines were spoken with new-coined freshness, driven home by 'all the hot emotion that was to wreck him later'.[53] Even in the flood-tide of declamation he maintained, John Anderson thought, 'an extraordinary balance which holds the luxury of the words without wallowing'.[54]

Joseph Holland's Caesar, as much a symbol as a man, was not Shakespeare's dictator, but an awesome creation in its own right. Holland conceived Caesar as 'such a great man that he needs no wild gestures. He knows that the slightest motion of his finger is quite sufficient to make things happen.'[55] There was no hint of weakness here, no talk of deaf ears. The portrait was a terrifying study in utter stillness. His words when they came carried the brutality of a physical blow. His presence alone vindicated Cassius' fears; this man indeed might well bestride the world.

The production's contemporary relevance, novelty, and pulsating theatricality made over-praise unavoidable. Examined in retrospect, Welles's effort was not, as Richard Watts Jr claimed, 'the great *Julius Caesar* of our times'; it is doubtful if a script so abridged could be called *Julius Caesar* at all. Rather it was an exploration of the political theme in *Julius Caesar* in a contemporary ambiance. For Shakespeare, however, politics and the personal and moral life of man were inseparable and continuous. To isolate the political features of the play was to mutilate its form. With Antony a shadow of himself, Octavius virtually non-existent, the Forum and Cinna scenes overblown, and the final act irreparably maimed, Shakespeare would have been hard put to recognize his creation.

Nevertheless, Welles's achievements are far from negligible. The production in its own right was a brilliant *coup-de-théâtre*. Togas, painted Forums, and statuesque rhetoric vanished; scenes long a mere classroom exercise took on a compelling reality when spoken colloquially by men in overcoats and dark felt hats. His stagecraft remains a model of speed, flexibility, and aptness to its subject. That Welles lavished his genius[56] on essentially a perversion of the play must remain a matter for regret.

In theory Welles's innovations should have given *Caesar* a new lease on life; but the facts are otherwise. The vitality, freshness, and relevance of the Mercury production in the long run did more harm than good. No director was willing to challenge Welles on his own ground, and the play was generally ignored for a dozen years. In 1949 it was resuscitated briefly by Margaret Webster for a tour of high schools and out-of-the-way cities. Since then major American productions may easily be counted on one's fingers.

II

London productions (1900–49)

From the dawn of the new century until the Second World War black-out, *Caesar* was a frequent and welcome feature on the London boards, and mirrors with fidelity the changing faces of Shakespeare production: the last flashes of Victorian paint and pomp; then the fresh-scrubbed complexion of Elizabethan Methodism; and finally the self-consciously chic features of modern dress revivals. With the outbreak of hostilities, in another of those curious reversals of fortune which mark the play's history, it disappeared from the city's stages for a decade.

Between 1900 and 1913, *Caesar* became a treasured heirloom of His Majesty's, a relic to be displayed at intervals for veneration. In 1900, 1905, and 1907 audiences packed the house to gape at the glory that was Rome, limned in paint and swarming supers, and to revel in the golden-toned, larger-than-life heroics of Lewis Waller, Basil Gill, Lyn Harding, and Tree himself. From 1909 to 1913 Tree made the play an annual highlight of his Shakespeare Festivals; and saw it greeted always with undiminished delight.

A year after Alma-Tadema's Forum was struck for the last time, Lilian Baylis resolved to add Shakespeare to the operatic fare featured at her cultural soup-kitchen, the Old Vic Theatre in the Waterloo Road. In the autumn of 1914 Ben Greet was recruited as stage director, and ordered to purvey the Bard to the workers with moral and theatrical punch at absolutely minimal cost.[1] With him he brought a clutch of veterans from his touring troupe, and he coaxed remarkable performances from some of them amid hand-me-down flats (often of shuddering inappropriateness), fit-up costumes, and antiquated gas lighting. Accompanied by the cheers of neighbourhood schoolchildren, the warm-hearted enthusiasm of their elders, and the pervasive odour of Baylis's frying sausages drifting from the wings, Shakespeare came to life with an earthy vitality undreamt of in the West End. Greet's work had only begun when the shortage of male performers occasioned by the First World War threatened to end it; but as actors departed for the front, actresses stepped gamely, if sometimes incongruously, into their roles. In emergencies even audience-members were pressed into service for crowd scenes. Ill-dressed and forever on the edge of disaster or absurdity, Ben Greet's Shakespeare defiantly kept the Old Vic boards throughout the war years.

In such catch-as-catch-can circumstances, Greet invited the veteran actor J. Fisher White to stage the Old Vic's first *Caesar* in 1915. A. Corney Grain undertook the title-role; William Stack played Brutus; White appeared as Cassius; and Jerrold Robertshaw tackled Antony. The next year Greet himself directed a revival with Ernest Walker as Caesar, William Stack as Brutus, Robert Atkins as Cassius, and Ernest Cassel as Antony. In 1917 came Greet's second and last Old Vic *Caesar*, with E. A. Ross as the Dictator, Mark Stanley as Brutus, Frederick Sargent as Cassius, and Russell Thorndike as Antony.

Under Greet's management all productions were 'Victorian Provincial' in style: texts were heavily cut; performances were more remarkable for vigour than subtlety; business was unlimited; and settings – drawn from whatever the scene-dock had to offer – were more a visual diversion than a functional adjunct of the dramatic action. Although 'The Master of the Greensward' respected the work of Poel and Granville-Barker, he found the neo-Elizabethan approach ill-suited to Old Vic exigencies. In a 1917 *Caesar* programme note he acknowledged with disarming frankness, 'Let us admit at once that the best way [to stage Shakespeare] is a plain stage representing as nearly as possible Shakespeare's own stage, and to give as much as possible – all in fact – of the text.' But Old Vic policy demanded a weekly change of bill, a feat made possible only by the actors' familiarity with traditional theatre texts and business. To make changes, especially under wartime stresses, would be to invite catastrophe. 'We can only give here – with our limited means – carefully arranged "acting" versions', he concluded somewhat apologetically; 'therefore, we do them with changes of scenery, to make them entertaining and interesting to ordinary audiences. The intellectual ones, and the youngsters who study the plays, can supply with their knowledge the omitted scenes. The regular playgoer can understand the plot as it stands, and imagination will help him to fill in the "gaps".'[2]

In 1920 Robert Atkins, who had acted at the Old Vic before his enlistment, returned as its new stage director;[3] and with him he brought a keen regard for William Poel. Free from the wartime woes which frustrated Greet, and undeterred by tradition, limited means, and production pressures, he proceeded to stage over the next five years every play in the Folio except *Cymbeline*. Using methods similar to those of Bridges-Adams, he demonstrated in a metropolitan context the commercial viability of Poel's notions.

Inside the massive Old Vic proscenium he installed a false arch of black velvet with doors in each pediment and a small apron in front. The smokey, paint-soaked drops and flats of earlier productions disappeared in favour of curtains and the occasional simple set scene. Despite Lilian Baylis's Spartan finances, audiences seldom found the décor wanting in interest. Atkins's flair for impressionistic detail, ingenious lighting, and telling composition were frequently the envy and sometimes the inspiration of the more prosperous West End managements.

Atkins's first *Caesar* revival, on 17 January 1921, rejected the tradition of realistic design even more firmly than Bridges-Adams had done. The Public Place of act I was merely a flight of white steps and a few columns backed by a drop of black velvet. Brutus' Orchard comprised three poplar trees silhouetted against a fragment of white wall, picked out by the merest touch of light from the enveloping blackness beyond. For the last act, with the drop drawn into perpendicular folds and washed with blue light, three pine trunks and a cypress or two suggested to the *Westminster Gazette* (18 January 1921) critic 'an astonishingly beautiful and tragic forest'. In happy contrast to the visual starkness, audiences heard spoken with swiftness and intelligibility the fullest *Caesar* text played in London since the Restoration.

The standard of acting, however, was less than superlative. The same dearth of competent Shakespearian actors which bedevilled Bridges-Adams also plagued Atkins; and a woefully inadequate two-week rehearsal period allowed scant opportunity to cultivate classical skills and fresh insights. Reviewers, understandably enough, were more taken with the production's clarity and vigour than the subtlety and originality of its characterization. Atkins's second revival two years later (6 November 1922) evinced the same strengths and weaknesses.[4]

Harcourt Williams, when he became stage director in 1929, took up the production cudgel where Atkins had dropped it.[5] Atkins's stage remained in place, and textual integrity continued to be a *sine qua non*. Most of Williams's energies, however, were directed toward making acting a worthier servant of the script. Movement took on a simpler, lighter quality, and speech became ever more rapid. The flow of dramatic action was minimally interrupted for set-changes, and fewer intervals were permitted. If critics sometimes missed the red-blooded drive and visual invention of Atkins's work, they found comfort in a subtle dramatic structure and rich characterization denied them earlier.

Even as Atkins took Poel as his mentor, Williams turned to Granville-Barker for whom he had often acted. 'Harley Granville-Barker was the one man I was determined to talk to before I plunged into the actual work of the [first] season', he tells us. 'He had just published his first volume of *Prefaces to Shakespeare* and I had been thrilled with *Julius Caesar*.'[6] On Granville-Barker's invitation, Williams visited him at his home in Devonshire where he spent a frantic fifteen hours taking advice. Williams records little of what was said; the substance of the conversation, however, reveals itself in the Old Vic style throughout Williams's tenure.

One of Williams's first productions (on 20 January 1930) was *Julius Caesar* with Granville-Barker's Preface as its inspiration. A full text was spoken, save for the excision of the second announcement of Portia's death – a cut with which Granville-Barker was in sympathy. Atkins's false proscenium and apron were retained, with a flight of stairs added to connect the stage with the orchestra pit. Columns, steps, and rostrum blocks placed in front of curtains constituted the only scenic elements; and changes were minor and infrequent. The Public Place of act I, for example, with the addition of a garden seat, did duty for Brutus' Orchard. Dramatic continuity was interrupted by only one interval – immediately after the assassination.

Williams seized at once upon Granville-Barker's suggestion that *Julius Caesar* represents Shakespeare's search for a new sort of hero, a quest which leads the dramatist to construct four figures in some depth before he can bring himself to choose a protagonist. In the end, Granville-Barker contends, Shakespeare opted for Brutus, not out of approval of Caesar's murder, but because he 'finds the spiritual problem of the virtuous murderer the most interesting in the story'.[7] Read thus, the play becomes primarily a set of intricately related psychological studies.

Brember Wills was cast as Caesar; Donald Wolfit played Cassius; and the young John Gielgud was selected as Antony. Gyles Isham rehearsed Brutus, but shortly before the opening he fell ill, and Williams took his place. Unfortunately the shift to some degree shattered the delicately-contrived interrelationships which had been planned; and instead of a structure the audience viewed a collection of individual portraits.

Wills's Caesar took his cue from one of Granville-Barker's readings of this problem figure as 'now no more than an empty shell, reverberating hollowly, the life and virtue gone out of him'.[8] Dignified and impressive in appearance, he seemed merely a tired and fretful old man, quite obviously living on his reputation. While this interpretation carried instant conviction, it weakened the play as Granville-Barker suggested it might. 'For will it be so desperate an enterprise to conspire against such a Caesar?' he asked. In the opinion of some reviewers, it decidedly was not.

Williams assessed his own Brutus as not 'more than up to team level'; but Wolfit found his performance 'sensitive and moving',[9] if somewhat detrimental to the production's fragile balance. Easy in movement and informal in speech, his stoic evinced throughout a mood of sombre gentleness, broken only by the cold, deadly anger of the quarrel. Wolfit's Cassius proved by contrast 'a highly-strung, nerve-ridden creature',[10] full of jealous fury and suspicion, altogether more vehement and less subtle than Granville-Barker would have wished.

The undeniable star was Gielgud. Although wanting something of the heroic grace of the old school, his 26-year-old Antony, shambling in gait but vocally electrifying, crossed the footlights as a compelling, multi-dimensional character. He abandoned traditional stage business in favour of natural dignity, simple gesture, and a keen concern for the psychology and poetry of the part. The ruthless, almost savage, side of Antony was not scanted, and revealed itself with particular cogency in 'the sharp bark of laughter with which he greeted Cassius's offer of a share of the spoils, and that other more derisive laugh when Cassius reminds Brutus whose fault it is that Antony is still alive'.[11]

The Forum scene was predictably superlative. Here Williams confined the crowd to the orchestra pit and the stone slabs which formed the steps, a stratagem designed to disguise the supers' want of numbers and experience. But in the end there was no cause for concern. Leading players voluntarily donned disguises and, incited by Margaret Webster as a Roman Madame Defarge, lent concentrated and effective support. Gielgud stood at the top of the steps with the body of Caesar at his feet; and the scene was played in silhouette except for a light on Antony's face. The very first line, spoken as 'a natural and hurried appeal for listeners in a tumult',[12] firmly identified the speech as a genuine and natural public event rather than a stock splendour of the stage.

Whatever its considerable merits, the revival fell short of success; and not only because of its impotent Caesar and *ad hoc* Brutus. The crucial defect was an absence of tragic dimension. As naturalism came through the door, spiritual grandeur went out at the window. 'To do the play in this everyday manner is to bury its greatness', contended C. B. Purdom.

These men were great figures in the world; they are placed by Shakespeare in a noble setting where they exhibit the high qualities of the soul. Unless that is brought out the play fails, and though I admire greatly what Mr. Harcourt Williams is doing at the Old Vic, I have to say that he makes this tragedy a commonplace affair.[13]

Two years later (25 January 1932) Williams dusted off his 1930 promptbook and staged another revival, this time with himself as Caesar, Ralph Richardson as Brutus, Robert Speaight as Cassius, and Robert Harris as Antony. 'We have tried to produce the play simply, and without any flourish of trumpets',[14] Williams explained; but with a meagre purse and three weeks of rehearsal he had little alternative. Again the psychology of Shakespeare's characters was kept uppermost; and once more individual readings were intriguing, but the overall production lacked balance and tragic force.

Williams's Caesar was, like Wills's, a tired old man, occasionally play-fully avuncular, sometimes haggard and distraught, but never a serious threat to the conspirators. 'Soaked as the name is in legend and tradition, the part is an extremely difficult one, and I never managed to get it steady on its feet',[15] he confessed later. Richardson was more fortunate. His Brutus, a dispassionate soldier, philosopher, and idealist, 'very conscious of his philosophy and his integrity, with a touch of donnish humour',[16] firmly placed himself at the play's centre. With the announcement of Portia's death, in line with Granville-Barker's suggestion, Williams handed Richardson the reins of the action and the remaining scenes were treated as the tale of Brutus' unregretful march toward doom. His 'clear-cut and magnificent' death scene, Williams thought, 'could hardly have been bettered';[17] and reviewers noted less of an anti-climax than usual after the Forum sequence. Nevertheless, the naturalistic method again seemed to rob Brutus of his tragic mystique. Herbert Farjeon found the character 'too much in the bread-and-butter vein';[18] the *New Statesman and Nation* critic dubbed him 'a *Gregers Werle de ses jours*';[19] and in retrospect Williams felt that Richardson missed 'the metaphysical something in the character that Shakespeare was to develop more fully in Hamlet'.[20] What was wanted was the elusive spirituality which Edwin Booth's Brutus embodied so poignantly.

Robert Speaight's Cassius, splendid-voiced if unheroically-proportioned, was considerably more satisfying than Wolfit's had been. 'I don't think I had any revolutionary ideas about him', Mr Speaight says. 'I saw him as an impulsive, envious character rather battering himself against the integrity of Brutus. I didn't see him as noble at all.'[21] The swift ease with which Cassius worked his fanatical will upon the ignorant idealism of Brutus caught the imagination of theatre-goers at the outset. Nervously alive and sensation-racked, the character grew compellingly as the play progressed by a cumulative series of deft touches rather than isolated flamboyant effects. A typically telling moment was the barely perceptible glance he exchanged with Brutus when Casca told them the tribunes had been put to silence.[22] But when untrammelled passion was needed, Speaight was not behindhand. 'In his outburst in the quarrel scene', Farjeon noted, 'his legs quivered with emotion. He showed from the first moment the agony with which his love for Brutus inspired his fury against him.'[23]

Robert Harris's Antony, lightweight, sentimental, and lachrymose, evinced a certain romantic appeal, but lacked the craft, authority, and ruthless charm of Gielgud's *arriviste*. The Forum scene, marred by the shortcomings of both actor and director, fell below the standard set in 1930. To permit more flexible blocking Williams placed a second staircase in the orchestra pit; and the size of the mob was substantially increased. Harris lacked the weight and elocutionary technique to dominate the ensuing rough and tumble, and frequent resemblances to a cup-final were not lost upon the critics. Harris was further handicapped by Williams's post-assassination interval. The emotional momentum of the action evaporated with the coffee and sandwiches, and Antony found himself unable to regain it. The simple sincerity of his delivery seemed curiously flat and spiritless – when it could be heard above the incessant shrieks from the orchestra well. Yet again the scene demonstrated its resistance to naturalistic treatment. A small and quiet crowd is absurd; and a large and vociferous one overwhelms all but the most splendid oratory. The search for a workable compromise has exercised every *Caesar* director throughout the past four decades.

Viewed in historical perspective, Williams's essays in the naturalistic style assume considerable importance. He clearly demonstrated in the metropolis, as Bridges-Adams had done at Stratford, that Shakespeare comes off best when full texts are played with simplicity, swiftness, and fluidity. His sensitivity to the psychological subtleties of the characters enabled him to discover their contemporary and compelling relevance – an achievement which largely eluded both Atkins and Bridges-Adams. But Williams's failure to realize *Caesar*'s tragic dimension despite his scholarly care cannot be ignored. Critics and directors alike found themselves asking whether the play's austere classicism, formal rhetoric, and august characters defy naturalism and demand epic treatment. Rightly or wrongly, the modern theatre has consistently rejected the grand style in an understandable reaction against its nineteenth-century excesses. And tragic magnificence has since graced Shakespeare's lofty scene on only the rarest of occasions.

On 22 October, 1935, Henry Cass directed, in the Williams vein, the last *Caesar* revival to be seen at the Old Vic for almost two decades. Again a full text was played, and the verse was admirably spoken. The décor, if simple, was more eye-catching than in previous productions; and constituted the chief novelty. Acting upon Granville-Barker's observation that the Roman Senate assembled may not have looked like the cooling-room of a Turkish bath, Betty Dyson designed a wardrobe which took account of Renaissance notions of classical costume. Hats, cloaks, and doublets could be spoken of without impropriety, and their vivid hues enlivened and lent sumptuousness to the action. Like Atkins, Cass took great pains with lighting, and had a flair for deft visual touches. His crowds, marshalled against skies of flame-red and cobalt-blue, were picturesque without pretentiousness or prettiness; and on the Plains of Philippi Brutus' tattered army, straggling in silhouette against the skyline, added a poignant resonance to the finale.

Cecil Trouncer's Caesar was universally praised. James Agate considered it the best he had seen, while Ivor Brown rated it 'one of the best'. Trouncer's portrait was a study in cold splendour, an inhuman, alarming figure with 'a mouth as ruthless as the maw of a shark'.[24] This Caesar, Brown thought, 'created exactly that sense of majesty a little over-matured which the part needs'.[25] Both 'the flash of greatness as well as the weakening assault of falling sickness' were clearly etched.[26]

Leo Genn's Brutus, young, handsome, and integrity personified, was 'a hero of the present rather than an exponent of outworn republican virtue'.[27] Acting on a hint from Granville-Barker, Genn made no effort to minimize the less attractive aspects of Brutus' idealism. Supercilious and unforgiving, he was too priggishly aware of himself as the 'soul of Rome': in the Quarrel scene his calm, irritating superiority taxed the audience's sympathy almost as highly as it did Cassius' patience. William Devlin's lean and hungry conspirator was distinguished by a 'look of livid intensity, and a feverish and leaping intelligence'.[28] Although an ever-erupting volcano of anger and envy, he managed to remain oddly likeable. Both men were persuasive politicos, but neither achieved anything like tragic stature.

By all accounts Old Bensonian Ion Swinley's Mark Antony acted everyone else off the stage. To Agate's mind, his virile passion reduced the conspirators to 'little more than boys'. In its way, Swinley's Antony was as modern as Genn's Brutus. Swilling wine with Octavius in the Proscription scene, the dissolute cynic and opportunist struck one reviewer as so up-to-date that 'one would scarcely be surprised to find him making a deal in armaments'.[29] Yet the part was never distorted to pander to naturalistic tastes. While Antony's psychology and behaviour were contemporary and credible, his delivery remained poetic and passionate, with a natural lyrical line and a fine sense of rhythm in the set speeches. The Forum sequence was a triumph. Once again the citizens were relegated to the orchestra pit, but they were permitted to surge over the top at the last. This time there was no question of who was in control; and oratorical finesse was never blemished by naturalistic bellowing. 'The easy rhetoric of the funeral oration became in his declamation a torrent of music swept by dissonance', Audrey Williamson tells us, 'a masterly playing on the feelings of the mob with enough core of genuine grief to lash his hearers to frenzy.'[30] Caesar audiences were not to witness another such blend of human passion and poetic splendour until the Gielgud Cassius some fifteen years later.

While Waterloo Road revivals pioneered a new production mode, Tree's Caesar format, with modifications, held periodic sway in the West End until near the outbreak of the Second World War.

In 1920 Stanley Bell, formerly an assistant to Tree, starred Henry Ainley in a spectacular revival at St James's (9 January, 1920). Bell both directed and designed the production. The text and three-act arrangement were Tree's;[31] but the settings, although pictorial, were a comparatively austere mixture of impressionism and simplified realism.[32] Ever-changing skies, silhouettes of buildings and trees, and a picturesque corner of Caesar's palace supplanted Alma-Tadema's epic spectacle. The spirit of Craig and Granville-Barker was clearly discernible in the décor, if totally absent elsewhere.

The play was of course Antony's; and it was soon evident that Ainley, who had played Cassius to the Antonys of both Tree (1910) and Benson (1911), had taken the latter as his master. Here was no cynical politician, no super-subtle trickster. 'He is instead', wrote Sydney Carroll, 'a fiercely emotional, woolly headed fellow, voluptuous yet virile, whose feelings force him to craft and eloquence, whose grief carries him and you into the clouds, whose passion blinds the mob, infuriates, and sets the fires of revenge blazing toward Heaven.'[33] To a role in which the actor too often relies exclusively upon his vocal gifts, Ainley brought a refreshing non-verbal quality. 'One could write a whole article merely on his variations of walk', maintained John Francis Hope, 'the amazed haste with which he bursts into the Senate, the sagging descent of the steps to the corpse, the stark, stricken immobility of his grief merging into a continued tremor of the leg revealed by the shivering toga.'[34]

Basil Gill's Brutus, a frequent partner of Tree's Antony in palmier days, was traditionally handsome, impassive, and declamatory. Milton Rosmer's Cassius, actuated more by personal jealousy of Caesar than by any higher motive, yet revealed the odd flash of nobility to mitigate somewhat his baser traits. Rosmer's sense of character was altogether more praiseworthy than his verse-speaking. 'If a technically correct stress, pause, or accentuation obscures the human verisimilitude or dims clear emotional expression, it goes!' he told his critics. 'It is humanity first I am out for.'[35] Clifton Boyne's Caesar was too senile, but not entirely devoid of dignity.

Apart from a disastrous attempt by Henry Baynton to stage *Caesar* with a young and bare-legged company at the Savoy in 1922, the play was a stranger to the West End until 1932 when Oscar Asche revived at His Majesty's a near replica of Tree's *fin de siècle* spectacle. Once again panoramic views of Rome, massed throngs of citizens, statuesque poses, and lofty elocution were the order of the day. The text spoken was basically Tree's, but the nine scenes were divided into four acts rather than Tree's three. Much of the original business was retained, including a black-garbed Calphurnia mourning her dead husband as the curtain fell on the Senate scene.

But the marmoreal glories of Augustan Rome had lost their power to charm. 'Shakespeare's Rome is not in the least like "ancient Rome",' insisted Desmond MacCarthy, 'and the dramatic atmosphere in the play is falsified when an attempt is made to resurrect it.'[36] Reviewers who had experienced the full texts and spirited playing at Stratford and the Old Vic had little patience with the wanton cuts and plodding pace. 'This is the old bad Shakespeare', charged C. B. Purdom, 'the dull and heavy Shakespeare that makes us sorry for the actors who have to speak such stale and dreary words. This is the resurrected Shakespeare that we have to pretend to enjoy. The tragedy is gloomily dug out of the buried past. There is no life or passion, nothing that comes straight from the heart, nothing that concerns us to-day. There is not even an echo of the gay, swift, living word that is the real Shakespeare.'[37]

Godfrey Tearle's Antony, rugged and impassioned rather than elegant and eloquent, was clearly of Benson lineage. But in the Forum scene, attired in a short black mantle over a red and white tunic and toga, he was more the rabid demagogue than Benson would have favoured. In a singular concession to contemporary practice, Asche placed the mob on orchestra pit steps with lictors stationed at the top to restrain them. Their behaviour was less contrived than that of Tree's supers; and at times the action approached a free-for-all. Tearle 'did not drop his words, as Tree did, "into a pool of silence". He was a mob-orator from first to last. He hurled the intruders physically from Caesar's body. He drowned the shouts with his own voice, and at times roared like a football-coach.'[38]

By contrast, Brutus (Basil Gill) was more sculpture than man. 'He intones the lines reverentially and as portions of an august ceremony rather than as vehicles of acute and anxious thought', Ivor Brown complained.[39] Baliol Holloway's Cassius, on the other hand, was a tornado of energy, speaking in Morse-like bursts of two syllables at a time through a sly, smouldering smile; but convincing nobility and craft were in short supply. Lyn Harding, heavily made up, was a Caesar more stagey than stately; resplendent in golden wreath and robes of Imperial purple, he spoke, Purdom thought, 'as though he were telling stories of the moon'.[40]

Two years later Gill and Tearle repeated their roles at the Alhambra (20 February 1934) in a production by Stanley Bell under Sir Oswald Stoll's management. Bell's *mise en scène* was, as in 1920, distinguished by an elegant simplicity, a quality curiously at variance with performances dubbed 'a Wagnerian opera of words'. Tearle and Gill echoed finely amid star-spangled skies and trumpet fanfares; Franklin Dyall imparted a sinister roughness to an otherwise conventional Cassius; and Edgar Owen's Caesar was much praised for his Roman profile. The play ended with the Plains of Philippi deserted; and to a sudden scurry of dead leaves over the empty stage, the curtain fell on the last spark of the beau idéal tradition.

On 5 July 1937 Robert Atkins directed in Regent's Park Open Air Theatre a *Caesar* reluctantly truncated to fit the park's closing hours. Stunning visual effects flowed from a few ingeniously lighted pillars and platforms. Unwontedly colourful and luxurious costumes were rented from Alexander Korda's suspended film *I Claudius*. Eric Portman's Brutus was 'a fine austere study, a man of sorrows, a Hamlet cast in the sterner mould of a more marmoreal civilization than that of Elsinore'.[41] Laidman Browne offered a febrile contrapuntal portrait of 'the alert, practical, ignoble politician, the man of intelligence without intellect'.[42] Ion Swinley once more spoke right on with an unmatched wedding of sense and sound; and Neil

Porter reanimated his Old Vic Caesar of more than a decade earlier, a gaunt hollow-eyed patrician with 'an Aristotelian magnanimity'.[43]

Shortly afterwards Orson Welles dropped his boulder into the pool of conventional *Caesar* production in America; and six months later the ripples reached England. In May of 1938 the Festival Theatre, Cambridge, staged a modern-dress revival in which the scene in Caesar's house found the Dictator busy with grapefruit and coffee while Calphurnia read out the horrors of the previous night from the pages of the *Daily Express*. Later Caesar used a telephone to contact the augurers. A special effort was made to give the verse the clipped cadences of twentieth-century conversation, but there was no overt attempt to force a contemporary political parallel.

Two months later (24 July) the BBC made the first television version of the play a full-dress study in power politics. The major characters appeared in Italian-style military uniforms, and the citizens in civilian dress. The Soothsayer wore a lounge suit and soft felt hat, and carried a hurdy-gurdy. The Senators sat on modish chairs of tubular stainless steel, but stabbed Caesar, somewhat incongruously, with daggers. Brutus and Cassius conducted their quarrel at a café table in a park with sky-scrapers in the background. Lucius was metamorphosed into a hovering waiter who served two lagers in lieu of a bowl of wine. In the battle scenes, tanks, gas-masks, and dugouts were commonplace; and revolvers served as the instruments of death. The play ended with the prophetic rattle of machine-guns, the whine of shells, and a flight of bombers passing over. Dallas Bower was the producer, and the cast featured Ernest Milton as Caesar, Sebastian Shaw as Brutus, Anthony Ireland as Cassius, and D. A. Clarke-Smith as Antony.

With the war fears of 1938 realized in the autumn of 1939, Henry Cass's modern-dress *Caesar* premiered on 30 November at the Embassy Theatre with compelling immediacy. Walter Hudd appeared in the title-role, with Godfrey Kenton as Brutus, Clifford Evans as Cassius, and Eric Portman as Antony. On 23 December the production transferred to His Majesty's with Godfrey Kenton as Caesar and Godfrey Tearle as Brutus.

On a bare stage set with platforms, steps, and a few curtains, Cass set out to delineate 'the struggle between decent modern idealism and Power supported by an undiscriminating public'.[44] Unlike Welles, he cut the text very little, and relied upon contemporary costumes, novel business, and colloquial speaking to point his anti-Fascist moral. Unfortunately, Cass's knack for gimmickry became an obsession, and the play and its message were engulfed by eye-catching gewgaws. In the Forum scene, for example, Antony harangued a mackintoshed, mufflered crowd massed on a flight of stairs under a spotlight, while lantern slides on a backcloth upstaged both the rhetoric and the mob's reaction to it. To add insult to injury, a distant newsboy intermittently bawled the headline, 'Caesar dead, special'. The battlefield confrontation between the opposing forces in v.i took place over field telephones, to its considerable detriment. Theatre-goers were less conscious of Brutus' words than of the upturned sugar boxes which furnished his dugout, or the figures in steel helmets with fixed bayonets who crouched distractingly beyond.

Hudd's Caesar was a harsh-voiced hypochondriac in a General Franco cap who when under stress kept snatching gold-rimmed spectacles from his nose. Godfrey Kenton played Brutus as Wells's grave liberal, 'the well-meaning democrat, uncomfortable and, alas, unsuccessful when he is forced to become a man of action'.[45] Dressed in a British naval officer's uniform in the military scenes, he was pathetically ineffective, fully realizing a temperamental unfitness brilliantly prefigured immediately after the assassination when he sentimentally appropriated Caesar's spectacles as a keepsake. Cass's choice of Tearle for the role when the play moved to the West End defies conjecture. Whatever the reasons, Tearle maintained his usual grand manner; undaunted by twentieth-century trappings, he wrapped his greatcoat about him like a toga and let fly whenever occasion offered. Clifford Evans was a prose Cassius, colloquial and convincing at the most obvious, naturalistic level; but the poetic dimension of the character eluded him. Eric Portman's Mark Antony in SS uniform – loyal, subtle, and rather stout – suggested an amalgam of Goering and Goebbels. Casca (Anthony Hawtrey) was perversely portrayed as a mincing, effeminate intellectual, despite the blunt decisiveness of his 'Speak hands for me.' Needless to say, this line was cut.

The Embassy production, while not without ephemeral success, shed little new light on the play. Intent on clarifying *Caesar*'s political ambivalence and giving it a modern look, Cass created more problems than he solved. Despite, or because of, its sensational gear and newsreel tone, the tragedy declined into unabashed melodrama, innocent either of poetry or spiritual energy. Unfortunately, Cass was not the last director to be frustrated by *Caesar*'s resistance to directorial manipulation; rather he serves merely as prologue to *Julius Caesar*'s stage history in the third quarter of this century – a tale of bold-spirited, if often futile, efforts to satisfy the conflicting claims of tragic grandeur, contemporary naturalness, and box-office novelty.

Donald Wolfit's odd revival at the King's Theatre, Hammersmith, in 1949, after the play's uncongenial theme and uncommon demand for male actors had kept it off the boards during the war,[46] concludes this century's first fifty years of *Julius Caesar* productions, and signals an era of perplexed, and often perplexing, directorial reassessment and experimentation. Wolfit's *Caesar*, in contrast to the Welles and Cass productions, was in style less modern-dress than fancy-dress. Or as he put it in a programme note, 'The uniforms are of no particular state or country but chosen for their colour value as applicable to the main characters.'[47] Mystified reviewers and audiences speculated fruitlessly upon the relevance of each costume's cut and colour to its wearer; and Wolfit was chary of enlightenment. Mused Ivor Brown:

To use modern uniforms for 'Julius Caesar' is surely to invite misunderstanding. Wolfit claims that the colours chosen fit the characters. But do they? Most of the Liberators in Wolfit's presentation wear black, which gives to the historical opponents of dictatorship a Nazi–Fascist look. Caesar resembles a Victorian Field Marshal in full fig. Brutus in white drill with black jack-boots suggests rather a Mussolini on holiday than the thoughtful maladroit liberal. Marc Antony in a bright blue tunic might have wandered along from Mr. Novello's Murania in order to deliver a king's rhapsody over the emperor's clay.[48]

A decade later Alan Dent revealed (*News Chronicle*, 12 August 1960) that a query about the appropriateness of the uniforms prompted a letter from the company's wardrobe-mistress 'to explain that the real reason for the modern dress was that modern laundries – in immediate post-war conditions – refused to wash togas'. But the curious colour-scheme apparently went unexplained.

The nature of Wolfit's Brutus was as enigmatic as his outfit. In the early part of the play he seemed the familiar agonized idealist, loath to act. Yet, in the Assassination scene, an astonished Harold Hobson noted that 'he picks up the gashed and bleeding Caesar by the shoulder, and sticks his sword through him with a deliberate and sadistic pleasure'.[49] Whatever Wolfit's directorial intentions, they died a-borning in the hands of inexperienced supporting players. Caesar (Jonathan Meddings), despite his scarlet regalia, was universally judged inadequate. Nigel Clarke, arrayed in a green uniform vaguely commodore-ish in style, was a vehement but patently insincere Cassius. Bryan Johnson, although virile and spirited, missed the full stature of Antony. 'He is dressed like a rowing Blue, and delivers his oration as might be expected of a man about to stroke Oxford to victory next spring', jibed Harold Hobson.[50] But he was little aided by a mob conceived as a Greek chorus, which affected stylized screams and poses to the undisguised hilarity of school parties in the audience. Hammersmith theatregoers were but the first of thousands to leave modern *Caesar* productions scratching their heads in wonderment or muttering darkly of wilful misinterpretation.

English and North American productions (1950–73)

Directors of *Caesar* after the Second World War inherited from the Old Vic a full text and flexible stagecraft. But with the legacy came the unsolved Waterloo Road dilemma: how best to reconcile the claims of tragic grandeur with those of contemporary naturalness and relevance. Throughout the 1950s the text was retained virtually intact, together with the Old Vic acting style and production techniques, in the hope that, Williams's experience notwithstanding, *Caesar*'s tragic stature would reveal itself if given a substantially Elizabethan treatment. Modernity and novelty were added by reshaping the playing space and tricking out the *mise en scène*; while business, summarily banned by Williams, was re-admitted. Whatever the theoretical virtues of the compromise between 'Elizabethan Methodism' (as Bridges-Adams called it) and innovation, the practical result was indifferent at best. The play stoutly proclaimed itself chronicle or melodrama, and yielded up its tragic splendour only in flashes.

The first major post-war *Caesar*, and the only significant Stratford revival since the Bridges-Adams era,[1] opened at the Shakespeare Memorial Theatre on 7 May 1950 under the joint direction of Antony Quayle and Michael Langham. Less than a hundred lines were cut, with the Camp Poet episode (IV.iii.124–38), the second announcement of Portia's death (IV.iii.176–95), and the preferment of Strato to Octavius (V.v.61–3, 66–7) the only excisions of consequence.[2] The play was divided into two parts in the Harcourt Williams manner, separated by an interval of twenty minutes. The first act, in nine scenes, closed with the Proscription episode; the shorter second act comprised only the military sequences in an effort to reduce the risk of anti-climax.

Warwick Armstrong's settings, although unlocalized, were considerably more complex and costly than those used at the Old Vic. Act I was staged in a two-storied arrangement of steps, columns, and arches. Behind the colonnade a cyclorama pictured skies of appropriate mood, and in front the familiar stairway joined stage and orchestra pit. Purple drapes suspended from the nearer pillars were added to suggest the Senate interior. Act II opened with the tent in place for the quarrel, flanked on either side by flights of steps. The tent was later struck by soldiers to reveal the Plains of Philippi behind – an agglomeration of broken columns and the suggestion of a low rock wall, framed by the steps, which remained in position. The curtain fell only at the interval.

Although Armstrong reverted to white togas and conventional Roman military dress, he was lavish of colour in cloaks, tunics, and properties. The severe architecture of the first act threw into glittering relief the civic processions which flowed diagonally up and down the orchestra steps and over the stage; while the perpetual twilight of the Plains of Philippi was fitfully brightened by the glint of armour and weapons on richly-hued fabrics.

Once more the play was viewed as a character study; and every effort was made to allow the actors full freedom to capture the complex interplay of personalities stressed by Granville-Barker. Action was swift and fluid. At the end of II.iii, for example, the conspirators and Caesar could still be seen moving up right as Artemidorus came down left to read his scroll.

The pivotal figure in the affair was clearly Cassius, played by John Gielgud. For the first time since Lawrence Barrett, and after more than half a century of uncomplex blends of waspishness, neuroticism, and general mean-mindedness, Cassius was allowed a measure of nobility. No longer merely a passionate foil to Brutus' tranquillity, Gielgud's lean and hungry Roman emerged as the coiled spring which vitalizes the tragedy.

In the early scenes he appeared as a fanatical crusader against totalitarianism, burningly sincere, and driven by a torrent of energy. 'Three or four times he looks not so much *at* as *into* the audience', Alan Dent noted, 'and we observe that his eyes have the curious sightless blaze of a man obsessed with an ideal.'[3] Cassius' political concern was not, in Gielgud's opinion, entirely disinterested, however; at the core of the man and pulsing with deadly vitality was 'an innate sense of frustrated power'.[4] Although mightily in awe of Brutus' moral and social superiority, he threw caution to the winds at their first encounter in a desperate attempt to grasp the reins of authority. Vehement and fiery-tongued, Gielgud delivered the Tiber speech as it had not been heard in living memory. 'It was a joy to hear the lines ringing from the Stratford stage in silver and beaten bronze', wrote J. C. Trewin.[5]

Gielgud's conspirator was an intellectual who clearly justified Caesar's disquiet. Once he had seized the initiative, neither political conviction nor power-lust was allowed to dim tactical acuity. 'Ardent, envious, weak, valiant, living between gusts of fury and depression',[6] he drove the conspiracy to its conclusion, confident that the sublimity of the end justified the baseness of the means. But on the eve of battle, long-repressed doubts momentarily gained the upper hand. At the close of the quarrel, 'exasperated by that stubborn idealism which drives Brutus to make every possible

15. The Quarrel scene (IV.iii) with John Gielgud as Cassius and Harry Andrews as Brutus. Quayle–Langham production at the Shakespeare Memorial Theatre, 1950

mistake in the campaign, yet secretly a little in awe of Brutus' moral ascendancy and, knowing himself the unworthier man',[7] he capitulated open-heartedly, sacrificed strategic judgement to noble impulse, and sealed the tragic outcome of the action.

Although Gielgud thought himself unsuited to military and aggressive roles, he rose to full heroic stature in the final scenes; and critics were led to ask 'why his power to represent a warrior, a man of action has so long been doubted'.[8] His farewells and his death were profoundly noble; and for once Brutus' valediction seemed well-earned. It is our good fortune to have this landmark interpretation preserved, albeit adapted to cinema, in the 1953 MGM film of the play produced by John Houseman and directed by Joe Mankiewicz.

Harry Andrews's bearded Brutus suggested to Richard Findlater 'a shepherd king in his white robe and stick, an impressive patriarchal figure'.[9] Inspired by Antony's epitaph, Andrews made gentleness the keynote of the character. Throughout the first colloquy with Cassius, he remained studiedly motionless, responding only mildly, if at all, to Cassius' frenzied harangue. Stroke by stroke the performance grew in quiet authority, and captured with conviction the dilemma of the liberal idealist 'who foolishly thinks it unnecessary to be a politician as well'.[10] During the quarrel, he made little effort to overawe Cassius; his calm integrity was more potent than any amount of frigid grandeur. As Brutus revealed Portia's death, Findlater discovered 'a deep and poignant tenderness, and a dignity of self-restraint that is a match for Mr. Gielgud's fire and tears'.[11] Awkward blocking, however, mitigated the fullest realization of the scene; separated by a table much of the time, the actors' interchanges wanted the support of fluid movement. On the battlefield Brutus behaved with patrician restraint, and died with becoming nobility. Andrews's reading, whatever its obvious virtues, seemed to some critics a trifle too subdued and intimate, with a certain reluctance to give the rhetoric its full value. 'Need this fear of "reciting"', asked Philip Hope-Wallace, 'be so general as to allow great speeches to drop as if they were perfunctory half-framed thoughts?'[12]

Antony Quayle's Mark Antony was a portrait in primary hues. In the early scenes he looked every inch the hedonist and sycophant, if somewhat too chubby an athlete. In the Senate sequence his grief and fury were compelling, although craft was little in evidence. Quayle directed his Forum speech at the theatre audience, treating them as part of the assembly, while the stage-mob rioted on the other three sides of him. The empty downstage space proved artificial and distracting, and the full-face and profile grouping of the crowd gave it exaggerated prominence. The forensic subtlety of the speech, the intricate and intimate interplay between demagogue and crowd, was lost in pandemonium. The fury-driven tirade of an Antony described as 'half-politician, half-medium, a man possessed with the crowd's delirium',[13] was theatrically sensational, but a poor substitute for the orator and the oration of Shakespeare's contriving.

Andrew Cruickshank's Caesar, senile, unctuous, and sour faced, was decidedly unsympathetic, but not without a certain faded majesty.

The first *Caesar* to be staged in-the-round, at New York's Arena Theatre[14] on 20 June 1950, promised a radical treatment of the play, but ultimately achieved less than the Quayle–Langham version. The action took place on a central platform, denuded of all but a broken column and three or four stone blocks;[15] and actors came and went through an audience of five hundred by way of four aisles which converged on the performing area. Players and director seemed ill-at-ease with the arena convention; and only the Forum scene profited markedly from it. Here, with the mob posted throughout the theatre, the audience participated more directly in the action than ever before. The acting, however, was less gripping. Joseph Holland, the Caesar of Welles's production, proved a too-flamboyant Brutus for intimate performance conditions, and the modernity of his style clashed sharply with the formal Bensonian rhetoric of Basil Rathbone's Cassius. Horace Braham's Caesar was 'crotchety and gone womanish with age', and 'noble Antony' merely a 'strutting bully-boy'.[16]

In 1953, after an absence of almost two decades, *Caesar* returned to the Old Vic in a production by Hugh Hunt; but little advance on Cass's 1935 effort was detectable. Tanya Moiseiwitsch designed a collection of massive murky pillars and steps for the civil scenes and an arrangement of tents for the Plains of Philippi. Alan Tagg enhanced the gloomy *ambiance* with costumes of Renaissance-classical cut, many of them in black.

The text was relatively full (only the Caius Ligarius and Camp Poet sequences were omitted), but Hunt seemed curiously unwilling to trust it. Played at breakneck speed and overwhelmed with trumpet and drum fanfares and alarums, an operatic storm, and the smoke and flame of burning Rome, Shakespeare's lofty scene dwindled into swashbuckling melodrama. Vocal music was muted; and the poetic line was freely fractured in the service of naturalism. The first three acts were dominated by a frenetic mob. At each appearance of Caesar, Cecil Wilson noted, 'the crowd surges, screaming, on to the stage as if tossed there by an earthquake'.[17] Their frequent emergence kept excitement at fever-pitch until their final terrifying exit after the lynching of Cinna, leaving 'the stripped body huddled head downwards on the steps'.[18] Wary of the anti-climactic hazards of the Plains of Philippi, Hunt interjected, by the *Daily Herald* reviewer's count, no less than sixteen hair-raising military skirmishes.

The pivotal importance of Cassius, so ably affirmed by Gielgud, was maintained to some degree by Paul Rogers. 'Tactically far ahead of Brutus and morally a bit behind him, unpriggish of mood and unrestrained of temper, waspish yet easily melting into comradeship', Ivor Brown awarded him 'all the sympathy of our sour time in which the Liberalism typified by Brutus dwindles and the romantic figure of an Antony is suspect'.[19] This 'tight-lipped, thrusting Cassius, impatient of every lost minute',[20] lacked the unique nobility and intellect of Gielgud's conspirator, but nonetheless set the pace.

William Devlin's Brutus trod in the footsteps of Harry Andrews's gentle idealist, although the external trappings of the 'shepherd king' were inexplicably rejected in favour of black robes and a Guy Fawkes beard. 'Alone, in the opening scenes', wrote Philip Hope-Wallace, 'he well enough reveals the man's divided soul and the flaw in his honour; the humourless, ponderous, kindly part of the character comes out well. But something falls short of emotional distinction: this was a Brutus with a small heart.'[21] Stephen Williams found him 'so high-principled that he is about as fit to lead a conspiracy against Caesar as a sick child'.[22] In the military scenes he remained 'a gentle philosopher who is obviously ill at ease in a breast-plate', entirely wanting 'that soldier-like authority becoming to one whose ancestor had driven the Tarquin from the streets of Rome'.[23]

Antony, accoutered in pink, was equally unheroic but theatrical to the core. 'Robin Bailey does not present Antony as a high Roman blazon', one critic tells us. 'The man is an opportunist . . . Mark Antony feels Caesar's loss keenly; but he does not let grief unman him: rather, his wit is sharpened.'[24] In the Forum, he delivered his speech in 'plain, blunt man' vein 'with an energetic but deliberate flatness, two or three words or phrases at a time, with a cunning gleam in the eye',[25] like 'a rising young modern Parliamentarian aware that he is in excellent form and enjoying a new found mastery over words'.[26]

Douglas Campbell's Caesar, pompous and dull in life, contrived to die with rather more flair, gaping at Brutus for a moment, and then, 'without staggering or sinking to his knees, falling flat on his back with the impact of a felled tree'.[27] Octavius, doubled by Campbell, was the epitome of frigid arrogance, defiantly keeping his hand at his side as the corpse of Brutus was borne from the field to the salutes of friends and foes.

The quest for contemporary relevance was given brief respite in the course of the next year or so when two revivals exhibited Caesar as an Elizabethan theatre artifact. On 29 June 1953 Michael MacOwan directed his youthful Elizabethan Theatre Company in a Tudor-dress production on a rudimentary platform at the Westminster Theatre. 'It is all too easy for a producer to impose a spurious interpretation on "Julius Caesar"', ran the programme note. 'The play has been transformed into a study of mob psychology, or an analysis of dictatorship . . . It is worthwhile remembering that it was not power politics that interested him [Shakespeare], but people.'[28] MacOwan's conception, however admirable, was betrayed by his actors' inexperience; utility costumes, daylight-type illumination, a minute

mob, and token armies served only to underline the puniness of the characterization. Equally brave, but hardly more fortunate, was a production on 8
March 1954 by the Nottingham Theatre Trust – a doublet, hose, and
nightgown affair in a replica Tudor playhouse.

The first major attempt to give *Caesar* a functional Elizabethan setting
came in June 1955, when the fledgling Shakespeare Festival in Stratford,
Ontario, revived the play on Tanya Moiseiwitsch's splendid thrust stage,
housed temporarily in a tent auditorium. With the audience seated on three
sides of the platform, and the actors coming and going in all directions, the
play revealed a fluid rhythm and complex texture undreamt of in proscenium settings, however flexible.

Michael Langham directed the drama as less tragedy than chronicle: the
ebb and flow of historic events transcended the men who made them.
Supers were employed in some numbers to lend glamour and verisimilitude
to the action; and Tanya Moiseiwitsch dressed them in Renaissance-
classical costumes, freely splashing their rich but muted colours over the
fumed oak of the stage. The naturalistic bustle of soldiers, citizens, and
peasant women launched the first act on a flood of vitality; and their
shamefaced retreat through the audience permitted only a moment's respite
before the stage exploded with the splendour of Caesar's procession.
'Imperial Rome delighted in banners and the insignia of power', remarks
Robertson Davies, 'and it was a pleasure to see these handsomely realized. A
great golden spreadeagle mounted on a pole; a ponderous standard with the
Senatus Populusque Romanus symbol; golden wreaths and sheaves of wheat
borne in procession; the splendid sceptre of Caesar himself, and the handsome chair in which he was carried; the banners topped with busts; the
armour and weapons of the soldiers; these things, no less than the bearded
priests of Jupiter, and the slaves and foreigners among the crowd, gave us
the feel of Rome.'[29]

The assassination was seen not as a grand culmination of the action but
simply as the mid-point in the tale. A largish company of senators lent
credibility to the event, and a handful served as a horrified chorus. When
Caesar 'reeled from one of his slayers to another, his mantle seeming
transformed into the blood that was being shed, we were concerned', recalls
Professor Davies, 'not only with him and the men about him, but with the
stricken few who were witnesses, and who at last fled shrieking from the
place'.[30]

The early moments of the Forum scene were played with comparative
restraint, initiating a splendidly-contrived rise in tension which reached its
zenith only with the death of Cinna. Langham disposed his mob throughout
the theatre, and they came and went by way of five aisles which converged
upon the stage. The speeches were given from the platform's upper level, a
triangular balcony supported by columns over part of the acting area.

Brutus, robed in ice-blue, climbed the stairs to the pulpit with assurance, spoke with sincerity, and descended with dignity. Only with difficulty did Antony manage to coax the crowd back. His use of space immediately set off his fervid emotionalism from Brutus' chilly rationality. When instructed to 'go up', he ignored the stairs and swung himself athletically aloft; later, with a reckless leap he flung himself down beside the body. As the mob stormed away at the end of the speech, he solemnly carried the corpse in his arms down one of the auditorium vomitories under the very feet of the hushed house. No sooner was Antony lost to sight when the sequence swept to its terrifying finale as the frenzied mob seized the unfortunate poet and literally tore him to pieces, 'so that limbs and a head were flung into the darkness, and only a litter of horrifying scraps was left'.[31]

Despite the verve of the earlier acts, the final third of the play retained its momentum, thanks largely to visual effects and hurtling action. Portable properties and vivid costumes lent the Proscription scene an air of oriental sensuousness, an effect enhanced by two lascivious courtesans with whom Antony toyed as he talked. In the battle scenes entrances were made from all sides of the auditorium through the public doors, making the audience almost as much participants as spectators. 'Soldiers swept in from one side and then the other', Arnold Edinborough tells us. 'They fought each other up the stage and down, banners were swished through the air giving both visual and audible support to the clash of arms. Soldiers tumbled down the steps and leaped off the balcony.'[32] As a bonus, Caesar's ghost, clad in bloody mantle, twice stalked the battlefield. With the tumult at last over and Brutus' body borne away, Antony and Octavius remained alone onstage as the lights faded, eyeing each other coldly in anticipation of struggles yet to come.

As an exercise in unfettered action and visual excellence, Langham's *Caesar* could hardly be bettered. But if the play derives its real thrust from character rather than event, as Granville-Barker argues, the production was critically flawed. 'Here was action and sound enough', maintained Edinborough, 'but we had not seen the clash of personalities and ideals which Shakespeare wrote about.'[33] Lorne Greene's Brutus, stalwart and full-voiced, was finely oratorical in the Forum, but monotonous and stodgy elsewhere. 'Brutus was unquestionably noble, honourable and unselfish', contended Professor Davies, 'but he was also a bore.'[34] Lloyd Bochner's Cassius wanted weight. Such a puny personality, it seemed, 'could never rise to the high command in an army, and when he sought to persuade Brutus to join the conspiracy he gave an effect less of subtlety than waspishness'.[35] Antony, played by Donald Davis, looked 'less like a sun-drenched Roman athlete than like Saint Sebastian on his way to the archery butts'.[36] Worse still, an intrusive intellectuality seriously weakened the contrast with Brutus and Cassius upon which the balance of the play depends. His Forum speech was well judged, however, and the concluding 'Now let it work' lines combined the glee of the triumphant demagogue with a unique daemonic quality. His 'He comes upon a wish' lines suggested 'not the high spirits of an adventurer and soldier, but rather the secret exultation of a man who feels himself to be in league with fate'.[37] Caesar (Robert Christie) struck Arnold Edinborough as 'a caricature, posturing and trembling by turns'.[38]

On 12 July 1955 the American Shakespeare Festival staged *Caesar* to open its new theatre at Stratford, Connecticut. Heavy-handedly directed by Denis Carey, confined to a proscenium stage with a shallow apron, and impeded by humdrum pillars and steps, the action lacked the fluid dash of the Canadian revival. Raymond Massey played Brutus, Brooks Atkinson thought, 'like a kindly deacon';[39] while Walter Kerr found Jack Palance's Cassius 'simply a sullen, bad-tempered opportunist'.[40] Christopher Plummer as Antony was refreshingly brisk and theatrical. 'As he works his way among the conspirators', Kerr noted, 'taking their bloodstained hands one by one but keeping his own fierce counsel, the actor suggests the whole course of the action to come. The nervous working of the mouth, the patient nods with which he listens to Brutus' self-justification foreshadow everything.'[41] Unfortunately, however, youthful inexperience led him to underplay Antony's guile and cunning. Caesar (Hurd Hatfield) was the familiar husk of greatness, 'a querulous, neurotic old man, a man so lost in his own grandeur that shrewd planning can guide and bend him'.[42]

In August of the same year, the Old Vic premiered a new *Caesar* at the Edinburgh Festival and later brought it home to the Waterloo Road.[43] Under Michael Benthall's direction the first four acts were played virtually uncut, save for the omission of the Camp Poet. The fifth act, however, was savaged. Brutus entered immediately after Cassius' suicide, discovered the body himself, spoke the 'O Julius Caesar, thou art mighty yet!' lines, and without more ado asked his companions to kill him. All the intervening matter was cut. In a curious reversion to Victorian practice, the play's final speeches were reversed to allow Antony's eulogy to bring down the curtain.

The setting, designed by Audrey Cruddas, featured two great columns, one on either side of the stage. Although only the bases could be seen, their massiveness testified overwhelmingly to Rome's eternality. In act V the same pillars were broken and crumbling, a monument to human folly. A vast flight of steps led from the forestage to the orchestra pit, and another stretched upward behind the pillars. Beyond the steps lay a pitch-black sky, and the stage was bathed in perpetual twilight. The mood throughout was one of unrelieved gloom: conspiracy and treachery were a way of life.

The constant flow of action up and down the steps proved wearying to audience and actor; but in the Senate scene the vertical dimension was used to fine effect. Caesar stood atop the highest steps, and the conspirators knelt below him. Once Casca had struck the first blow, the Dictator tottered from level to level, savagely hacked by the conspirators as he went. When he reached Brutus, the latter with surprising decisiveness killed him in one clean, deliberate thrust. For a long moment the conspirators stood silent, overwhelmed by their temerity, until Cinna broke the silence in a hoarse, unbelieving whisper, 'Liberty!' At the conclusion of the scene, a grim-faced Antony carried the corpse into the orchestra pit and out of sight.

For his Forum speech Brutus stood on the topmost step in a shaft of light with the crowd silhouetted in the semi-darkness in front of him. Antony, in an impromptu display of athleticism, vaulted to the base of the right-hand column for his oration. The unfortunate Cinna later took refuge on one of these same columns, and was callously hurled from it to the ravening mob below.

The Proscription scene was distinguished by a telling piece of business. Lepidus sat on Caesar's throne-like seat, and the other members of the triumvirate stood. When Lepidus prepared to go, Antony and Octavius approached the vacant chair, and Antony took it a moment before Octavius reached it. As Antony in turn moved off, Octavius 'could not resist sitting for a moment, as if to taste majesty. Antony, turning back, noticed the action and surveyed Octavius with a smile, half jealous, half amused, as the curtain fell.'[44]

The Plains of Philippi battles were presumed to take place offstage. Brutus made his final entrance over the highest steps, and wearily stumbled down front to die. Lucius, not Strato, held the sword!

As in the Canadian and American revivals, the acting held little to startle. Paul Rogers's black-bearded Brutus was 'high-minded and perplexed: the well-meaning man wholly unfitted to cope with the situation which he has guilelessly allowed to develop about himself'. The weakness of this reading, the *Times* critic argued, is 'that there is no true relationship between the figurehead of the conspiracy and its driving force'.[45] Cassius came off as less 'a blunt, impatient fighter prepared to back his incitements with his life', than 'a wily political priest insinuating his doubts in minds simpler than his own and watching the doubts harden into sinister resolution with a rather malign satisfaction'.[46] John Neville's Antony was a more complex creation, capturing

the gamesome youth, happy enough in the favour of Caesar, growing up in a day, as it were, into the man fighting for his life with all the weapons he can command and swiftly graduating, after his oratorical triumph over Caesar's body, into the ruthless leader of men who can harshly patronise the manifestly weak Lepidus but is careful to keep a narrow watch on the young Caesar he suspects to be made of tougher stuff.[47]

Anthony Hartley, however, found him 'a little too noble for the part' and 'not quite gross enough for this debauched and merciless triumvir'.[48] Caesar, in the hands of Gerald Cross, cut so mild-mannered and unambitious a figure as to pass almost unnoticed.

Two years later (28 May 1957) Glen Byam Shaw returned *Caesar* to the Shakespeare Memorial Theatre in a revival graced with fine scholarship and rare dramatic art.[49] Taking Shakespeare's title at face value, Shaw placed Caesar firmly at the play's centre. The action was divided into two major movements: the conspiracy leading to Caesar's death, with the physical presence of the Dictator as the dominant motif; and the fate of the leaderless state after the assassination, with Caesar's spirit, symbolized by a blazing star, never far away.

Shaw shortened the text by some 175 lines, but most of his cuts were designed to clarify syntax and eliminate obscurities. The only significant excisions were a dozen lines from Brutus' idealistic outburst during the conspiracy sequence (II.i.129–40), the division of the citizens prior to the Forum speeches, some of the mob's comments during the orations, the second announcement of Portia's death, the 'Ride, ride, Messala' episode (v.ii), and Titinius' garlanding of Cassius.

In the first part of the play, Caesar's grandeur was splendidly reflected in the dimensions of Rome itself. Six majestic grey-white stone slabs, designed by Motley, slid smoothly to and fro, altering their positions and relationships to suggest each locale. For the second part, they opened to their fullest extent to reveal in turn Antony's house, the camp near Sardis, and the long rocky escarpment on the Plains of Philippi. Costumes were of the traditional sort, and dyed in the rich strong colours of Roman and Pompeian paintings of the classical period.[50]

As the curtain rose, the slabs were arranged in triangular formation. At the apex, on a plinth, stood a huge gold statue of the Dictator. Once the image was 'disrobed', it slid out of sight, and the blocks parted to reveal the living Caesar, breathtakingly posed in procession upstage against the blue empyrean. 'The statue might easily have dwarfed the human figure', wrote Roy Walker,

but the magnificence of the gold-embroidered crimson toga and the majesty of Cyril Luckham's bearing made him the incarnation of an immutable and pivotal principle of order. This ordered Rome was visible in the massive fluted monoliths of light grey stone, ranged outwards from Caesar as their personal centre in two symmetrical lines, continued in the tall stone portals flanking the fore-stage. Here was the wide perspective of Caesar's Rome with Caesar himself as the keystone.[51]

At the end of the scene the sky darkened rapidly, save for a patch of crimson above where Caesar had stood; and lightning ricocheted blindingly back and forth between cliff-like shapes during the storm.

In the Senate House Caesar sat at centre-stage upon an elevated throne backed by a sheet of burnished gold. Behind lay a limitless expanse of blue sky. The assassination was bold, but not wrathful; and Caesar became, in terrifying reality, the sacrificial victim of Brutus' imagining. Tottering from conspirator to conspirator, fighting desperately to remain upright, he was received by each on the point of his sword until Brutus dealt the *coup de grâce*. Anthony Hopkins's nerve-shattering score for brass and gong audibly intensified the horror, and as Caesar fell, lightning raked the suddenly-overcast sky.

The Forum scene unfolded at sunset, with the great stone slabs now towering in sombre disorder. The pulpit was placed at centre-stage, and Caesar's coffin, draped with his crimson and gold robe, stood just in front. The crowd, adroitly portrayed as an anonymous force rather than a collection of disparate individuals, shuffled and growled in the shadows. In the course of the orations, the daylight faced; and as Antony cried, 'Here was a Caesar! when comes such another?' (III.ii.252), a star appeared, a reminder of vanished constancy in the midst of cataclysm.[52] Suddenly Cinna entered, and the mob surged back, bearing lighted torches. When they left, the mutilated body of the poet hung, like some bloodstained rag, over the pulpit. And in the blue-black heavens the star shone on, a dispassionate witness to bloodlust and anarchy as the curtain fell.

The military sequences of the second half were more sensitively handled than usual, and careful attention to the smallest roles gave them unflagging interest. As Brutus exclaimed, 'O Julius Caesar, thou art mighty yet', the star once more appeared, and remained, a symbol of icy Nemesis, until the final curtain.

Byam Shaw's concern with the play's wholeness, with what Granville-Barker called its 'constant, varied ebb and flow and interplay of purpose, character and event', was not calculated to foster star performances; and the ensemble was probably the best seen for decades. Even the smallest parts – Cato, Lucilius, and Pindarus – caught the eye of reviewers.

Cyril Luckham's Caesar, present and absent, occupied centre-stage. On his first entrance he seemed to Rosemary Anne Sisson 'indeed, the conqueror of the world'; and manifested throughout 'that almost selfless sense of removal from other men which great men own'.[53] 'The declining invalid was there', Ivor Brown records, 'and so was the flash of greatness.'[54]

Alec Clunes's Brutus combined something of the heroic nobility of Davenport's interpretation with the spiritual sensibility of Booth's reading. This Brutus was no intellectual, and arguably even stupid enough to become the tool of lesser men. But his nobility of soul, his purity of motive, and his humane instincts were beyond question. 'Mr. Alec Clunes' Brutus is the natural leader', the *Times* critic reported, 'serene in authority and more sensitively delineating than most the Hamlet-like nature of his dilemma: the reluctant distaste he gives to such a line as "kill him in the shell" stresses both the noble strain and idealist's conscience.'[55] Geoffrey Keen's Cassius, a fussy, waspish figure, was less than an ideal foil; and unhappy comparisons with the superhuman drive, the corrosive bitterness, and the emotional brilliance of Gielgud's Cassius were inevitable.

Richard Johnson's Antony was a triumph. Over six feet in height, darkly handsome, and a fine verse speaker, he gave the character an extraordinary physical and rhetorical magnetism. Antony's grief in the Senate was utterly unfeigned, and his determination to revenge, single-minded. In the Forum it was his passionate sincerity, rather than his tactics, which moved the mob. But once aware of his gifts as a spellbinder, latent vanity, ambition, and ruthlessness rapidly surfaced. One reviewer notes that as he said, 'Belike they had some notice of the people, how I had moved them', 'he stresses the "I" – and a great conceit flashes through his grief'.[56] From this moment onwards, relentless self-interest was his ruling passion.

Byam Shaw's revival, if it did not scale the tragic heights, at least came close enough to put its immediate successors *hors de combat*. An Old Vic production on 8 October 1958, confined by hackneyed steps and columns and smothered in crimson drapery, was tedious by comparison. Its minute mob, half a dozen according to Philip Hope-Wallace, must have been the smallest since the eighteenth century. Its only other novelty was the absence of Caesar's ghost in the Tent scene, although his voice was heard there, and later on the battlefield as well. The next year (15 August 1959) Joseph Papp's New York Shakespeare Festival staged an outdoor performance in Central Park under Stuart Vaughan's direction; but much of the play's subtlety leached away into the open air. In intriguing contrast to Byam Shaw's almost operatic assassination, Vaughan created a devastating hush 'as Caesar spun silently from one conspirator to the other, the only sound his grunts as they stabbed him'.[57]

In 1960 (11 August) Michael Croft brought his National Youth Theatre to the Queen's in the first modern-dress revival for more than two decades.[58] Roman teenagers rock 'n' rolled happily in the sunshine; Casca plunged about with abandon in a plastic raincoat during the storm; and the senators donned black jackets and pin-striped trousers for the assassination. Teddy Boys mocked Antony on the fringes of the Forum crowd, and later killed an effeminate Cinna with flick-knives. Played with fine vitality, the production had many enjoyable moments, even if its young performers were unable fully to take the measure of the play's heroic theme.

Before venturing further into the 1960s, an era dominated by the director, it is well to remark his changing role in Shakespeare production during the pre- and post-war eras. Bridges-Adams, Atkins, and Williams served primarily as matchmakers, bringing text and actors into a relationship out of which a performance would ultimately be born. Décor was viewed merely as an environment to facilitate and complement the performer. All subscribed implicitly to the notion that a Shakespeare text had a stable identity ready to reveal itself when played with competence. Welles, on the other hand, made no such assumption. For him a text was a rough block from which a director carved his own interpretation. A production had to be constructed round a theme or idea, and impelled by a gimmick. The designer became a full partner in the theatrical process, creating a visual vehicle for the director's conception. In this scheme of things the actor became less an artist than the creature of director and designer.

Between 1946 and 1960 both approaches to Shakespeare production co-existed uneasily on the English stage. Michael Benthall, Hugh Hunt, and Glen Byam Shaw, artistic heirs of Bridges-Adams, Atkins, and Williams, kept faith with both text and actors, although they gave the designer more rein than their predecessors would have done. Meanwhile, Tyrone Guthrie, Peter Brook, and Peter Hall, among others, pressed the Wellesian doctrine of directorial inspiration, with originality the artistic be-all and end-all. Assumptions, they argued, should not be made about meaning or manner for any Shakespearian play. Everything must be re-examined. The theatre was seen as a laboratory, the text as a subject for experimentation, and the director as supervisor of research. 'If a well-known play is pulled to pieces and reconstructed', wrote Brook, 'it is an attempt to understand more fully how certain structures work at certain times. If an audience is put in strange positions in unusual surroundings, it is to help both actors and audiences to discover what is gained and what is lost if certain apparently accepted conventions are broken.'[59] Throughout the 1950s, 'accepted conventions' fell like ninepins. When, near the end of the decade, Hall took the helm of the Memorial Theatre, laboratory Shakespeare found an international showcase. 'The whole thing . . . is all in a state of finding', Hall asserted, 'of not expecting final solutions, but keeping open . . . We want to be in a world of experiment.'[60]

Brook joined Hall (and Michel Saint-Denis) in the directorate of the new-baptized Royal Shakespeare Theatre and Company (RSC) in 1963; and their work, together with that of John Barton, John Blatchley, Clifford Williams, and others, made Stratford the avant-garde Mecca of the 1960s. With daemonic energy directors tore into the texts, reading and re-reading them through the eye-glasses of Artaud, Brecht, Grotowski, or Beckett. Film, television, the circus, and the playground were ransacked for techniques to animate new concepts. Décor, ranging from non-existent to opulent, worked in tandem with the director's vision. Sometimes the plays spoke with freshness; at others dramatic integrity was sacrificed to meretricious novelty. Hall's epic *Wars of the Roses* (1963–4) and Brook's *Lear* (1962) and *Midsummer Night's Dream* (1970) are safe in memory. Even outright disasters were not without flashes of blinding illumination;

although, it must be admitted, such moments came as often despite the
director as because of him.

During the 1950s, *Caesar* attracted only directors in the
Atkins–Williams–Bridges-Adams tradition. Even Croft's superficially
iconoclastic production in 1960 tampered mainly with trappings; the text
and actors retained their wonted importance. Two years later, however,
Greek scholar-director Minos Volanakis in his Old Vic revival (17 April
1962) brought *Caesar* modestly but firmly into the mainstream of contemporary aesthetics. Less concerned with interpreting the play than with
playing an interpretation, his inspiration was a set of ideas about *Caesar*
rather than *Caesar* itself. In a lengthy programme apologia, typical of the
didacticism of director's theatre, he claimed the play was Shakespeare's
attempt 'to examine and exhaust the possibility of salvation through
politics'. 'When *Julius Caesar* was written (1599)', he argued,

the Renaissance was dying between Puritanism and Counter-Reformation. Its
humanism had been bred on the Graeco–Roman belief that a heroic and just life is
possible and complete within the State, that goodness and politics are compatible.
The manly virtues of Republican Rome provided the inspiration, and *Plutarch's
Lives* the illustrious examples. Yet Shakespeare ... knew that the Republic had
transmuted itself into the Empire, and the very virtues of Rome had hammered each
other through civil strife, into their evil counterparts ... He chooses precisely the
turning point of Rome's transformation: Caesar's greatness ensured the Republic of
its last year of stability by transforming it into Caesarism. Brutus, the very embodiment of the ideals that fired the Renaissance and fostered modern liberalism, tries to
resist this transformation by killing Caesar, *his best lover*. The murder released
precisely the dark forces Brutus was fighting. Haunted by Caesar's spirit and his own
sense of Justice, he keeps stubbornly choosing the virtuous rather than the
expedient, and through his very integrity destroys himself. The play ends with the
ascent of Octavius. He left a ruthlessly efficient state-machine to his successors:
Tiberius – and Caligula.

Volanakis the scholar had obviously done his homework; but somehow the
conception of *Caesar* as an ideological piece had to be translated into the
idiom of the stage. And here Volanakis the director foundered.

Rejecting any hint of marmoreal Rome, designer Nicholas Georgiadis
created a tiered Meccano-kit structure, lighted variously in shades of
grey, pink, and rust. Critics, unable to make anything of it, took refuge
in witty metaphor. Kenneth Tynan called it 'the perfect all-purpose
construction set',[61] while J. C. Trewin pondered 'such odd matters
as imperfectly articulated skeletons, or toy building sets uncertainly
used, or the scaffold-poles of a housing project after some weeks in the
rain'.[62]

The most theatrical notion in Volanakis' rationale was the release of the
'dark forces' by Caesar's murder; and this was the only idea to materialize

with absolute clarity on stage. The first acts of the play were wrapped in Stygian gloom. The streets were abnormally hushed and deserted; crowds, when they passed, were small and subdued. Rome stood still, supernaturally visited and braced for monstrous events. The assassination unfolded with all the solemnity of religious ceremonial. 'It is no ordinary killing', remarked Harold Hobson, 'no swift affair of flashing knives. The slaughterous arms descend slowly, sacrificially; Joseph O'Conor's grave Caesar moves deliberately towards Brutus, his best lover, who stabs him in an embrace; it is a ritual that is being enacted, the falling knives a counterpoint to the elevation of the Host.'[63] When Caesar fell, Cinna tried to cry 'Liberty!' but could not. 'His voice is choked and strangled', Hobson noted, 'his face blanched. This is the supreme moment of the performance, the moment when one knows that the god has appeared, and that his aspect is terrible.'[64]

The unchained deity was seen incarnate in the mob's animalism. With the assassination over, the empty streets suddenly leapt to horrific life as screaming, sub-human figures savaged their enemies and strung them up from impromptu scaffolds provided by the set. It was this primal force that Antony harnessed to confound his friends and shape his destiny. He met the other members of the triumvirate, appropriately enough, in a grove hung with dangling corpses, mute reminders of the destructive forces at his command. But Octavius refused to be cowed; indeed, his ambition was only whetted. In the final scene he endured Antony's sentimental valedictory with frigid cynicism, then callously kicked Brutus' sword out of his way as he pushed forward to insist, 'Within *my* tent his bones to-night shall lie.'[65] The dogs of war were once more straining at the leash.

Apart from this imaginative stroke, the play moved ponderously. Long pauses, heavy emphases on key words, and mindless recitation wearied the ear. Intent upon the play's ideas, Volanakis overlooked the fact that Shakespeare clothes his thought in human flesh. The Old Vic characters were of flimsiest pasteboard. Brutus, comedian John Gregson's first Shakespearian role, was an honest, prosaic soul, without conspicuous magnetism, either physical or spiritual. The Cassius of Robert Eddison seemed an altogether more likely leader. Taller than Brutus, musical of voice and graceful of carriage, Eddison's conspirator was a man of sorrows, little given to scorn and not at all to envy. The fundamental contrasts between the two men, implicit in the subtle psychology which gives their relationship point and power, were missed. And the spine of the play, it goes without saying, was irreparably damaged.

Where Volanakis viewed *Caesar* as Shakespeare's exploration of the chances of salvation through politics, John Blatchley, in his 1963 Royal Shakespeare revival (9 April), proclaimed it the dramatist's disillusioned rejection of any such notion. 'There is a great deal of talk about nobility in

Julius Caesar . . . but how many of the actions are noble?' he asked in a programme note. 'For me it is a play about the way political and diplomatic life works; I wanted to display this machinery of power and the necessities it puts upon men. It seemed to me that Shakespeare's theme was that "the ends do not justify the means".'

An unheroic vision demanded an unromantic setting; and the bare stage and leather costumes of Brook's Beckettian *Lear* a year earlier offered a ready example. Designer John Bury located Blatchley's political exposé on a long, sloping, dun-coloured ramp, a series of abstract planes, and two staircases, the whole textured with light in the Appian mode. Almost the sole items of décor were a Henry Moore-ish statue of Pompey in the Senate scene and a hanging tapestry to suggest Brutus' tent.

Bury's costumes were of all periods and no period. Rudimentary togas were worn over First World War uniforms; motorcycle suits marched cheek by jowl with cloaks and leather tunics; and jack-boots peeped out where sandals were wont to be. The unrelieved use of grey, brown, and black fabrics reduced the *mise en scène* to a deadly monochrome. Although the audience could hardly fail to infer that politics in all times and places was a dusty, dirty business, the price paid for the insight was a visual monotony which threatened concentration and made it difficult to distinguish friend from foe.

Blatchley retained a full text,[66] save perhaps for a hundred scattered lines, and stoutly refused to garnish it with any hint of the theatre theatrical. Crowds and processions in the early scenes were small, drab, and lifeless. The storm consisted of a brief clash of cymbals and a flicker of light; and the assassination was a hole-and-corner affair. In the Forum scene, Antony, in profile, faced some half-dozen souls restrained in the wings by what appeared to be London bobbies; and their shouts, patently taped, boomed with ludicrously disproportionate strength over the theatre's sound system. Battles were little more than perfunctory gestures. The play's final speeches, far from the traditional hymn to altruism, became a wry sneer at the very notion.

The lines were spoken with commendable clarity, but at a plodding pace. The sweep of the verse was forever arrested by significant pauses, heavy emphases, and pregnant business. Interrupted by only one fifteen-minute interval (after the Proscription scene), the production ran for an exhausting three and a quarter hours.

Blatchley's unheroic conception made little call on classical tragedians; creators of credible contemporary politicians were what was wanted. Tom Fleming's Brutus was a gangling, craggy-faced political innocent, 'not clever but respected, personally brave but without a clear understanding of what was happening, standing out for principles his policies cannot match'.[67] Cassius, played by Cyril Cusack, was older and brainier, the sort of politician who might just miss the leadership of a party in modern times, and remain, in J. C. Trewin's words, 'the voice of the corridors and the private conference; the probing urging voice; the power behind the plot; the maker of policy; the bitter ambitious intriguer'.[68] Stringy and shrivelled, his grey hair sparse and his voice a mocking rasp, he was well-nigh a travesty of the noble patrician of Barrett or Gielgud. Kenneth Haigh was, the *Times* critic thought, 'a flyweight Antony'. Although his 'combination of sensuality and shrewd self-interest'[69] was accurate enough, the character was shorn of the emotional splendour crucial to its texture.

Roy Dotrice's Caesar, the only figure allowed to wear white, dominated the play visually and morally. 'A carved statue, saturated with the diffidence of greatness: just crumbling within, and still clinging to the power-politics without',[70] he was a prisoner of his own mythology. Drawn to the virility of the near-naked Antony, fearful of the dynamism of the wiry Cassius, sweating with fever even as he proclaimed his invulnerability, he was an ageing lion; but still with claws of steel. In the Senate scene, he recognized the inevitability of death, and met it with equanimity. Covering his face with his mantle, he deliberately hurled himself on Brutus' sword in one last triumph of will over circumstance. No symbolic star was needed to keep his memory green at Sardis and Philippi.

In the end, however much one may admire Blatchley's ingenuity, his *Caesar* must be reckoned primarily an intellectual exercise. The spectator found little for the eye and ear, and nothing for the heart. 'It is as though the theatre he is attending is an operating one', observed Peter Roberts, 'and the stage an operating table on which the Body Politic is dissected before his interested but unmoved gaze. He watches the removal of the tyrannical growth from the diseased body, but remains detached and uninvolved.'[71] This method might be admirably suited to Brecht; but to play Shakespeare from the head alone is not so much to interpret as to misrepresent him.

Lindsay Anderson's radical assault on *Caesar* at the Royal Court (26 November 1964), however, makes Blatchley's treatment seem almost conventional. 'My approach', Anderson explained in a *Times* article (15 December 1964),

was admittedly subjective. Never having directed anything but new plays – or at least plays new to London – it was exciting to tackle a classic in the same spirit. With a spirit of discovery, that is to say, rather than reverence. And having been generally bored by Shakespeare on the stage, I want to find out for myself if his writing has really become as unmeaning as it often seems.

With determined irreverence Anderson cut the play heavily on the grounds of tedium. The exchange between the tribunes and the cobbler was blue-pencilled as unfunny; and lengthy speeches, including Brutus' orchard soliloquy, were abbreviated to eliminate 'rhetorical embroidery'. Convinced that 'the battles today are boring; and Shakespeare's slavish cribbing from Plutarch is mere padding', Anderson eliminated, he tells us, 'three pages of text and linked the deaths of Cassius and Brutus with an entrance and a speech of our own composition, and spoken by young Metellus Cimber with the accents of a messenger of fate'.[72] Speeches were juggled and redistributed with Victorian abandon. Artemidorus' letter, for example, was read offstage while Caesar welcomed the conspirators to his house; and later, in the Senate scene, Popilius Lena was inexplicably ousted in favour of Cicero.[73]

Anderson's production style was, like Blatchley's, decidedly anti-romantic, even Brechtian; but the aesthetic unity which marked the Stratford revival was absent. The Royal Court version dwindled into a studio exercise, a series of novel flourishes without cohesion or cumulative thrust.

Jocelyn Herbert's décor for the first half of the play featured abstract metal shapes. The major one, looming in bronze outline over the Public Place, Brutus' Orchard, and the Capitol, subliminally suggested a colossal statue of Caesar. The second part of the action unfolded before a huge white concrete-textured screen over which back projections and lighting effects played at intervals. In the final scenes, monstrous metallic birds of prey cast their shadow over the dying conspirators. In keeping with Brechtian convention, lighting equipment and fire hoses were clearly visible. Actors wore black trousers and jerseys topped by rudimentary togas of stippled rubbery material. In the military episodes the togas were discarded.

To forestall any hint of melodramatic thrill, the crowd was kept small, dingy, and inactive throughout. Caesar was slain in slow motion, the swords of the conspirators penetrating his body with an almost sensual pleasure. Brutus' and Cassius' deaths, already abridged, were drowned in electronic roars. Bored reviewers found themselves reflecting upon crop-spraying airplanes, helicopters, and motorbikes on the Naples Autostrada as the heroes sighed their last.

Anderson's style was not merely anti-heroic, but very nearly anti-actor. Performers of sterling talent were constrained to create muted and one-dimensional characters; and verse was reduced uniformly to muddy prose. Underemphasis, false emphasis, slurred speech, and fractured rhythm were cultivated as deliberate techniques. Bernard Levin noted twenty-eight instances of mis-scansion before he wearied of counting.[74]

Douglas Campbell's revival, on 16 June 1965 at Stratford, Ontario, was also a product of the director's unease with *Caesar*'s well-thumbed familiarity; but any wholesale modernization along the lines of Blatchley or Anderson was rejected. 'I do not disapprove of productions that are given a contemporary flavour and setting,' Campbell explained, but I would stop short at *Julius Caesar*. Why? As Rome is the hero of the piece, surely any production must present the city-state as Shakespeare very clearly drew it. To do otherwise is, for me, to remove the most important element of the piece and to artificially impose new concepts, which bear no relation to the playwright's original purpose.[75]

Campbell's Roman *ambiance*, splendidly realized in traditional dress and spectacular mobs, processions, and battles, lent the action a brazen grandeur all too rare in recent times. Unfortunately Campbell's anti-modernist convictions did not extend much beyond matters of décor; and he proved just as disinclined to play the text 'straight' as the next man. Although he did not offer any novel reading, he fiddled freely with the lines and introduced extraneous business with abandon. Theatrical effects became an end in themselves, obscuring the play's ideas and smudging its crisp outline.

The production opened with the Soothsayer on stage alone, delivering his warning under a spotlight. Portia, when she appeared a little later, betrayed her overwrought condition by a compulsively twitching mouth. The assassination was a highly elaborate affair. Caesar approached each conspirator with stately formality, and was met with a well-urged weapon point. When he reached Brutus, the latter placed an arm tenderly around him in the Mansfield manner, and, holding him close, sank his dagger with unexpected decision. The Forum oratory of both Brutus and Antony was marred by the to-ing and fro-ing of a mob which monopolized audience interest with its alternating realistic and stylized antics. During the crucial moment just before Antony produced the will, the crowd broke into a sports-arena chant of 'The will, the will', even turning round to the audience at one point as if to fellow-citizens. All the while Antony was left to his own devices, and the breathtaking ascent of his oratory stopped short. Examples of over-production could be multiplied.

Actors predictably played business rather than text, and pallid characterization was endemic. William Hutt's Brutus, 'unyielding and troubled and searching',[76] was on the whole more solid than subtle. Cassius (Peter Donat) was sympathetic in his 'untethered passion, in his sudden switches from wild enthusiasm to despair, from jubilation to tears',[77] but hardly the scourge of tyranny. Bruno Gerussi as Antony suggested 'an eye-rolling, curly-haired Italian playboy',[78] but little more. Robert Shaw's Caesar seemed more martinet than monarch.

If Campbell's revival typifies the danger of one kind of over-production – the smothering of the text with alien trivia – John Barton's 1968 Royal Shakespeare revival epitomizes the hazards of the opposite extreme – the combing of every line for super-subtle readings to the neglect of overall dramatic design. Barton shared Blatchley's anti-romantic bias, but had no political point to make.[79] He considered the play, as did Granville-Barker, to be a character study; although he preferred to read it through dark lenses. In his hands *Caesar* became a veritable portrait gallery, paying lip service to a warts-and-all vision, but specializing in warts. Each scene, slowed by tortured readings and frequent pauses, seemed to be treated as an isolated unit of characterization, to the neglect of the play's structural integrity.

The action was located on a dark grey ramp, set with four triumphal arches and three brick-textured plinths which rearranged themselves in varying patterns to create new venues; an environment which permitted flexible stagecraft and solid architecture a ready co-existence. The military scenes were staged on an absolutely bare platform. Costumes comprised a mixture of gowns, cloaks, hats, jerkins, rudimentary togas, breeches, and jackboots. Once again the colour scheme was uniformly murky; the only bright note seen throughout the evening was the crimson of blood.

Barton's scholarly care for the text led him to cut only about fifty lines, most of which were removed to simplify syntax or clarify thought.[80] The verse was delivered with admirable sensitivity and intelligence, if painfully slowly. A single intermission was permitted, after the Proscription scene.

Caesar, as in most recent Stratford revivals, gave the play its heartbeat. Brewster Mason's Dictator was, as Cassius reckoned him, a real and present menace. Robert Speaight found himself reminded of General de Gaulle. 'The remoteness, the self-sufficiency, the sense of political incarnation and personal indispensability, the *grandeur* and the *hauteur* were all there, reinforced by a large presence and a quiet address.'[81] In the Senate scene he repulsed the senators' pleas with serene contempt; and when trapped a moment later, a victim of his own miscalculation, he remained indomitable to the last. Bearing down on Brutus as he fell, he seized with scorn the Stoic's faltering hand and forced the dagger home. His '*Et tu, Brute*' was not a reproach, but a wrathful taunt.

Barton gave his ghost, in addition to the tent visit, two further appearances. Just after the farewells of Brutus and Cassius, his wrathful presence crossed the battlefield; and, finally, as Brutus lay dead at the end of the play, he stood, gleaming, over the body, the last thing visible as the lights faded. To make assurance doubly sure, his bloody mantle was flourished at intervals. Antony produced it as a red rag to incite the Forum mob, bore it as a banner on the battlefield, and finally laid it to rest as a shroud for Brutus' corpse. Never in the stage history of the play has Caesar's claim to the title role been so rigorously pressed.

The conspirators were in reality the petty men of Cassius' tortured imagination. The squalid collection of misfits announced by Lucius had about them an air so self-consciously sinister as to be almost comic. One could hardly take their ambitions seriously. Yet in the Capitol their flailing, ill-timed thrusts were as deadly as those more heroically dealt. As each man stabbed, he recoiled into a crouch, waiting retribution in huddled shock. Moments later, in trembling disbelief, they rose and approached the gargantuan blood-stained corpse, clinging together and chattering in near-hysteria, 'Liberty, freedom, tyranny is dead.' Caesar was less stricken by princes than stung to death by insects.

Brutus, played by Barrie Ingham, suffered most from Barton's derogation. A young man, not over-bright and obsessed with family pride, his actions were dictated less by liberalism than a thirst for the power his heritage merited. Peter Roberts found him 'a self-deceiver, a man who in fact casts himself in the role of noble sacrificer but who in fact is so puny a leader he cannot even bring himself to knife the victim'.[82] When Caesar fell he shared the terror of his fellows, but soothed by visions of his place in history, fear soon faded. With revealing absent-mindedness he ensconced himself on Caesar's throne and toyed idly with his wand of office. His denial of knowledge of Portia's death became a crude stratagem to impress Cassius with his stoic control; and on the battlefield, his 'ill request' seemed motivated more by cowardice than moral scruple. Antony's last lines were no ringing valedictory for a hero, but simply one fallible mortal's muttered recognition of another.

Ian Richardson's Cassius, although less obviously iconoclastic, was a compelling portrait. Obsessed by a lust for greatness, the febrile Roman found himself wanting when weighed on the Caesarian scale. The present standard of measurement, then, must be destroyed, and another set up more favourable to his gifts. His motivation seemed hardly more complex than that. The key to his character lay, Hilary Spurling aptly noted, in 'an emotional desperation which, if it intensifies his venom towards Caesar, makes him at once cunning and defenceless in his need for Brutus's admiration'. There was something almost womanish and uniquely touching in 'his feverish, self-forgetful exultation as he strides unbuttoned through the storm ... or in his jealousy and his shrill, aggrieved self-pity in the quarrel'.[83] Fortitude and leadership there was too, when needed; but throughout his vulnerable humanity was kept uppermost. Regrettably, however, the performance missed maximum resonance for want of a Brutus of moral stature to throw it into relief. His praise of Brutus' virtue suggested that he was a bad judge of character; and his yielding to him in the Quarrel episode seemed less a pathetic capitulation than the diplomatic concession of a strong man to a weaker one.

Charles Thomas convincingly limned Antony in the early scenes as an athletic, curly-haired voluptuary. Stripped for the race at his first entrance and lounging indolently about, he radiated brooding sensuality. On the morning of the Ides he arrived at Caesar's house rumpled and blear-eyed from the excesses of the night before. In the Senate scene he was unashamedly emotional, profoundly grieved at the loss of his friend and irrevocably bent on revenge. Wit and guile were foreign to the earthy directness of his character, and he used none. In the Forum, confronted by a minute but vocal mob, the sleek reveller degenerated into a leather-jacketed bully, belabouring the crowd in thoroughly unpatrician style. The harangue resembled nothing so much as a vicious puppet show, with a malicious puppeteer savouring his own cynicism throughout. His ruffianism intensified in the later scenes as athletic grace and personal charm were brutalized by power-hunger. There was perhaps just the slightest flutter of feeling as he closed Brutus' eyes and mumbled the final eulogy; but it died a-borning.

Edward Payson Call's *Caesar*, on 26 June 1969 at the Guthrie Theatre, Minneapolis, was the very antithesis of the RSC mood. Colour, spectacle, and novel business were everything; and somehow characterization, poetry, and even meaning got lost in the shuffle. Call set the play in a nameless Latin American dictatorship, and left the period indeterminate to permit a God's plenty of costumes ranging from Aztec slave-wear to contemporary military fatigues. The setting was simple, merely a raked thrust with a spiralling ramp and a huge Mayan idol. Visual interest was furnished by brilliantly-garbed peons in fiesta gear, troops of marching soldiery in full dress, senators in diplomatic cutaways, and, above all, Caesar, an aspiring sun-god in white and gold.

Whatever the theoretical advantages of a geographical venue famed for a volatile populace and power-mad dictators, and however apt the parallels between Caesar and Peron or Antony and Castro, the conception did not stir an American audience. South American politics was even more incomprehensible than Roman history; and the actors seemed unable to reveal familiar passions beneath the alien clothes.

Americans had fresh cause to marvel at the strange ways of *Caesar* directors when Jonathan Miller's production for the Oxford and Cambridge Shakespeare Company toured universities in 1972; and Londoners professed the same amazement during its brief season at the New Theatre afterwards.

Capitalizing upon frequent references in the play to sleep and waking, appearance and reality, the natural and the supernatural, Miller staged it as an expressionistic fantasy with the terrifying illogic and persuasive reality of dreams. 'But whose dream is it and what's he dreaming about?' Milton Schulman wanted to know.[84] Jeremy Kingston guessed it to be 'a nightmare fantasy on parricide. Brutus and Cassius destroy the tyrant father-figure and then become inhibited with guilt, bickering blunderers who lack the wish to survive. Antony and Octavius identify themselves with the father and go on to triumph.'[85] Most of his confrères skirted the question by treating the production as an improvisation upon *Caesar* rather than an interpretation of it.

16. *Julius Caesar* in Latin American dress at The Guthrie Theatre, Minneapolis, 1969. Directed by Edward Payson Call. Scenic designer, Douglas Schmidt; costume designer, Carrie Fishbein Robbins

The *mise en scène*, by Bernard Culshaw, suggested a blood-red medieval Italian fortress with a soaring panel behind. Actors wore parti-coloured tights and jerkins, the former geometrically scored in the manner of text-book illustrations, and the latter slashed at an angle like some cutaway anatomical diagram. With the casual incongruity of dreams, Caesar appeared as a southern gambler, complete with white frock coat and top hat, cigar and cane. Actors' faces were uniformly pale and impassive; movement throughout was somnambulistic, akin to modern dance and frequently frozen for long periods. Speech was slow, and silences protracted. Most properties, including weaponry, were imagined. Caesar was slain by what appeared to be a karate chop, while the conspirators fluttered their hands above him like butterflies. The Forum speech was spouted at a masked mob who remained totally silent. The final battles were wrestling-matches in hypnotic slow-motion, as if underwater.

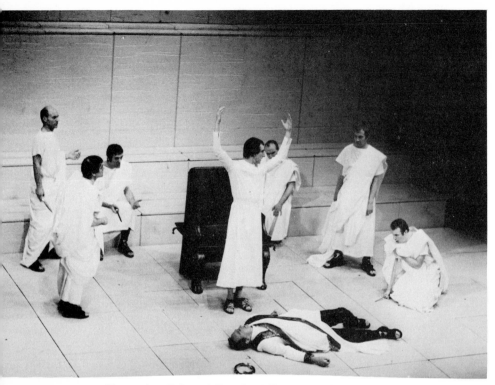

17. Cinna cries, 'Liberty! Freedom! Tyranny is dead!' (III.i.78). Trevor Nunn's
production at the Royal Shakespeare Theatre, 1972. Designed by Christopher
Morley with Ann Curtis. Cinna, John Atkinson (standing); Brutus, John Wood
(kneeling); Caesar, Mark Dignam

John Mortimer's conclusion that Miller's production started 'at some
distant and private point and coincides only occasionally with the author's
intentions'[86] was probably apt enough. The same could not be said, however, of Trevor Nunn's Royal Shakespeare revival a few months later (2
May 1972). Not only did Nunn (Peter Hall's successor as Artistic Director
of the RSC) and his associates, Buzz Goodbody and Euan Smith, scrupulously respect *Caesar*'s wholeness, but presented it for only the second time
in its history[87] in company with Shakespeare's other three Roman dramas.

No attempt was made to achieve the close-textured coherence between
individual plays which marked the *Wars of the Roses* epic; yet Nunn did not
feel the Roman dramas were quite disparate. *Coriolanus*, *Julius Caesar*, and
Antony and Cleopatra were, he argued,

three different explorations of the requirements of a system of good government, of
world politics as opposed to what it is that's rich and rare individually in people.
Individuals are destroyed.

By the time you get to *Caesar* the aristocratic group have taken over completely, and they're fighting for their survival against a new outsider, Julius Caesar. He's a military man, who's realized that if you control the army you control the world. Therefore he's bent on destroying all previous Roman institutions. So Rome closes its ranks and destroys him. But by then all that ancient world is gone. With the murder of Caesar republicanism is over.[88]

Just previous to 'The Romans', the Royal Shakespeare stage was radically redesigned. A forestage slab forty feet in width and eighteen and a half feet deep was installed in front of the proscenium with a sloping ceiling suspended above. Upstage of the arch, huge wing-blocks were inset at an angle on either side. The entire setting was textured to resemble rough white marble. Thanks to hydraulic lifts, revolving periaktoi, and an apron which could be tilted, an almost cinematic flexibility became possible. At the touch of a button hills rose, walls fell, steps soared, or plains stretched away to infinity.

Like Blatchley and Barton, Nunn saw Caesar as the play's pivotal figure – a Fascist overreacher aspiring to divinity. Julian Rome, in Christopher Morley's design for the first scene, was a stark white box, blindingly illuminated. Residents of the Eternal City no longer skulked in shadow, but cowered under the harsh glare of Fascist intelligence. Privacy, concealment, or escape were alike chimerical. In an interpolated overture to act I, a scarlet carpet hurled itself down the naked forestage to a deafening roll of drums; and Caesar entered in a splendid procession, dressed in black leather and surrounded by sycophantic senators chanting 'Hail, Caesar!' like a well-paid claque. Grimly he strode downstage through a corridor of black-garbed SS types to stare with chilling arrogance at the audience as Brutus crowned him with laurel. Cassius' description of the looming Colossus seemed no more than the literal truth. The assassination became an act of responsible statesmanship; and the conspirators' ultimate defeat owed less to a relentless Nemesis than to their own flawed personalities.

The Public Place sequence opened in a deliberately low key. Holidaymakers were few and dingy, and Flavius and Marullus were patently uneasy. Two of Caesar's blackshirts passed as the tribunes talked, and the pair fell abruptly silent. Spontaneity and vitality had all but vanished; Rome was clearly 'groaning underneath this age's yoke'. Caesar's entry revealed with devastating impact the tainted fountain-head of the social and political system. White-robed senators, black-uniformed military, red, gold, and purple banners, and effigies of Caesar endlessly multiplied all spoke of a state machine programmed to snuff out individuality with mindless efficiency.

The assassination was made the axis of the production. Caesar arrived at the Capitol in majesty, borne on an eagle-backed chair amid the aggressive panoply of a police state. For the Senate House itself, four great statues were flown in, complete with cornices and plinths; and three tiers of seats rose from the floor to meet them. If Blatchley's assassination smacked of the hospital, Nunn's reeked of the abattoir. As Casca struck, the conspirators all rushed in, the blood staining their white gowns like butcher's aprons. Brutus, bent on sacrifice not bloodlust, pushed into the mêlée, grasped Caesar reluctantly, and flicked his knife against a throat artery, only to recoil in revulsion as blood spurted into his face. Meantime Cassius stabbed at the corpse with insatiable fury until Brutus dragged him off. Gradually, however, the assassins became aware of the blood on their hands and clothes. Their eyes wandered to the bleeding hulk at their feet; and they were struck dumb by their own temerity.

The Forum harangue was hurled from a minute rostrum at a knot of unindividualized citizens; and the military episodes unfolded supply on a hill, a stretch of road, and broad plains. The battles were restrained. Both sides wore identical uniforms, presumably to underline visually the horror of a community battening on itself; but the effect, however felicitous in theory, was untheatrical. Distinctions between parties could not readily be made, and narrative clarity suffered. The play ended on a pointedly ambiguous note. 'Octavius' invitation to Antony to "*part* the glories of this *happy* day" was followed by his immediate brisk exit *right*. Alone on stage, Antony shook his head slightly, and slowly walked off *left*.'[89] *Antony and Cleopatra* was already in the wings.

While the Roman cycle let some daylight into odd corners of the plays, it offered little of the cumulative enlightenment which distinguished *The Wars of the Roses*. Nunn reaffirmed that Shakespeare was a great believer in law and order, and that the preservation of social structures must, in his view, transcend all human aspirations. But that was hardly news. On balance *Julius Caesar*, spoken sensibly and almost uncut,[90] gained little from the experiment, and remained thematically and stylistically independent. Apart from its theatrical conjunction with the other Roman dramas, Nunn's *Caesar* will be remembered mainly for John Wood's Brutus, one of this century's most telling portraits of him.

Young, tall, somehow El Grecoesque, this Brutus struck John Mortimer as the complete 'intellectual revolutionary, whose calm smile is the result, not of happiness, for he is never happy, but of having solved life as if it were a proposition of logic or a mathematical equation'.[91] His friendship for Caesar was patent, but at the same time Caesar's totalitarianism pained him deeply. As Cassius probed him at their first meeting, it was apparent that he was hearing merely the echo of his own thoughts. On the occasions when he deigned to speak, his voice was sharp, and the words were articulated with an almost spinsterish precision. In the Orchard soliloquy Jeremy Kingston found himself reminded that Brutus was a lawyer. Here he seemed 'a man levering himself into an attitude with specious arguments, a man who cannot act until action has assumed a verbal structure'.[92] Later, in the presence of the conspirators, he was aristocratic, self-contained, fastidious, and chary of casual physical contact; but a fit of violent shivering after their exit betrayed the turmoil so carefully repressed. Alone with Portia and Lucius, he rounded on them in bursts of impatience unknown to any previous Brutus. Those nearest this Roman knew less a self-possessed philosopher than a tormented neurotic, torn between impossible dreams and sordid reality.

The Senate scene brought him face to face not with the abstract proposition of his night imaginings, but a man and a friend. Despite retching revulsion, his liberal principles urged him on. He decisively entered the fray, flicked his knife, and waited for the nausea to subside. In the Forum, quite unable to comprehend the temper of the times, he merely appealed in dry, subdued tones for a return to republican virtues, and quit the field secure in the triumph of reason. The Quarrel scene found him near exhaustion; yet while Cassius battered the table he remained 'cool and prim', walking about 'picking up the scattered papers one by one, mild exasperation in his voice, a mocking smile on his face, condescension in every gesture'.[93] The abrupt entry of the Camp Poet (a soldier in drag) at the moment of reconciliation caught him off his guard. Cassius only laughed, but Brutus struck the man full in the face, his feelings inadvertently loosed. Past caring for appearances, he made no effort to stifle his sobs or curb his tears as he announced Portia's death. Here Wood managed once more 'to suggest the real strength of Brutus's self-control and self-awareness by suggesting also . . . the depth of his feelings'.[94] The sight of him crawling over the barren hillside in his final moments, pleading for death with dignity, evoked a pity as profound as it was unexpected.

Cassius and Antony, although competently played, were largely foils to Brutus. Patrick Stewart's tempestuous Roman was a red-blooded individualist, impatient of restriction and passionately sincere. A hard-headed realist, Cassius recognized among other facts of life his own 'yearning for human affection, a hungriness which makes him emotionally raw and as demanding and undeniable as a child'.[95] Brutus' refusal to recognize the validity of emotional hunger ultimately lay at the root of the tensions between them.

Richard Johnson's Antony, fifteen years older than when last seen at Stratford, was not so much a playboy or voluptuary as a black-bearded adventurer. He knew nothing of the moral turmoil of a Brutus or the psychological insecurities of a Cassius. He accepted the world as he found it, wresting from it as much as his strength and wits permitted. He was genuinely grieved by Caesar's death; but even as he lamented he weighed the opportunities for material advantage. Brutus and Cassius were easy prey to a man without either social needs or ethical scruples. The Forum speech was a supreme demonstration of how an individual unashamed of and unimpeded by his own passions could callously exploit those of others to serve his turn. In the end he met his match in Octavius (Corin Redgrave), the fair, clean-shaven, icy *arriviste*. With no feelings to be played upon, he offered Antony no target; and Antony's own passionate nature suddenly rendered him highly vulnerable. In the final moments of the play as Octavius froze Antony's sentimental elegy in mid-air, Antony realized he had been challenged to combat; and the choice of weapons was with the other side.

Mark Dignam played Caesar, no doubt on directorial advice, as an individual with no private self. Myth and man were one; and the effect was horrific. He bestrode the action of the early scenes like some omnipotent robot bent on subjugating every last vestige of individuality to the national will. At the same time he evinced a magnetism very nearly irresistible. One was forced to recognize his greatness, however malign; and one instantly understood Brutus' admiration for the man, and his reluctance to annihilate a veritable symbol of human potential. Although a bolder and less complex portrait than many of its predecessors, the impact of Dignam's Colossus was immediate, overwhelming, and all pervasive throughout.

In 1973 the production, with the same principals, was restaged with considerable success at the Aldwych.

Afterword

Julius Caesar's stage history, it must be acknowledged, is a tale of unrealized potential. To reveal itself fully the play requires an uncut text, fluid stagecraft, and actors of heroic power. And these three factors, sadly enough, have never conjoined. The eighteenth-century theatre played a relatively full text with flexible settings, but actors of mettle were few. The nineteenth-century stage, although graced with superb performers, mutilated the script, sacrificed ensemble effects to the star system, and hobbled the action by ponderous settings and business. The first half of this century saw the text restored and Elizabethan stagecraft rediscovered; but by then the classical acting tradition was almost extinct. In more recent times, although *Caesar* has been played whole, and for the most part fluidly, its splendour has gleamed only fitfully. Our leading players, like Garrick, Kean, and Irving before them, have shied at the play. Sir Laurence Olivier and Paul Scofield have never appeared in it; and Sir John Gielgud, a fine Antony and a brilliant Cassius, has not essayed Brutus, although the part might have been written for him.[1] Good actors, if not the greatest, have attempted the major roles with some degree of ensemble; but their efforts have been frequently misdirected toward playing an interpretation rather than interpreting the play. Their directors, bent upon novelty and contemporary relevance, have all too often been less concerned with *Caesar* itself than a set of ideas about it.

The challenge to future *Caesar* directors lies primarily in the integration of a complete text, supple staging, and first-class acting with emphasis on ensemble performance. But were these elements magically to meet and mingle, the problems posed by *Caesar*'s style, structure, and characters remain formidable. Before taking leave of the play, I venture to add a few personal comments on these vexed topics. My views are admittedly subjective, but they have their roots, I think, in the theatre's experience of *Caesar* throughout almost four centuries. I offer them, nevertheless, in only the most tentative way; for their validity cannot be demonstrated on paper, but ultimately must stand or fall by that harshest of all practical tests, performance in the contemporary theatre.

A major challenge for the modern director lies in *Caesar*'s style. The majesty of its rhetoric, the stately progress of its scenes, the heroic stances of its characters give it a formal quality alien to our easy-going times; and its unique nature demands to be recognized and dealt with. To treat its action as a workaday account of sordid politics is only to underscore its artificiality, and, worse still, to rob it of tragic power. Under our anti-heroic onslaughts, its epic character has dwindled into melodrama or chronicle; and the words 'tragic' and 'tragedy' have almost vanished from contemporary reviews. The nineteenth-century theatre enjoyed a different experience. If Kemble, Macready, and Booth and Barrett scuttled *Caesar*'s structure by their cavalier cutting, they nonetheless revealed a tragic dimension in its characters, an element of profound grandeur – physical, intellectual, and spiritual in varying blends. Kemble's heroic frame doubtless lent conviction to his reading; but Booth demonstrated that physical size is not crucial, provided the spirit is great, the movement graceful, and the verse vocally splendid. Our grandeur cannot be that of centuries past; we must find it freshly for ourselves. But the effect upon the audience must be the same, a sense of awe and wonder.

Caesar's epic scale is inseparable from its spectacle – its crowds, processions, costumes, armour and weapons. Rome to the Elizabethan mind, however variously it interpreted Roman politics,[2] spoke of glory. The archaeological panoply of Booth, Tree, and the Meininger ran to excess; but some degree of magnificence is needed to give Rome and Caesar their due, and to lend visual brilliance to the high heroism and rich rhetoric with which the play abounds. Throngs of supers are not *de rigueur*: the audience will happily divide one man into a thousand parts provided the convention is rigidly adhered to. And there is no call for elaborate scenery either. Brechtian drabness or niggardly quality, however, have no place here. Costumes should be colourful, appropriate, and telling; and mobs, whatever their size, vivid and vital. The military episodes, although few, demand close attention to uniforms, accessories, and blocking if they are not to suffer by comparison with earlier scenes and strike the heroic note the tragic conclusion demands. Dress need not be slavishly Elizabethan or pedantically Roman. Some arrangement along Renaissance–classical lines will permit Shakespeare's allusions to hats, cloaks, and doublets to be incorporated without jar, and yield the treat for the eye so often missed during the reign of the Talma toga. Michael Langham's 1955 production at Stratford, Ontario, brilliantly designed by Tanya Moiseiwitsch, offers an instructive example of spectacle which enriches the action without constituting an interest in itself or retarding dramatic flow.

The return of a full text to the stage in this century might have been expected to prompt a long-awaited appreciation of *Caesar*'s structure; but this has not been the case. Modern directors, while staging the play fairly fluidly, have been almost as insensitive to its overall rhythm as were Benson or Tree. For Harcourt Williams speed was everything; and dignified, quiet sequences were often hurtled through. At the other extreme, recent RSC revivals have featured readings so subtle and laboured that the cumulative sweep of the action has often ground to a halt. At other times, a perverse tendency to underplay the grander moments has reduced peaks and valleys alike to one monotonous plain.

Caesar's overall rhythm is stately and unhurried. Yet there is no want of excitement; processions, mob scenes, violent events, and military alarums take care of that. But there must be time allowed for the formal beat of the poetry, the omen-laden imagery, the intricately-wrought set speeches, and the subtlety of intellectual debate to have their full effect. It is worth noting, perhaps, that major rhetorical passages are strategically placed to have the most telling effect. Marullus' speech to the plebeians in I.i is preceded by the physical excitement of Caesar's Lupercal procession. The conversation of Brutus and Cassius which ensues is enclosed by the departure and return of the same procession. The declamatory flights of Cassius and Casca in I.iii are introduced and punctuated by the storm and terminate with the breathless arrival and hurried exit of Cinna. Brutus' Orchard soliloquy opens in thunder and lightning and closes with the quickened heartbeat precipitated by the sinister arrival of the conspirators. Examples could be multiplied. Unless this interplay of theatrical bustle and formal rhetoric is marked and savoured, the intrinsic majesty of the play evaporates, and with it our response to its larger rhythms.

Caesar's content, most modern directors agree, divides itself into two parts: the first leads up to and includes the assassination; the second details the results which follow from it. Yet their location of the interval often seems eccentric; and the balance between the two movements suffers. Granville-Barker and Glen Byam Shaw both break the action after act III. Indeed, Byam Shaw considers it 'ridiculous' to allow an interval before then.[3] This arrangement has the advantage of sweeping the action in an unbroken crescendo from the start of the play to the death of Cinna; but certain risks attend it. The Forum and Cinna episodes, as the climax of this section, may upstage the assassination; and the second half, shorn of much of its matter, may appear to lack weight. Contemporary directors (e.g. Blatchley, Barton, and Nunn), who pause after the Proscription scene, simply compound the problem. With only the military sequences left for after the intermission, some sense of anti-climax is inevitable. Audiences at Nunn's 1972 RSC production waited a gruelling two hours for the intermission, and returned for a mopping-up operation of merely fifty-five minutes.

Bridges-Adams placed a seven-minute interval after the assassination, and the production seems to have been no worse for it. The experiment might be worth repeating with a longer break allowed. True, the first part would lack some of the continuity it now enjoys; but the compensations are significant. Caesar's murder, when used to mark the mid-point of the performance, assumes a central importance, and profits from being separated somewhat from the more overtly spectacular events which follow. The latter half of the play not only gains in bulk, but the Forum scene opens it on a high note. The presence of Caesar's corpse neatly bridges the two parts.

Caesar's major scenes have traditionally been regarded, rightly enough, as the Assassination, the Forum, and the Quarrel; but they have not always been seen in their right relationship to each other and to the drama as a whole. The quarrel, although almost always well-managed throughout the play's history, obtruded unduly in eighteenth-century revivals to the detriment of its companion pieces. The Assassination scene acquired status and grandeur for the first time at the hands of Kemble, although he over-ritualized it somewhat. Macready took his cue from Kemble, while nudging the action firmly in the direction of realism. Booth, in his turn, treated the sequence mainly as a majestic and isolated historical pageant. The Forum scene was viewed mainly as a declamatory exercise for Brutus and Antony until the Meininger demonstrated the interdependence of crowd and speakers. Tree and Benson, bettering their instruction, made it the play's central feature, topping the assassination and making the quarrel almost an irrelevance. In this century the balance between these scenes has been better preserved; although the standard of performance has seldom matched the brilliance of nineteenth-century revivals.

The assassination is the fulcrum of the play, and will appear so if it is staged with dignity and respect for its form. It falls into two major movements. The first takes its rise with Caesar's procession to the Capitol and concludes with the blood-ritual. The second discovers the avenging spirit of the dead dictator, now incarnate in Antony and venting itself in doom-stricken prophecy.

The first movement, although growing steadily in excitement, cannot be rushed. There is a marked formality in Caesar's stately progress to his destiny; and each step must be well-defined. The Soothsayer is scorned; Artemidorus' paper is repulsed; Mark Antony is lured out of the way; Casca slips with precision into position; Metullus offers his petition, and the other conspirators kneel one by one in his support. Caesar's swelling oratory, almost Agamemnon-like in its hubris (Benson made no mistake about *Caesar*'s resemblance to Greek tragedy), demands to be given full value. The murder itself, as the keystone of the drama, needs an air of sublimity about it. The artificial ballet of Kemble is excessive, but the savagery of Benson and Blatchley is equally undesirable. Karate chops, gangland brutality, and slow-motion posturings are no less than perversions of the scene's stately mood. Earlier Brutus asks that the affair be sacrifice, not butchery;

and the fact that he conducts the blood-rite implies that his humane hopes have been realized. To suggest otherwise is to make Brutus a victim of the conspirators' savage impulses rather than of his own delusion that murder can ever be anything but what it is.

The arrival of Antony's servant, insensitively cut by Benson, initiates the scene's second major movement. It offers both a moment of release from tragic strain and preparation for Antony's forthcoming rise to dominance. With Antony's entrance the scene begins to soar towards its conclusion. His great laments and final imprecation (III.i.148–64; 194–210; 254–75) give the episode its orientation; and all else falls into position in relation to these cardinal points. The speeches must be given full rhetorical and emotional scope if the spirit of Caesar and the dramatic action itself are to take wing. Naturalistically-spoken and underplayed, as so often happens in contemporary productions, tragic splendour fades and Antony's heroic charm is eclipsed. It is well to remember that his abandoned passion in this scene when juxtaposed with Brutus' well-meaning rationality foreshadows the clash of styles which lends the Forum encounter its character. The dealings with the conspirators need not be rushed; but they do not benefit from the tedious business characteristic of the Booth-Barrett era. And Antony must retain primacy throughout. The entry of Octavius' servant, far from being an anti-climax, serves to relieve audience-tension, lowering the dramatic temperature somewhat in anticipation of its sustained rise in the next sequence.

The Forum scene is required to sweep the dramatic tension upward without rendering the assassination puny by comparison; a difficult task, but one made somewhat easier if the Senate scene is well-handled.

The action begins with the division of the crowd between Brutus and Cassius, a significant moment, but one usually excised a century ago. It serves to start the scene on a low note, reminds us briefly that Cassius is still a fully-fledged member of the conspiracy, and lends an air of realism to the proceedings.

However hackneyed the traditional face-on-centre-stage position of the rostrum may seem to a director, that is where it belongs – as Blatchley found to his cost; and the crowd should stand in front and to the sides, not in the wings. Thrust stage productions, such as those at Stratford, Ontario, appear to profit from placing crowd members in the auditorium. Mob-size is of relatively little importance; although the munificence of Tree and the parsimony of Blatchley are obviously not ideal. Numbers should simply be sufficient to be credible; and today's restricted theatre budgets permit no more in any case. What matters is the amount and kind of activity the crowd engages in. Brutus and Antony must be allowed to treat their orations as the vocal set pieces that they are; and extraneous crowd-business ought not to mar the delicate structure of the rhetoric, nor excessive noise force the actor into tonal ugliness. On the other hand, the crowd should not be so subdued as to make the orations seem patently artificial or lacking in effect. The solution is to tailor the size and reactions of the mob to the capacity of the performers. Above all, the shape of the entire play must be kept in mind, and the Forum scene fitted within it. Without the greatest care, Caesar can be raised to so high a pitch at this point that all that follows seems anaemic.

The orations are not pieces of contemporary political spouting as they are so often made to appear, but exercises in styles of argumentation designed for an Elizabethan audience which 'could be relied upon to follow the turns and twists of an argument, to note the skill, the adroitness, the fumbles, as readily as a modern crowd notes these points in a football game'.[4] A modern director can make no such assumptions on the part of his audience; and we doubtless miss much of the charm the speeches held for the Tudor play-goer.[5] At the very least, however, our actors should be able to capture the overall rhetorical contour of each speech and make clear the different personalities at work behind them. Brutus' rational prose, composed of *logos* and *ethos*, is the product of an intellectual. The slower rhythm, the formal pause for a reply, the appeal to the mind, should be clearly marked. But formality need not imply detached frigidity. The speech asks for utter conviction and sincerity without condescension. Brutus' transparent honesty and nobility are what ultimately move his hearers. His conquest must not appear to be easy, as in Tree's production or Benson's; and his success must be convincing. Too much should not be made of it, however, or Antony's oration suffers.

Antony's speech, while not deficient in *logos* and *ethos*, a fact sometimes forgotten by those who would make him a mere rabble-rouser, incorporates the vital element of *pathos*. He remembers, as Brutus does not, that the word can be used to inflame as well as inform. His intricately-structured verse, the outpouring of a finely-tuned sensibility, has a colour and warmth which Brutus' appeal does not, and it sweeps the scene to a flaming finale which needs no support from chemical blazes of the Booth, Benson, or Tree variety. To do so, however, the poetry needs to be given its head, and the crowd-responses carefully orchestrated so as not to fracture its rhythm at crucial moments.

The Quarrel scene, long overblown but frequently underplayed today, contributes its share to the cumulative thrust of the military sequences but should not upstage the scenes which follow. The military mood is firmly established at the outset by Shakespeare's call for 'Drum . . . and the army' and reinforced by orders to 'Stand'. Whatever is available by way of martial display can do no harm here, and will serve to underscore the heroic ambiance proper to the final scenes. The entry of Cassius is neatly prepared for in the conversation between Brutus and Lucilius, a stratagem made necessary by his long absence from the action.

The quarrel, in telling contrast to the Forum oratory, takes the form of dialectic with the opponents face to face. The debate, however, is not about abstract intellectual matters, but Cassius' passionate allegations of a personal wrong done him. The personalities of the protagonists are thus more important than the validity of their arguments. While the scene pits Brutus' predominant rationality against Cassius' febrile passion with telling effect, the interplay between the two characters is more complex than it at first appears. To interpret Brutus as a majestic and frigid stoic as Kemble did, or as an insensitive prig as he so often seems in contemporary revivals, is to shortchange him and the scene. Brutus does value objectivity and strives for emotional restraint, but this is not to say he is unfeeling. The fact that he has to struggle for self-control, as John Wood so aptly demonstrated, reveals the depth of his sensibility. Cassius, despite a long history of misrepresentation, is no mere raving Hector, but a highly-sensitive soul, outraged at what he feels to be an injustice, and desperate for understanding and warmth from a man he profoundly respects. True, he is high-mettled, and even womanishly pettish at times, but he is no tortured neurotic. His military competence is never questioned, save by Brutus; and events tragically vindicate his strategic insight. Unless both characters are allowed a full measure of human dignity in the early part of the scene, Cassius' pathetic capitulation and Brutus' moving revelation of Portia's death will lack point and power.

The conference sequence poses no particular problem, save for Brutus' denial of knowledge of Portia's suicide. There is no pressing reason to cut this passage, as some directors have done. If played without undue emphasis, it merely indicates Brutus' reluctance to re-open a matter so painful that it may unman him at a moment when undivided concentration is imperative. The almost lyrical episode with Lucius, offering an interlude of peace in which Brutus' humaneness further asserts itself, has been generally well played throughout *Caesar*'s stage history. The treatment of the apparition, however, has not always been so fortunate. To downplay its significance by making it a figment of Brutus' diseased imagination as Mansfield did, or to render its presence almost casual as in many modern productions, is to deny Caesar the dominance accorded him by the play's title, and to weaken the sense of Nemesis so crucial to the play's tragic spirit. The exit of the ghost, Brutus' staccato questions, and his orders to Cassius to 'set on his powers before' initiates the climactic movement of the play which now climbs with crescendo effect to its majestic finale.

The Plains of Philippi episodes, frequently regarded as minor and treated perfunctorily, are in fact major, and must be developed with care if the play is to keep its shape. The action is of one piece throughout, almost cinematic in technique, and cumulative in its effect. To fully realize its potential, the act must be played in its entirety. The preliminary skirmish between

Octavius and Antony and the slanging-match between the rival generals, riddled as they are with scorn and contempt, give the scene a firm beginning, and contrast finely with the touching farewells of Brutus and Cassius and the latter's pathetic birthday speech. The 'Ride, ride, Messala' episode, brief though it is, accelerates the dramatic momentum and lends a touch of martial authenticity to the action, without any prolonged diversion of attention from the protagonists who are Shakespeare's main concern. Protracted battles or interpolated military tableaux, in the manner of Phelps or Benson, only slow the action and seem artificial. Naturalism of this sort is difficult to capture in the stage idiom.

Brutus' and Cassius' deaths, although broadly similar, are more remarkable for their differences; and they complement each other if the frequently-cut scene of Lucilius' capture (V.iv) is allowed to separate them, and if the distinctive nature of each is carefully noted. Cassius is stabbed by Pindarus without a word of protest by the latter. Brutus hurls his body on the sword held by Strato only after three rejections – by Clitus, Dardanius, and Volumnius – each intensifying his desperate quest for death. Cassius takes leave of the world, appropriately enough, with an abrupt line or two addressed to Caesar; Brutus quits it with a formal and dignified farewell. The eulogies, too, are different in quality. Brutus' lines over Cassius' corpse are spoken by a friend among friends, and are subjective and deeply-felt. Brutus' eulogy is enunciated by an enemy with heroic formality against a background of military pageantry. There is no need to detract from Antony's gallantry and Octavius' noble response to it by making their speeches serve as prologue to *Antony and Cleopatra*. There are indeed hints of future turmoil here and there throughout the play, but they are best left at that.

Julius Caesar has no single tragic hero as do *Hamlet* and *Lear*, although Brutus comes closer to being so than anyone else. But the play must not be warped to become simply Brutus' tragedy. Caesar is the pivotal figure; and from their relationship to him Brutus, Cassius, and Antony derive their relative importance. These four characters, like the action, are constructed on a grand scale, and function as an ensemble. One is again reminded of Moulton's conception of the play as a sculptured grouping. At the centre stands Caesar, physical in the first half of the drama, spiritual in the second part; but never far from our minds. Arranged about him in clearly-defined relationships to him and to each other are Brutus, Cassius, and Antony. At some distance stand a host of other figures, smaller but sharply-etched, which lend perspective and dimension to the major characters.

Caesar is undoubtedly the most difficult part to cast. Here we need an actor capable of capturing a majesty profound enough to give the conspirators' crime tragic significance, and yet sufficiently vulnerable to make credible the talk of deaf ears and falling sickness. The performer is required to create his effects in comparatively few lines, and to register them strongly enough to resonate throughout the play. Actors in the main are not impressed by talk of Caesar's spiritual dominance after death; a character who appears so seldom and dies so early seems minor, whatever the critics may say. In the eighteenth century, at the mercy of the theatre's lesser lights, Caesar degenerated into a ranting buffoon. Nineteenth-century portraits of him as a pompous puppet were no great improvement. Early in this century his senile frailty was so patent that the assassination lacked motive. More recently, Dotrice, Dignam, and others have struck a welcome balance between authority and infirmity, only to see his stature diminished anew by the anti-heroic stances of Brutus, Cassius, and Antony.

The role of Brutus poses similar difficulties. Brutus is a man of reason and a stoic; but he is no frigid monument. Stoicism leads him to repress emotion, but does not obliterate it; and his humane impulses peek out with startling frequency when the lines are spoken with intelligence and sensitivity. Brutus is noble, however Blatchley may argue to the contrary, and he must be seen to be so in bearing, in speech, and, above all, in spirit. Kemble, Macready, and Davenport endowed him with physical and intellectual grandeur, while Booth gave him a spiritual elevation; but his superiority to other men was never in doubt. His chilly rationality was at times too much stressed in eighteenth- and nineteenth-century readings, and his repressed sensibility was made too little of. Yet this bias is surely less dangerous than the contemporary trend toward making him a prig, a bore, or a neurotic incompetent. Brutus is, after all, the central figure in the conspiracy; if he wants distinction, the plot lacks a focus, and Cassius seems merely a bad judge of character.

From the Restoration performances of Mohun until the mid-Victorian revivals of Macready, no leading player brought his talents to the role of Cassius; and in the past century only Barrett and Gielgud have risked their reputations in it. The unpopularity of the part no doubt arose from a chronic misconception of it as merely a foil to Brutus. A long line of glacial Stoics forced Cassius to counter with untrammelled, if simplistic, emotionalism; and few stars were prepared to devote their skills to so undemanding an exercise. Barrett, however, finally restored to him the nobility which made Brutus his friend; and gave the latter's 'Noble, noble Cassius' and his promise of tears at his death a poignant truth long missed. Gielgud, in his turn, revealed to us the intellectual gifts of the fiery Roman; no longer a mere spoiled child, he emerged as a clever strategist, a keen reader of men, a competent general. More important still, Gielgud demonstrated that Cassius' energy, if not dissipated in sheer histrionic display, can serve to propel *Caesar*'s entire dramatic action.

Cassius has, it is true, a less pleasant side: he makes undue demands on his friends; he is quick-tempered and sometimes violent. But so devastating is the sweep of his emotional drives that we are caught up with him, and suffer a sense of tragic waste when his impulsive suicide withdraws him from the play. To portray him otherwise is to deprive the drama of texture, colour, energy, and tragic force.

The role of Antony requires a fine presence, athletic good looks, and superb verse-speaking talents. Throughout the eighteenth and nineteenth centuries, with the Proscription scene cut and unflattering remarks about him excised elsewhere, little more was demanded of Antony's interpreter; and Robert Wilks, Spranger Barry, Charles Kemble, and Frank Benson did what was asked for superbly. His place in the later scenes has been explored mainly in our own time, and the emphasis has been, as for Brutus and Cassius, upon his baser traits.

The role is difficult, although less so than the other major parts. Prior to the death of Caesar, Antony is allowed only four brief appearances (including two with the procession), and is given little to say. Yet he must suggest a friendship with Caesar which makes credible his later grief, and simultaneously confirm his reputation as a rake if his transformation in the Senate scene is to have full effect. The complex splendours and challenges of the Senate and Forum scenes, so splendidly realized by Booth, Benson, and, to a lesser degree, Tree, are self-evident.

The current proneness to denigrate Antony from the Forum scene onwards warrants some concern. His shabby side is unmistakably delineated in the text, and must be given full value. He is the shrewd contriver Cassius says he is, and a first-class opportunist as well. But he, like his companion characters, cannot be shorn of all nobility. He must be seen, whatever his faults, as the living instrument of Ate in the military scenes, and the magnanimous hero at the play's close. The epic nature of the conflict and its tragic dénouement ask no less.

It is a mistake, I think, to coarsen and brutalize him in the Forum as did Charles Thomas. He discovers his power over men only in the course of the scene; and he speaks gracefully and treads warily throughout. Nor is it wise for courtesans to intrude upon the Proscription episode, as they did in Douglas Campbell's revival. Sensuality, temporarily at least, has been left behind in the Senate House. Such ploys serve only to divert attention from the scene's main interest – the naked quest for power and its callous side-effects. The ringing eulogy at the play's conclusion is the tribute of a hero to a hero, and loses its thrust if it is spoken by a drably-dressed thug who mumbles the words mechanically or, worse still, ironically.

Sir John Gielgud thinks, in view of *Caesar*'s manifold production problems, that it '*might* be more satisfactory in the cinema than it can ever be in the theatre, save under the most exceptional circumstances'.[6] Perhaps Sir John is right; but there will be no lack of attempts to prove him wrong. The theatre is a unique medium, and its immediacy and three-dimensional effect cannot be duplicated. Somewhere, it is safe to conjecture, a production is being planned at this moment. Some director, fired by *Caesar*'s characters and its political and social relevance, is even now weighing its challenges – the casting of four male leads, the consequence or lack of it to be given the crowd, the nature and scale of the pageantry, the anti-climactic dangers of the final scenes. Will he, one wonders, also consider a return to grandeur of style? Not simply a frigid artificiality, but a radiance of speech and greatness of spirit. A failure would be counted only a daring experiment; a success would restore to the stage a tragic splendour almost unknown in our time.

CHRONOLOGICAL HANDLIST OF PERFORMANCES
1599–1973

As a calendar of *Julius Caesar* performances in London, Stratford-upon-Avon, and New York, the following is, I hope, as complete as documentation permits. I have also included revivals elsewhere in Great Britain and North America when these are of special interest. Cast-lists are, regrettably, not always available. Actors are listed by surname only, except when one actor might be confused with a contemporary of the same name. In such cases I have distinguished them by initials. Performances take place in London unless otherwise indicated. For long-run and repertory revivals in the late-nineteenth and twentieth centuries, only the date of the première is noted.

For records of eighteenth-century London performances I am indebted to *The London Stage* and Charles Beecher Hogan's *Shakespeare in the Theatre 1701–1800*. The catalogue of nineteenth-century New York productions owes much to the work of Thomas Allston Brown, Joseph Norton Ireland, and George C. D. Odell. In most cases, however, I have checked secondary sources against the original playbills or newspaper advertisements.

21 September 1599	? The Globe. No cast-list. E. K. Chambers, *The Elizabethan Stage*, 1923, II, p. 365.
Winter 1612–13	At Court. No cast-list. E. K. Chambers, *William Shakespeare*, 1951, II, p. 343.
31 January 1636/7	St James's. No cast-list. *The Dramatic Records of Sir Henry Herbert*, ed. Joseph Quincy Adams, New Haven, 1917, p. 75.
13 November 1638	The Cockpit. No cast-list. *The Dramatic Records of Sir Henry Herbert*, p. 77.
May 1663–June 1665	Theatre Royal, Drury Lane. No cast-list. John Downes, *Roscius Anglicanus*, 1708, p. 8. Allardyce Nicoll, *A History of English Drama*, 1952, I, p. 299.
c. 1671	Theatre Royal, Drury Lane. JC–Bell; B–Hart; C–Mohun; A–Kynaston. Downes, *Roscius Anglicanus*, p. 8.
4 December 1676	? Hall ? Drury Lane. No cast-list. Nicoll, *History of English Drama*, I, p. 346.
c. 1678–82	Theatre Royal, Dublin. JC–Cudworth; B–Richards; C–Ashbury; A–Smith. R. C. Bald, 'Shakespeare on the

	Stage in Restoration Dublin', *PMLA*, LVI (June 1941), pp. 369–78.
1684	Theatre Royal, Drury Lane. JC–Goodman; B–Betterton; C–Smith; A–Kynaston. John Genest, *Some Account of the English Stage*, 1832, I, pp. 422–3.
18 April 1687	At Court. United Company. No cast-list. Nicoll, *History of English Drama*, I, p. 351.
14 February 1703/4	Lincoln's Inn Fields. No cast-list.
14 March 1705/6	Queen's. No cast-list.
14 January 1706/7	Queen's. JC–Booth; B–Betterton; C–Verbruggen; A–Wilks. Repeated 15 Jan.; 1 Apr.
22 December 1709	Drury Lane. JC–?; B–Booth; C–Powell; A–?
22 April 1710	Drury Lane. JC–Keene; B–Booth; C–Powell; A–?
5 April 1712	Drury Lane. No cast-list.
8 April 1712	Drury Lane. No cast-list.
24 April 1712	Drury Lane. No cast-list.
15 November 1712	Drury Lane. No cast-list.
11 December 1712	Drury Lane. No cast-list.
20 January 1712/13	Drury Lane. No cast-list.
16 March 1712/13	Drury Lane. JC–Mills; B–Booth; C–Powell; A–Wilks. Repeated 6 Apr.; 4 May.
26 September 1713	Drury Lane. No cast-list.
27 October 1713	Drury Lane. No cast-list.
23 January 1713/14	Drury Lane. No cast-list.
12 April 1714	Drury Lane. No cast-list.
9 October 1714	Drury Lane. No cast-list.
24 January 1714/15	Drury Lane. JC–Mills; B–Booth; C–Elrington; A–Wilks.
13 May 1715	Drury Lane. No cast-list.
24 November 1715	Drury Lane. No cast-list.
22 March 1715/16	Drury Lane. No cast-list.
24 May 1716	Drury Lane. No cast-list.
20 October 1716	Drury Lane. No cast-list.
27 October 1716	Lincoln's Inn Fields. JC–?; B–Keene; C–Elrington; A–? Repeated 8 Nov.
3 January 1716/17	Lincoln's Inn Fields. JC–?; B–Keene; C–Elrington; A–? Repeated 4 Apr.; 3 May.
27 April 1717	Drury Lane. No cast-list.
7 November 1717	Lincoln's Inn Fields. No cast-list.
16 November 1717	Drury Lane. No cast-list.
1 March 1717/18	Lincoln's Inn Fields. JC–[J.] Leigh; B–Keene; C–Ryan; A–Quin.
17 March 1717/18	Lincoln's Inn Fields. No cast-list.
1 November 1718	Lincoln's Inn Fields. JC–?; B–Quin; C–Ryan; A–?
13 November 1718	Drury Lane. JC–Mills; B–Booth; C–?; A–Wilks.

25 November 1718	Lincoln's Inn Fields. JC–Ogden; B–Quin; C–Ryan; A–[J.] Leigh.
28 January 1718/19	Drury Lane. JC–Mills; B–Booth; C–Elrington; A–Wilks.
24 April 1719	Drury Lane. No cast-list.
25 April 1719	Lincoln's Inn Fields. No cast-list.
19 November 1719	Lincoln's Inn Fields. JC–Ogden; B–Quin; C–Ryan; A–[J.] Leigh.
9 April 1720	Lincoln's Inn Fields. JC–Ogden; B–Quin; C–Ryan; A–[J.] Leigh.
1 November 1720	Lincoln's Inn Fields. JC–Boheme; B–Quin; C–Ryan; A–[J.] Leigh.
26 January 1720/1	Drury Lane. No cast-list.
4 March 1720/1	Drury Lane. No cast-list.
26 April 1721	Drury Lane. JC–Thurmond; B–Booth; C–Mills; A–Wilks. Repeated 3 Oct.
25 May 1721	Lincoln's Inn Fields. JC–Boheme; B–Quin; C–Ryan; A–[J.] Leigh.
16 January 1721/2	Drury Lane. JC–Thurmond; B–Booth; C–Mills; A–Wilks. Repeated 19 Oct.
18 October 1722	Lincoln's Inn Fields. JC–[J.] Leigh; B–Quin; C–Boheme; A–Walker.
10 January 1722/3	Lincoln's Inn Fields. JC–[J.] Leigh; B–Quin; C–Boheme; A–Walker. Repeated 14 May; 31 Oct.; 31 Dec.
13 February 1722/3	Drury Lane. JC–Thurmond; B–Booth; C–Mills; A–Wilks. Repeated 24 Sept.
9 May 1723	Drury Lane. No cast-list.
11 January 1723/4	Drury Lane. JC–Thurmond; B–Booth; C–Mills; A–Wilks. Repeated 19 Sept.
2 January 1724/5	Drury Lane. JC–Thurmond; B–Booth; C–Mills; A–Wilks. Repeated 18 June; 30 Sept.
11 March 1724/5	Lincoln's Inn Fields. JC–Ryan; B–Quin; C–Boheme; A–Walker. Repeated 22 May; 15 Dec.
3 April 1725	Drury Lane. No cast-list.
26 January 1725/6	Drury Lane. JC–Thurmond; B–Booth; C–Mills; A–Wilks. Repeated 16 Apr.
11 November 1726	Lincoln's Inn Fields. JC–Ryan; B–Quin; C–Boheme; A–Walker.
5 April 1727	Drury Lane. No cast-list.
31 May 1727	Drury Lane. No cast-list.
3 October 1727	Drury Lane. JC–Williams; B–Booth; C–Mills; A–Wilks.
4 January 1727/8	Drury Lane. JC–Williams; B–Booth; C–Mills; A–Wilks.
20 November 1728	Lincoln's Inn Fields. JC–Ryan; B–Quin; C–Boheme; A–Walker.

13 November 1729   Lincoln's Inn Fields. JC–Ryan; B–Quin; C–Boheme; A–Walker.

1 December 1732   Goodman's Fields. JC–Huddy; B–Delane; C–? A–Giffard. Repeated 2 Dec. [C–Hulett]; 4, 5, 6, 7, 8, 9, 11, 12, 13, 14, 26 Dec.

3 January 1732/3   Goodman's Fields. JC–Huddy; B–Delane; C–Hulett; A–Giffard. Repeated 22 Jan.; 6 Apr.; 15 May; 10 Sept.; 10 Oct.

21 January 1733/4   Goodman's Fields. JC–Huddy; B–Delane; C–Hulett; A–Giffard. Repeated 20 Sept.

14 February 1733/4   Goodman's Fields. No cast-list.

1 April 1734   Goodman's Fields. No cast-list.

8 November 1734   Goodman's Fields. JC–[W.] Mills; B–Quin; C–Mills; A–Milward. Repeated 9, 11, 12, 13 Nov.; 4 Dec.

18 January 1734/5   Drury Lane. JC–[W.] Mills; B–Quin; C–Mills; A–Milward. Repeated 1 Sept.; 1 Oct.; 9 Dec.

13 March 1734/5   Goodman's Fields. JC–Huddy; B–Delane; C–Hulett; A–Giffard.

22 November 1735   Covent Garden. JC–Bridgwater; B–Delane; C–Ryan; A–Walker.

16 April 1736   Drury Lane. JC–[W.] Mills; B–Quin; C–Mills; A–Milward. Repeated 19, 29 May; 21 Sept.; 28 Oct.

24 January 1736/7   Drury Lane. JC–Berry; B–Quin; C–Milward; A–[W.] Mills. Repeated 17 Feb.; 28 Apr.

19 January 1737/8   Drury Lane. JC–[W.] Mills; B–Quin; C–Milward; A–Wright. Repeated 8 Feb.; 28 Apr.; 21 Sept.; 29 Nov.; 12 Dec.

29 March 1739   Drury Lane. JC–[W.] Mills; B–Quin; C–Milward; A–Wright. Repeated 10 Oct.; 11 Dec.

17 January 1739/40   Drury Lane. JC–[W.] Mills; B–Quin; C–Milward; A–Wright. Repeated 13 Mar.; 4 Oct.; 19 Dec.

24 February 1740/1   Drury Lane. JC–[W.] Mills; B–Quin; C–Milward; A–Wright. Repeated 3 Apr.

16 November 1741   Drury Lane. JC–Berry; B–Delane; C–Milward; A–[W.] Mills.

20 November 1742   Covent Garden. JC–Bridgwater; B–Quin; C–Ryan; A–Hale. Repeated 20 Dec.

22 January 1742/3   Covent Garden. JC–Bridgwater; B–Quin; C–Ryan; A–Hale. Repeated 15 Feb.; 8 Dec.

3 January 1743/4   Covent Garden. JC–Bridgwater; B–Quin; C–Ryan; A–Hale. Repeated 19 Jan.

18 April 1744   Covent Garden. JC–Bridgwater; B–Sheridan; C–Ryan; A–Hale. Repeated 31 Oct.; 10 Nov.

2 February 1744/5   Covent Garden. JC–Bridgwater; B–Quin; C–Ryan; A–Hale.

28 March 1746/7	Drury Lane. JC–[W.] Mills; B–Delane; C–[L.] Sparks; A–Barry. Repeated 2 Apr.; 30 Apr. [A–Giffard].
20 April 1747	Covent Garden. JC–Bridgwater; B–Quin; C–Ryan; A–Havard.
24 November 1748	Covent Garden. JC–Bridgwater; B–Quin; C–Ryan; A–Delane. Repeated 25 Nov.; 8 Dec.
19 October 1749	Covent Garden. JC–Bridgwater; B–Quin; C–Ryan; A–Delane. Repeated 28 Nov.
12 January 1749/50	Covent Garden. JC–Bridgwater; B–Quin; C–Ryan; A–Delane.
24 November 1750	Covent Garden. JC–[L.] Sparks; B–Quin; C–Ryan; A–Barry. Repeated 26, 27 Nov.; 27 Dec.
19 February 1751	Covent Garden. JC–Sparks; B–Quin; C–Ryan; A–Barry. Repeated 7 Mar.; 1 May.
7 May 1753	Covent Garden. JC–Bridgwater; B–Sparks; C–Ryan; A–Barry. Repeated 14 May.
9 March 1754	Covent Garden. JC–Bridgwater; B–Sparks; C–Ryan; A–Barry. Repeated 12, 16 Mar.
28 January 1755	Covent Garden. JC–Sparks; B–Sheridan; C–Ryan; A–Smith.
14 April 1758	Covent Garden. JC–Clarke; B–Sparks; C–Ryan; A–Barry.
31 January 1766	Covent Garden. JC–Clarke; B–Walker; C–Smith; A–Ross. Repeated 3, 7, 24 Feb.
25 April 1767	Covent Garden. JC–Clarke; B–Walker; C–Smith; A–Hull.
11 September 1769	Haymarket. JC–[J.] Aickin; B–Sheridan; C–Sowdon; A–A Young Gentleman [Miller, according to Hogan, II, p. 317].
1 June 1770	Southwark Theatre, Philadelphia. American Company. JC–?; B–?Hallam; C–?Henry; A–A Gentleman [Goodman].
4 May 1773	Covent Garden. JC–Clarke; B–Bensley; C–Hull; A–Smith.
20 April 1774	Charleston Theatre. American Company. JC–?; B–?Hallam; C–?Henry; A–?Goodman.
24 January 1780	Drury Lane. JC–Packer; B–[J.] Palmer; C–Henry; A–Smith. Repeated 25 Jan.; 15 [C–Bensley], 19 Feb.; 11 Mar; 27 Apr.
28 April 1788	John Street Theatre, New York. American Company. JC–?; B–?Hallam; C–?Henry; A–?
29 January 1791	Southwark Theatre, Philadelphia. Old American Company. JC–?; B–?Hallam; C–?Henry; A–?
14 March 1794	John Street Theatre, New York. Old American Company. JC–Richards; B–Hallam; C–Henry; A–Hodgkinson.

28 May 1802	Park Theatre, New York. JC–Tyler; B–Hodgkinson; C–Hallam; A–Cooper.
23 March 1803	Federal Street Theatre, Boston. JC–Powell; B–Barrett; C–Harper; A–Downie.
6 April 1807	Boston Theatre. JC–A Gentleman; B–Fennell; C–Caulfield; A–Usher.
19 February 1808	Federal Street Theatre, Boston. JC–?; B–Fennell; C–Caulfield; A–Cooper.
14 March 1808	Park Theatre, New York. JC–Tyler; B–Green; C–Robertson; A–Cooper.
16 December 1808	Chestnut Street Theatre, Philadelphia. JC–Warren; B–Wood; C–M'Kenzie; A–Cooper.
29 February 1812	Covent Garden. JC–Egerton; B–[J.P.] Kemble; C–Young; A–[C.] Kemble. Repeated 3, 7, 10, 14, 17, 21, 29 Mar.; 1, 4, 8, 16, 20, 30 Apr.; 7, 14, 21, 28 May; 4, 12 June.
13 July 1812	Theatre Royal, Liverpool. JC–Banks; B–[J.P.] Kemble; C–Rae; A–Bartley.
3 March 1813	Chestnut Street Theatre, Philadelphia. No cast-list.
23 April 1813	Park Theatre, New York. JC–Green; B–A Gentleman; C–Simpson; A–Cooper.
3 June 1813	Covent Garden. JC–Egerton; B–Sowerby; C–Young; A–[C.] Kemble.
9 December 1813	Theatre Royal, Dublin. JC–Thompson; B–[J.P.] Kemble; C–Hackett; A–[C.] Connor.
4 February 1814	Covent Garden. JC–Egerton; B–Kemble; C–Young; A–Conway. Repeated 9, 16 Feb.; 25 May.
21 March 1814	Theatre-Royal, Edinburgh. No cast-list. Repeated 24 Mar.
29 October 1814	Covent Garden. JC–Egerton; B–Kemble; C–Young; A–Conway. Repeated 5 Nov.; 1, 13 Dec.
17 April 1815	Covent Garden. JC–Egerton; B–Kemble; C–Young; A–Conway.
4 April 1816	Theatre-Royal, Edinburgh. No cast-list.
6 May 1816	Covent Garden. JC–Egerton; B–Kemble; C–Young; A–Conway. Repeated 13 May.
5 July 1816	Theatre-Royal, Liverpool. JC–M'Gibbon; B–Kemble; C–Vandenhoff; A–Cooper.
15 November 1816	Covent Garden. JC–Egerton; B–Kemble; C–Terry; A–[C.] Kemble. Repeated 9 Dec.
10 January 1817	Park Theatre, New York. JC–?; B–Pritchard; C–Simpson; A–Cooper.
14 February 1817	Chestnut Street Theatre, Philadelphia. JC–?; B–?; C–?; A–Cooper.
29 April 1817	Covent Garden. JC–Egerton; B–Kemble; C–Young; A–[C.] Kemble. Repeated 6, 17, 31 May; 9, 19 June.

14 January 1818	Park Theatre, New York. JC–?; B–?; C–?; A–Cooper.
19 February 1818	Boston Theatre. JC–Wheatley; B–Duff; C–Brown; A–Cooper. Repeated 24 Feb.
29 September 1818	Park Theatre, New York. JC–Graham; B–Pritchard; C–Simpson; A–Cooper.
10 November 1818	Theatre-Royal, Chester. JC–Crisp; B–Musgrave; C–Ormond; A–Powell.
16 November 1818	Federal Street Theatre, Boston. JC–Wheatley; B–Duff; C–Price; A–Cooper.
21 April 1819	Bath. JC–?; B–Warde; C–Young; A–Conway.
8 June 1819	Covent Garden. JC–Egerton; B–Young; C–Macready; A–[C.] Kemble. Repeated 14 June.
13 December 1819	Federal Street Theatre, Boston. JC–Pelby; B–Duff; C–[H.] Williams; A–Cooper.
5 January 1820	Theatre-Royal, Birmingham, JC–Ward; B–Cordell; C–Yates; A–Mude.
8 June 1820	Theatre-Royal, Liverpool. JC–M'Gibbon; B–Young; C–Vandenhoff; A–Bass.
25 October 1820	Theatre-Royal, Liverpool. JC–M'Gibbon; B–Vandenhoff; C–Younge; A–Bass.
30 October 1820	New Theatre-Royal, Birmingham. JC–Musgrave; B–Conway; C–Hamblin; A–Mude.
7 December 1820	Drury Lane. JC–Thompson; B–Wallack; C–Booth; A–Cooper. Repeated 12 Dec.
17 February 1821	New Theatre-Royal, Dublin. JC–Armstrong; B–Young; C–Cobham; A–Barton.
26 February 1821	Theatre, Savannah, Ga. JC–Green; B–Finn; C–Robertson; A–Cooper.
18 December 1821	Bath. JC–?; B–Young; C–Hamblin; A–Mude. Genest, *Some Account of the English Stage*, IX, p. 121.
11 February 1822	Theatre-Royal, Newcastle. JC–Pope; B–Mude; C–Younge; A–Carter.
22 April 1822	Covent Garden. JC–Egerton; B–Young; C–Macready; A–[C.] Kemble. Repeated 27 Apr.; 2, 6, 10, 22, 27, 29 May; 3 June.
31 October 1822	Federal Street Theatre, Boston. JC–?; B–Finn; C–Barrett; A–Cooper. Repeated 6 Nov.
5 February 1823	Theatre-Royal, Edinburgh. No cast-list. Repeated 10 Feb.
8 February 1823	Chestnut Street Theatre, Philadelphia. JC–Wilson; B–[J.] Wallack; C–[H.] Wallack; A–Cooper. Repeated 12 Feb.
13 June 1823	City Theatre, New York. A–Mrs Baldwin.
29 September 1823	Park Theatre, New York. JC–Woodhull; B–Maywood; C–[John H.] Clarke; A–Cooper.
27 October 1823	Holliday Street Theatre, Baltimore. JC–Perkins; B–Wood; C–Brown; A–Duff.

14 November 1823	Boston Theatre. JC–Clarke; B–Finn; C–Barrett; A–Cooper.
15 December 1823	Chestnut Street Theatre, Philadelphia. JC–Darley; B–Duff; C–Wallack; A–Cooper.
22 December 1823	Covent Garden. JC–Egerton; B–Young; C–Cooper; A–[C.] Kemble. Repeated 1 Jan 1824.
26 January 1824	Theatre-Royal, Bristol. JC–Bass; B–Butler; C–Williams; A–Montague. Repeated 6, 16 Feb.; 31 May [C–Macready].
18 February 1824	Park Theatre, New York. JC–Woodhull; B–Cooper; C–? A–Conway.
23 February 1824	Theatre-Royal, Newcastle. No cast-list. Repeated 29 Mar.
17 March 1824	Boston Theatre. JC–Clarke; B–Cooper; B–Barrett; A–Conway. Repeated 26 Mar. [B–Conway; A–Cooper].
19 March 1824	Theatre-Royal, Edinburgh. JC–Denham; B–Young; C–Vandenhoff; A–Calcraft. Repeated 25 Mar.
12 April 1824	Park Theatre, New York. JC–?; B–Conway; C–?; A–Cooper.
8 May 1824	Chestnut Street Theatre, Philadelphia. JC–Darley; B–Conway; C–[H.] Wallack; A–Cooper. Repeated 19 May [B–Cooper; A–Conway].
31 May 1824	Theatre-Royal, Bristol. JC–Bass; B–Butler; C–Macready; A–Montague.
19 July 1824	Theatre, Leeds. JC–Crook; B–Calvert; C–Faulkner; A–Marlow.
19 February 1825	Theatre-Royal, Bath. JC–?; B–Warde; C–Hamblin; A–Montague.
23 May 1825	Covent Garden. JC–Egerton; B–Young; C–Cooper; A–[C.] Kemble. Repeated 30 May, 7 July.
7 July 1825	Theatre, Leeds. JC–Stanley; B–Calvert; C–Faulkner; A–Crook.
26 September 1825	Covent Garden. JC–Egerton; B–Warde; C–Cooper; A–[C.] Kemble. Repeated 3, 10 Oct.; 14 Nov.
25 October 1825 (c.)	South Pearl Street Theatre, Albany. JC–?; B–Conway; C–?; A–Forrest.
31 October 1825	Park Theatre, New York. JC–Woodhull; B–Conway; C–Clarke; A–Cooper.
21 December 1825	Theatre, Newark. JC–Frazer; B–Hart; C–Hazelton; A–[W.] Robertson.
2 January 1826	Covent Garden. JC–Egerton; B–Warde; C–Cooper; A–[C.] Kemble. Repeated 15 May.
30 January 1826	Park Theatre, New York. JC–?; B–Conway; C–Clarke; A–Cooper.
8 March 1826	Theatre-Royal, Edinburgh. JC–Denham; B–Young; C–Vandenhoff; A–Pritchard. Repeated 17 Mar.

26 June 1826	Chatham Garden, New York. JC–[J.M.] Scott; B–Conway; C–[H.] Wallack; A–Duff.
2 October 1826	Covent Garden. JC–Egerton; B–Young; C–Warde; A–[C.] Kemble. Repeated 9 Oct.
17 November 1826	Chatham Garden, New York. JC–[J.M.] Scott; B–Hamblin; C–Booth; A–[H.] Wallack.
1 December 1826	The Bowery, New York. JC–Young; B–Conway; C–Barrett; A–Duff. Repeated 12 Dec. [A.] Forrest.
1 January 1827	Covent Garden. JC–Egerton; B–Young; C–Warde; A–[C.] Kemble. Repeated 18, 25 Apr.; 3 May; 18 June.
21 February 1827	Park Theatre, New York. JC–Woodhull; B–Conway; C–Macready; A–Barry.
29 March 1827	Theatre-Royal, Edinburgh. JC–Denham; B–Young; C–Vandenhoff; A–Pritchard.
12 June 1827	Park Theatre, New York. JC–Woodhull; B–Conway; C–[H.] Wallack; A–Barry.
1 October 1827	Covent Garden. JC–Egerton; B–Young; C–Warde; A–[C.] Kemble. Repeated 23 Nov.
8 February 1828	Theatre-Royal, Edinburgh. JC–Denham; B–Young; C–Vandenhoff; A–Pritchard.
24 April 1828	Covent Garden. JC–Egerton; B–Young; C–Warde; A–[C.] Kemble.
3 May 1828	Chestnut Street Theatre, Philadelphia. JC–?; B–Cooper; C–Wood; A–Forrest.
13 May 1828	The Bowery, New York. JC–?; B–Cooper; C–Barrett; A–Forrest.
25 August 1828	Theatre-Royal, Liverpool. JC–Raymond; B–Warde; C–Vandenhoff; A–Elton.
12 November 1828	The Bowery, New York. JC–?; B–Hamblin; C–[H.] Wallack; A–Forrest.
13 April 1829	Park Theatre, New York. JC–?; B–[J.] Wallack; C–[H.] Wallack; A–Hamblin.
22 June 1829	Theatre, Leeds. JC–Anderton; B–Calvert; C–Stuart; A–Carton.
18 July 1829	Theatre-Royal, Liverpool. JC–Raymond; B–Warde; C–Vandenhoff; A–Montague.
26 October 1829	Drury Lane. JC–[H.] Wallack; B–Young; C–Cooper; A–[J.] Wallack. Repeated 2 Nov. [JC–Thompson].
26 February 1830	Theatre-Royal, Edinburgh. JC–Denham; B–Young; C–Vandenhoff; A–Pritchard.
21 June 1830	Surrey Theatre. No cast-list.
11 August 1830	The Bowery, New York. JC–[J.M.] Scott; B–Hamblin; C–Blake; A–Cooper.
20 October 1830	Theatre-Royal, Liverpool. JC–Haines; B–Young; C–Aitkin; A–Vandenhoff.
8 March 1831	Theatre-Royal, Dublin. JC–Matthews; B–Young; C–Calcraft; A–Vandenhoff.

9 May 1831	Theatre-Royal, Manchester. JC–Clarkson; B–Vandenhoff; C–Mude; A–Fredericks.
16 June 1831	The Bowery, New York. JC–[J.M.] Scott; B–Hamblin; C–Booth; A–Cooper.
11 July 1831	Walnut Street Theatre, Philadelphia. JC–Rowbotham; B–Barton; C–Booth; A–Cooper.
18 August 1831	The Bowery, New York. JC–?; B–Hamblin; C–Booth; A–Cooper.
14 September 1831	The Bowery, New York. JC–?; B–Barton; C–Pearson; A–Hamblin.
5 October 1831	The Bowery, New York. JC–?; B–Barton; C–Pearson; A–Hamblin.
16 November 1831	Theatre-Royal, Liverpool. JC–Clarkson; B–Vandenhoff; C–Cooke; A–Fredericks.
23 February 1832	Theatre-Royal, Manchester. JC–Clarkson; B–Vandenhoff; C–Cooke; A–Fredericks.
25 February 1832	Walnut Street Theatre, Philadelphia. JC–Rowbotham; B–Hamblin; C–Booth; A–Smith.
5 March 1832	Surrey Theatre. JC–[D.] Pitt; B–Osbaldiston; C–Cobham; A–Elton. [Described in playbill as 'a Drama of Five Acts, founded on Shakespeare's Historical Play Julius Caesar! or, the Battle of Pharsalia'.] Repeated 6 Mar.
25 April 1832	Covent Garden. JC–Egerton; B–Young; C–Warde; A–[C.] Kemble. Repeated 30 Apr.
6 July 1832	Walnut Street Theatre, Philadelphia. JC–?; B–Wood; C–Booth; A–Smith.
12 November 1832	Covent Garden. JC–Egerton; B–Warde; C–Bennett; A–Butler.
5 January 1833	The Bowery, New York. JC–?; B–Hamblin; C–Booth; A–Cooper.
8 April 1833	Walnut Street Theatre, Philadelphia. JC–Rowbotham; B–Hamblin; C–Booth; A–Cooper.
3 June 1833	The Bowery, New York. JC–Jones; B–Hamblin; C–Forbes; A–Cooper.
21 November 1833	The Bowery, New York. JC–?; B–Hamblin; C–Booth; A–[H.] Wallack.
15 February 1834	The Bowery, New York. JC–Jones; B–Hamblin; C–Cooper; A–Forrest.
21 March 1834	Surrey Theatre. JC–[D.] Pitt; B–Osbaldiston; C–Elton; A–Serle.
25 April 1834	Davidge's Royal Surrey Theatre. JC–Heslop; B–Lyon; C–Bennett; A–Marston.
28 April 1834	The Bowery, New York. JC–Jones; B–Hamblin; C–Booth; A–Parsons.
25 August 1834	The Bowery, New York. JC–?; B–Parsons; C–Ingersoll; A–[J.R.] Scott.

13 October 1834	The Bowery, New York. JC–?; B–Hamblin; C–Booth; A–[J.R.] Scott.
19 January 1835	Covent Garden. JC–Diddear; B–Wallack; C–Warde; A–Cooper.
27 February 1835	Drury Lane. JC–Diddear; B–Vandenhoff; C–Warde; A–Cooper.
18 March 1835	Walnut Street Theatre, Philadelphia. JC–Blaike; B–[A.] Addams; C–Booth; A–Jackson.
1 September 1835	Walnut Street Theatre, Philadelphia. JC–Muzzy; B–[A.] Addams; C–Booth; A–Conner.
21 September 1835	The Bowery, New York. JC–Pickering; B–Hamblin; C–Ingersoll; A–Cooper.
24 November 1835	The Bowery, New York. JC–Pickering; B–Hamblin; C–Booth; A–Cooper.
23 December 1835	The Bowery, New York. JC–Pickering; B–Hamblin; C–Booth; A–[J.R.] Scott.
7 March 1836	Arch Theatre, Philadelphia. JC–Rowbotham; B–[J.] Wallack; C–Maywood; A–Abbott.
30 May 1836	Covent Garden. JC–?; B–Knowles; C–Macready; A–[C.] Kemble.
8 June 1836	Walnut Street Theatre, Philadelphia. No cast-list.
30 June 1836	Drury Lane. JC–?; B–Paumier; C–Warde; A–Cooper.
14 November 1836	Covent Garden. JC–Bennett; B–Macready; C–Vandenhoff; A–[C.] Kemble. Repeated 18, 21, 24, 29 Nov.; 5, 10, 15, 20 Dec.; 12 Apr. 1837; 14, 19 Apr.; 20 May.
28 January 1837	Walnut Street Theatre, Philadelphia. No cast-list.
1 June 1837	Royal Surrey Theatre. JC–?; B–Vandenhoff; C–Serle; A–Knowles.
21 July 1837	Walnut Street Theatre, Philadelphia. No cast-list.
25 September 1837	National Theatre, New York. JC–?; B–[J.] Vandenhoff; C–[H.] Wallack; A–Abbott.
13 October 1837	Theatre-Royal, Birmingham. JC–Whyte; B–Mude; C–Stuart; A–Lacey.
20 February 1838	Covent Garden. JC–Bennett; B–Macready; C–Phelps; A–Elton. Repeated 10 May.
12 July 1838	Walnut Street Theatre, Philadelphia. No cast-list.
26 July 1838	Theatre, Swansea. JC–Barry; B–Balmanno; C–Shaw; A–Mude.
7 September 1838	Walnut Street Theatre, Philadelphia. No cast-list.
27 April 1839	Covent Garden. JC–Bennett; B–Macready; C–Phelps; A–Vandenhoff.
4 November 1839	Theatre, Leeds. JC–Taylor; B–Waldron; C–Welsh; A–Courtney.
25 December 1839	The Bowery, New York. JC–Proctor; B–Hamblin; C–[Charles] Kean; A–Barry. Repeated 27 Dec.
4 June 1840	The Bowery, New York. JC–?; B–Hamblin; C–Jamieson; A–Forrest.

13 July 1840	The Chatham, New York. JC–Proctor; B–Cline; C–Booth; A–[J.R.] Scott.
25 September 1840	New National Theatre, Philadelphia. JC–?; B–Graham; C–Abbott; A–[J.R.] Scott.
27 August 1841	The Chatham, New York. JC–?; B–?; C–Kirby; A— [J.R.] Scott.
16 October 1841	Arch Theatre, Philadelphia. JC–Thompson; B–Harrison; C–Eaton; A–Smith.
7 January 1842	The Chatham, New York. JC–Goodenow; B– [C.J.] Smith; C–Kirby; A–[J.R.] Scott. Repeated 26 Jan.
20 June 1842	The Bowery, New York. JC–McCutcheon; B–Hamblin; C–Abbott; A–Addams.
27 June 1842	The Bowery, New York. JC–McCutcheon; B–Hamblin; C–[J.W.] Wallack Jr; A–[J.M.] Scott.
28 July 1842	The Chatham, New York. JC–Proctor; B–Hield; C–Kirby; A–[J.R.] Scott.
8 November 1842	Theatre-Royal, Birmingham. JC–Cullenford; B–Butler; C–Howard; A–Wyndham. Repeated 9 Nov.
10 November 1842	The Bowery, New York. JC–?; B–Hamblin; C–?; A–[G.] Vandenhoff.
30 December 1842	The Bowery, New York. JC–[J.M.] Scott; B–Hamblin; C–[J.W.] Wallack Jr.; A–[J.R.] Scott.
20 April 1843	Walnut Street Theatre, Philadelphia. No cast-list.
1 May 1843	Drury Lane. JC–Ryder; B–Macready; C–Phelps; A–Anderson. Repeated 16 May; 5 June.
16 August 1843	The Chatham, New York. JC–[J.M.] Scott; B–Vandenhoff; C–Jamieson; A–Forbes.
14 September 1843	Arch Theatre, Philadelphia. No cast-list.
9 October 1843	Arch Theatre, Philadelphia. No cast-list.
9 October 1843	Covent Garden. JC–Diddear; B–Vandenhoff; C–Phelps; A–Anderson. Repeated 13 Oct.
18 October 1843	Arch Theatre, Philadelphia. No cast-list.
13 November 1843	Park Theatre, New York. JC–Barry; B–[J.] Wallack; C–Booth; A–Wheatley.
22 January 1844	Walnut Street Theatre, Philadelphia. No cast-list.
29 March 1844	Walnut Street Theatre, Philadelphia. No cast-list.
19 June 1844	Walnut Street Theatre, Philadelphia. No cast-list.
8 November 1844	Theatre-Royal, Birmingham. JC–Barton; B–Creswick; C–[C.] Pitt; A–Conway.
3 March 1845	Theatre-Royal, Edinburgh. JC–Bedford; B–Glover; C–Couldrock; A–Leigh.
27 May 1845	Walnut Street Theatre, Philadelphia. JC–Davenport; B–Leman; C–Booth; A–Wheatley.
12 June 1845	Theatre-Royal, Birmingham, JC–Barton; B–Macready; C–Ryder; A–Hield. Repeated 19 June.

1 September 1845	The Bowery, New York. JC–Davenport; B–Henkins; C–[C.W.] Clarke; A–[J.R.] Scott. Repeated 2 Sept.
6 October 1845	Arch Theatre, Philadelphia. No cast-list.
11 November 1845	The Bowery, New York. JC–?; B–Davenport; C–Clarke; A–[J.R.] Scott.
2 December 1845	Chestnut Street Theatre, Philadelphia. No cast-list.
27 February 1846	Walnut Street Theatre, Philadelphia. No cast-list.
6 April 1846	The Bowery, New York. JC–Chanfrau; B–Davenport; C–Clarke; A–[J.R.] Scott. Repeated 7 Apr.
5 May 1846	Sadler's Wells. JC–Mellon; B–Phelps; C–Bennett; A–Marston.
30 July 1846	Sadler's Wells. JC–Mellon; B–Phelps; C–Creswick; A–Marston. Repeated 31 July; 1, 5, 6, 7, 19, 20 Aug.
28 December 1846	Walnut Street Theatre, Philadelphia. No cast-list.
22 November 1847	Theatre-Royal, Manchester. JC–Reynolds; B–[G.V.] Brooke; C–[B.] Sullivan; A–Hall.
5 April 1848	Princess's. JC–Fisher; B–Macready; C–Ryder; A–Cooper. Repeated 7, 10 Apr.
13 May 1848	The Bowery, New York. JC–Tilton; B–Marshall; C–Clarke; A–Dyott.
16 October 1848	Niblo's Astor Place Theatre, New York. JC–Clarke; B–Macready; C–Ryder; A–Vandenhoff.
1 June 1849	The Bowery, New York. JC–Duff; B–Hamblin; C–Ryder; A–Gilbert.
20 November 1849	Theatre-Royal, Birmingham. JC–Barton; B–[J.] Bennett; C–Horsman; A–Glydon.
1 February 1850	Windsor Castle. JC–Fisher; B–Macready; C–[J.] Wallack; A–[C.] Kean.
6 February 1850	Theatre-Royal, Birmingham. JC–Barton; B–[J.] Bennett; C–Horsman; A–Mortimer.
14 February 1850	Drury Lane. JC–Fisher; B–Vandenhoff; C–Cathcart; A–Anderson. Repeated 18, 20 Feb.; 30 Apr. [C–Cooper].
3 April 1850	Theatre-Royal, Birmingham. JC–Barton; B–Macready; C–Bennett; A–Saville.
21 October 1850	Royal Surrey Theatre. JC–?; B–Creswick; C–Mead; A–Montague. Repeated 22, 23, 29 Oct.; 2 Nov.
23 October 1850	Sadler's Wells. JC–Younge; B–Phelps; C–Bennett; A–Marston. Repeated 24 Oct.
28 October 1850	Theatre-Royal, Birmingham. JC–Barton; B–Anderson; C–[J.] Bennett; A–Bland. Repeated 28 Nov.
18 November 1850	Haymarket. JC–Stuart; B–Macready; C–Davenport; A–Howe. Repeated 23 Nov. [B–Davenport; C–Macready]; 20 Jan. 1851; 24 Jan [B–Macready; C–Davenport].

19 January 1852	Chestnut Street Theatre, Philadelphia. No cast-list. Repeated 28 Jan.
12 June 1852	The Bowery, New York. JC–?; B–Hamblin; C–Eddy; A–Goodall.
3 September 1852	National Theatre, Philadelphia. No cast-list.
8 February 1853	The Bowery, New York. JC–Hamilton; B–Johnston; C–Eddy; A–[William] Hamblin.
1 July 1853	National Theatre, New York. JC–[N.B.] Clarke; B–[C.F.] Addams; C–Pope; A–[J.R.] Scott.
11 October 1854	National Theatre, New York. JC–?; B–?; C–?; A–[J.R.] Scott.
17 October 1854	The Great Metropolitan Theatre, New York. JC–?; B–Marshall; C–Eddy; A–Pope.
27 October 1856	Theatre-Royal, Newcastle. No cast-list.
1 November 1856	Sadler's Wells. JC–[A.] Ryder; B–Phelps; C–Marston; A–Robinson. Repeated 3, 4, 5 Nov.; 29, 30, 31 Dec.; 1 Jan. 1857.
26 January 1857	Queen's Theatre and Opera-House, Edinburgh. JC–Tindell or Tyndall; B–Vandenhoff; C–Mead; A–Moorhouse.
29 April 1857	Broadway Theatre, New York. JC–?; B–Davenport; C–[J.W.] Wallack Jr.; A–Loraine. Repeated 30 Apr.
25 September 1857	The Bowery, New York. JC–Clarke; B–Fenno; C–Eddy; A–Foster.
26 April 1858	Boston Theatre. JC–Donaldson; B–Davenport; C–Howe; A–Proctor.
2 July 1858	The Bowery, New York. JC–[N.B.] Clarke; B–Buchanan; C–Eddy; A–Johnston.
12 February 1859	Sadler's Wells. JC–?; B–Phelps; C–?; A–? Repeated 14, 15, 16 Feb.
16 June 1859	Niblo's Garden, New York. JC–Pearson; B–Davenport; C–Eddy; A–Perry.
27 February 1860	Old Bowery, New York. JC–Carden; B–Johnston; C–Allen; A–Jamieson.
28 May 1860	New Bowery, New York. JC–Nunan; B–[F.B.] Conway; C–Wallack; A–Boniface. Repeated 30 May.
26 February 1861	Sadler's Wells. JC–Harald; B–Phelps; C–Marston; A–Vezin. Repeated 27, 28 Feb.; 1, 2 Mar.
3 June 1861	Howard Athenaeum, Boston. JC–McCullough; B–Davenport; C–[E.] Booth; A–[L.P.] Barrett. Repeated 6, 8 June.
13 December 1861	New Bowery, New York. JC–?; B–Davenport; C–[J.W.] Wallack Jr; A–Boniface. Repeated 16 Dec.
15 January 1862	Niblo's Garden, New York. JC–Ryer; B–Davenport; C–[J.W.] Wallack Jr; A–Wheatley. Repeated 16, 17 Jan.

6 November 1862	Sadler's Wells. JC–Edgar; B–Phelps; C–Creswick; A–[E.] Phelps.
25 November 1864	Winter Garden, New York. JC–Varrey; B–[E.] Booth; C–[J.B.] Booth; A–[J.W.] Booth.
6 April 1865	Drury Lane. JC–?; B–Phelps; C–Montgomery; A–Anderson. Repeated 8 Apr.
4 September 1865	New Bowery, New York. JC–?; B–Grisdale; C–Thompson; A–Boniface.
28 October 1865	Drury Lane. JC–?; B–Phelps; C–Swinbourne; A–Anderson. Repeated 30, 31 Oct.; 1, 2, 3 Nov.
12 November 1866	Prince's Theatre, Manchester. No cast-list.
30 September 1868	Stadt-Theatre, New York. JC–Lange; B–Dombrowsky; C–Collmer; A–Hendrick.
5 September 1870	Niblo's Garden, New York. JC–Hamilton; B–Davenport; C–Barrett; A–Montgomery. Repeated 7, 8, 10 Sept. (JC–Levick).
26 April 1871	Boston Theatre. JC–Aldrich; B–Creswick; C–Bennett; A–Montgomery.
25 December 1871	Booth's Theatre, New York. JC–Waller; B–[E.] Booth; C–Barrett; A–Bangs. 19 Feb.–2 Mar. 1872: C–[J.B.] Booth. 4–9 Mar. 1872: B–Creswick; C–[E.] Booth. 11–16 Mar. 1872: B–Bangs; C–Creswick; A–[E.] Booth.
27 March 1872	Walnut Street Theatre, Philadelphia. JC–Morrison; B–Bangs; C–Walcot; A–[E.] Booth.
4 October 1872	Davidson Theatre, Milwaukee. JC–Vroom; B–Lane; C–Barrett; A–Hanley.
22 October 1872	DeBar's Opera House, New Orleans. JC–[J.] Barrett; B–Robinson; C–[L.] Barrett; A–Norton.
7 December 1872	DeBar's Grand Opera, St Louis. JC–Knowles; B–Krone; C–Barrett; A–Norton.
20 October 1873	Park Theatre, Brooklyn. JC–Plympton; B–Sheridan; C–Barrett; A–Norton.
29 May 1874	Boston Theatre. JC–Richmond; B–Norton; C–Barrett; A–Murdoch.
27 December 1875	Booth's Theatre, New York. JC–Levick; B–Davenport; C–Barrett; A–Bangs.
22 April 1876	Academy of Music, Brooklyn. JC–Levick; B–Davenport; C–Barrett; A–Warde.
22 May 1876	Booth's Theatre, New York. JC–Levick; B–Davenport; C–Barrett; A–Bangs.
2 October 1876	California Theatre, San Francisco. JC–Edwards; B–McCullough; C–Keene; A–[E.] Booth.
27 November 1876	Brooklyn Theatre. JC–Collier; B–Davenport; C–Barrett; A–Warde.
19 March 1878	Boston Museum. JC–McDowell; B–Barron; C–Barrett; A–Cotter.

25 May 1878   Booth's Theatre, New York. JC–Morton; B–McCul-
                     lough; C–Levick; A–Warde.
27 November 1878   Park Theatre, Brooklyn. JC–Little; B–McCullough;
                     C–Hardie; A–Stuart.
13 January 1879   Boston Theatre. JC–Price, B–McCullough; C–James;
                     A–Edwards.
1 October 1879   Grand   Opera   House,   Chicago.   JC–Langdon;
                     B–McCullough; C–Lane; A–Warde.
2 December 1880   Park Theatre, Brooklyn. JC–?; B–James; C–Barrett;
                     A–Bock.
18 March 1881   Grand Opera House, New York. JC–?; B–James;
                     C–Barrett; A–Bock. Repeated 19 Mar.
30 May 1881   Drury Lane. Meiningen Court Company. JC–Richard;
                     B–Nesper; C–Teller; A–Barnay. Repeated 3, 23, 30
                     June; 8, 20 July.
14 October 1881   Haverly's Fifth Avenue Theatre, New York. JC–Skin-
                     ner; B–James; C–Barrett; A–Bock. Repeated 15 Oct.
2 January 1882   Academy of Music, New York. JC–Skinner; B–James;
                     C–Barrett; A–Bock.
7 March 1882   Haverly's Fifth Avenue Theatre, New York. JC–Skin-
                     ner; B–James; C–Barrett; A–Bock.
20 December 1882   Windsor Theatre. JC–?; B–?; C–Barrett; A–?
10 March 1883   Grand Opera House, New York. JC–?; B–?; C–Barrett;
                     A–?
19 March 1883   Thalia Theatre, New York. JC–Alexander; B–Reinau;
                     C–Kierschner; A–Barnay. Repeated 21, 23, 26 Mar.
12 April 1883   Niblo's Garden. JC–Vance; B–McCullough; C–Lane;
                     A–Collier.
30 April 1883   Dramatic Festival, Cincinnati. JC–James; B–McCul-
                     lough; C–Barrett; A–Murdoch.
21 April 1884   Second Dramatic Festival, Cincinnati. JC–Hanford;
                     B–Warde; C–Hill; A–Keene.
26 January 1885   Star Theatre, New York. JC–Springer; B–James;
                     C–Barrett; A–Mosley. Repeated until 7 Feb.
25 January 1886   Boston Museum. JC–Kent; B–Booth; C–Barron;
                     A–Mason.
22 February 1886   Star Theatre, New York. JC–Robertson; B–Sheridan;
                     C–Barrett; A–Mosley. Repeated 23, 24, 27 Feb.
26 February 1886   Fifth Avenue Theatre, New York. JC–Kent; B–Booth;
                     C–Barron; A–Mason. Repeated 27 Feb.
31 August 1886   Grand Opera House, New York. JC–?; B–?; C–?;
                     A–Jones.
4 September 1886   Star Theatre, New York. JC–?; B–?; C–Barrett; A–?
                     Repeated 23 Sept.
11 June 1887   Windsor Theatre, New York. No cast-list.
26 December 1887   Academy of Music, New York. JC–Lane; B–Booth;
                     C–Barrett; A–Buckley.

31 March 1888	Salt Lake City Theatre. JC–Lane; B–[E.] Booth; C–Barrett; A–Hanford.
9 April 1888	National Standard Theatre. JC–Bentinck; B–[E.] Tearle; C–Lever; A–Paley. Repeated 11, 13 Apr.
23 April 1888	Sadler's Wells. JC–Bentinck; B–[E.] Tearle; C–Lever; A–Paley.
14 May 1888	Amphion Academy, New York. JC–Lane; B–[E.] Booth; C–Barrett; A–Hanford. Repeated 19 May.
15 June 1888	Windsor Theatre, New York. JC–Jackson; B–Collier; C–Lane; A–Keene.
10 December 1888	Fifth Avenue Theatre, New York. JC–Lane; B–[E.] Booth; C–Barrett; A–Hanford. Nightly until 22 Dec. Repeated 25 Dec. (mat.) and 2 Jan.
12 February 1889	Colosseum Theatre. JC–Bentinck; B–[E.] Tearle; C–Gathercole; A–Paley.
27 March 1889	Amphion Academy, New York. JC–Vroom; B–Booth; C–Barrett; A–Lane.
22 April 1889	Shakespeare Memorial Theatre. JC–Beverly; B–[O.] Tearle; C–Lever; A–[F.B.] Conway.
30 April 1889 (mat.)	People's Theatre, New York. JC–Jackson; B–Elliot; C–Learock; A–Keene.
27 May 1889	Sadler's Wells. JC–Bentinck; B–[E.] Tearle; C–Gathercole; A–Paley.
10 February 1890	Lee Avenue Academy, New York. No cast-list.
20 February 1890	Fourteenth Street Theatre, New York. JC–Hennig; B–Keene; C–Learock; A–Humphrey.
25 March 1890	Windsor Theatre, New York. JC–Leighton; B–James; C–Ferry; A–Mosley.
5 March 1891	Broadway Theatre, New York. JC–Vroom; B–Booth; C–Barrett; A–Lane. Repeated 6 Mar.
17 November 1891	Thalia Theatre, New York. JC–Knorr; B–Pfeil; C–Kober; A–Tichy.
15 January 1892	People's Theatre, New York. JC–Boag; B–?; C–?; A–Downing.
16 April 1892	New Olympic. JC–Bentinck; B–[E.] Tearle; C–Scarth; A–Hardy.
20 April 1892	Shakespeare Memorial Theatre. JC–Lewis; B–Swete; C–Mollison; A–Benson.
25 September 1893	Star Theatre, New York. JC–Kyle; B–James; C–Herman; A–Warde. Repeated 26, 27 (mat.), 30 (mat.) Sept.
4 December 1893	Boston Museum. JC–Wright; B–James; C–Herman; A–Warde.
27 November 1894	Prince's Theatre, Bristol. JC–Fitzgerald; B–Calvert; C–Rodney; A–Benson.
9 March 1896	Broadway Theatre, New York. JC–Dixon; B–Malone; C–Jewett; A–Miln.

21 April 1896	Shakespeare Memorial Theatre. JC–Fitzgerald; B–Asche; C–Rodney; A–Benson.
13 November 1896	Star Theatre, Buffalo. JC–Temple; B–Ahrendt; C–Keene; A–Hanford.
22 January 1898	Her Majesty's. JC–Fulton; B–Waller; C–McLeay; A–Tree.
11 April 1898	Shakespeare Memorial Theatre. JC–Fitzgerald; B–Asche; C–Rodney; A–Benson.
12 April 1898	Star Theatre, New York. No cast-list.
27 September 1898	Grand Opera House, Chicago. JC–?; B–James; C–?; A–Warde. Repeated 28 Sept. (mat.).
21 April 1899	Herald Square Theatre, New York. JC–Milton; B–MacLean; C–Wolfe; A–Hanford.
30 August 1900	Theatre-Royal, Birmingham. JC–Lowe; B–[O.] Tearle; C–Shepherd; A–[C.] Tearle.
6 September 1900	Her Majesty's. JC–Carson; B–Waller; C–Taber; A–Tree.
14 October 1902	Grand Opera House, Chicago. JC–Greenaway; B–Mansfield; C–Johnstone; A–Forrest.
1 December 1902	Herald Square Theatre, New York. JC–Greenaway; B–Mansfield; C–Haworth; A–Forrest.
27 April 1904	Shakespeare Memorial Theatre. JC–Hampden; B–Whitby; C–Keightley; A–Benson.
29 April 1905	His Majesty's. JC–Neville; B–Gill; C–Harding; A–Tree.
20 November 1905	Mendelssohn Hall, New York. Ben Greet Players.
4 January 1906	Ford's Theatre, Baltimore. JC–Lindsley; B–Mantell; C–Campbell; A–McGinn.
26 February 1906	Castle Square Theatre, Boston. JC–McVay; B–Craig; C–Waldron; A–Mackay.
25 April 1906	Shakespeare Memorial Theatre. JC–Buchanan; B–Pittar; C–Keightley; A–Benson.
28 April 1906	His Majesty's. JC–Neville; B–Gill; C–Harding; A–Tree.
29 October 1906	Castle Square Theatre, Boston. JC–Waldron; B–Hansel; C–Johnson; A–Miller.
26 November 1906	Academy of Music, New York. JC–Lindsley; B–Mantell; C–Owen; A–McGinn.
21 March 1907	Garden Theatre, New York. Ben Greet Players. Repeated 22, 23; 3, 6 April.
25 April 1907	His Majesty's. JC–Neville; B–Harding; C–Gill; A–Tree.
29 April 1907	New Amsterdam Theatre, New York. JC–Lindsley; B–Mantell; C–Burby; A–McGinn.
2 May 1908	Shakespeare Memorial Theatre. JC–Carrington; B–Warburton; C–Buchanan; A–Benson.

3 September 1908	Theatre-Royal, Bolton. JC–Neill; B–Marsh; C–Ryde; A–Wilkie.
19 April 1909	Shakespeare Memorial Theatre. JC–Carrington; B–Warburton; C–Keightley; A–Benson.
26 July 1909	His Majesty's. JC–Haviland; B–Gill; C–Harding; A–Tree.
17 January 1910	Garden Theatre, New York. Ben Greet Players.
2 April 1910	His Majesty's. JC–Haviland; B–Harding; C–Ainley; A–Tree.
4 May 1910	Shakespeare Memorial Theatre. JC–[G.] Rathbone; B–[O.] Stuart; C–Maxon; A–Benson.
27 July 1910	Shakespeare Memorial Theatre. JC–Carrington; B–Stuart; C–Maxon; A–Benson.
17 April 1911	Daly's Theatre, New York. JC–Lindsley; B–Mantell; C–Sawyer; A–Leiber.
25 April 1911	Shakespeare Memorial Theatre. JC–Carrington; B–Stuart; C–Ainley; A–Benson.
5 May 1911	Shakespeare Memorial Theatre. JC–Carrington; B–Brydone; C–Keightley; A–Benson.
22 May 1911	His Majesty's. JC–George; B–Bourchier; C–Gill; A–Tree.
11 September 1911	Manhattan Opera House, New York. JC–Lindsley; B–Mantell; C–Crawley; A–Leiber.
29 April 1912	Shakespeare Memorial Theatre. JC–Johnston; B–Carrington; C–Ayrton; A–Benson.
3 June 1912	His Majesty's. JC–George; B–Gill; C–Harding; A–Tree.
14 October 1912	Majestic Theatre, Brooklyn. JC–Lindsley; B–Mantell; C–Royce; A–Leiber.
4 November 1912	Lyric Theatre, New York. JC–Mellish; B–Power; C–Keenan; A–Faversham.
27 January 1913	Garrick Theatre, Detroit. JC–Mellish; B–Churchill; C–Keenan; A–Faversham.
4 February 1913	Shubert Theatre, New York. JC–Lindsley; B–Mantell; C–Royce; A–Leiber.
29 April 1913	Court Theatre. JC–Wiltshire; B–Bland; C–[G.] Tearle; A–Berry.
7 May 1913	Majestic Theatre, Brooklyn. JC–Mellish; B–MacLean; C–Arden; A–Faversham.
2 June 1913	Castle Square Theatre, Boston. JC–Ernst; B–Carleton; D–Meek; A–Craig.
23 June 1913	His Majesty's. JC–George; B–Gill; C–Merivale; A–Tree.
17 October 1913	Gaiety Theatre, Manchester. JC–Wills; B–Casson; C–[J.] Shaw; A–Vigors.
12 November 1913	The Potter Theatre, Santa Barbara. JC–Tracey; B–MacLean; C–Rowan; A–Faversham.

11 August 1914	Shakespeare Memorial Theatre. JC–Conrick; B–Carrington; C–Ayrton; A–Benson.
25 January 1915	Boston Opera House. JC–Tonge; B–MacLean; C–Jewett; A–Relph.
1 February 1915	44th Street Theatre, New York. JC–Lindsley; B–Mantell; C–Burke; A–Leiber.
19 April 1915	Shakespeare Memorial Theatre. JC–Johnston; B–Stuart; C–Warburton; A–Benson.
26 April 1915	Old Vic. JC–Grain; B–Stack; C–White; A–Robertshaw. Repeated 28 Apr.
22 March 1916	Old Vic. JC–Walker; B–Stack; C–Atkins; A–Cassel. Repeated 23, 24 Mar.
2 May 1916	Drury Lane. Shakespeare Tercentenary Performance. JC–Benson; B–Bourchier; C–[H.B.] Irving; A–Ainley.
19 May 1916	Beechwood Amphitheatre, Hollywood. Shakespeare Tercentenary Performance. JC–Roberts; B–Power; C–Keenan; A–Farnum.
16 April 1917	44th Street Theatre, New York. No cast-list.
7 November 1917	Old Vic. JC–Ross; B–Stanley; C–Sargent; A–Thorndike. Repeated 8, 12, 14, 15, 16, 20 Nov. (first evening performance 12 Nov.).
15 March 1918	Cort Theatre, New York. JC–Kyle; B–Power; C–Keightley; A–Hampden. Repeated 16, 22, 23 Mar.; 5, 6, 12, 13 Apr. (series of matinées).
10 March 1919	Old Vic. JC–Barnett; B–Thorndike; C–Milton; A–Warburton. Repeated 12, 13, 14, 15, 17, 19, 20, 21 Mar.; 25, 26 Apr.
5 August 1919	Shakespeare Memorial Theatre. JC–Hannam-Clark; B–Dale; C–[B.] Rathbone; A–Carrington.
9 January 1920	St James's. JC–Boyne; B–Gill; C–Rosmer; A–Ainley.
26 January 1920	Old Vic. JC–Paterson; B–Shaw; C–Warburton; A–Thorndike. Repeated 31 Jan.; 2, 4, 5, 6 Feb.
7 June 1920	Prince's Theatre, Manchester. JC–Harris; B–Gardiner; C–Rains; A–Ainley.
28 December 1920	Lexington Theatre, New York. JC–Roberts; B–Hall; C–Burke; A–Leiber.
17 January 1921	Old Vic. JC–Harker; B–Harvey; C–Atkins; A–Milton. Repeated 19, 20, 21 Jan.
30 December 1921	Lexington Theatre, New York. JC–Quin; B–Hall; C–Burke; A–Leiber.
16 January 1922	48th Street Theatre, New York. No cast-list.
24 January 1922 (mat.)	Savoy Theatre. JC–Vernon; B–Kinnell; C–Dunstan; A–Baynton.
19 April 1922	Shakespeare Memorial Theatre (Spring Festival). JC–Lathbury; B–Colbourne; C–Stack; A–Holloway.
24 April 1922	New National Theatre, Washington. JC–Lindsley, B–Mantell; C–Deering; A–Alexander.

29 July 1922	Shakespeare Memorial Theatre (Summer Festival). Cast as for Spring Festival.
6 November 1922	Old Vic. JC–Atkins; B–Burbidge; C–Harvey; A–Walter. Repeated 8, 9, 10, 18 Nov.
29 January 1923	Alexandra Palace Theatre. JC–Brook; B–[W.] Anderson; C–Stirling; A–Oscar.
8 February 1926	Old Vic. JC–Porter; B–Yarrow; C–Holloway; A–Vosper. Repeated 10, 11, 12, 15, 17, 18, 19, 20, 22, 24, 25, 26 Feb.
16 July 1926	Shakespeare Memorial Theatre (Summer Festival). JC–Wicksteed; B–Skillan; C–Worrall-Thompson; A–Ayrton.
17 September 1926	Hollywood Bowl, Hollywood. JC–Gordon; B–MacLean; C–Humphrey; A–Farnum. Repeated 18 Sept.
6 June 1927	New Amsterdam Theatre, New York. Players' Revival. JC–Courtleigh; B–Power; C–Rathbone; A–Rennie.
25 January 1928	Capitol Theatre, Albany. JC–Adams; B–Mantell; C–Conklin; A–Alexander.
11 April 1928	Shakespeare Memorial Theatre (Spring Festival). JC–Wicksteed; B–Maxon; C–Hayes; A–Walter.
12 July 1928	Shakespeare Memorial Theatre (Summer Festival). Cast as for Spring Festival.
21 October 1929	Repertory Theatre of Boston. JC–Kyle; B–Taylor; C–Rhea; A–Nourse.
22 October 1929	Pasadena Community Playhouse, Pasadena. JC–Levison; B–Brown; C–Walgamott; A–Bushman. Repeated until 2 Nov.
20 January 1930	Old Vic. JC–Wills; B–Williams; C–Wolfit; A–Gielgud. Repeated 22, 23, 24, 25, 27, 29, 30, 31 Jan.; 3, 5, 6, 7, 8 Feb.
3 April 1930	Shubert Theatre, New York. Chicago Civic Shakespeare Society. JC–Jenks; B–Courtleigh; C–Cecil; A–Leiber.
22 April 1930	Shakespeare Memorial Theatre (Spring Festival). JC–Wicksteed; B–Hayes; C–Maxon; A–Walter.
12 July 1930	Shakespeare Memorial Theatre (Summer Festival). Cast as for Spring Festival.
17 November 1931	Royale Theatre, New York. Chicago Civic Shakespeare Society. JC–Jenks; B–Power; C–de Cordoba; A–Leiber.
25 January 1932	Old Vic. JC–Williams; B–Richardson; C–Speaight; A–Harris.
25 January 1932	'Q' Theatre. JC–?; B–Gill; C–West; A–Lewisohn.
8 February 1932	His Majesty's. JC–Harding; B–Gill; C–Holloway;

A–[G.] Tearle. From 20 Feb., A–Skillan. From 2 Mar., B–Tearle. From 26 Mar., B–Dale; A–Tearle. Run ended 2 Apr.

26 April 1932   Shakespeare Memorial Theatre (Spring Festival). JC–Ayrton; B–Isham; C–Maxon; A–Walter.

28 June 1932   Shakespeare Memorial Theatre (Summer Festival). Cast as for Spring Festival.

19 December 1932   The Shakespeare Theatre, New York. JC–Joyner; B–Cooksey; C–Austen; A–[S.] Smith.

12 January 1933   The Guildhall, Winchester. JC–Ledgard; B–O'Hanlon; C–[S.] Thompson; A–Tindall.

20 February 1934   Alhambra. JC–Owen; B–Gill; C–Dyall; A–Tearle.

19 April 1934   Shakespeare Memorial Theatre (Spring Festival). JC–Maxon; B–Wyse; C–Holloway; A–Porter.

22 October 1934   Gate Theatre, Dublin. JC–Edwards; B–Mason; C–Gill; A–MacLiammoir.

22 October 1935   Old Vic. JC–Trouncer; B–Genn; C–Devlin; A–Swinley.

14 April 1936   Shakespeare Memorial Theatre. JC–Eccles; B–Dale; C–Wolfit; A–Glenville.

13 July 1936   Pasadena Community Playhouse, Pasadena. JC–McKinley; B–Brown; C–Ankrum; A–King.

22 October 1936   Prince's Theatre, Bristol. JC–Wood; B–Trollope; C–Layne-Smith; A–Yarrow.

5 July 1937   Open Air Theatre, Regent's Park. JC–Porter; B–Portman; C–Browne; A–Swinley.

26 July 1937   CBS Music Box Theatre. Radio Production. JC–Denny; B–Mitchell; C–Rains; A–[R.] Massey.

6 November 1937   Mercury Theatre, New York. JC–Holland; B–Welles; C–Gabel; A–Colouris.

16 May 1938   Festival Theatre, Cambridge. JC–Clark; B–Wattis; C–Longman; A–Young.

24 July 1938   BBC Radio Production. JC–Milton; B–Shaw; C–Ireland; A–Clarke-Smith.

29 November 1939   Embassy Theatre. JC–Hudd; B–Kenton; C–Evans; A–Portman. Transferred to His Majesty's 23 Dec. B–Tearle.

15 April 1941   Shakespeare Memorial Theatre. JC–Souper; B–Hayes; C–Holloway; A–Kenton.

19 January 1948   Sheffield Repertory Co. JC–Wilson; B–Davies; C–Wearing; A–MacNee.

19 April 1948   Theatre Royal, Huddersfield. JC–Milton; B–Howlett; C–Foster; A–Hepton.

19 April 1948   Opera House, Scarborough. JC–Lovell; B–Dyce; C–Whiting; A–Norris.

12 March 1949   CBS-TV. JC–Post; B–Keith; C–O'Shaughnessy; A–Bourneuf.

19 September 1949	Kings, Hammersmith. JC–Meddings; B–Wolfit; C–Clarke; A–Johnson.
6 October 1949	Woodstock, New York. The Margaret Webster Shakespeare Company. JC–Rolf; B–Lewis; C–Straub; A–Clark. Tour ended in New Haven, Conn., 29 Apr. 1950.
25 April 1950	Theatre Royal, Bristol. Bristol Old Vic Co. JC–Cannan; B–Coulouris; C–Winter; A–King-Wood.
2 May 1950	Shakespeare Memorial Theatre. JC–Cruickshank; B–Andrews; C–Gielgud; A–Quayle.
20 June 1950	The Arena, New York. JC–Braham; B–Holland; C–Rathbone; A–Ryder.
16 October 1950	Colchester Repertory Theatre. JC–Woodfield; B–Van Eyssen; C–Rye; A–Aldridge.
1 December 1952	Royalty Theatre, Morecambe Repertory Theatre. JC–Pinney; B–Stephens; C–Thorpe; A–Wyatt.
24 February 1953	Old Vic. JC–Campbell; B–Devlin; C–Rogers; A–Bailey.
29 June 1953	Westminster Theatre. The Elizabethan Theatre Company. JC–Jeffrey; B–David; C–George; A–Robertson.
8 March 1954	Nottingham Playhouse. JC–Crowden; B–Stone; C–Barrington; A–Godfrey.
26 April 1954	Oldham Repertory Theatre. JC–Bennett; B–Magill; C–Lomax; A–Kennaby.
20 April 1955	Cleveland Playhouse. JC–Allman; B–Cover; C–Sostek; A–Corzatte.
27 June 1955	Shakespeare Festival, Stratford, Ontario. JC–Christie; B–Greene; C–Bochner; A–Davis.
12 July 1955	American Shakespeare Festival, Stratford, Conn. JC–Hatfield; B–Massey; C–Palance; A–Plummer.
22 August 1955	Old Vic at Lyceum, Edinburgh. JC–Cross; B–Rogers; C–Wordsworth; A–Neville. Opened at Old Vic, London, 7 Sept.
14 February 1956	Citizens' Theatre, Glasgow. JC–Maguire; B–Judd; C–Keir; A–Gale.
14 February 1956	Library Theatre, Manchester. JC–Barry; B–Warwick; C–Stephens; A–Brett.
17 April 1956	Birmingham Repertory Theatre. JC–Rowe; B–MacKintosh; C–Bayldon; A–[G.] Taylor.
25 February 1957	Gaiety Theatre, Dublin. JC–Edwards; M–McMaster; C–Gaffney; A–MacLiammoir.
11 March 1957	Guildford Theatre. JC–[R.] Mason; B–Howell; C–Kelsey; A–Chinnery.
28 May 1957	Shakespeare Memorial Theatre. JC–Luckham; B–Clunes; C–Keen; A–Johnson.
23 October 1957	The Shakespearewrights, New York. JC–Walker; B–Graves; C–Ruskin; A–Mandan.

8 October 1958   Old Vic. JC–May; B–Phillips; C–Hordern; A–Lewis.
15 August 1959   New York Shakespeare Festival. JC–Cotsworth;
                     B–Harkins; C–Graves; A–Madden.
11 August 1960   Queen's Theatre. The Youth Theatre. JC–Shrapnel;
                     B–Stacy; C–Allkins; A–Weston.
21 February 1962   Hechscher Theatre, New York. JC–Raphel; B–Hicks;
                     C–McGonagill; A–Roat.
17 April 1962   Old Vic. JC–O'Conor; B–Gregson; C–Eddison;
                     A–Good.
22 May 1962   Nottingham Playhouse. JC–Magill; B–George; C–Cur-
                     ram; A–Spenser.
30 August 1962   Sadler's Wells. National Youth Theatre. JC–Rowe;
                     B–Stacy; C–Allkins; A–Cadman.
13 November 1962   Bristol Old Vic. JC–Tuckey; B–Eddington; C–Barron;
                     A–Burke.
9 April 1963   Royal Shakespeare Theatre. JC–Dotrice; B–Fleming;
                     C–Cusack; A–Haigh.
24, 31 May 7 June 1963   BBC-TV. Three-part performance in series of revivals
                     of Shakespeare's Roman plays titled 'The Spread of the
                     Eagle'. JC–[B.] Jones; B–Eddington; C–Cushing;
                     A–Michell.
16 September 1963   Scala Theatre. National Youth Theatre. JC–Rowe;
                     B–Stacy; C–Allkins; A–Cadman.
26 November 1964   Royal Court. JC–Curran; B–Bannen; C–McKenna;
                     A–[D.] Massey.
16 June 1965   Shakespeare Festival, Stratford, Ontario. JC–Shaw,
                     B–Hutt; C–Donat; A–Gerussi.
23 June 1966   American Shakespeare Festival, Stratford, Conn.
                     JC–Sommer; B–Watson; C–Sparrer; A–Joyce.
21 September 1966   Nottingham Playhouse. JC–Innocent; B–Neal;
                     C–Hancock; A–Turner.
15 November 1966   Belgrade Theatre, Coventry. JC–Wilkinson;
                     B–Danby; C–Needham; A–Forgeham.
3 March 1967   Tavistock Repertory Company, Tower Theatre.
                     JC–Walker; B–Marlow; C–Barnes; A–Mudie.
7 March 1967   Victoria Theatre, Stoke-on-Trent. JC–Collins;
                     B–Daniels; C–Hayes; A–Martin.
3 April 1968   Royal Shakespeare Theatre. JC–[B.] Mason;
                     B–Ingham; C–Richardson; A–Thomas. Transferred to
                     the Aldwych 20 Nov., 1968.
12 May 1969   New Theatre, Bromley. JC–Purcell; B–Hely; C–Dar-
                     row; A–Voss.
26 June 1969   Guthrie Theatre, Minneapolis. JC–Pastene; B–Hamil-
                     ton; C–Ramsey; A–Keating.
7 September 1970   Collegiate Theatre. National Youth Theatre.
                     JC–Payne; B–Smerczac; C–O'Brien; A–Phillips.
13 March 1972   New Theatre. The Oxford and Cambridge Shakespeare

	Company. JC–James-Moore; B–Hilton; C–Snodin; A–Harris.
2 May 1972	Royal Shakespeare Theatre. JC–Dignam; B–Wood; C–Stewart; A–Johnson.
17 August 1972	Young Vic. JC–Beale; B–Hawthorne; C–McEnery; A–Bennett.
2 November 1972	Harrogate Theatre. JC–Brown; B–Lawton; C–Marinker; A–Shaw.
21 July 1973	Aldwych Theatre. JC–Dignam; B–Wood; C–Stewart; A–Johnson. Revival of 1972 RSC production with altered sets.
26 July 1973	American Shakespeare Festival, Stratford, Conn. JC–Pendleton; B–Kerr; C–Richardson; A–Levin.

NOTES

Introduction

1 Thomas Rymer, *Critical Works*, ed. Curt A. Zimansky, New Haven, 1956, p. 165.
2 *Saturday Review*, 29 January 1898.
3 Rymer, *Critical Works*, p. 165.
4 John Dennis, *Critical Works*, ed. Edward Niles Hooker, Baltimore, 1939, II, pp. 5, 10.
5 Mrs Elizabeth Montague, *An Essay on the Writings and Genius of Shakespeare*, 1769, p. 232.
6 William Hazlitt, *Characters of Shakespeare's Plays*, 1818, p. 33. *The Complete Works*, ed. P. P. Howe, 1930, IV, p. 195.
7 Charles Gildon, Preface to *Julius Caesar, The Works of Mr. William Shakespeare*, ed. Nicholas Rowe, 1710, VII, p. 377.
8 Dennis, *Critical Works*, II, p. 10.
9 Leigh Hunt, *Dramatic Criticism (1808–1831)*, ed. Lawrence Husten Houtchens and Carolyn Washburn Houtchens, 1950, p. 66.
10 Gildon, Preface to *Julius Caesar*, p. 377.
11 Montague, *Writings and Genius of Shakespeare*, p. 229.
12 Samuel Taylor Coleridge, *Shakespearean Criticism*, ed. Thomas Middleton Raysor, 1960, I, p. 14.
13 Hunt, *Dramatic Criticism*, p. 66.
14 A. C. Swinburne, *A Study of Shakespeare*, 1879, p. 159.
15 Gildon, Preface to *Julius Caesar*, VII, p. 377.
16 D. E. Baker, *Biographia Dramatica*, 1782, II, p. 177.
17 Gildon, Preface to *Julius Caesar*, VII, p. 363.
18 Dennis, *Critical Works*, II, p. 5.
19 Montague, *Writings and Genius of Shakespeare*, p. 211, 228.
20 Francis Gentleman, *The Dramatic Censor*, 1770, II, p. 1.
21 Rymer, *Critical Works*, pp. 166–7.
22 Gentleman, *The Dramatic Censor*, 1770, II, pp. 3, 7. Cuts and alterations in eighteenth-century acting editions on the grounds of impropriety of expression will be more fully treated in chapter 2.
23 Charles Gildon, *Miscellaneous Letters and Essays*, 1694, Sig. F 5ʳ.
24 John Dryden, Preface to *Troilus and Cressida*, 1695, Sig. aʳ. Reprinted by W. P. Ker in *Essays of John Dryden*, 1900, vol. I.
25 Samuel Johnson, *Johnson on Shakespeare*, ed. Walter Raleigh, 1931, p. 179.

26 Baker, *Biographia Dramatica*, II, p. 177.
27 Coleridge, *Shakespearean Criticism*, I, p. 116.
28 Gildon, Preface to *Julius Caesar*, VII, pp. 377–8.
29 Montague, *Writings and Genius of Shakespeare*, p. 227.
30 Hazlitt, *Characters of Shakespeare's Plays*, IV, pp. 196, 197.
31 Gildon, Preface to *Julius Caesar*, VII, pp. 377–8.
32 Hazlitt, *Characters of Shakespeare's Plays*, IV, p. 195.
33 Hunt, *Dramatic Criticism*, p. 66.
34 Johnson, *Johnson on Shakespeare*, p. 15.
35 Ibid., p. 30.
36 Hermann Ulrici, *Shakespeare's Dramatic Art*, trans. A. J. W. M[orrison], 1846, p. 355.
37 See G. G. Gervinus, *Shakespeare Commentaries*, trans. F. E. Bunnètt, 1863; A. Lindner, 'Die Dramatische Einheit im Julius Caesar', *Jahrbuch*, II (1866), pp. 90–5; and Edward Dowden, *Shakspere: His Mind and Art*, 1875.
38 H. N. Hudson, *Shakespeare: His Life, Art, and Characters*, 1872, II, p. 234.
39 Richard G. Moulton, *Shakespeare as a Dramatic Artist*, 1885, p. 169.
40 René E. Fortin discusses this trend in '*Julius Caesar*: An Experiment in Point of View', *Shakespeare Quarterly*, XIX (Autumn 1968).
41 J. C. Maxwell outlines major critical studies in the first half of this century in 'Shakespeare's Roman Plays: 1900–1956', *Shakespeare Survey*, 10 (1957).
42 Harley Granville-Barker, *Prefaces to Shakespeare*, first series, 1927.
43 *Shakespeare Quarterly*, V (Summer 1954).
44 Sir Mark Hunter, 'Politics and Character in Shakespeare's "Julius Caesar"', *Essays By Divers Hands, Transactions of the Royal Society of Literature*, X (1931), p. 114.
45 Ernest Schanzer, *The Problem Plays of Shakespeare*, New York, 1963, p. 32.
46 Mark Van Doren, *Shakespeare*, New York, 1953, p. 161.
47 Gordon Ross Smith, 'Brutus, Virtue, and Will', *Shakespeare Quarterly*, X (Summer 1959), p. 378.
48 William R. Bowden, 'The Mind of Brutus', *Shakespeare Quarterly*, XVII (Winter 1966), p. 67.
49 Ernest Schanzer, 'The Tragedy of Shakespeare's Brutus', *ELH*, 22 (March 1955), p. 1.
50 John Palmer (*Political Characters of Shakespeare*, 1945) and J. I. M. Stewart (*Character and Motive in Shakespeare*, 1949) also hold relatively favourable opinions of Brutus.
51 T. J. B. Spencer, *Shakespeare: The Roman Plays*, 1963, p. 19.
52 See J. E. Phillips, *The State in Shakespeare's Greek and Roman Plays*, 1940; Brents Stirling, *The Populace in Shakespeare*, 1949, and 'Or Else Were This a Savage Spectacle', in his *Unity in Shakespearian Tragedy*, 1957; T. J. B. Spencer, 'Shakespeare and the Elizabethan Romans', *Shakespeare Survey*, 10 (1957); Geoffrey Bullough, *Narrative and Dramatic Sources of Shakespeare*, V (1964); Northrop Frye, *Fools of Time*, 1965; and L. C. Knights, 'Personality and Politics in *Julius Caesar*', *Further Explorations*, 1965.
53 British Museum, MS 22, 629. See G. Blakemore Evans, 'The Problem of

Brutus: An Eighteenth Century Solution', *Studies in Honour of T. W. Baldwin*, Urbana, 1958.

54 *The Works of John Sheffield, Earl of Mulgrave, Marquis of Normanby, and Duke of Buckingham*, 1723, vol. I.

55 François Voltaire, *Oeuvres Complètes*, Paris, 1877, vol. III.

56 *Caesar's Revenge* was first published in the posthumous *Works of the Late Aaron Hill, Esq.*, 1753, vol. I. The title-page asserts that it was played at Bath.

57 Lewis Casson staged an Elizabethan style *Caesar* for a brief run in Manchester in 1913. See chapter 9, n. 2.

58 I also mention Casca from time to time when his performance warrants attention. There is surprisingly little to be said of Portia and Calphurnia. Although they have been played by actresses of the calibre of Peg Woffington, Sybil Thorndike, and Edith Evans, no one has won much critical acclaim in these roles.

1. Seventeenth-century productions

1 E. K. Chambers, *The Elizabethan Stage*, 1923, II, p. 365.

2 e.g. John Dover Wilson, (Introduction to) *Julius Caesar*, Cambridge edition, 1949, pp. ix–x; E. K. Chambers, *William Shakespeare*, 1951, I, p. 397; T. S. Dorsch, (Introduction to) *Julius Caesar*, Arden edition, 1961, pp. vii–viii.

3 Chambers, *The Elizabethan Stage*, IV, p. 158.

4 Ibid., III, p. 309.

5 Ibid., IV, p. 216.

6 Ben Jonson, *Every Man Out of His Humour* (III.iv.32–3), ed. C. H. Herford and Percy Simpson, 1927. For a fuller treatment of Jonsonian references to Shakespeare and their implications, see J. Dover Wilson, 'Ben Jonson and *Julius Caesar*', *Shakespeare Survey* 2 (1949), 36–43.

7 *Shakespeare Jahrbuch*, XLIII (1907), p. 210.

8 E. Koeppel, *The Wisdome of Doctor Dodypoll*, Old English Drama: Students' Facsimile edition, Sig. E1ʳ, lines 26–7.

9 Ibid., Sig. D3ʳ, lines 16–19.

10 Ibid., Sig. B1ᵛ, lines 1–3.

11 Leonard Digges, *Poems: Written by Wil. Shake-speare Gent.*, 1640.

12 This is to suppose with most scholars that 'Caesars Tragedye' is Shakespeare's play. See *Julius Caesar*, ed. H. H. Furness, Jr, New Variorum edition, 1913, p. 437.

13 Chambers, *William Shakespeare*, II, p. 343.

14 *The Dramatic Records of Sir Henry Herbert*, ed. Joseph Quincy Adams, New Haven, 1917, pp. 75–7.

15 John Downes lists it as one of 'their Principal Old Stock Plays', but exactly what he means by 'old' is difficult to determine. *Roscius Anglicanus*, 1708, p. 8.

16 Downes, *Roscius Anglicanus.*, p. 8.

17 Allardyce Nicoll, *A History of English Drama*, 1952, I, p. 354.

18 It is likely that this cast-list refers to performances which took place some time

between 2 October 1669 and 25 January 1671/2, since the name of Richard Bell occurs. According to Professor Nicoll, Bell's name first appears in a livery warrant on the first date, and he died when the theatre burned on the second. See Nicoll, *History of English Drama*, I, pp. 298–9, 322.

19 Downes, *Roscius Anglicanus*, p. 8. A 1691 edition of *Julius Caesar* in the British Library (C131C14) contains a manuscript cast-list which includes Downes's cast and adds the following characters: Octavius Caesar–William Wintershall; Casca–Philip Griffin; Trebonius–Thomas Gradwell; Ligarius–Nicholas Burt; Decius Brutus–Cardell Goodman; Metellus Cimber–Thomas Clark; Cinna the Poet–Robert Shatterell; Flavius–Thomas Loveday; Plebeians–John Lacy, William Cartwright, and Walter Clun. The dating of this cast-list poses numerous problems, but it probably relates to a revival within two or three years after the issue of the warrant. See Edward A. Langhans, 'New Restoration Manuscript Casts', *Theatre Notebook*, XXVII (Summer 1973), pp. 149–57.

20 James Wright, *Historia Histrionica*, 1699, p. xxiv.

21 Ibid., p. xxix.

22 Downes, *Roscius Anglicanus*, p. 16.

23 Downes, *Roscius Anglicanus*, p. 16. Downes's comment gives us another clue to the frequency of *Julius Caesar* performances in the immediate post-Restoration period; for it seems unlikely that the perspicacious Killigrew would have missed any chance to present Hart in a part so suited to his powers and so profitable to the box-office.

24 '"Major" Mohun . . . is recorded as a boy apprenticed to Beeston, he was certainly at the Cockpit between 1637 and 1640'. Nicoll, *History of English Drama*, I, p. 288. See also Gerald Eades Bentley, *The Jacobean and Caroline Stage*, 1949, II, pp. 511–12, and Leslie Hotson, *The Commonwealth and Restoration Stage*, Cambridge, Mass., 1928, p. 198 passim.

25 Mohun summarizes his military career in a petition to Charles II following the union of the companies. See Nicoll, *History of English Drama*, I, p. 366.

26 Downes, *Roscius Anglicanus*, p. 17.

27 Francis Fane Jr, *Love in the Dark*, 1675. See also John Genest, *Some Account of the English Stage*, 1832, I, 376–7; Bentley, *Jacobean and Caroline Stage*, II, pp. 511–12; Cibber's *Apology*, ed. Edmund Bellchambers, 1822, note to pp. 80–3; Nicoll, *History of English Drama*, I, p. 67.

28 Cibber's *Apology*, ed. Bellchambers, note to p. 128.

29 According to Bellchambers (p. 130) he retired from the stage some time between 1695 and 1706.

30 George Powell, in his 'Epistle Dedicatory' to *The Treacherous Brothers*, 1690, makes the theatrical influence of Hart and Mohun abundantly clear:

as Old *Ben* ended his Grace with God bless me, and God bless *Ralph* . . . so some Modern Authors with the same Equity, might full as Pathetically have furnish'd out one Article of their Prayers, (not forgetting the present Props of the Stage) with God bless Mohun and God bless Hart, the good actors that got 'em their good third Days; and consequently more Patrons than the greatest gay Name in the Frontispiece of the proudest Dedication.   Sig. A2ᵛ

31 Of Hart's ability to establish memorable characterizations one admirer remarked that it was 'the sense of all mankind, that the best tragedies of the

English stage received their lustre from Mr. Hart's performance' (Henry Barton Baker, *Our Old Actors*, 1878, I, p. 49).

32 Little is known of Richard Bell, who played Caesar.

33 Langbaine recalls that the play was 'reviv'd and acted divers times in the reign of the late King Charles II' (Gerard Langbaine, *The Lives and Characters of the English Dramatic Poets*, 1702, p. 128).

34 See below.

35 It may have taken place at the Theatre Royal, Drury Lane or, according to Miss Boswell, at the Hall Theatre. See Eleanore Boswell, *The Restoration Court Stage*, Cambridge, Mass., 1932, p. 286, and *The London Stage*, Part I: *1660–1700*, ed. William Van Lennep, Carbondale, Illinois, 1960, p. 252.

36 Nicoll, *History of English Drama*, I, p. 346.

37 For the same period, Jaggard lists only two quarto editions of *Macbeth* (1687, 1689), and these Davenant's alteration, two of the Tate version of *King Lear* (1689, 1690), one of Dryden's *Othello* (1687), one of the Dryden–Davenant *Tempest* (1690), and one of Shadwell's *Timon of Athens* (1688). The other plays did not appear at all.

38 Henrietta C. Bartlett, 'Quarto Editions of *Julius Caesar*', *The Library*, third series, IV (1913), pp. 129, 130.

39 Hazelton Spencer, *Shakespeare Improved*, Cambridge, Mass., 1927, p. 362.

40 George C. D. Odell, *Shakespeare From Betterton to Irving*, 1920, I, p. 58.

41 See Francis Gentleman, *Julius Caesar*, Bell's Edition, 1773, p. 53.

42 This much is apparent from the acting edition. He may, however, have commenced playing the role soon after Hart's retirement in 1682.

43 Colley Cibber, *An Apology for the Life of Mr.*, ed. Robert W. Lowe, 1889, I, pp. 103–4.

44 Ibid., I, p. 104.

45 'The time of his retirement is not known ... He had left [the stage], however, before 1707, when Betterton and Underhill have been specified by Downes, as "being the only remains of the Duke of York's servants at that time before the public".' Bellchambers (ed.), Cibber's *Apology*, p. 130.

46 Cibber describes him as 'celebrated'. *Apology*, ed. Lowe, I, p. 79.

47 [Charles Gildon], *The Life of Mr. Thomas Betterton*, 1710, p. 84.

48 Cibber's *Apology*, ed. Lowe, I, pp. 153–4.

49 Ibid.

50 Nicoll, *History of English Drama*, I, p. 351.

51 Ibid., I, p. 336.

52 Perhaps John Verbruggen, who acted at Lincoln's Inn Fields from 1 Jan 1695/6 onwards (see Nicoll, *History of English Drama*, I, 339), and whose name occurs opposite the role of Cassius in the *Daily Courant* advertisement for the 1707 revival.

53 *The Daily Courant*, 14 February 1704.

54 For detailed discussion of post-Restoration dramatic tastes see: Allardyce Nicoll, *British Drama*, 1958, pp. 223–41; Allardyce Nicoll, 'Political Plays of the Restoration', *Modern Language Review*, XXI (1921), pp. 224–42; George

W. Whiting, 'The Condition of the London Theatres, 1679–83. A Reflection of the Political Situation', *Modern Philology*, XXVI (1927–8), pp. 195–206.

2. Eighteenth-century productions

1 In all, *Julius Caesar* was performed 163 times in the years 1701 to 1750 as compared with *Macbeth* (378), *Hamlet* (358), *Othello* (265), *1 Henry IV* (214), *The Merry Wives* (202), *Richard III* (200), *The Tempest* (186), *King Lear* (186), *Romeo and Juliet* (96), *Henry V* (49), *Richard II* (25), *Coriolanus* (16). These figures take into account performances in all versions. See Charles Beecher Hogan, *Shakespeare in the Theatre 1701–1800*, 1952, I, pp. 460–1.

2 Thomas Davies (*Memoirs of the Life of David Garrick*, 1774, p. 19) writes, 'I have seen the character of Cassius accurately delineated in Mr. Garrick's own hand-writing . . . and it is very probable that he had given his consent to act the part, but that, on serious reflection, he had renounced his intention, as the weight of applause, in the much-admired scene between these great men in the fourth act of the play, must have fallen to the share of Brutus. There was another reason for rejecting Cassius, which, in all probability had its force with him; he would never willingly put on Roman habit.' John Bernard claims that Earl Conyngham told him he had seen Garrick and Quin play Cassius and Brutus, perhaps in Bath (*Retrospections of the Stage*, 1830, II, p. 29).

3 See Allardyce Nicoll, *A History of English Drama*, 1952, II, pp. 19–21.

4 *A Collection and Selection of English Prologues and Epilogues*, 1779, III, pp. 1–2.

5 Not only did Booth and Wilks provide regular revivals at Drury Lane, but their financial success was responsible for a number of other productions as the rival playhouses were stirred to emulation.

6 Mrs Inchbald (*Remarks* [prefatory to] *Julius Caesar* [1808]) writes:

It has been thought advisable, for some years past, that this tragedy should not appear upon the stage.

When men's thoughts are deeply engaged on public events, historical occurrences, of a similar kind, are only held proper for the contemplation of such minds as know how to distinguish, and to appreciate, the good and evil with which they abound. Such discriminating judges do not compose the whole audience of a playhouse; therefore, when the circumstances of certain periods make certain incidents of history most interesting, those are the very seasons to interdict their exhibition.

7 No acting version will represent the text exactly as spoken, since they do not take into account readings either traditional or peculiar to certain actors. One such example is cited by Thomas Davies (*Dramatic Miscellanies*, 1783–4, II, p. 248):

Cassius. – What, durst not tempt him?
Brutus. For your life, you durst not.

In this last line of Brutus', the actors from time immemorial, have made a small alteration, which I suppose they imagined would convey the sentiment with stronger emphasis, and make a deeper impression on their auditors. Brutus said, instead of

For your *life*, you durst not,
No, for your *soul*, you durst not.

8 A number of editions claim to represent the play 'as acted', but all prove to be either reprints of critical editions or derivative versions of the Dryden–Davenant or Bell texts.

9 R. C. Bald, 'Shakespeare on the Stage in Restoration Dublin', *PMLA*, LVI (June 1941), pp. 369–78. William Van Lennep, 'The Smock Alley Players of Dublin', *A Journal of English Literary History*, XIII (September 1946), pp. 216–22.

10 Montague Summers, *The Restoration Theatre*, 1934, p. 184.

11 In 1676 John Richards, who played Brutus in the Smock Alley production, returned to London. See Nicoll, *History of English Drama* (1952), I, p. 301.

12 Van Lennep, 'Smock Alley Players', p. 217.

13 It is unlikely that this entry should be an error. The compiler was not merely entering names opposite a printed cast-list, but wrote out the *dramatis personae* in full; thus virtually eliminating the possibility that he inadvertently left the name of Marullus standing.

14 It may be worth noting that, according to Chetwood, Richards was a great encourager of Robert Wilks in the 1690s. Wilks played in *Caesar* at least as early as 1707, and his name appears in the cast-list of the Dryden–Davenant version.

15 David Erskine Baker, *Biographia Dramatica*, 1782, II, p. 177.

16 The 2478 lines of *Julius Caesar* make it the third shortest of Shakespeare's tragedies – after *Macbeth* (2108) and *Timon* (2373). Hence little cutting is needed merely to fit it to the time of performance.

17 These changes are discussed at length by Hazelton Spencer, *Shakespeare Improved* (1927), pp. 365ff.

18 Gentleman (ed.), *Julius Caesar*, p. 17.

19 Spencer, *Shakespeare Improved*, p. 364.

20 Gentleman (ed.) (*Julius Caesar*, p. 28) notes that 'this short soliloquy is usually omitted, in representation'.

21 Writes Rymer (*Critical Works*, pp. 168–9), 'Two philosophers, two generals . . . the *ultimi Romanorum* . . . are to play a prize, a tryal of skill in huffing and swaggering, like two drunken Hectors, for a two-penny reckoning.'

22 Gentleman (ed.), *Julius Caesar*, p. 75.

23 I.i. Cited by Nicoll, *History of English Drama*, II, p. 20.

24 The last instance of Brutus' killing himself occurred at a 1932 performance at His Majesty's (producer – Oscar Asche) in which Godfrey Tearle played Brutus. Brutus' last lines, however, were those of John Philip Kemble who revised somewhat the Dryden–Davenant death-speech. See Sir Vincent Troubridge, 'Oral Tradition in the Theatre', *Theatre Notebook*, V (October 1951), pp. 87–8.

25 Van Lennep, in a note on the flyleaf of the promptbook, associates the script with Drury Lane and identifies the prompter's hand as George Garrick's, citing in evidence the conclusions of Elizabeth Stein (*David Garrick, Dramatist*, 1938, pp. xi–xii).

Recent research by Professor Leo Hughes (University of Texas) establishes that the hand is in fact that of Covent Garden actor and prompter, Joseph

Younger. In a forthcoming article, Professor Hughes convincingly links this book with the Covent Garden revival of 31 January 1766. I am most grateful to Professor Hughes for making his unpublished findings available to me.

26 When the short conversation between Cassius and Messala (v.i) was performed (according to Gentleman it was 'sometimes, but very improperly rejected'), Casca apparently took Messala's lines.

27 Interestingly enough, Caius Ligarius appears in the cast-list to Bell's edition (played by Mr Holtom), although his scene is eliminated from the text. At times, at least, it must have been retained in performance.

28 Gentleman (ed.), *Julius Caesar*, p. 39.

29 Ibid., p. 61.

30 Ibid., p. 68.

31 Ibid., p. 66.

32 Directions are frequently altered, but both the original and corrected versions appear to be in the same hand. I cite the corrected form throughout; but when the original note is of particular interest I include it in parentheses.

33 Only one instance of new scenery for *Caesar* is recorded. A *Daily Courant* advertisement for Tuesday, 24 September 1723 informs the public that the play will be presented 'with an intire new Sett of Scenes representing Ancient Rome, Painted by Monsieur Devoto'. E. Croft Murray provides a brief study of Devoto's work entitled *John Devoto. A Baroque Scene Painter*, 1953. He is unfortunately unable to throw any light on the *Caesar* settings.

34 It is almost certain that all the early scenes were played well forward, since the Capitol had to be pre-set behind.

35 My reconstruction presupposes the use of only three grooves, although the theatre may well have had more. See Richard Leacroft, *The Development of the English Playhouse*, 1973, p. 110.

36 I assume that groove 3 is reserved for a pre-set Capitol. It is possible, however, that the Capitol flat was a backscene (i.e. a drop or flat set against the back wall of the stage), in which case groove 3 would be available for the Marble Hall shutter.

37 If Marble Hall was run on in groove 3, the Town shutter could be placed in groove 1 or groove 2.

38 Nicholas Dall (d. 1776), a Scandinavian landscape artist, was employed as scene painter at Covent Garden from 1757 until his death. See Sybil Rosenfeld and Edward Croft-Murray, 'Checklist of Scene Painters Working in Great Britain and Ireland in the 18th Century', *Theatre Notebook*, 1964–6, vols. 19, 20.

39 Davies, *Dramatic Miscellanies*, 1783–4, II, p. 237.

40 Eighteenth-century critical views of Brutus' lines are discussed by Leo Kirschbaum in 'Shakespeare's Stage Blood and its Critical Significance', *PMLA*, LXIV (June 1949), pp. 517–29.

41 Brents Stirling provides a stimulating study of the ritual aspect of *Julius Caesar* in 'Or Else This Were a Savage Spectacle', *PMLA*, LXVI (September 1951), pp. 765–74. This article is reprinted in his *Unity in Shakespearian Tragedy*, 1956.

42 If a backshutter had been run on in front of Dall's Palace, there would have been no need to employ the curtain. The curtain, as this and later directions

indicate, was used to hide the stage when two deep scenes followed one another, thus allowing properties to be removed and new ones brought on.

43 Voltaire, *Oeuvres Complètes*, II, p. 317. Cited by A. C. Sprague, *Shakespeare and the Actors*, 1948, p. 323.

44 Gentleman (ed.) *Julius Caesar*, p. 47.

45 The term 'discovery' indicates that a backshutter is withdrawn or a curtain raised to reveal a scene set with furniture and properties. The characters are already in position.

46 John Laguerre (*fl.* 1719–48) was a Covent Garden actor and scene painter. See Rosenfeld and Croft-Murray, 'Checklist of Scene Painters'.

47 Probably a simple woodland scene. It is described as 'Short Wood' to distinguish it from 'Long Wood'. See below.

48 'Short' and 'Long' settings are discussed briefly by Richard Southern in *Changeable Scenery*, 1952, p. 207.

49 This direction makes it clear that Cassius did not die on the apron, an area reserved for Brutus' death. He probably fell behind the proscenium, just far enough back to be masked by the falling curtain.

50 See W. M. Merchant, 'Classical Costume in Shakespearian Productions', *Shakespeare Survey* 10 (1957), p. 71.

51 See Muriel St Clare Byrne, *A History of Shakespearean Production in England*, Part I, *1700–1800*. 1949, p. 19.

52 Merchant, 'Classical Costume', p. 71.

53 Caesar, without doubt, wore some sort of cloak since the 'mantle' was an essential property for the Forum scene. See below.

54 I am inclined to accept this engraving as strongly influenced by theatre practice, if not depicting an actual performance. The setting sorts well with the Town backshutter called for in the prompt-copy. Caesar lies on the prescribed bier, and the smallness of the group of citizens agrees with what we know about the size of the mob. See Merchant, 'Classical Costume', p. 49 and T. S. R. Boase, 'Illustrations of Shakespeare's Plays in the Seventeenth and Eighteenth Centuries', *Journal of the Warburg and Courtauld Institutes*, X (1947), p. 87.

55 British Library. Add. MSS. 12, 201. Selected Folios 34–73. This inventory was prepared by John Rich when he was seeking a mortgage from Martha Launder.

56 Tate Wilkinson, *Original Anecdotes Respecting the Stage*, [*c.* 1801], pp. 7–8.

57 Aaron Hill, *The Works of the late Aaron Hill Esq.*, 1753, II, p. 159.

58 Two years earlier, however, he had played Caesar to Betterton's Brutus in the Queen's Theatre subscription performance.

59 In 1700 Booth left Dublin, where he had played for two years, and joined Betterton's company in which he remained until Betterton's withdrawal to the Queen's in 1709. At this point he decided to stay on with Collier at Drury Lane.

60 Davies, *Dramatic Miscellanies*, II, p. 278.

61 Ibid.

62 Thomas Whincop. *A Compleat List of all the English Dramatic Poets*, 1747, p. 179.

63 Theophilus Cibber, *The Lives and Characters of the Most Eminent Actors and Actresses of Great Britain and Ireland*, 1753, p. 44.

64 Ibid., p. 45.

65 Ibid., p. 44.
66 William Cooke, *Memoirs of Charles Macklin*, 1806, p. 364.
67 Ibid.
68 Ibid.
69 He may well have played with Booth in earlier performances, but cast-lists for revivals prior to 1713 are incomplete.
70 *The Tatler*, 8 June 1710.
71 Davies, *Dramatic Miscellanies*, II, p. 241.
72 Ibid., II, p. 244.
73 Cibber's *Apology*, ed. Bellchambers, p. 305 n.
74 Cibber's *Apology*, ed. Lowe, II, p. 242.
75 Davies, *Dramatic Miscellanies*, I, p. 249.
76 Sir John Hill, *The Actor*, 1755, p. 22.
77 Davies, *Garrick*, I, p. 28.
78 Davies, *Dramatic Miscellanies*, I, p. 356.
79 Davies, *Garrick*, I, p. 28.
80 *A Source Book in Theatrical History*, ed. A. M. Nagler, New York, 1952, pp. 356–7. It is clear from this passage that Quin reverted to the pre-Restoration stage practice of a quarrel threatening a duel. This interpretation must have been dispensed with by Betterton and Booth to judge from their restrained manner of playing this scene. See A. C. Sprague, *Shakespeare and the Actors*, 1948, p. 324.
81 Davies, *Dramatic Miscellanies*, II, p. 248.
82 Ibid., II, p. 250.
83 Sir John Hill, *The Actor*, p. 205.
84 Quin had the greatest aversion to any actor who played at full capacity in scenes where the honours were equally shared. When Bowman played Ligarius with 'great vigour' and 'truly Roman spirit', Quin attempted to decrease his applause by neglecting 'to pay that attention to the character that he ought'. See Davies, *Dramatic Miscellanies*, II, p. 214.
85 John Mills played the role from 1734 until his death in 1736.
86 Ryan was probably Quin's partner in the scene to which Smollett refers in the passage cited above, note 80.
87 Gentleman, *The Dramatic Censor*, 1770, II, p. 17.
88 Davies, *Dramatic Miscellanies*, II, p. 246.
89 Davies, *Garrick*, I, p. 27.
90 Davies, *Dramatic Miscellanies*, II, p. 246.
91 William Cooke, *Memoirs of Charles Macklin*, p. 178.
92 Wilkes, *A General View of the Stage*, 1759, p. 291.
93 Davies, *Dramatic Miscellanies*, II, p. 244.
94 Gentleman, *The Dramatic Censor*, II, p. 18.
95 Davies, *Dramatic Miscellanies*, II, p. 240.
96 Aaron Hill, *Works*, I, p. 167.
97 Ibid., II, p. 55.
98 Wilkes, *A General View of the Stage*, pp. 313–14.
99 Gentleman, *The Dramatic Censor*, II, p. 16. See Illustration 3.
100 Ibid.

101 *The Present State of the Stage in Great Britain and Ireland*, 1763, p. 52.
102 Gentleman, *The Dramatic Censor*, II, p. 16.
103 *The Present State of the Stage*, p. 52.
104 Ibid.
105 [Hugh Kelly], *Thespis*, 1766, p. 26.
106 Bensley also played the part for several performances in 1780.
107 Gentleman, *The Dramatic Censor*, I, p. 210.

3. John Philip Kemble (1812)

1 'Memoranda of J. P. Kemble', British Library Add. MSS. 31972–5, Vol. IV.
2 Julian Charles Young, *A Memoir of Charles Mayne Young*, 1871, p. 58.
3 James Boaden, *Memoirs of the Life of John Philip Kemble Esq.*, 1825, I, p. 279. Details of Kemble's life and work are also provided by Percy Fitzgerald, *The Kembles*, 1871, and Herschel Baker, *John Philip Kemble*, 1942.
4 Sir Joshua Reynolds, 'The Third Discourse', *Fifteen Discourses Delivered in the Royal Academy* (Everyman Edition, n.d.), pp. 27, 30.
5 Boaden, *Kemble*, II, p. 2.
6 James Boaden, *Memoirs of Mrs. Siddons*, 1827, II, p. 250.
7 Reynolds, 'The Thirteenth Discourse', p. 220.
8 Facsimile edition published by the Cornmarket Press, 1972, with an introduction by John D. Ripley.
9 J. R. Planché, *The Recollections and Reflections of*, 1872, I, p. 54. According to Thomas Goodwin (*Sketches and Impressions*, 1887, p. 33) the scenic artist was Peugh.
10 Young, *A Memoir of Charles Mayne Young*, p. 59.
11 'The costumes are correct; and the architectural scenes, though dingy – being the same, we believe, that were used in JOHN KEMBLE's time – are in good taste, and preserve the classic keeping of the stage pictures.' *The Spectator*, 19 November 1836.
12 John Finlay, *Miscellanies*, 1835, p. 255.
13 Henry Crabb Robinson, *Diary, Reminiscences and Correspondence of*, ed. Thomas Sadler, 1896, I, pp. 373–4.
14 Finlay, *Miscellanies*, p. 255.
15 [Joseph Haslewood], *The Secret History of the Green-Room*, 1795, p. 16.
16 Finlay, *Miscellanies*, p. 255.
17 See Lily B. Campbell, 'A History of Costuming on the English Stage between 1660 and 1823', *University of Wisconsin Studies in Language and Literature*, Madison, 1918.
18 This book, and another written in an 1811 edition, are in the Wister Collection at the Folger Shakespeare Library. A similar book, containing a note by Charles Kemble in which he asserts that his brother marked it 'with his own hand for representation' is also at the Folger (*JC* 6). The Garrick Club has another, but less fully annotated book (*JC* 5). Two copies of the originals also survive: one, once owned by Richard Jones (*JC* 8), is at the Shakespeare Centre Library in Stratford-upon-Avon, and another, which belonged to Henry Siddons (*JC* 7) is at the Folger.

19 This book and the other *Caesar* book in the Wister Collection (see n. 18) appear in *John Philip Kemble Promptbooks*, ed. Charles H. Shattuck, vol. 4, published for the Folger Shakespeare Library by the University Press of Virginia, Charlottesville, 1974. Professor Shattuck's general introduction in vol. 1 and his prefatory essay in vol. 4 on Kemble's treatment of *Caesar* are invaluable.

20 The playbill lists twenty-five plebeians, but Kemble's book calls for twenty-six men and six boys.

21 Entrances were designated by number according to the groove immediately behind; thus IEL or, more commonly, LIE, was the entrance at stage left between the first groove and the curtain line. Kemble frequently uses R and L in this book instead of RIE and LIE.

22 House-lights were left on during the performance, so complete stage darkness was never possible.

23 I am grateful to Professor Shattuck for clarifying the action at this point. The direction simply states that Caesar enters MLUE. On the basis of his wide experience with Kemble promptbooks, Professor Shattuck explains that the actor came on stage from LUE and then passed through the arch in the middle (M) of the backshutter.

24 With so many supernumeraries to be arranged behind, he no doubt concluded that the brief conversation between the conspirators after the exit of the procession left him too little time.

25 Sir Theodore Martin, 'An Eye-Witness of John Kemble', *The Nineteenth Century* (February 1880), p. 281.

26 Kemble's alteration of Shakespeare's 'Lend me your hand.' cf. the eighteenth-century 'Take up the body'.

27 Another of Kemble's minor alterations.

28 The previous scene seems to have been set in groove 2. Everything above that must be kept free for the final tableau.

29 Kemble alters 'rest on this rock' (V.v.1) to read 'let's rest us here'. Scenic pieces were seldom, if ever, placed on the apron.

30 Sir Walter Scott, Review of Boaden's *Kemble*, *The Quarterly Review* (June 1826), p. 223.

31 Bertram Joseph, *The Tragic Actor*, 1959, p. 187.

32 *The News*, 8 March 1812.

33 Scott, review of Boaden's *Kemble*, p. 215.

34 *The News*, 28 December 1823.

35 *Bell's Weekly Messenger*, 8 March 1812.

36 *St. James's Chronicle*, 3 March 1812.

37 *Bell's Weekly Messenger*, 8 March 1812.

38 Finlay, *Miscellanies*, p. 261.

39 *The Times*, 7 May 1816.

40 Finlay, *Miscellanies*, p. 261.

41 James Henry Hackett, *Notes and Comments upon Certain Plays and Actors of Shakespeare*, New York, 1864, pp. 136–7. Hackett's account is actually based on Young's imitation of Kemble's performance.

42 *The Examiner*, 5 April 1812. Reprinted in *Leigh Hunt's Dramatic Criticism*

1808–1831, ed. Lawrence Husten Houtchens and Carolyn Washburn Houtchens, 1950.

43 William Hazlitt, *Criticisms and Dramatic Essays of the English Stage*, 1854, p. 296.

44 *The Examiner*, 5 April 1812.

45 Hackett, *Notes and Comments*, p. 132.

46 J. W. Cole, *Life and Theatrical Times of Charles Kean F.S.A.*, 1859, I, p. 201.

47 Hackett, *Notes and Comments*, p. 132.

48 Young, *A Memoir of Charles Mayne Young*, pp. 61, 85.

49 *The News*, 8 March 1812.

50 *The Examiner*, 5 April 1812.

51 *Bell's Weekly Messenger*, 8 March 1812.

52 *The Times*, 2 March 1812.

53 *Blackwood's Edinburgh Magazine*, XXXI (April 1832), p. 676.

54 *The Examiner*, 5 April 1812.

55 Young, *A Memoir of Charles Mayne Young*, p. 61.

56 *The Morning Herald*, 2 October 1827.

57 *The News*, 28 December 1823.

58 *The Morning Herald*, 23 December 1823.

59 *The Morning Post*, 23 December 1823.

60 *The Drama, or, Theatrical Pocket Magazine*, May 1822.

61 *The Times*, 2 March 1812.

62 *The News*, 8 March 1812.

63 *The Morning Post*, 23 December 1823.

64 *The Morning Herald*, 23 December 1823.

65 *The Examiner*, 5 April 1812.

4. From Young to Phelps (1819–65)

1   The acting editions of this period – Oxberry's (1822) and Cumberland's (*c.* 1827–9) – are virtual reprints of Kemble's version.

2   *The Morning Chronicle*, 8 December 1820.

3   Cole, *Life and Theatrical Times of Charles Kean*, I, p. 108.

4   23 April 1822.

5   23 April 1822.

6   *The News*, 28 December 1823.

7   *The Sunday Times*, 1 November 1829.

8   R. H. Horne, *A New Spirit of the Age* (World's Classics edition, 1907), p. 304. Cited by Nicoll, *A History of English Drama*, IV, pp. 171–2.

9   William Archer, *William Charles Macready*, 1890, p. 23.

10 Between 1822 and 1836 he played Cassius in London only once – to Sheridan Knowles's Brutus at Covent Garden on 30 May 1836.

11 For further discussion of Macready's production practice see John Forster and George Henry Lewes, *Dramatic Essays*, ed. William Archer and Robert W. Lowe, 1896; Charles H. Shattuck, *William Charles Macready's King John*, Urbana, 1962; and Alan S. Downer, *The Eminent Tragedian: William Charles Macready*, Cambridge, Mass., 1966.

12 *Macready's Reminiscences, and Selections from His Diaries and Letters*, ed. Sir Frederick Pollock, 1876, II, p. 150.
13 *The Examiner*, 2 November 1850.
14 George Vandenhoff, *Dramatic Reminiscences*, 1860, p. 206.
15 Ellis played a plebeian in the 1843 performance and in the following season became Drury Lane's chief prompter. He made two other copies, one for Charles Kean (*JC* 14) and one for Hermann Vezin (*JC* 15). Neither is as full as *JC* 13. See Charles H. Shattuck, 'Macready Prompt-Books', *Theatre Notebook*, XVI (Autumn 1961), p. 9.
16 2 May 1843.
17 Macready's *Reminiscences*, II, p. 53.
18 Macready restores the fourth Plebeian's splendidly ironic line, 'Caesar's better parts / Shall be crown'd in Brutus' (III.ii.51–2).
19 This engraving was obviously inspired by a theatre performance, but its date is uncertain.
20 Vandenhoff, *Reminiscences*, p. 207.
21 W. May Phelps and John Forbes-Robertson, *The Life and Life-Work of Samuel Phelps*, 1886, p. 48.
22 John Ranken Towse, *Sixty Years of the Theater*, New York, 1911, pp. 38–9.
23 John Coleman, 'Phelps as I Knew Him', *The Theatre*, 1 October 1885.
24 Westland Marston, *Our Recent Actors*, 1888, II, p. 5.
25 *The Sunday Times*, 7 May 1843.
26 Marston, *Our Recent Actors*, II, p. 5.
27 *The Sunday Times*, 7 May 1843.
28 Ibid.
29 Of course, it must not be assumed that Macready's style would be considered natural by present-day standards. Indeed, the exaggerated elocution and stilted movement would seem as classical to us as the Kemble school appeared to the age of Kean and Macready.
30 Hackett, *Notes and Comments*, p. 138.
31 *The Diaries of William Charles Macready 1833–1851*, ed. William Toynbee, 1912, I, p. 359.
32 Macready's *Reminiscences*, II, p. 365.
33 *The Morning Chronicle*, 15 November 1836.
34 *The Spectator*, 19 November 1836.
35 *The Examiner*, 20 November 1836.
36 Ibid.
37 *John Bull*, 20 November 1836.
38 Ibid.
39 *The Examiner*, 8 April 1848.
40 *John Bull*, 20 November 1836.
41 *The News and Sunday Herald*, 20 November 1836.
42 *John Bull*, 20 November 1836.
43 *The Morning Herald*, 15 November 1836.
44 *The Examiner*, 8 April 1848.
45 Forster and Lewes, *Dramatic Essays*, p. 34.
46 For a fuller discussion of these roles see Marston, *Our Recent Actors*, II, pp. 37ff.

47 *Tallis's Dramatic Magazine*, January 1851.
48 Forster and Lewes, *Dramatic Essays*, p. 35.
49 Macready's *Reminiscences*, 1, p. 178.
50 *The Critic*, 1 December 1850.
51 *The Examiner*, 30 November 1850.
52 *Tallis's Dramatic Magazine*, January 1851.
53 *The Critic*, 1 December 1850.
54 *The Examiner*, 30 November 1850.
55 Ibid.
56 *Tallis's Dramatic Magazine*, January 1851.
57 Macready must have re-arranged their entry to take place after the announcement of Portia's death.
58 *The Examiner*, 30 November 1850.
59 *Tallis's Dramatic Magazine*, January 1851.
60 Phelps and Forbes-Robertson, *Samuel Phelps*, p. 213.
61 Henry Morley, *The Journal of a London Playgoer*, 1866, p. 152. For further details of Phelps's production practice see Shirley S. Allen, *Samuel Phelps and Sadler's Wells Theatre*, Middletown, Conn., 1971; Sidney Lee, *Shakespeare and the Modern Stage*, 1906; Odell, *Shakespeare from Betterton to Irving*, 1, pp. 237ff; and Phelps and Forbes-Robertson, *Samuel Phelps*.
62 Phelps and Forbes-Robertson, *Samuel Phelps*, p. viii.
63 In the Folger Shakespeare Library. Another book (*JC* 17) is in the New York Public Library.
64 Emendations to the above procession are marked 'Procession 1849', but I have been unable to locate any record of a performance in that year. A revival may have been contemplated, but seems not to have taken place.
65 Phelps and Forbes-Robertson, *Samuel Phelps*, p. 12.
66 Ibid., p. 29.
67 *The Morning Herald and Advertiser* (n.d.) Cited by Phelps and Forbes-Robertson, *Samuel Phelps*, p. 211.
68 *The Athenaeum*, 8 August 1846.
69 *The Illustrated London News*, 8 November 1856.
70 *John Bull*, 22 August 1846.
71 *The Morning Herald and Advertiser* cited above.

5. American productions (1770–1870)

1 Esther Cloudman Dunn, *Shakespeare in America*, New York, 1939, pp. 92–3, 95.
2 *Dunlap's American Daily Advertiser*, Philadelphia, 29 January 1791.
3 *The Pennsylvania Journal*, Philadelphia, 31 May 1770. Thirty years later, with independence achieved, Dunlap and Hodgkinson's bills epitomized Brutus and Cassius as 'those preservers of the Republic' (*New York Evening Post*, 27 May 1802). The orations remained a strong selling-point in advertisements. In 1791 the managers designated 'the remarkable Orations of Brutus and Antony over the Corpse of Caesar, &c. &c.' (*Dunlap's American Daily Advertiser*, Philadelphia, 29 January 1791) as a feature of the production. In 1802 these speeches

were again highlighted, this time as 'the two most celebrated Orations of the Roman People' (*New York Evening Post*, 27 May 1802).

4 See 'On Elocution', *The Emerald*, Boston, 12 March 1808. The history of oratory in American education, and the use of Shakespeare in teaching it are treated in L. F. Snow's *College Curriculum in the United States*, New York, 1907, and Henry W. Simon's *The Reading of Shakespeare in American Schools and Colleges*, New York, 1932.

5 George O. Seilhamer, *History of the American Theatre During the Revolution and After*, 3 vols, Philadelphia, 1888–91.

6 *The Pennsylvania Journal*, Philadelphia, 31 May 1770, and *Dunlap's American Daily Advertiser*, Philadelphia, 29 January 1791.

7 Seilhamer, *American Theatre During the Revolution and After*, III, p. 94.

8 For contemporary accounts of Hallam's appearance and acting style see John Bernard, *Retrospections of America 1797–1811*, ed. Mrs Bayle Bernard, with an introduction, notes and index by Laurence Hutton and Brander Matthews, New York, 1887. Reissued by Benjamin Blom, Inc., New York, 1969, p. 265; William Dunlap, *History of the American Theatre*, New York, 1832. Reissued by Burt Franklin, New York, 1963, p. 155; [Alexander Graydon], *Memoirs of a Life, Chiefly Passed in Pennsylvania*, Harrisburgh, Pennsylvania, 1811, p. 77; William Wood, *Personal Recollections of the Stage*, Philadelphia, 1855, p. 120.

9 For contemporary accounts of Hodgkinson's appearance and acting style see *The Mirror of Taste and Dramatic Censor*, Philadelphia, November, 1810; Dunlap, *History of the American Theatre*, p. 187; John Durang, *The Memoir of*, ed. Alan S. Downer, Pittsburgh, 1966, p. 36.

10 Dunlap, *History of the American Theatre*, p. 155.

11 Durang, *Memoir*, p. 31.

12 *The Francis Letters By Sir Philip Francis and Other Members of the Family*, ed. Beata Francis and Eliza Keary, 1901, I, p. 118. Henry may not, of course, have appeared at this performance; but Mackrabie's remark about eccentric pronunciation reinforces our conjecture that he is the Cassius referred to. On 18 October 1779 the *Morning Chronicle* reviewer criticized his Othello at Drury Lane for calling a handkerchief a 'hand-kercher'. See *The London Stage 1660–1800*, Part 5 *1776–1800*, Carbondale, Illinois, 1968, I, p. 289.

13 Ibid., I, p. 316.

14 *New-England Palladium*, Boston, 22 March 1803.

15 *New-England Galaxy & Masonic Magazine*, Boston, 20 November 1818.

16 Joseph Ireland, *A Memoir of the Professional Life of Thomas Abthorpe Cooper*, New York, 1888 Reissued by Burt Franklin, New York, 1970, p. 42.

17 In the Theatre Collection, New York Public Library.

18 *Boston Weekly Magazine*, 5 July 1817.

19 *New-England Galaxy & Masonic Magazine*, Boston, 4 December 1818.

20 *The Minerva*, New York, 24 April 1824.

21 See Noah M. Ludlow, *Dramatic Life As I Found It*, St Louis, 1880, p. 234; James E. Murdoch, *The Stage or Recollections of Actors and Acting*, Philadelphia, 1880; Francis Courtney Wemyss, *Theatrical Biography*, Glasgow, 1848; *The Polyanthos*, Boston, December, 1805.

22 *The New-York Mirror*, 27 September 1823.

23 *Boston Weekly Magazine*, 7 March 1818.
24 Ibid.
25 *The New-York Mirror*, 15 October 1823.
26 *The Mirror of Taste, and Dramatic Censor*, Philadelphia, May 1810.
27 *The New-York Mirror*, 15 October 1823.
28 *The Polyanthos*, Boston, April 1807.
29 *Boston Weekly Magazine*, 7 March 1818.
30 *New-England Galaxy*, Boston, 19 March 1824.
31 Ibid.
32 *The Minerva*, New York, 24 January 1824.
33 *The Minerva*, New York, 24 April 1824.
34 *The Truth-Teller*, 16 December 1826.
35 Thomas R. Gould, *The Tragedian*, New York, 1868, p. 19.
36 Ibid.
37 For further treatment of Booth's life and work, see Asia Booth Clarke, *Booth Memorials*, New York, 1866; William Winter, *The Life and Art of Edwin Booth*, 1893; and Stanley Kimmel, *The Mad Booths of Maryland*, New York, 1969.
38 Gould, *The Tragedian*, p. 152.
39 Ibid.
40 *The New-York Mirror*, 27 August 1831.
41 *The Albion*, New York, 18 November 1843.
42 *National Advocate*, New York, 24 September 1823.
43 *Reminiscences of an Idler*, New York, 1880, p. 76.
44 Henry Dickinson Stone, *Personal Recollections of the Drama*, Albany, 1873, p. 80.
45 *The New-York Mirror*, 27 August 1831.
46 Walt Whitman, *November Boughs*, Philadelphia, 1888, p. 90.
47 *The Albion*, New York, 2 June 1849.
48 Hackett, *Notes and Comments*, p. 125.
49 Ibid.
50 T. Allston Brown, *A History of the New York Stage*, New York, 1903, I, p. 129.
51 *The New-York Mirror*, 25 June 1831.
52 *New York Herald*, 16 January 1862.
53 Henry P. Goddard, 'Recollections of Edward L. Davenport', *Lippincott's Magazine*, April 1878, p. 463.
54 Ibid.
55 *New-York Daily Tribune*, 8 September 1870.
56 Goddard, 'Recollections of Edward L. Davenport', p. 464.
57 *New-York Daily Tribune*, 8 September 1870.
58 John Ranken Towse, *Sixty Years of the Theater*, New York, 1916, pp. 84–5.
59 *New-York Daily Tribune*, 8 September 1870.
60 Goddard, 'Recollections of Edward L. Davenport', p. 464.
61 William Winter, *Shakespeare on the Stage*, third series, New York, 1915, p. 601.
62 Ibid.
63 *New-York Daily Tribune*, 8 September 1870.

6. The Booth–Barrett–Davenport era

1 Asia Booth Clarke, *The Elder and the Younger Booth*, [n.d.], p. 121.

2 Major Booth biographies include William Winter, *Life and Art of Edwin Booth*, New York, 1893; Edwina Booth Grossman, *Edwin Booth: Recollections By His Daughter*, New York, 1894; Richard Lockridge, *Darling of Misfortune*, New York, 1932; Otis Skinner, *The Last Tragedian*, New York, 1939; and Eleanor Ruggles, *Prince of Players*, New York, 1953.

3 Booth's managerial career is treated in some detail in Charles Shattuck's essay 'The Theatrical Management of Edwin Booth', *The Theatrical Manager in England and America*, ed. Joseph W. Donohue, Jr, Princeton, N.J., 1971.

4 On 23 November 1870 he wrote to Lawrence Barrett regarding the engagement of Edwin Adams, 'You and he can be so placed as not to clash – in the production of pieces ("Julius Caesar", for instance) or at different times' (Skinner, *The Last Tragedian*, p. 154).

5 Professor Shattuck provides an illuminating analysis of Booth's intellectual and aesthetic development in 'The Theatrical Management of Edwin Booth', and *The Hamlet of Edwin Booth*, Urbana, Illinois, 1969.

6 All known Booth promptbooks for *Julius Caesar* are described, and identified as far as possible, in Charles H. Shattuck's *The Shakespeare Promptbooks*, Urbana, Illinois, 1969.

7 He claimed to have studied the text of *Hamlet* in a dozen or so modern editions. See Shattuck, *The Hamlet of Edwin Booth*, p. xvi.

8 Booth was, however, thoroughly familiar with the best contemporary sources of archaeological information. He wrote to Winter, 'The pages on costume you sent are from Hope [Thomas Hope, *Costume of the Ancients*, 1841], it seems; I have Hope – but unfortunately, he is packed with other books . . . I send you, however, "Becker's Gallus" [Wilhelm Adolf Becker, *Gallus; or Roman Scenes of the Time of Augustus*, 1844] & "Carr's Antiquities" [Thomas Swinburne Carr, *A Manual of Roman Antiquities*, 1836] which will give you – I think – all that Hope possesses.' Daniel J. Watermeier, *Between Actor and Critic*, Princeton, New Jersey, 1971, p. 116.

9 A note for the Assassination scene in the 1871 promptbook allocates thirteen citizens and between thirty-nine and forty-six senators to this scene, depending apparently on their availability on different nights of the week. I have roughly divided this total of fifty-two to fifty-nine supers into about fifteen for the crowd and forty for the procession for act I.

10 Unidentified newspaper clipping, *Julius Caesar* file, Theatre Collection, New York Public Library.

11 Winter, *Shakespeare on the Stage*, third series, p. 583.

12 See C. H. Stranahan, *A History of French Painting*, 1889, p. 315.

13 The promptbook for the 1871 production calls for forty senators on Thursday, forty-six on Friday, and thirty-nine for a matinée.

14 Although this comment refers to Davenport's performance, Witham's design indicates that Booth employed this same piece of business.

15 *Spirit of the Times*, 30 December 1871.

16 30 December 1871.

17 31 December 1871.
18 Grossman, *Edwin Booth*, p. 167.
19 Winter, *Life and Art of Edwin Booth*, p. 153.
20 Ibid., p. 136.
21 At the Rodgers and Hammerstein Archives of Recorded Sound (New York Public Library) I listened to Booth's recording of Othello's speech to the Senate beginning 'Most potent, grave, and reverend signiors' (1890) and compared it with Tree's reading of Mark Antony's lament over Caesar's body (1906) and the Mercury Theatre recording of *Julius Caesar* (Columbia, *c.* 1938). I was struck by the contrast between the easy, mellifluous rhythms of Booth's speech and the forced, quavering recitative of Tree. Booth spoke as naturally, I thought, as the Mercury actors, and his voice was richer in tone colour and subtler in inflection than that of Orson Welles.
22 *New-York Daily Tribune*, 14 March 1872; Winter, *Shakespeare on the Stage*, third series, p. 586.
23 Winter, *Shakespeare on the Stage*, third series, p. 587.
24 Ibid., p. 587.
25 *The New York Herald*, 31 December 1871.
26 *The Guardian*, New York, 18 January 1872.
27 Winter, *Life and Art of Edwin Booth*, p. 218.
28 Ibid., p. 217.
29 *San Francisco Chronicle*, 28 May 1889.
30 Winter, *Life and Art of Edwin Booth*, p. 221.
31 Winter, *Shakespeare on the Stage*, third series, p. 587.
32 *The Chicago Tribune*, 25 September 1888.
33 John Creahan, *The Life of Laura Keene*, Philadelphia, 1897, p. 90.
34 Winter, *Shakespeare on the Stage*, third series, p. 587.
35 *The New York Evening Post*, 26 December 1871.
36 *The New York Evening Express*, 28 February 1872.
37 Skinner, *The Last Tragedian*, pp. 130–1.
38 William Winter, *Other Days*, New York, 1908, p. 249.
39 William Winter, *Shadows of the Stage*, Edinburgh, 1892, p. 222.
40 Winter, *Life and Art of Edwin Booth*, p. 119.
41 *New-York Daily Tribune*, 27 December 1887.
42 *New-York Daily Tribune*, 27 January 1885.
43 *Spirit of the Times*, 1 January 1876.
44 Winter, *Shakespeare on the Stage*, third series, pp. 593–4.
45 *New-York Daily Tribune*, 11 December 1888.
46 *The New York Herald*, 27 January 1885.
47 The Becks book has the note 'Cas Xs C reading scroll – cold salute to Caesar & none to Antony.'
48 *New-York Daily Tribune*, 27 January 1885.
49 *St. Louis Republic*, 23 October 1888.
50 Winter, *Shakespeare on the Stage*, third series, p. 594.
51 *The Guardian*, New York, 18 January 1872.
52 Winter, *Shakespeare on the Stage*, third series, p. 595.
53 *New-York Daily Tribune*, 6 March 1891.

54 *Spirit of the Times*, 1 January 1876.
55 *New-York Daily Tribune*, 6 March 1891.
56 Winter, *Shakespeare on the Stage*, third series, p. 596.
57 *The Chicago Tribune*, 4 October 1887.
58 *New-York Daily Tribune*, 15 October 1881.
59 He wrote to Barrett 3 July 1871, 'I desire Ned Adams to do *Anthony* – a part as well suited to him as *Cassius* and *Brutus* are adapted to us' (Skinner, *The Last Tragedian*, p. 160).
60 Although on tour later in the year Bangs seems to have got out of hand. Booth wrote Barrett, '*Mark Antony* has ruined Bangs – *he* wants to *star* & asked me the other day to give him the four weeks that I am in Phila! I expect trouble with him' (Skinner, *The Last Tragedian*, p. 170).
61 *The Standard*, New York, 1 January 1872.
62 *New-York Daily Tribune*, 28 December 1875.
63 O. B. Bunce, '"Julius Caesar" at Booth's Theatre', *Appleton's Journal*, XV (22 January 1876), p. 116.
64 *The World*, New York, 2 January 1876.
65 Bunce, 'Julius Caesar', p. 116.
66 *The New York Herald*, 31 December 1871.
67 *The New York Times*, 31 December 1871.
68 The Jones copy of Kemble's promptbook (*JC* 8), once in Creswick's possession, contains rough sketches of the Grand Square, Senate, and Forum settings for Booth's production. Whether Creswick made them himself is uncertain.
69 Unidentified newspaper clipping in scrapbook titled 'Booth Newspaper Clippings 1871–1873' in the Walter Hampden Memorial Library, The Players, New York.
70 Winter, *Shakespeare on the Stage*, third series, p. 593.
71 *New York Evening Express*, 6 March 1872.
72 Unidentified clipping cited above n. 69.
73 *New-York Daily Tribune*, 14 March 1872.
74 Unidentified clipping cited above, n. 69.
75 *The Evening Post*, New York, 5 March 1872.
76 *The New York Times*, 5 March 1872.
77 *New York Evening Express*, 6 March 1872.
78 Unidentified clipping cited above, n. 69.
79 Ibid.
80 Winter, *Life and Art of Edwin Booth*, pp. 219–20.
81 Winter, *Shakespeare on the Stage*, third series, p. 588.
82 16 March 1872.
83 *New-York Daily Tribune*, 14 March 1872.
84 Creahan, *Life of Laura Keane*, p. 91.
85 *Weekly Review*, New York, 16 March 1872.
86 Ibid.
87 *New-York Daily Tribune*, 14 March 1872.
88 Winter, *Shakespeare on the Stage*, third series, p. 590.
89 Creahan, *Life of Laura Keane*, p. 91.
90 Richard Benson analyses Voigtlin's alterations in some detail in his unpub-

lished Ph.D. dissertation, 'Jarrett and Palmer's 1875 Production of *Julius Caesar*: a Reconstruction' (University of Illinois, Urbana, 1968), p. 155. Mr Benson's excellent study has been of great help in the preparation of this chapter.

91 Bunce, 'Julius Caesar', p. 117. Winter says (*Shakespeare on the Stage*, third series, p. 603) that this scene was 'originally used in a revival of "Coriolanus" effected by William Wheatley, November 2, 1863, at Niblo's Garden, with Edwin Forrest as the arrogant patrician'. Barrett introduced the same effect during his tours with Booth. Booth wrote to his daughter from Chicago, 24 September 1888, 'To-night I begin with *Brutus*, with some new scenic effects – burning the body of *Brutus*, anthem, etc.' See Grossman, *Edwin Booth*, p. 88.

92 Vincent's book calls for '140 Supers – 19 Ballet – 5 Children'. Allston Brown (*History of the New York Stage*, III, p. 117) says there were 'over one hundred and sixty persons on the stage, besides the regular cast'. An advertisement for a performance at Booth's Theatre on 22 May 1876 says 'The grand finale scenic effect illustrating the burning of the body of Brutus . . . requires an auxiliary force of 400 people' (*The New York Herald*, 21 May 1876). This figure is probably exaggerated.

93 Details of the procession in the Becks and Vincent books differ somewhat. See also the description in *The New York Herald*, 25 December 1875.

94 For details of Davenport's performance I have relied mainly on the Vincent, Mason, and Becks books noted above.

95 Winter, *Shakespeare on the Stage*, third series, pp. 603–4.

96 Ibid., p. 604.

97 Ibid.

98 Winter, *Shakespeare on the Stage*, third series, p. 604.

99 Ibid.

100 Goddard, 'Recollections of Edward L. Davenport', p. 467.

101 Winter, *Shakespeare on the Stage*, third series, p. 604.

102 Ibid., p. 605.

103 Goddard, 'Recollections of Edward L. Davenport', p. 467.

104 Winter, *Shakespeare on the Stage*, third series, p. 605.

105 For biographical information and general treatment of McCullough's acting see Joseph I. C. Clarke, *My Life and Memories*, New York, 1925; Percy MacKaye, *Epoch: The Life of Steele MacKaye*, 1927; Augustus Pitou, *Masters of the Show*, 1914; J. R. Towse, *Sixty Years of the Theatre*, 1911, and New York, 1916; and Winter, *Other Days* and *Shakespeare on the Stage*, third series.

106 Winter, *Shakespeare on the Stage*, third series, pp. 608–9. See also *New York Daily Tribune*, 13 April 1883.

107 See E. H. Southern's *My Remembrances*, 1917, for a diverting account of his tour with McCullough's company as a young actor.

108 Otis Skinner gleefully recalls this accident-prone production in *Footlights and Spotlights*, Indianapolis, 1924, pp. 121–2.

109 Winter, *Shakespeare on the Stage*, third series, p. 610.

110 *The New York Times*, 1 May 1883.

111 Winter, *Shakespeare on the Stage*, third series, p. 611.

112 Skinner, *Footlights and Spotlights*, p. 121.

7. The Meiningen Court Company (1881) and Beerbohm Tree (1898)

1 Osmond Tearle's touring company in 1889 and 1892 staged uninspired revivals in the Kemble manner, but they would have been of little assistance.
2 *The Times*, 31 May 1881.
3 The programme is in the Enthoven Collection, Victoria and Albert Museum.
4 *The Illustrated London News*, 4 June 1881.
5 *The Academy*, 4 June 1881.
6 *The Illustrated London News*, 4 June 1881.
7 *The Saturday Review*, 4 June 1881.
8 Brander Matthews, 'Shakesperian Stage Traditions', *Shakesperian Studies*, ed. Brander Matthews and Ashley Horace Thorndike, 1916, p. 18.
9 4 June 1881.
10 *The Saturday Review*, 4 June 1881.
11 Matthews, 'Shakesperian Stage Traditions', pp. 18–20.
12 Herbert Beerbohm Tree, *Thoughts and After-Thoughts*, 1913, p. 49.
13 University of Bristol Theatre Collection.
14 It is difficult to understand how the ultra-realistic Meiningen could have played a full text. However, by eliminating the curtain-raiser, speaking more swiftly than English actors, and extending the time of performance slightly, they might just have been able to manage it. Of course, it is possible that they abridged individual speeches without substantially reducing the number of characters.
15 Hesketh Pearson, *Beerbohm Tree His Life and Laughter*, 1956, p. 119.
16 Ibid., p. 104.
17 The painting itself was carried out by Joseph Harker and Walter Hann, both highly competent scenic artists who had worked under Irving.
18 *The Daily Telegraph*, 24 January 1898.
19 Ibid.
20 Ibid.
21 Percy Simpson, Appendix to *Julius Caesar*, ed. Mark Hunter, 1900. Reprinted by H. H. Furness Jr, Appendix to *Julius Caesar*, New Variorum edition, 1913, p. 442.
22 *The Daily Telegraph*, 24 January 1898.
23 Simpson, Appendix to *Julius Caesar*, p. 442.
24 Ibid., p. 443.
25 Ibid.
26 Ibid., pp. 443–4.
27 *The Daily Mail*, 24 January 1898.
28 *The Westminster Gazette*, 24 January 1898.
29 Souvenir Program (1898)
30 See Joseph, *The Tragic Actor*, 1959, pp. 360ff.
31 In the Rodgers and Hammerstein Archives of Recorded Sound, New York Public Library.
32 'From the Stalls', *Herbert Beerbohm Tree*, ed. Max Beerbohm, n.d., p. 224.

33 *Thoughts and After-Thoughts*, p. 196.
34 *The Era*, 29 January 1898.
35 *The Daily Mail*, 24 January 1898.
36 *The Era*, 29 January 1898.
37 *The Daily Mail*, 24 January 1898.
38 Lady Tree, 'Herbert and Me', *Herbert Beerbohm Tree*, p. 108.
39 *Illustrated Sporting and Dramatic News*, 29 January 1898.
40 Gordon Crosse, *Shakespearean Playgoing (1890–1952)*, 1953, p. 41.
41 24 January 1898.
42 *The Daily Telegraph*, 24 January 1898.
43 Richard Dickins, *Forty Years of Shakespeare on the English Stage*, 1907, p. 89.
44 *The World*, 2 February 1898.
45 *The Era*, 29 January 1898.
46 Dickins, *Forty Years of Shakespeare on the English Stage*, p. 89.
47 *The Westminster Gazette*, 24 January 1898.
48 *The Pall Mall Gazette*, 24 January 1898.
49 Crosse, *Shakespearean Playgoing (1890–1952)*, p. 43.
50 *The Westminster Gazette*, 24 January 1898.
51 *The Queen*, 29 January 1898.
52 *The Pall Mall Gazette*, 24 January 1898.
53 This, it will be recalled, was a practice of Kemble. Perhaps Waller learned the trick from Calvert (Casca) who was an authority on stage tradition.
54 *The Daily Telegraph*, 24 January 1898.
55 *The Pall Mall Gazette*, 24 January 1898.
56 *The Era*, 29 January 1898.
57 25 January 1898.
58 *The Saturday Review*, 29 January 1898.
59 Ibid.
60 24 January 1898.
61 *The Era*, 29 January 1898.
62 Ibid.

8. F. R. Benson at Stratford (1892–1915)

1 J. C. Trewin, *Benson and the Bensonians*, 1960, p. 184.
2 The only previous *Julius Caesar* production had been a mediocre effort staged by Osmond Tearle during the Shakespeare Festival of 1889.
3 Sir Frank Benson, *My Memoirs*, 1930, p. 184.
4 For biographical details and treatment of Benson's production practice see Benson, *My Memoirs*; Lady Benson, *Mainly Players*, 1926; Sidney Lee, 'Mr. Benson and Shakespearean Drama', *Shakespeare and the Modern Stage*, 1906; and J. C. Trewin, *Benson and the Bensonians*.
5 Lee, 'Mr. Benson and Shakespearean Drama', p. 112.
6 Mrs Dennis Roberts, Benson's assistant stage manager and keeper of the promptbooks in the 1920s, assured me in 1963 that on all basic points it conforms to the production pattern followed by Benson throughout his career. There was little real change from the first Benson books to the last. Minor

business was occasionally inserted or deleted; lighting was altered to reflect technical progress; and new scenery replaced the outworn pieces; but the text, groupings, entrances and exits, and positions of settings and properties remained unchanged.

7 Both in the Shakespeare Centre Library, Stratford-upon-Avon.
8 W. A. S. Benson, '"Agamemnon" At Oxford', *Cornhill Magazine*, new series, XLVI (May 1919), p. 544.
9 Sir Frank Benson, *My Memoirs*, p. 145.
10 *The Stratford-upon-Avon Herald*, 30 April 1915.
11 According to the promptbook, the seat was later moved to the left.
12 It will be recalled that Tree introduced the same business. Perhaps he learned of it from Oscar Asche who toured with Benson before entering the employ of Tree.
13 *The Stratford-upon-Avon Herald*, 24 April 1896.
14 This photograph, although not taken during a performance, differs only in the absence of the corpse of Caesar and the use of a makeshift rostrum.
15 By the 1920s, according to Mr Roberts, Benson had dispensed with the gauze and staged the appearance of the ghost by an ingenious system of lighting.
16 Foreward to *The Shakespeare Memorial Theatre* by Ruth Ellis, 1948, p. xii.
17 Hesketh Pearson, *The Last Actor-Managers*, 1950, p. 33.
18 *The Scotsman*, 1 January 1940.
19 *The Birmingham Post*, 22 April 1896.
20 Trewin, *Benson and the Bensonians*, p. 227.
21 *The Birmingham Post*, 28 April 1904.
22 *The Birmingham Daily Mail*, 22 April 1896.
23 *The Stratford-upon-Avon Herald*, 22 April 1892.
24 Conversation with Mr Roberts, 18 June 1963.
25 Ibid.
26 *The Birmingham Daily Gazette*, 12 April 1898.
27 *The Stratford-upon-Avon Herald*, 24 April 1896.
28 *The Stratford-upon-Avon Herald*, 22 April 1892.
29 *The Stratford-upon-Avon Herald*, 27 April 1906.
30 *The Stratford-upon-Avon Herald*, 23 April 1909.
31 *The Stratford-upon-Avon Herald*, 24 April 1896.
32 Trewin, *Benson and the Bensonians*, p. 227.
33 *The Stratford-upon-Avon Herald*, 29 July 1910.
34 Ibid.
35 *The Stratford-upon-Avon Herald*, 6 May 1910.
36 *The Stratford-upon-Avon Herald*, 23 April 1915.
37 Ibid.
38 *The Birmingham Mail*, 26 April 1911.
39 *The Birmingham Mail*, 26 April 1911.
40 Ibid.
41 *The Stratford-upon-Avon Herald*, 28 April 1911.
42 3 May 1912.
43 *The Stratford-upon-Avon Herald*, 14 August 1914.
44 *The Birmingham Daily Mail*, 22 April 1896.

45 *The Stratford-upon-Avon Herald*, 24 April 1896.
46 *The Stratford-upon-Avon Herald*, 28 April 1911.
47 *The Stratford-upon-Avon Herald*, 23 April 1909.
48 *The Birmingham Express*, 20 April 1909.

9. William Bridges-Adams at Stratford (1919–34)

1 Later he changed his surname to Bridges-Adams. In the interests of clarity I use this form throughout.
2 Lewis Casson staged *Caesar* uncut at The Gaiety Theatre, Manchester, in 1913. Played in a more or less permanent setting of pillars, arches, and steps in the Granville-Barker manner, the production was well-received by critics but largely ignored by audiences. Miss Horniman, the theatre proprietor, considered the production 'freakish', and Casson, much irritated, resigned. See Rex Pogson, *Miss Horniman and the Gaiety Theatre*, Manchester, 1952, pp. 159ff.
3 Although Poel in practice made 'alterations and reconstructions when the plays are considered to be unactable . . . and when it seemed to me that the success of the performance needed some alteration in the play' (Robert Speaight, *William Poel and the Elizabethan Revival*, 1954, p. 262). Poel articulates his ideas in *Shakespeare in the Theatre*, 1913, *Monthly Letters*, selected and arranged by A. M. T. [rethewy], 1929, and 'Some Notes on Shakespeare's Stage and Plays', *Bulletin of the John Rylands Library*, III (April–December 1916).
4 *The Stratford-upon-Avon Herald*, 25 July 1919.
5 W. Bridges-Adams, *Looking at a Play*, 1947, p. 27.
6 Ibid.
7 *The Stratford-upon-Avon Herald*, 25 July 1919.
8 Both books are in the Shakespeare Centre Library, Stratford-upon-Avon.
9 William Archer and John Drinkwater warmly debated the merits of *Caesar* cut and uncut in *The Nation*, 9 August and 16 August 1919.
10 8 August 1919.
11 16 August 1919.
12 W. Bridges-Adams, letter to writer, 17 July 1963.
13 W. Bridges-Adams, letter to writer, 8 July 1963.
14 W. Bridges-Adams, letter to writer, 17 July 1963.
15 Harcourt Williams had introduced this idea in his Old Vic *Caesar* in 1930.
16 W. Bridges-Adams, letter to writer, 17 July 1963.
17 20 April 1934.
18 Here Craig's influence makes itself felt. 'Among all the dreams that the architect has laid upon earth', he wrote, 'I know of no more lovely things than his flights of steps leading up and leading down' (Janet Leeper, *Edward Gordon Craig*, 1948, p. 17).
19 18 June, 1934.
20 Hudson, *Shakespeare: His Life, Art, and Characters*, II, p. 234.
21 W. Bridges-Adams, letter to writer, 17 July 1963.
22 Bridges-Adams was doubtless familiar with Reinhardt's spectacular use of steps. For the Assassination scene in his production of *Julius Caesar* at the

Grosses Schaupielhaus, Berlin, on 25 May, 1920, Reinhardt arranged a flight of thirty or forty steps leading up to Caesar's throne. After being stabbed from behind by Casca, Caesar tumbled from step to step with the conspirators savagely striking at him as he fell. See Oliver M. Sayler, *Max Reinhardt and His Theatre*, New York, 1924, p. 13.

23 Harcourt Williams dispensed with the rostrum in his Old Vic revivals in 1930 and 1932.
24 *The Birmingham Gazette*, 20 April 1934.
25 *The Birmingham Evening Despatch*, 20 April 1934.
26 1 June 1934.
27 W. Bridges-Adams, letter to writer, 17 July 1963.
28 *The Stage*, 19 April 1928. The promptbook makes it clear that Bridges-Adams did not see the part thus.
29 *The Observer*, 4 May 1930.
30 *The Stratford-upon-Avon Herald*, 1 June 1934.
31 *The Stage*, 1 May 1930.
32 *The Stratford-upon-Avon Herald*, 1 June 1934.
33 *The Stratford-upon-Avon Herald*, 20 April 1928.
34 *The Morning Post*, 20 April 1922.
35 *The Daily Telegraph*, 5 May 1932.
36 *The Stratford-upon-Avon Herald*, 9 May 1930.
37 *The Birmingham Mail*, 20 April 1934.
38 *The Birmingham Gazette*, 20 April 1934.
39 *The Times*, 20 April 1934.
40 *The Stratford-upon-Avon Herald*, 21 April 1922.
41 *The Stratford-upon-Avon Herald*, 9 May 1930.
42 Ibid.

10. American productions (1892–1949)

1 The standard biographies of Mansfield are Paul Wilstach, *Richard Mansfield – The Man and the Actor*, 1908, and William Winter, *The Life and Art of Richard Mansfield*, 2 vols., New York, 1910.
2 For detailed discussion of these scenes see Sybil Rosenfeld, 'Alma-Tadema's Designs for Henry Irving's *Coriolanus*', *Deutsche Shakespeare – Gesellschaft West Jahrbuch 1974*, ed. Hermann Heuer, pp. 84–95; and Phéné Spiers, 'The Architecture of *Coriolanus*', *Architectural Review*, x (July 1901), pp. 3–21. The latter article is lavishly illustrated.
3 Unidentified newspaper clipping dated 2 January 1908 in the Theatre Collection, New York Public Library.
4 *The Sun*, New York, 2 December 1902.
5 The playbill for the Chicago production divides the play into five acts, but the titles and order of the scenes are identical.
6 *The World*, New York, 2 December 1902.
7 Ibid.
8 *The Evening Post*, New York, 2 December 1902.
9 Joseph I. C. Clarke, *My Life and Memories*, 1925, p. 310.

10 Unidentified newspaper clipping in the Theatre Collection, New York Public Library.
11 Paul Stapfer, *Shakespeare and Classical Antiquity*, trans. Miss E. J. Carey, 1880.
12 *Munsey's Magazine*, March 1907, p. 775.
13 Unidentified clipping cited above.
14 Winter, *Richard Mansfield*, II, p. 159.
15 *The Sun*, New York, 2 December 1902.
16 *The Detroit Free Press*, 7 November 1902.
17 Winter, *Richard Mansfield*, II, p. 161.
18 Wilstach, *Richard Mansfield – The Man and the Actor*, p. 398.
19 *The Sun*, New York, 2 December 1902.
20 Unidentified Tulane newspaper clipping dated 17 March 1903 in the Theatre Collection, New York Public Library.
21 *The Evening Journal*, New York, 2 December 1902.
22 Wilstach, *Richard Mansfield – The Man and the Actor*, p. 399.
23 Unidentified newspaper clipping related to a Detroit performance in the Theatre Collection, New York Public Library.
24 Mantell's promptbook (*JC* 17) is in the Folger Shakespeare Library.
25 Winter, *Shakespeare on the Stage*, third series, p. 620.
26 William Winter (ed.), *Edwin Booth's Prompt-Book of Julius Caesar*, Philadelphia, 1904.
27 *Chicago Record-Herald*, 20 October 1912.
28 *New York American*, 6 November 1912.
29 *The World*, New York, 5 November 1912.
30 See *The Christian Science Monitor*, Boston, 23 May 1916.
31 Orson Welles and John Houseman, 'Plan for a New Theatre', *The New York Times*, 29 August 1937. Welles was not, however, the first to stage a modern-dress *Caesar*. In February of the same year Robert C. Schnitzer directed the Delaware Federal Theatre in a revival costumed in Fascist uniforms and street clothes. See *Wilmington Morning News*, 4 February 1937 and 11 February 1937.
32 John Houseman, *Run-through*, 1973, p. 298.
33 *The Mercury, A Weekly Bulletin of Information Concerning The Mercury Theatre* [n.d.].
34 Interview with Michel Mok, *New York Post*, 24 November 1937.
35 In the Theatre Collection, New York Public Library.
36 *Everybody's Shakespeare*, ed. Roger Hill and Orson Welles, Woodstock, Illinois, 1934, p. 6.
37 Orson Welles, *The Director in the Theatre Today*. Talk given at the Theatre Education League *c.* 1934 and later published as an undated pamphlet.
38 Houseman, *Run-through*, p. 307.
39 *Time*, 22 November 1937.
40 *The New York Sun*, 27 November 1937.
41 *New York Post*, 12 November 1937.
42 Houseman, *Run-through*, p. 306.
43 Ibid., p. 312.
44 *World-Telegram*, New York, 15 November 1937.

45 *New York Daily News*, 13 November 1937.
46 *Time*, 22 November 1937.
47 *The New York Sun*, 27 November 1937.
48 *World-Telegram*, New York, 12 November 1937.
49 Houseman, *Run-through*, p. 308.
50 'The American Ides of March', *The Nation*, 145 (4 December 1938), p. 617.
51 Houseman, *Run-through*, p. 307.
52 *The New Republic*, 29 December 1937.
53 Euphemia Van Rensselaer Wyatt, *The Catholic World*, CXLVI (January 1938), p. 466.
54 *New York Journal-American*, 12 November 1937.
55 Interview with Joseph Holland, *New York Herald Tribune*, 19 December 1937.
56 Professor Richard France's excellent study, *The Theatre of Orson Welles*, Lewisburg, 1977, published since this chapter was written, examines the Mercury *Caesar* in the context of Welles's total theatre career.

11. London productions (1900–49)

1 For details of Old Vic productions during the First World War, see John Booth, *The 'Old Vic'*, 1917; Cicely Hamilton and Lilian Baylis, *The Old Vic*, 1926; Matheson Lang, *Mr. Wu Looks Back*, 1941; Harcourt Williams (ed.), *Vic-Wells, The Work of Lilian Baylis*, 1938; Harcourt Williams, *Old Vic Saga*, 1949.
2 Programme in the Enthoven Collection.
3 Greet left the theatre in 1918, and was succeeded by George R. Foss, a Shakespeare scholar and erstwhile producer at the Oxford University Dramatic Society, who staged a modest *Caesar* along traditional lines in 1919. Early in 1920, a few months after Foss's departure, Russell Thorndike and Charles Warburton staged a makeshift revival. See Chronological handlist.
4 For further treatment of Atkins's work see Crosse, *Shakespearean Playgoing (1890–1952)*, pp. 50ff; Norman Marshall, *The Other Theatre*, 1947, pp. 129–30; Robert Speaight, *Shakespeare on the Stage*, 1973, pp. 148–9; J. C. Trewin, *Shakespeare on the English Stage 1900–1964*, 1964, pp. 89–90.
5 For further details of Harcourt Williams productions see Robert Speaight, *Shakespeare on the Stage*; J. C. Trewin, *Shakespeare on the English Stage 1900–1964*; and Harcourt Williams, *Four Years at the Old Vic*, 1935, and *Old Vic Saga*.
6 Williams, *Four Years at the Old Vic*, p. 12.
7 Granville-Barker, *Prefaces to Shakespeare*, first series, 1927, p. 43.
8 Ibid., p. 83.
9 Donald Wolfit, *First Interval*, 1954, p. 135.
10 *The Daily Telegraph*, 21 January 1930.
11 Crosse, *Shakespearean Playgoing (1890–1952)*, p. 69.
12 *The Times*, 21 January 1930.
13 *Everyman*, 30 January 1930.
14 *The Morning Post*, 26 January 1932.
15 Williams, *Four Years at the Old Vic*, p. 138.

16 Crosse, *Shakespearean Playgoing (1890–1952)*, p. 68.
17 See Williams, *Old Vic Saga*, p. 117, and *Four Years at the Old Vic*, p. 139.
18 Herbert Farjeon, *The Shakespearean Scene*, 1949, p. 126.
19 6 February 1932.
20 Williams, *Old Vic Saga*, p. 117.
21 Writer's conversation with Mr Speaight, London, 22 August 1976.
22 Crosse, *Shakespearean Playgoing (1890–1952)*, p. 68.
23 Farjeon, *The Shakespearean Scene*, p. 126.
24 *The Sunday Times*, 27 October 1935.
25 *The Observer*, 27 October 1935.
26 Audrey Williamson, *Old Vic Drama*, 1953, p. 36.
27 *The Times*, 25 October 1935.
28 Williamson, *Old Vic Drama*, p. 35.
29 *The Times*, 25 October 1935.
30 Williamson, *Old Vic Drama*, p. 35.
31 Bell altered Tree's version slightly. The storm was allotted a separate scene in act I and the Plains of Philippi action was played as three scenes instead of the single continuous episode of Tree's production.
32 For excellent photographs of this production see *Play Pictorial*, February 1920.
33 *The Sunday Times*, 11 January 1920.
34 *The New Age*, 22 January 1920.
35 Letter to *The Times*, 4 February 1920.
36 'No Change', *The New Statesman and Nation*, 20 February 1932.
37 C. B. Purdom, 'The Museum Shakespeare', *Everyman*, 18 February 1932.
38 *The Morning Post*, 9 February 1932.
39 *The Observer*, 14 February 1932.
40 Purdom, 'The Museum Shakespeare'.
41 *The Times*, 6 July 1937.
42 *Evening Standard*, 6 July 1937.
43 *The Times*, 6 July 1937.
44 *Daily Herald*, 30 November 1939.
45 Ibid.
46 Andrew Leigh directed an unremarkable production at Stratford which opened on 15 April 1941.
47 Programme in the Enthoven Collection.
48 'Tailoring the Bard', *The Observer*, 25 September 1949.
49 'Mr. Wolfit's Brutus', *The Sunday Times*, 25 September 1949.
50 Ibid.

12. English and North American productions (1950–73)

1 In 1936 John Wyse directed an unremarkable *Caesar* along Old Vic lines on a permanent set consisting of columns and flights of steps. The columns were shown as broken in the Plains of Philippi scenes. The crowd was again located on orchestra-well stairs for the Forum speech. A director's workbook for this production (*JC* 81) is in the Shakespeare Centre Library. The promptbook was

erased and freshly marked for Andrew Leigh's production in 1941, but many of the original directions are still legible.

Andrew Leigh's wartime production re-used the Wyse settings with some modification. The text was abbreviated by over 400 lines. Many of the traditional cuts reappeared (e.g. the sequences with the servants of Antony and Octavius, the Cinna the Poet scene, the Proscription scene, the Camp Poet episode, and Cassius' birthday speech). This promptbook (*JC* 84) is also in the Shakespeare Centre Library.

2 The promptbook for this revival has disappeared. A partial copy (*JC* 86) is in the Shakespeare Centre Library. This book indicates the text played, and much of the stage business for act I is marked.

3 *News Chronicle*, 3 May 1950.

4 John Gielgud, *Stage Directions*, 1963, p. 45.

5 *John O'London's Weekly*, 26 May 1950.

6 *Tribune*, 12 May 1950.

7 *Evening News*, 5 May 1950.

8 *Sketch*, 24 May 1950.

9 *Tribune*, 12 May 1950.

10 *Truth*, 12 May 1950.

11 *Tribune*, 12 May 1950.

12 *Time & Tide*, 10 June 1950.

13 *Tribune*, 12 May 1950.

14 The Arena Theatre, a renovated ballroom in the Hotel Edison on Forty-Seventh Street, was jointly operated by David Heilweil and Derrick Lynn-Thomas. Their productions were the first Broadway ventures in arena staging. *Julius Caesar* was directed by Dan Levin.

15 See A. C. Sprague, *Shakespearian Players and Performances*, Cambridge, Mass., 1954, p. 155.

16 *New Republic*, 3 July 1950.

17 *Daily Mail*, 25 February 1953.

18 *New Statesman and Nation*, 7 March 1953.

19 *Observer*, 1 March 1953.

20 *Daily Mail*, 25 February 1953.

21 *Manchester Guardian*, 26 February 1953.

22 *Evening News*, 25 February 1953.

23 *The Times*, 25 February 1953.

24 *Sketch*, 11 March 1953.

25 *Manchester Guardian*, 24 February 1953.

26 *The Times*, 25 February 1953.

27 *Daily Mail*, 25 February 1953. The trick was an old one. Otis Skinner was taught it by the nineteenth-century veteran, Joe Nagle, and used it on tour with Barrett. 'It was a rigid backdrop', writes Skinner, 'straight from the heels with arms extended so as to strike the stage simultaneously with my shoulders and save my spine and the back of my head. The whack on the planking never failed to shock the audience into applause. I knew Barrett thought it inartistic, and he was right.' See Skinner, *Footlights and Spotlights*, p. 115.

28 Programme in the Enthoven Collection.

29　Robertson Davies, *Thrice the Brinded Cat Hath Mewed*, Toronto, 1955, pp. 8–9.

30　Ibid., p. 27.

31　Ibid.

32　Arnold Edinborough, 'Shakespeare Confirmed: At Canadian Stratford', *Shakespeare Quarterly*, VI (Autumn 1955), p. 437.

33　Ibid.

34　Davies, *Thrice the Brindèd Cat Hath Mewed*, p. 25.

35　Ibid., p. 23.

36　Ibid., p. 21.

37　Ibid., p. 22.

38　Edinborough, 'Shakespeare Confirmed', p. 437.

39　*New York Times*, 13 July 1955.

40　*New York Herald-Tribune*, 17 July 1955.

41　*New York Herald-Tribune*, 13 July 1955.

42　*Morning Telegraph*, New York, 14 July 1955.

43　For further details of this production see the promptbook (*JC* 89) at the Old Vic; also Roger Wood and Mary Clarke, *Shakespeare at the Old Vic*, 1956, vol. 3.

44　Wood and Clarke, *Shakespeare at the Old Vic*, n.p.

45　8 September 1955.

46　Anthony Cookman, 'An Off-Key Triumph', *The Tatler and Bystander*, 21 September 1955.

47　Ibid.

48　*The Spectator*, 26 August 1955.

49　The promptbook (*JC* 90) is in the Shakespeare Centre Library.

50　See Glen Byam Shaw's introduction to the Folio Society edition of *Julius Caesar*, 1962.

51　Roy Walker, 'Unto Caesar: A Review of Recent Productions', *Shakespeare Survey* 12 (1959), p. 132.

52　Mr Walker apparently suggested the idea of the emblematic star to Mr Byam Shaw. See note 5 to Mr Walker's article cited above.

53　*Stratford-upon-Avon Herald*, 31 May 1957.

54　Ivor Brown, Introduction to *Shakespeare Memorial Theatre 1957–1959*, 1959, p. 8.

55　29 May 1957.

56　*Coventry Evening Telegraph*, 29 May 1957.

57　Alice Griffin, 'The Shakespeare Season in New York 1958–1959', *Shakespeare Quarterly*, X (Autumn 1959). p. 572.

58　Croft revived the production with new casts and updated costumes and business at Sadler's Wells in 1962, at the Scala in 1963, and at the Collegiate Theatre in 1970.

59　'We are all menaced', *Flourish*, II.i (1968), p. 7. See also Brook's *The Empty Space*, New York, 1968, and J. C. Trewin's *Peter Brook: a Biography*, 1971.

60　J. C. Trewin, *Peter Brook*, p. 51n.

61　*Observer*, 22 April 1962.

62　*Illustrated London News*, 17 April 1962.

63　'Volanakis Releases the God', *The Sunday Times*, 22 April 1962.

64 Ibid.
65 See J. C. Trewin, 'The Old Vic and Stratford-upon-Avon 1961–62', *Shakespeare Quarterly*, XIII (Autumn 1962), p. 510.
66 The promptbook is in the Shakespeare Centre Library.
67 *Spectator*, 20 April 1963.
68 *Birmingham Post*, 10 April 1963.
69 10 April 1963.
70 *Stratford-upon-Avon Herald*, 12 April 1963.
71 *Plays and Players*, June 1963.
72 The interpolated lines, inserted after v.iii.103 ran as follows:
> Brutus, the day is lost.
> Octavius' legions in their disarray,
> Meeting with Antony did take new strength.
> Together they have routed all our hopes,
> Vanquished our soldiers, set our tents ablaze.
> Our expectation hath this day an end
> And we no longer are defensible.

Mr Anderson kindly supplied me with this speech in a letter dated 2 March 1977.
73 Jonathan Griffin attacked Anderson's alterations in a letter to *The Times*, 19 December 1964; and Robert Speaight commented in another letter on 31 December 1964.
74 *Daily Mail*, 27 November 1964.
75 Director's Preface to the Festival Edition of *Julius Caesar*, ed. John Saxton, Toronto, 1970, p. xxxiii.
76 *New York Times*, 2 July 1965.
77 Unidentified newspaper clipping in Theatre Section, Metropolitan Toronto Public Library.
78 Arnold Edinborough, 'The Canadian Shakespeare Festival', *Shakespeare Quarterly*, XVI (Autumn 1965), p. 327.
79 Anti-romanticism was a feature of productions during the Peter Hall era. See Gareth Lloyd Evans, 'Shakespeare, the Twentieth Century and "Behaviourism"', *Shakespeare Survey* 20 (1967), pp. 133–42.
80 The promptbook is in the Shakespeare Centre Library.
81 'Shakespeare in Britain', *Shakespeare Quarterly*, XIX (Autumn 1968), p. 373.
82 *Plays and Players*, June 1968.
83 'Politicians down the ages', *Spectator*, 12 April 1968.
84 *Evening Standard*, 14 March 1972.
85 *Punch*, 22 March 1972.
86 *Observer*, 19 March 1972.
87 In 1963 the BBC televised all four plays under the title 'The Spread of the Eagle'. In 1972 the American Shakespeare Festival staged an uneventful joint revival of *Julius Caesar* and *Antony and Cleopatra* at Stratford, Connecticut.
88 'Direction and Design. Trevor Nunn and Christopher Morley Talk to Margaret Tierney', *Plays and Players*, September 1972, p. 26.
89 Peter Thomson, 'No Rome of Safety: The Royal Shakespeare Season 1972 Reviewed', *Shakespeare Survey* 25 (1972), p. 139.

90 The promptbook is in the Shakespeare Centre Library.
91 *Observer*, 7 May 1972.
92 *Punch*, 10 May 1972.
93 *New Statesman*, 11 May 1972.
94 *Stratford-upon-Avon Herald*, 5 May 1972.
95 Ibid.

Afterword

1 Since this study was written Sir John has played Julius Caesar (National Theatre, 1977).
2 See Terence Spencer, 'Shakespeare and the Elizabethan Romans', *Shakespeare Survey* 10 (1957).
3 Introduction to *Julius Caesar*, Folio Society Edition, 1962, p. 3.
4 Sister Miriam Joseph Raugh, *Shakespeare's Use of the Arts of Language*, 1947, p. 240.
5 Sister Miriam Joseph's analysis of *Julius Caesar*'s rhetoric has greatly enriched my understanding of the play.
6 Sir John Gielgud, *Stage Directions*, 1963, p. 48.

BIBLIOGRAPHY

BOOKS

Place of publication is noted only when it is other than London.

Adams, Joseph Quincy (ed.). *The Dramatic Records of Sir Henry Herbert*. New Haven, 1917.

Alger, William Rounseville. *Life of Edwin Forrest*. 2 vols. Philadelphia, 1877.

Allen, Shirley S. *Samuel Phelps and Sadler's Wells Theatre*. Middletown, Conn., 1971.

Archer, William. *William Charles Macready*. 1890.

Baker, David Erskine. *The Companion to the Play-House*. 2 vols., 1764.

—— *Biographia Dramatica*. 2 vols., 1782.

Baker, Henry Barton. *Our Old Actors*. 2 vols., 1878.

Baker, Herschel. *John Philip Kemble*. Cambridge, Mass., 1942.

Baylis, Lilian. *See* Hamilton, Cicely.

Becker, William Adolf. *Gallus; or Roman Scenes of the Time of Augustus*, 1844.

Beerbohm, Max (ed.). *Herbert Beerbohm Tree* [n.d.]

Benson, Lady. *Mainly Players*. 1926.

Benson, Sir Frank. *My Memoirs*. 1930.

Benson, Richard Lee. *Jarrett and Palmer's 1875 Production of Julius Caesar: A Reconstruction*. Unpublished Ph.D. dissertation, University of Illinois, Urbana, 1968.

Bentley, Gerald Eades. *The Jacobean and Caroline Stage*. 2 vols. Oxford, 1949.

Bernard, John. *Retrospections of the Stage*. 2 vols., 1830.

—— *Retrospections of America 1797–1811*. Edited by Mrs Bayle Bernard, with an introduction, notes and index by Laurence Hutton and Brander Matthews. New York, 1887. Reissued by Benjamin Blom, Inc. New York, 1969.

Boaden, James. *Memoirs of the Life of John Philip Kemble Esq*. 2 vols., 1825.

—— *Memoirs of Mrs. Siddons*. 2 vols., 1827.

Bonjour, Adrien. *The Structure of Julius Caesar*. 1958.

Booth, John. *The 'Old Vic'*. 1917.

Boswell, Eleanore. *The Restoration Court Stage*. Cambridge, Mass., 1932.

Bridges-Adams, W. *Looking at a Play*. 1947.

Brook, Peter. *The Empty Space*. New York, 1968.

Brown, Ivor. *Shakespeare Memorial Theatre 1957–1959*. 1959.

Brown, Thomas Allston. *A History of the New York Stage*. 3 vols. New York, 1903.

Bullough, Geoffrey. *Narrative and Dramatic Sources of Shakespeare*. 8 vols. 1957–75.

Byrne, M. St Clare. *A History of Shakespearean Production in England*. 1949.

Campbell, Lily B. 'A History of Costuming on the English Stage between 1660 and 1823', *University of Wisconsin Studies in Language and Literature*. Madison, 1918, pp. 187–223.

—— *Scenes and Machines on the English Stage During the Renaissance*. Cambridge, Mass., 1923.

Carr, Thomas Swinburne. *A Manual of Roman Antiquities*. 1836.

Chambers, E. K. *The Elizabethan Stage*. 4 vols. Oxford, 1923.

—— *William Shakespeare*. 2 vols. Oxford, 1951.

Charney, Maurice. *Shakespeare's Roman Plays*. 1963.

Child, H. *The Shakespearian Productions of John Philip Kemble*. 1935.

Churchill, Charles. *The Poetical Works*. Edited by Douglas Grant, 1956.

Cibber, Colley. *An Apology for the Life of*. Edited by Edmund Bellchambers, 1822.

—— *An Apology for the Life of*. 2 vols. Edited by Robert W. Lowe, 1889.

Cibber, Theophilus. *The Lives and Characters of the Most Eminent Actors and Actresses of Great Britain and Ireland*. 1753.

Clarke, Asia Booth. *Booth Memorials*. New York, 1866.

—— *The Elder and the Younger Booth* [n.d.].

Clarke, Joseph I. C. *My Life and Memories*. New York, 1925.

Clarke, Mary. *See* Wood, Roger.

Cole, J. W. *Life and Theatrical Times of Charles Kean F.S.A.* 2 vols., 1859.

Coleridge, Samuel Taylor. *Shakespearean Criticism*. 2 vols. Edited by Thomas Middleton Raysor, 1960.

A Collection and Selection of English Prologues and Epilogues. 3 vols., 1779.

Cooke, William. *Memoirs of Charles Macklin*. 1806.

Creahan, John. *The Life of Laura Keene*. Philadelphia, 1897.

Crosse, Gordon. *Shakespearean Playgoing (1890–1952)*. 1953.

Davies, Robertson. *Thrice the Brinded Cat Hath Mewed*. Toronto, 1955.

Davies, Thomas. *Dramatic Miscellanies*. 3 vols., 1783–4.

—— *Memoirs of the Life of David Garrick*. 2 vols., 1780, 1784.

Dennis, John. *The Critical Works*. 2 vols. Edited by Edward Niles Hooker. Baltimore, 1939.

Dickins, Richard. *Forty Years of Shakespeare on the English Stage*. 1907.

Dowden, Edward. *Shakspere: His Mind and Art*. 1875.

Downer, Alan S. *The Eminent Tragedian: William Charles Macready*. Cambridge, Mass., 1966.

Downes, John. *Roscius Anglicanus*. 1708.

Dryden, John. Preface to *Troilus and Cressida*. 1695.

—— *Essays*. 2 vols. Edited by W. P. Ker, 1900.

Dunlap, William. *History of the American Theatre*. New York, 1832. Reissued by Burt Franklin. New York, 1963.

Dunn, Esther Cloudman. *Shakespeare in America*. New York, 1939.

Durang, John. *The Memoir of*. Edited by Alan S. Downer. Pittsburgh, 1966.

Ellis, Ruth. *The Shakespeare Memorial Theatre*. 1948.

Evans, G. Blakemore. 'The Problem of Brutus. An Eighteenth Century Solution', *Studies in Honour of T. W. Baldwin*. Urbana, 1958.

Fane, Francis, Jr. *Love in the Dark*, 1675.
Farjeon, Herbert. *The Shakespearean Scene*, 1949.
Finlay, John. *Miscellanies*. Dublin, 1835.
Fitzgerald, Percy. *The Kembles*. 2 vols., 1871.
Foakes, R. A., and Rickert, R. T. (eds.). *Henslowe's Diary*. 1961.
Forbes-Robertson, John. *See* Phelps, W. May.
Forster, John, and Lewes, George Henry. *Dramatic Essays*. Edited by William Archer and Robert W. Lowe, 1896.
The Francis Letters By Sir Francis and Other Members of the Family. Edited by Beata Francis and Eliza Keary, 1901.
Frye, Northrop. *Fools of Time*. 1965.
Genest, John. *Some Account of the English Stage*. 10 vols. Bath, 1832.
Gentleman, Francis. *The Dramatic Censor*. 2 vols., 1770.
Gervinus, G. G. *Shakespeare Commentaries*. Translated by F. E. Bunnètt, 1877.
Gielgud, John. *Stage Directions*. 1963.
Gildon, Charles. *Miscellaneous Letters and Essays*. 1694.
—— *The Life of Mr. Thomas Betterton*, 1710.
—— Preface to *Julius Caesar*. Vol. VII: *The Works of Mr. William Shakespeare*. Edited by Nicholas Rowe, 1710.
Goodwin, Thomas. *Sketches and Impressions*, 1887.
Gould, Thomas R. *The Tragedian*. New York, 1868.
Granville-Barker, Harley. *Prefaces to Shakespeare*. First series, 1927.
[Graydon, Alexander]. *'Memoirs of a Life, Chiefly Passed in Pennsylvama*. Harrisburgh, Pennsylvania, 1811.
Grossman, Edwina Booth. *Edwin Booth: Recollections By His Daughter*. New York, 1894.
Hackett, James Henry. *Notes and Comments upon Certain Plays and Actors of Shakespeare*. 1864.
Hamilton, Cicely, and Baylis, Lilian. *The Old Vic*. 1926.
[Haslewood, Joseph]. *The Secret History of the Green-Room*. 1795.
Hazlitt, William. *Criticisms and Dramatic Essays of the English Stage*. 1854.
—— *The Complete Works*. 21 vols. Edited by P. P. Howe, 1930–4.
Hill, Aaron. *The Works of the Late Aaron Hill, Esq.* 4 vols., 1753.
Hill, Roger, and Welles, Orson. *Everybody's Shakespeare*. Woodstock, Illinois, 1934.
Hill, Sir John. *The Actor*. 1755.
Hogan, Charles Beecher. *Shakespeare in the Theatre 1701–1800*. 2 vols., 1952.
Hope, Thomas. *Costume of the Ancients*. 1841.
Horne, R. H. *A New Spirit of the Age*. (World's Classics Edition), 1907.
Hotson, Leslie. *The Commonwealth and Restoration Stage*. Cambridge, Mass., 1928.
Houseman, John. *Run-through*. 1973.
Hudson, H. N. *Shakespeare: His Life, Art, and Characters*. 2 vols., Boston, 1872.
Hunt, Leigh. *Dramatic Criticism 1808–1831*. Edited by Lawrence Huston Houtchens and Carolyn Washburn Houtchens, 1950.
Hunter, Sir Mark. 'Politics and Character in Shakespeare's "Julius Caesar"', *Essays By Divers Hands, Transactions of the Royal Society of Literature*, X (1931).
Inchbald, Mrs. *Remarks* [prefatory to *Julius Caesar*] 1808.

Ireland, Joseph Norton. *A Memoir of the Professional Life of Thomas Abthorpe Cooper.* New York, 1888. Reissued by Burt Franklin. New York, 1970.

—— *Playbills and Advertisements of Mr. Cooper's Performances for 1795 to 1836.* 2 vols., Bridgeport, 1888.

—— *Records of the New York Stage.* New York, 1866.

Jaggard, William. *Shakespeare Bibliography.* Stratford-on-Avon, 1911.

Johnson, Samuel. *Johnson on Shakespeare.* Edited by Walter Raleigh, 1931.

Jonson, Ben. *Every Man Out of his Humour. The Complete Works of Ben Jonson.* Edited by C. H. Herford and Percy Simpson. Vol. III, 1927.

Joseph, Bertram. *The Tragic Actor.* 1959.

[Kelly, Hugh]. *Thespis.* 1766.

Kemble, John Philip. *John Philip Kemble Promptbooks.* Edited by Charles H. Shattuck. Published for The Folger Shakespeare Library by the University Press of Virginia. 11 vols. Charlottesville, 1974.

—— 'Memoranda of J. P. Kemble', British Library Ad. MSS. 31972–5, vol. IV.

Kimmel, Stanley. *The Mad Booths of Maryland.* New York, 1969.

Knight, G. Wilson. *The Wheel of Fire.* 1930.

—— *The Imperial Theme.* 1931.

Knights, L. C. *Further Explorations.* 1965.

Lang, Matheson. *Mr. Wu Looks Back.* 1941.

Langbaine, Gerard. *The Lives and Characters of the English Dramatic Poets.* 1702.

Lee, Sidney. *Shakespeare and the Modern Stage.* 1906.

Leeper, Janet. *Edward Gordon Craig.* 1948.

Lewes, G. H. *See* Forster, John.

Lockridge, Richard. *Darling of Misfortune.* New York, 1932.

The London Stage. Part 1: *1660–1700.* Edited by William Van Lennep. Carbondale, Illinois, 1960.

Part 2: *1700–1729.* Edited by Emmett L. Avery. Carbondale, Illinois, 1960.

Part 3: *1729–1747.* Edited by Arthur Scouten. Carbondale, Illinois, 1961.

Part 4: *1747–1776.* Edited by George Winchester Stone. Carbondale, Illinois, 1962.

Part 5: *1776–1800.* Edited by Charles Beecher Hogan. Carbondale, Illinois, 1968.

Ludlow, Noah M. *Dramatic Life As I Found It.* St Louis, 1880.

MacCallum, M. W. *Shakespeare's Roman Plays.* 1910.

MacKaye, Percy. *Epoch: The Life of Steele MacKaye.* 1927.

Macready, William Charles. *Reminiscences.* Edited by Sir Frederick Pollock. 2 vols., 1875.

—— *The Diaries 1833–1851.* Edited by William Toynbee. 2 vols., 1912.

Marshall, Norman. *The Other Theatre.* 1947.

Marston, Westland. *Our Recent Actors.* 2 vols., 1888.

Matthews, Brander, and Thorndike, Ashley Horace (eds.). *Shakesperian Studies.* 1916.

Merchant, W. M. *Shakespeare and the Artist.* 1959.

The Mercury, A Weekly Bulletin of Information Concerning The Mercury Theatre. [n.d.].

Montague, Mrs Elizabeth. *An Essay on the Writings and Genius of Shakespear.* 1769.

Morley, Henry, *The Journal of a London Playgoer.* 1866.

Moulton, Richard G. *Shakespeare as a Dramatic Artist*. Oxford, 1885.
Murdoch, James E. *The Stage or Recollections of Actors and Acting*. Philadelphia, 1880.
Murray, E. Croft. *John Devoto. A Baroque Scene Painter*. 1953.
Nagler, A. M. (ed.). *A Source Book in Theatrical History*. 1952.
Nicoll, Allardyce. *The Development of the Theatre*, 1948.
—— *British Drama*, 1958.
—— *A History of English Drama*. Vols. I–V, Cambridge, 1952–9.
—— *English Drama 1900–1930: The Beginnings of the Modern Period*. Cambridge, 1973.
Odell, George C. D. *Shakespeare From Betterton to Irving*. 2 vols., 1920.
—— *Annals of the New York Stage*. 15 vols. New York, 1927–49.
Palmer, John. *Political Characters of Shakespeare*. 1945.
Pearson, Hesketh. *The Last Actor-Managers*. 1950.
—— *Beerbohm Tree: His Life and Laughter*. 1956.
Phelps, W. May, and Forbes-Robertson, John. *The Life and Life-Work of Samuel Phelps*. 1886.
Phillips, J. E. *The State in Shakespeare's Greek and Roman Plays*. 1940.
Pitou, Augustus, *Masters of the Show*. 1914.
Planché, J. R. *The Recollections and Reflections of*. 1872.
Poel, William. *Shakespeare in the Theatre*, 1913.
—— *Monthly Letters*. Selected and arranged by A. M. T. [rethewy], 1929.
Pogson, Rex. *Miss Horniman and the Gaiety Theatre*. Manchester, 1952.
Powell, George. *The Treacherous Brothers*. 1690.
The Present State of the Stage in Great Britain and Ireland. 1763.
Reynolds, Sir Joshua. *Fifteen Discourses Delivered in the Royal Academy*. (Everyman Edition) [n.d.].
Rich, John. 'Covent Garden Inventory', British Library Add. MSS. 12, 201. Selected Folios 34–73.
Rickert, R. T. *See* Foakes, R. A.
Robinson, Henry Crabb. *Diary, Reminiscences and Correspondence*. 2 vols. Edited by Thomas Sadler, 1869.
Rosenfeld, Sybil. *Strolling Players and Drama in the Provinces, 1660–1765*, Cambridge, 1939.
Ruggles, Eleanor. *Prince of Players*. New York, 1953.
Rymer, Thomas. *The Critical Works*. Edited by Curt A. Zimansky. New Haven, 1956.
Sayler, Oliver M. *Max Reinhardt and His Theatre*. New York, 1924.
Schanzer, Ernest. *The Problem Plays of Shakespeare*. New York, 1963.
Seilhamer, George O. *History of the American Theatre During the Revolution and After*. 3 vols. Philadelphia, 1888–91.
Shakespeare, William. *Julius Caesar*. Edited by Nicholas Rowe, 1710.
—— *Julius Caesar*. John Bell. Edited by Francis Gentleman, 1773.
—— *Julius Caesar*. J. P. Kemble Acting Edition, 1814. Facsimile published by Cornmarket Press, 1970.
—— *Julius Caesar*. New Variorum edition. Edited by H. H. Furness Jr, 1913.
—— *Julius Caesar*. Cambridge edition. Edited by John Dover Wilson, 1949.

—— *Julius Caesar*. Arden edition. Edited by T. S. Dorsch, 1961.

—— *Julius Caesar*. Folio Society edition. Introduction by Glen Byam Shaw, 1962.

—— *Julius Caesar*. Festival edition. Edited by John Saxton, Toronto, 1970.

—— *The Pictorial Edition of the Works of Shakspere*. Edited by Charles Knight [1846], vol. II.

—— *Poems: Written by Wil. Shake-speare. Gent.* 1640.

The Tragedy of 'Julius Caesar' . . . alter'd by Sir William Davenant and John Dryden. 1719.

Shattuck, Charles H. *William Charles Macready's King John*. Urbana, Illinois, 1962.

—— *The Shakespeare Promptbooks*. Urbana, Illinois, 1965.

—— *The Hamlet of Edwin Booth*. Urbana, Illinois, 1969.

—— 'The Theatrical Management of Edwin Booth', *The Theatrical Manager in England and America*. Edited by Joseph W. Donohue, Jr. Princeton, New Jersey, 1971.

—— (ed.) *John Philip Kemble Promptbooks*. Published for The Folger Shakespeare Library by the University Press of Virginia. 11 vols. Charlottesville, 1974.

Shaw, Bernard. *Three Plays for Puritans*. (Standard edition), 1931.

The Works of John Sheffield, Earl of Mulgrave, Marquis of Normanby, and Duke of Buckingham, 1723, vol. I.

Simon, Henry W. *The Reading of Shakespeare in American Schools and Colleges*. New York, 1932.

Skinner, Otis. *Footlights and Spotlights*. Indianapolis, 1924.

—— *The Last Tragedian*. New York, 1939.

Snow, L. F. *College Curriculum in the United States*. New York, 1907.

Southern, E. H. *My Remembrances*. 1917.

Speaight, Robert. *William Poel and the Elizabethan Revival*. 1954.

—— *Shakespeare on the Stage*. 1973.

Spencer, Hazelton. *Shakespeare Improved*. Cambridge, Mass., 1927.

Spencer, T. J. B. *Shakespeare: The Roman Plays*. 1963.

Sprague, A. C. *Shakespeare and the Actors*. Cambridge, Mass., 1945.

—— *Shakespearian Players and Performances*. Cambridge, Mass., 1954.

Stapfer, Paul. *Shakespeare and Classical Antiquity*. Translated by Miss E. J. Cary, 1880.

Stein, Elizabeth P. *David Garrick, Dramatist*. 1938.

Stewart, J. I. M. *Character and Motive in Shakespeare*. 1949.

Stirling, Brents. *The Populace in Shakespeare*. 1949.

—— *Unity in Shakespearian Tragedy*. 1956.

Stone, Henry Dickinson. *Personal Recollections of the Drama*. Albány, 1873.

Stranahan, C. H. *A History of French Painting*. 1889.

Summers, Montague. *The Restoration Theatre*. 1934.

Swinburne, Algernon Charles. *A Study of Shakespeare*. 1879.

Thorndike, Ashley Horace. *See* Matthews, Brander.

Towse, John Ranken. *Sixty Years of the Theater*. 1911; and New York, 1916.

Traversi, D. A. *Shakespeare's Roman Plays*. 1963.

Tree, Herbert Beerbohm. *Thoughts and After-Thoughts*. 1913.

Trewin, J. C. *Benson and the Bensonians*. 1960.
—— *Shakespeare on the English Stage 1900–1964*. 1964.
—— *Peter Brook: A Biography*. 1971.
Ulrici, Hermann. *Shakespeare's Dramatic Art*. Translated by A. J. W. M[orrison], 1846.
Vandenhoff, George. *Dramatic Reminiscences*, 1860.
Van Doren, Mark. *Shakespeare*. New York, 1953.
Voltaire, François. *Oeuvres Complètes*. Vols. II and III. Paris, 1877.
Watermeier, Daniel J. *Between Actor and Critic*. Princeton, New Jersey, 1971.
Welles, Orson. *The Director in the Theatre Today*. Theatre Education League pamphlet [n.d.]. *See also* Hill, Roger.
Wemyss, Francis Courtney. *Theatrical Biography*. Glasgow, 1848.
Whincop, Thomas. *A Compleat List of all the English Dramatic Poets*. 1747.
Whitman, Walt. *November Boughs*. Philadelphia, 1888.
Wikoff, Henry. *Reminiscences of an Idler*. New York, 1880.
Wilkes, Thomas. *A General View of the Stage*. 1759.
Wilkinson, Tate. *Memoirs of His Own Life*. 2 vols., 1790.
—— *Original Anecdotes Respecting the Stage* [c. 1801].
Williams, Harcourt. *Four Years at the Old Vic*. 1935.
—— *Old Vic Saga*. 1949.
—— (ed.). *Vic-Wells, The Work of Lilian Baylis*, 1938.
Williamson, Audrey. *Old Vic Drama*. 1953.
Wilstach, Paul. *Richard Mansfield – The Man and the Actor*, 1908.
Winter, William
—— *Shadows of the Stage*. Edinburgh, 1892.
—— *The Life and Art of Edwin Booth*. New York, 1893.
—— *Other Days*. New York, 1908.
—— *The Life and Art of Richard Mansfield*. 2 vols., New York, 1910.
—— *Shakespeare on the Stage*, third series. New York, 1915.
—— (ed.). *Edwin Booth's Prompt-Book of Julius Caesar*. Philadelphia, 1904.
The Wisdome of Doctor Dodypoll. 1600. (Old English Drama, Students' Facsimile edition).
Wolfit, Donald. *First Interval*. 1954.
Wood, Roger, and Clarke, Mary. *Shakespeare at the Old Vic*. Vol. 3., 1956.
Wood, William. *Personal Recollections of the Stage*. Philadelphia, 1855.
Wright, James. *Historia Histrionica*. 1699.
Young, Julian Charles. *A Memoir of Charles Mayne Young*. 1871.

Articles in periodicals

Anderson, Lindsay. 'No Nonsense About Shakespeare', *The Times*, 15 December 1964.
Bald, R. C. 'Shakespeare on the Stage in Restoration Dublin', *PMLA*, LVI (June 1941).
Bartlett, Henrietta C. 'Quarto Editions of *Julius Caesar*', *The Library*, third series, IV (1913).

Bassett, Abe J. 'The Capitol Setting for *Julius Caesar*', Ohio State University Theatre Collection Bulletin (Spring 1959).

Benson, W. A. S. '"Agamemnon" At Oxford', *Cornhill Magazine*, new series, XLVI (May 1919).

Boase, T. S. R. 'Illustrations of Shakespeare's Plays in the Seventeenth and Eighteenth Centuries', *Journal of the Warburg and Courtauld Institutes*, X (1947).

Bowden, William R. 'The Mind of Brutus', *Shakespeare Quarterly*, XVII (Winter 1966).

Brook, Peter. 'What About Real Life?' *Crucial Years*, Royal Shakespeare Company booklet, 1963.

—— 'We are all menaced', *Flourish*, II. 1 (1968).

Brown, Ivor. 'Tailoring the Bard', *The Observer*, 25 September 1949.

Bunce, O. B. '"Julius Caesar" at Booth's Theatre', *Appleton's Journal*, XV (22 January 1876).

Coleman, John. 'Phelps as I Knew Him', *The Theatre*, 1 October 1885.

Cookman, Anthony. 'An Off-Key Triumph', *The Tatler and Bystander*, 21 September 1955.

Edinborough, Arnold. 'Shakespeare Confirmed: At Canadian Stratford', *Shakespeare Quarterly*, VI (Autumn 1955).

—— 'The Canadian Shakespeare Festival', *Shakespeare Quarterly*, XVI (Autumn 1965).

Evans, Gareth Lloyd. 'Shakespeare, the Twentieth Century and "Behaviourism"', *Shakespeare Survey* 20 (1967).

Foakes, R. A. 'An Approach to *Julius Caesar*', *Shakespeare Quarterly*, V (Summer 1954).

Fortin, René E. '*Julius Caesar*: An Experiment in Point of View', *Shakespeare Quarterly*, XIX (Autumn 1968).

Goddard, Henry P. 'Recollections of Edward L. Davenport', *Lippincott's Magazine*, April 1878.

Griffin, Alice. 'The Shakespeare Season in New York 1958–1959', *Shakespeare Quarterly*, X (Autumn 1959).

Hobson, Harold, 'Mr. Wolfit's Brutus', *The Sunday Times*, 25 September 1949.

—— 'Volanakis Releases the God', *The Sunday Times*, 22 April 1962.

Kirschbaum, Leo. 'Shakespeare's Stage Blood and its Critical Significance', *PLMA*, LXIV (June 1949).

Koeppel, E. Note in *Shakespeare Jahrbuch*, XLIII (1907).

Langhans, Edward A. 'New Restoration Manuscript Casts', *Theatre Notebook*, XXVII (Summer 1973).

Lindner, A. 'Die Dramatische Einheit im Julius Caesar', *Jahrbuch*, II (1866).

MacCarthy, Desmond. 'No Change', *The New Statesman and Nation*, 20 February 1932.

MacLeish, Archibald. 'The American Ides of March', *The Nation*, 145 (4 December 1938).

Martin, Sir Theodore. 'An Eye-Witness of John Kemble', *The Nineteenth Century* (February 1880).

Maxwell, J. C. 'Shakespeare's Roman Plays: 1900–1956', *Shakespeare Survey* 10 (1957).

Merchant, W. M. 'Classical Costume in Shakespearian Productions', *Shakespeare Survey* 10 (1957).

Nicoll, Allardyce. 'Political Plays of the Restoration', *Modern Language Review*, XXI (1921).

'On Elocution', *The Emerald*, Boston, 12 March 1808.

Poel, William. 'Some Notes on Shakespeare's Stage and Plays', *Bulletin of the John Rylands Library*, III (April–December 1916).

Purdom, C. B. 'The Museum Shakespeare', *Everyman*, 18 February 1932.

Rosenfeld, Sybil. 'Alma-Tadema's Designs for Henry Irving's *Coriolanus*', *Deutsche Shakespeare – Gesellschraft West Jahrbuch* 1974, ed. Hermann Heuer.

Rosenfeld, Sybil, and Croft-Murray, Edward. 'Checklist of Scene Painters Working in Great Britain and Ireland in the 18th Century', *Theatre Notebook*, 1964–6, vols. 19, 20.

Rostron, David. 'John Philip Kemble's *Coriolanus* and *Julius Caesar*', *Theatre Notebook*, XXIII (Autumn 1968).

—— 'F. R. Benson's Early Productions of Shakespeare's Roman Plays at Stratford', *Theatre Notebook*, XXV (Winter 1970–1).

Schanzer, Ernest. 'The Tragedy of Shakespeare's Brutus', *ELH*, 22 (March 1955).

Scott, Sir Walter. Review of Boaden's *Kemble*, *The Quarterly Review*, XXXIV (June 1826).

Shattuck, Charles H. 'Macready Prompt-Books', *Theatre Notebook*, XVI (Autumn 1961).

Smith, Gordon Ross. 'Brutus, Virtue, and Will', *Shakespeare Quarterly*, X (Summer 1959).

Speaight, Robert. 'Shakespeare in Britain', *Shakespeare Quarterly*, XIV (Autumn 1963).

—— 'Shakespeare in Britain', *Shakespeare Quarterly*, XVI (Autumn 1965).

—— 'Shakespeare in Britain', *Shakespeare Quarterly*, XIX (Autumn 1968).

Spencer, T. J. B. 'Shakespeare and the Elizabethan Romans', *Shakespeare Survey* 10 (1957).

Spiers, Phéné. 'The Architecture of *Coriolanus*', *Architectural Review*, X (July 1901).

Stirling, Brents. '"Or Else Were This a Savage Spectacle"', *PMLA*, LXVI (September 1951).

Thomson, Peter. 'No Rome of Safety: The Royal Shakespeare Season 1972 Reviewed', *Shakespeare Survey* 25 (1972).

Tierney, Margaret. 'Direction and Design. Trevor Nunn and Christopher Morley Talk to Margaret Tierney', *Plays and Players*, September 1972.

Trewin, J. C. 'The Old Vic and Stratford-upon-Avon 1961–62', *Shakespeare Quarterly*, XIII (Autumn 1962).

Troubridge, Sir Vincent. 'Oral Tradition in the Theatre', *Theatre Notebook*, V (October 1951).

Tynan, Kenneth. 'Caesar smaller than life', *The Observer*, 14 April 1963.

Van Lennep, William. 'The Smock Alley Players of Dublin', *ELH*, XIII (September 1946).

Walker, Roy. 'Unto Caesar: A Review of Recent Productions', *Shakespeare Survey* 12 (1959).

Whiting, George W. 'The Conditions of the London Theaters, 1679–83. A Reflection of the Political Situation', *Modern Philology*, XXVI (1927–8).
Wilson, J. Dover. 'Ben Jonson and *Julius Caesar*', *Shakespeare Survey* 2 (1949).

Newspapers and magazines
Place of publication is London unless otherwise indicated.

The Academy: 4 June 1881.
The Albion, New York: 18 November 1843; 2 June 1849; 30 December 1871.
Appleton's Journal, New York: 20 January 1872.
The Athenaeum: 8 August 1846; 4 June 1881.
Bell's Weekly Messenger: 8 March 1812.
The Birmingham Daily Gazette: 12 April 1898.
The Birmingham Daily Mail: 22 April 1896.
The Birmingham Evening Despatch: 20 April 1934.
The Birmingham Express: 20 April 1909.
The Birmingham Gazette: 20 April 1934.
The Birmingham Mail: 26 April 1911; 20 April 1934.
The Birmingham Post: 22 April 1896; 28 April 1904; 10 April 1963.
Blackwood's Edinburgh Magazine: XXXI (April 1832).
Boston Weekly Magazine: 5 July 1817; 7 March 1818.
The Catholic World: CXLVI (January 1938).
Chicago Record-Herald: 20 October 1912.
The Chicago Tribune: 4 October 1887; 25 September 1888.
The Christian Science Monitor, Boston: 23 May 1916.
Columbian Sentinel, Boston: 2 November 1822.
Country Life Illustrated: 29 January 1898.
Coventry Evening Telegraph: 29 May 1957.
The Coventry Herald: 21 April 1928.
The Critic: 1 December 1850.
The Daily Courant: 14 February 1704; 14 March 1706; 14 January 1707; 24 September 1723.
The Daily Herald: 30 November 1939.
The Daily Mail: 24 January 1898; 16 August 1919; 25 February 1953; 27 November 1964.
The Daily Telegraph: 24 January 1898; 21 January 1930; 5 May 1932.
The Detroit Free Press: 7 November 1902.
The Drama, or, Theatrical Pocket Magazine: May 1822; January 1824.
Dunlap's American Daily Advertiser, Philadelphia: 29 January 1791.
The Era: 4 June 1881; 29 January 1898.
The Evening Journal, New York: 2 December 1902.
Evening News: 5 May 1950; 25 February 1953.
Evening Standard: 6 July 1937; 14 March 1972.
Everyman: 30 January 1930; 18 February 1932.
The Examiner: 29 March 1812; 5 April 1812; 28 April 1822; 20 November 1836; 8 April 1848; 2 November 1850; 30 November 1850; 8 February 1851.
The Guardian, New York: 18 January 1872; 3 February 1872; 6 February 1872.

The Illustrated London News: 8 November 1856; 4 June 1881; 29 January 1898; 17 January 1920; 17 April 1962.
Illustrated Sporting and Dramatic News: 29 January 1898.
John Bull: 20 November 1836; 16 April 1837; 22 August 1846.
John O'London's Weekly: 26 May 1950.
Manchester Guardian: 24 February 1953; 26 February 1953.
The Minerva, New York: 24 January 1824; 14 February 1824; 24 April 1824; 12 June 1824.
The Mirror of Taste and Dramatic Censor, Philadelphia: May 1810; November 1810.
The Morning Chronicle: 18 October 1779; 8 December 1820; 3 October 1826; 15 November 1836; 2 May 1843.
The Morning Herald: 8 December 1820; 23 April 1822; 23 December 1823; 2 October 1827; 15 November 1836; 2 May 1843.
The Morning Post: 23 December 1823; 26 April 1911; 20 April 1922; 26 January 1932; 9 February 1932.
Morning Telegraph, New York: 14 July 1955.
Munsey's Magazine, New York, March 1907.
The Nation: 9 August 1919; 16 August 1919.
National Advocate, New York: 24 September 1823.
The New Age: 22 January 1920.
New-England Galaxy, Boston: 15 December 1820; 8 November 1822; 19 March 1824.
New-England Galaxy & Masonic Magazine, Boston: 27 February 1818; 20 November 1818; 4 December 1818.
New-England Palladium, Boston: 22 March 1803.
The New Republic, New York: 29 December 1937; 3 July 1950.
New Statesman: 11 May 1972.
The New Statesman and Nation: 6 February 1932; 20 February 1932; 7 March 1953.
The New Times: 24 April 1822.
New York American: 6 November 1912.
The New York Citizen: 30 December 1871; 6 January 1872.
New York Daily News: 13 November 1937.
New York Daily Tribune: 8 September 1870; 26 December 1871; 23 February 1872; 14 March 1872; 28 December 1875; 15 October 1881; 13 April 1883; 27 January 1885; 27 December 1887; 11 December 1888; 6 March 1891.
The New York Evening Express: 26 December 1871; 28 February 1872; 6 March 1872.
The New York Evening Post: 27 May 1802; 26 December 1871; 5 March 1872; 28 December 1875; 27 December 1887; 2 December 1902; 18 November 1931.
The New York Herald: 16 January 1862; 26 November 1864; 26 December 1871; 31 December 1871; 25 December 1875; 21 May 1876; 27 January 1885; 11 December 1888.
New York Herald Tribune: 19 December 1937; 13 July 1955; 17 July 1955.
New York Journal-American: 12 November 1937.
The New York Mirror: 20 September 1823; 27 September 1823; 15 October 1823; 3 April 1824; 16 December 1826; 25 June 1831; 27 August 1831.
New York Post: 12 November 1937; 24 November 1937.

The New York Times: 6 September 1870; 31 December 1871; 5 March 1872; 28 December 1875; 1 May 1883; 29 August 1937; 14 November 1937; 13 July 1955; 2 July 1965.
The News: 8 March 1812; 28 December 1823.
The News and Sunday Herald: 20 November 1836.
News Chronicle: 3 May 1950; 12 August 1960.
The Observer: 25 April 1920; 4 May 1930; 14 February 1932; 27 October 1935; 25 September 1949; 1 March 1953; 22 April 1962; 19 March 1972; 7 May 1972.
The Pall Mall Gazette: 24 January 1898.
The Pennsylvania Journal, Philadelphia: 31 May 1770.
Play Pictorial: February 1920.
Plays and Players: June 1963; June 1968.
The Polyanthos, Boston: December 1805; April 1807.
The Port Folio, Philadelphia: March 1809; October 1810.
The Prompter: 24 January 1735.
Punch: 4 June 1881; 22 March 1972; 10 May 1972.
The Queen: 4 June 1881; 29 January 1898.
St. James's Chronicle: 3 March 1812.
St. Louis Republic: 23 October 1888.
San Francisco Chronicle: 28 May 1889.
The Saturday Review: 4 June 1881; 29 January 1898.
The Scotsman: 1 January 1940.
Sketch: 24 May 1950; 11 March 1953.
The Spectator: 19 November 1836; 26 August 1955; 20 April 1963; 12 April 1968.
Spirit of the Times, New York: 30 December 1871; 1 January 1876.
The Stage: 19 April 1928; 1 May 1930.
The Standard, New York: 30 December 1871; 1 January 1872.
The Star: 25 January 1898.
The Star, New York: 31 December 1871.
The Stratford-upon-Avon Herald: 22 April 1892; 24 April 1896; 15 April 1898; 27 April 1906; 23 April 1909; 6 May 1910; 29 July 1910; 28 April 1911; 3 May 1912; 14 August 1914; 23 April 1915; 30 April 1915; 25 July 1919; 8 August 1919; 21 April 1922; 20 April 1928; 9 May 1930; 29 April 1932; 1 June 1934; 31 May 1957; 12 April 1963; 5 May 1972.
The Sun, New York: 26 December 1871; 2 December 1902; 27 November 1937.
The Sunday Times: 1 November 1829; 7 May 1843; 9 April 1865; 11 January 1920; 27 October 1935; 25 September 1949; 22 April 1962.
Tallis's Dramatic Magazine: January 1851.
The Tatler: 16 July 1709; 8 June 1710.
The Theatrical Journal: 20 May 1843.
The Theatrical Observer: 23 April 1822.
Time, New York: 22 November 1937.
Time and Tide: 10 June 1950.
The Times: 2 March 1812; 7 May 1816; 27 October 1829; 31 May 1881; 24 January 1898; 4 February 1920; 21 January 1930; 27 April 1932; 20 April 1934; 25 October 1935; 6 July 1937; 25 February 1953; 29 May 1957; 10 April 1963; 15 December 1964; 19 December 1964; 31 December 1964.

Tribune: 12 May 1950.
Truth: 12 May 1950.
The Truth-Teller, New York: 16 December 1826.
Weekly Review, New York: 16 March 1872.
The Westminster Gazette: 24 January 1898; 18 January 1921.
Wilmington (Delaware) *Morning News:* 4, 11 February 1937.
Woodhull & Claflin's Weekly, New York: 13 January 1872.
The World: 2 February 1898.
The World, New York: 8 September 1870; 2 January 1876; 2 December 1902; 5 November 1912.
World-Telegram, New York: 12 November 1937; 15 November 1937.
The Yorkshire Post: 18 January 1934.

INDEX

370